Between Hope and Despair

Culture and Education Series

Between Hope and Despair

Pedagogy and the Remembrance of Historical Trauma

edited by
Roger I. Simon, Sharon Rosenberg,
and Claudia Eppert

ROWMAN & LITTLEFIELD PUBLISHERS, INC.
Lanham • Boulder • New York • Oxford

ROWMAN & LITTLEFIELD PUBLISHERS, INC.

Published in the United States of America
by Rowman & Littlefield Publishers, Inc.
4720 Boston Way, Lanham, Maryland 20706
http://www.rowmanlittlefield.com

12 Hid's Copse Road
Cumnor Hill, Oxford OX2 9JJ, England

British Library Cataloguing in Publication Information Available

Library of Congress Cataloging-in-Publication Data

Between hope and despair : pedagogy and the remembrance of historical trauma /
edited by Roger I. Simon, Sharon Rosenberg, and Claudia Eppert.
     p. cm.—(Culture and education series)
    Includes bibliographical references and index.
    ISBN: 978-0-8476-9463-1

    1. Historiography. 2. Atrocities. 3. Suffering. I. Simon, Roger I. II.
Rosenberg, Sharon, 1964- III. Eppert, Claudia, 1962- IV. Series.

D16.9 B426 1999
907'.2—dc21

                              99-046274

Printed in the United States of America

♾ ™ The paper used in this publication meets the minimum requirements of
American National Standard for Information Sciences—Permanence of Paper for
Printed Library Materials, ANSI Z39.48–1992.

Contents

Introduction

Between Hope and Despair:

The Pedagogical Encounter of Historical Remembrance

Roger I. Simon, Sharon Rosenberg, and Claudia Eppert

Dedicating oneself to the remembrance of traumatic history is a curious practice, one often viewed not just with critical skepticism, but with dismissive suspicion. Those of us who spend considerable time pursuing questions of the remembrance of specific acts of mass violence are frequently asked: Why your enduring concern with the memory of pain, loss, degradation, and death? Why subject yourself to a seemingly never-ending attention to human suffering through practices of genocide, enslavement, population displacement, and organized terror? These questions are rarely innocent, but are symptomatic of a double doubt with regard to the desires, or perhaps needs, to dwell with such memories. Underpinning such doubts is a worry that perseverating on difficult remembrance is not only unhealthy but politically suspect and socially unwise. Quite often these misgivings are driven by the apprehension—not altogether unrealistic—that remembrance of mass violence may become an irrational, obsessive practice, an "indulgence" in pain or a "dementia" in which one is possessed by ghosts. Equally, remembrance may be judged as a rational, but cynical, calculated endeavor to mobilize support for particular interests. On the basis of such distrust of remembrance, memorial practices are thought to produce nothing but anguish, grief, and a righteous, desperate rage that only risks fueling more violence. Rather than offering the possibility of a reconciled future, memories of victimization seem to fester social division and conflict.

No wonder, then, there is an anxiety that attaches to "too much" remembering. Herein lies the root for the oft-stated comment that past suffering and destruction cannot be undone, that our tragic histories must be put behind us in efforts to move toward a more positive future.

LEARNING AND REMEMBRANCE

Commonly and often intensively held, the above suspicions are contested through the promise of learning that remembrance is assumed to offer. In its most basic form, the pedagogical justification of remembrance asserts that, in order to avoid repeating the mistakes of the past, we must learn the lessons of history. While recognizing the pervasiveness of this claim, our edited collection begins from a position that a defense of remembrance, on these terms alone, will hardly do. Repeated and repeated, it remains an ad hominem argument. What is missing from this justification of remembrance is a sustained consideration of what "learning the lessons of the past" could mean. Such consideration requires us to begin with the recognition that different forms of remembrance carry different conceptions of what might be taught, what might be learned (by whom), and how this learning/teaching is to be accomplished within engagements with the traces of traumatic history.

In invoking these concerns, we are introducing the importance of conceptualizing remembrance as pedagogical. Our standpoint is that remembrance does not simply *become* pedagogical when representations of the past are situated and engaged in educational sites such as schools and museums. Rather, whatever its site and social form, remembrance is an inherently pedagogical practice in that it is implicated in the formation and regulation of meanings, feelings, perceptions, identifications, and the imaginative projection of human limits and possibilities. Indeed, to initiate a remembrance practice is to evoke a *remembrance/pedagogy,* an indissoluble couplet that echoes Foucault's (1980) pivotal dialexis "knowledge/power." In binding remembrance and pedagogy, we are suggesting that all formations of memory carry implicit and/or explicit assumptions about what is to be remembered, how, by whom, for whom, and with what potential effects.

In this sense, remembrance/pedagogies are political, pragmatic, and performative attempts to prompt and engage people in the development of particular forms of historical consciousness. The historical consciousness we refer to here is not simply a "state of mind," the cognitive accumulation that comprises one's knowledge of the past. Quite counter to epistemic traditions that grasp consciousness as singular and learning as taking place "within" individuals, we view historical consciousness as always requiring another, as an indelibly social praxis, a very determinate set of commitments and actions held and enacted by members of collectivities. As a praxeological consciousness, learning is situated in that series of interlinked performances through which members of a community "pass-on" and revisit something of the substance and significance of past events. Thus, the historical remembrance we are most interested in takes its form as communicative acts that re-cite and re-site what one is learning—not only about what happened to others at/in a different space/time but also (and key in regard to the social memory of mass vi-olence) what one is learning of and within the disturbances and disruptions inher-ent in comprehending these events.

What we are beginning to lay out here is a conception of remembrance in which the traces of traumatic histories remain present, arriving as a return of memory, hopeful of an attention not indifferent to the experiences and events these traces ref-erence—however incompletely. On these terms, the central problem of this edited collection is structured by the questions: What is to be the character of this non-in-difference? What does it mean, on both ethical and pedagogical terms, to "learn the lessons of the past"? How might we understand a mindful attentiveness to, learning from, and participation in the memory of the traces of traumatic history?

In order to extend the implications of this discussion, we will begin by briefly considering how two predominant remembrance/pedagogies articulate and partic-ipate in the preservation of social memories of traumatic history. In the first, re-membrance is constituted as a *strategic practice* in which memorial pedagogies are de-ployed for their sociopolitical value and promise. In the second, remembrance is enacted as a *difficult return,* a psychic and social responsibility to bring the dead into presence, a responsibility that concurrently involves learning to live with, and in relation to, loss. While we would argue that ultimately these two approaches to "the project" of remembrance are not as disaggregated as this distinction suggests, our purpose is to exemplify the importance of considering the pedagogical pre-sumptions of these different practices of remembrance, marking the conceptions of learning that each variably foregrounds and occludes.

REMEMBRANCE AS STRATEGIC PRACTICE

Remembrance as a strategic practice constitutes social memory as a sociohistorical formation incorporating what Raymond Williams once termed a determinate "structure of feeling" (1977). That is, social memories are produced as bounded sets of symbolizations (texts, images, songs, monuments, and rituals) and associated emotions. Collectivities share these as ways of stabilizing and transmitting particu-lar versions of past events and, in so doing, attempt to offer perspectives on present dilemmas and future aspirations. Formations of memory, in this view, are efforts to mobilize attachments and knowledge that serve specific social and political inter-ests within particular spatiotemporal frameworks. Certainly there is a long history of deploying remembrance practices on such terms to bolster hegemonic, emer-gent, and, at times, insurgent nationalisms and ethnocultural identifications.

On the terms of remembrance as strategic practice, the remembrance of mass violence has sustained the demand for institutionalized practices of justice, repara-tion, and reconciliation, through not only memorial recognition but also legal prosecution, institutional apology, and state-funded compensation. Thus, as strategic practice, remembrance is aligned with the anticipation of a reconciled future in which one hopes that justice and harmonious social relations might be secured. This is a hope that anxiously attends to a horrific past in expectation of the promise that, by investing attention in narratives that sustain moral lessons, there will be a better tomorrow. It is a tomorrow fully cognizant of the warning that forgetting could lead to a return to the horrors of history. Ironically, on these terms, no matter how horrible its stories, a strategic remembrance of mass systemic violence is consolatory. The hope enacted in and through such remembrance is dependent on a moralizing pedagogy: the provision of images and narratives against which the future is defined as different, a time in which the past "must never happen again."

While the promise of remembrance is that of a moral vigilance that stands over and against indifference, the continuation of local and global violence suggests that such a pedagogy rarely serves as an effective safeguard. This ongoing failure of social memory simply ups the ante of remembrance as an educative, strategic practice. As if caught in some form of repetition compulsion, such remembrance practices can only respond with further directives to tell again, and to tell with increased urgency, thereby invoking an absolutist moral demand that one must listen. However, if the repetition of terrible stories provides no guarantee of a redeemed society, are we not compelled to rethink what it means to remember and what practices might constitute its pedagogical character?

REMEMBRANCE AS A DIFFICULT RETURN

Breaking with the promise of strategic memorial practice, remembrance as a difficult return is situated in a different set of pedagogical premises. Remembrance here endeavors to bring forth into presence specific people and events of the past in order to honor their names and to hold a place for their absent presence in one's contemporary life. Implicated in this remembrance is a learning to live with loss, a learning to live with a return of a memory that inevitably instantiates loss and thus bears no ultimate consolation, a learning to live with a disquieting remembrance. On these terms, the memorial impulse to turn to and return traumatic history is an *assignment,* not simply a matter of choice. This demanding assignment is driven by an "unworked-through past," a past that continues to pose questions of what it means to live in the shadows of mass violence. As a difficult return, remembrance attempts to meet the challenge of what it might mean to live, not *in* the past but *in relation with* the past, acknowledging the claim the past has on the present. In this relation, the social and psychic ruptures coincident with the return of a traumatic past unsettle and put into question the very terms of the redemptive promise of a strategic remembrance: that the future will be better if one remembers. What remembrance as a difficult return clarifies are the limits of a consolatory assurance that the past can be discursively integrated into coherent—and pragmatic—contemporary frames of social memory. It makes evident that certain events of mass violence, through the ruptures they initiate, create an instability in practices of remembrance, rendering impossible any final stable assimilation. Living in the wake of this displacement of the recuperative impulse of social memory, remembrance as a difficult return then becomes a series of propositions of how to live with what cannot be redeemed, what must remain a psychic and social wound that bleeds.

At issue in both remembrance as "difficult return" and as "strategic practice," however, is how the relation between the living and the dead is configured and enacted. Remembrance as a strategic response posits a continuity between the living and the dead by collapsing the latter's specificities into our contemporary political and social use-value. Remembrance as a difficult return also risks, on different terms, overprivileging such a continuity through practices of identification that threaten to collapse differences across space/time and through performances of surrogacy that may leave the living in the breach of melancholia. Recognizing the costs of such risks, we posit the need for a remembrance/pedagogy that introduces *discontinuity* as necessary to a learning from the past, a learning that resides in a relationality that respects differences while honoring continuity.

HOPEFUL TRAUMA?

The chapters in this collection incorporate, as problem *and* resource, the recognition that the taken-for-granted frames of reference that orient people in their daily lives are deeply disrupted in attempts to respond to the traces of mass violence. Our collective interests lie in the possibilities of remembrance/pedagogies capable of bearing witness to historical trauma, through memorial enactments that interminably unsettle what it means to be invested in and guided by (consciously and unconsciously) the normative frames that govern our existence. In this respect, what one is faced with—in facing traumatic history through critical practices of remembrance—is the ongoing task of opening ourselves to a reworking of these normalized frames of daily life, a task that is rooted in attempts to remain in relation with loss without being subsumed by it. This is the charge of finding hope in the necessary task of reopening the present through an obligation to accept the demands of this relation, a relation that risks our becoming wounded in the attendance to the wounds of another. When experienced as an insufficiency of the present, such a wounding may indeed set the terms for a critical pedagogy of remembrance. What we are beginning to gesture toward, then, and what this collection centrally concerns itself with, is the conceptualization of a third form of pedagogy. This pedagogy devolves on the question of the character of the learning that enacts the possibilities of hope through a required meeting with traumatic traces of the past.

The chapters collected here are seeking remembrance practices that do not simply deploy strategic or persuasive historical narratives or formulate acts of eloquent and compelling memorialization but crucially invoke the requirement of critical learning. Such an endeavor engages us fundamentally in the difficult problems of hearing, understanding, and knowing; in other words, as Freud taught us, in learning not only *about,* but *from* past lives and events (Britzman 1998). This means remembrance must find a way to initiate a continual unsettling and an interminable asking of pedagogical questions regarding what it means to be taught by the experience of others. Taking this unsettlement seriously creates an ongoing problem of how to attend to and hold on to remembrance of the past without foreclosing the possibility that this attempt to remember will rupture the adequacy of the very terms on which a memory is being held.

Remembrance as a hopeful practice of critical learning extends to reworking notions of community, identity, embodiment, and relationship. In effect, this reworking requires us to contemplate a revised notion of the political beyond conventional questions of power—questions, for example, of who gets to decide for whom what privileges, opportunities, and resources will be made available and withheld within any given community. While never disregarding this dimension of the political, what we are attempting to bring to the fore is the recognition that remembrance as learning fundamentally reconfigures a "politics of relationality." In saying this, by no means do we diminish the importance of contesting ongoing systemic structures of violence such as racism, sexism, and anti-Semitism. Rather, we emphasize that a politics of relationality is additionally needed, implicating us in an examination of how it is each of us listens, learns, and responds to those whose identities, bodies, and memories have been fundamentally impacted by such violences— impacts that cannot ever be reduced to versions of our own troubles and traumas.

The ongoing awareness and increasing importance of the reconsideration of the remembrance of events of mass systemic violence is part of the growing cognizance that the very hope for a just and compassionate future lies, at least in part, in working through the traumatic catastrophes we have inherited. The chapters in *Between Hope and Despair* start with the recognition that the taking up and carrying of this inheritance is a necessary yet difficult task. The book's contributors discuss the complexities of remembrance/pedagogy in relation to: the Nazi genocide of European Jews (Baum, Britzman, Liss, Simon), the events comprising the period of the trans-Atlantic "Middle Passage" and the legacy of slavery it initiated (Walcott), the forced internment and dispersal of Japanese-Canadians during and following World War II (Eppert), the "Montreal Massacre" and its emblemization in relation to systemic violence against women (Rosenberg), the state-initiated atrocities against peoples in Argentina during the period commonly known as the "Dirty War" (Di Paolantonio), the recent genocide in Rwanda (Ranck), and the widespread proliferation of antipersonnel land mines that have maimed and killed civilian populations (Salverson). The purpose of gathering these contributions into one volume is not to contrast or compare these events or to collapse their uniqueness into the amorphous category of "mass violence." Rather, it is to allow each author to address, in relation to the specificity of the events under consideration in their chapter, how the difficulties of remembrance/pedagogy need to be conceptualized when the historical events to be remembered are underscored by a logic that seems difficult to comprehend and, moreover, makes problematic any assumptions about the "humane," and therefore hopeful, character of human existence.

REMEMBRANCE AS CRITICAL LEARNING

This collection seeks to foreground difficulties that center on not only the representation of "what happened" but also the attempt to respond to and hold in remembrance the traces of these events. What is at issue here is not only what gets remembered, by whom, how, and when, but, as well, the problem of the very limits of representing and engaging events that in their extremity shock and resist assimilation into already articulated discourses. The overriding question that the various contributions address is how remembrance might become an opening into learning—an opening of the present in which the identities and identifications, the frames of certitude that ground our understandings of existence, and the responsibilities to history are displaced and rethought. Each author accents different aspects of the problem of how to be vigilant, how to attend to traces of past people and events through practices of remembrance.

Taken together, the authors' conceptualizations of remembrance as practices of critical learning open up a new set of pedagogical concerns. One such concern is how to attend to stories and images that attempt to communicate various aspects of traumatic historical moments and the experiences of people who lived (and died) through them. The attentiveness referenced here is not just an idle encounter or a self-directed search for material that might support one's previously held knowledge or identifications. Rather, it is an embodied cognizance that opens the one who attends to the very terms of reading, listening, and viewing, to grasping the sense of one's limits and to what must be disturbed in order to realize remembrance as a radical position of learning.

A related concern is how to enact tellings of traumatic histories that encompass not only a repetition (a retelling) of the story of another but also the *story of the telling of the story*. What this signals is the struggle to work through one's own affiliations with and differences from the "original" narrative or memory one is engaging, a working through that takes into account the particularities of the space/time of one's engagement, the particular investments one brings to remembrance, and the continuities and discontinuities one enacts in relation to it. This is the very task of "remembering well," a remembering that humbles any design to master the past and requires a serious reflexivity rooted in a recognition that the historical character of one's partial and mediated remembrance is contingent and thus can always be otherwise.

As the chapters in this collection point out, we cannot underestimate the importance of remembrance as a practice of holding historical memories through a relation of continuity and discontinuity, of connection and disconnection between (present) self and (past) others. It is only in the staging and preservation of this dynamic, a dynamic both of oscillation and commingling, that one's engagement with traumatic histories enacts a possibility of a transformative breaking in on the present. This very specific "holding on to" historical memories is, in fact, a new memorial space, a boundary space that marks a third concern of a practice of critical learning in which to explore the fundamental terms of relationality with an absent presence. This is a space that invigorates what Derrida (1994) calls "learning to live with ghosts," a condition that disavows the modernist project of consolidation of self and the maintenance and perpetuation of subject-object binaries.

Perhaps what all of the chapters finally move toward is a critical and risk-laden learning that seeks to accomplish a shift of one's ego boundaries, that displaces engagements with the past and contemporary relations with others out of the narrow, inescapably violent and violative confines of the "I," to a receptivity to others, to an approaching of others. Remembrance is, then, a means for an ethical learning that impels us into a confrontation and "reckoning" not only with stories of the past but also with "ourselves" as we "are" (historically, existentially, ethically) in the present. Remembrance thus is a reckoning that beckons us to the possibilities of the future, showing the possibilities of our own learning.

Our own learning in regard to questions of remembrance and pedagogy has been amplified and extended by many conversations with colleagues. We are grateful, in particular, to past and present members of the Testimony and Historical Memory Project at the University of Toronto. In addition, we are deeply appreciative of the insight and attention to detail provided by the contributors to this book—as well as their patience and responsiveness in regard to our editorial suggestions. We are also indebted to the encouragement and attention we have received from Jill Rothenberg, Karen Johnson, and the staff of Rowman & Littlefield. Thanks to all for helping us to bring this project to completion. Collaborative work is never easy. During the three years that this book has been in the making, we have learned much—not only about remembrance but also about the importance of persistence, patience, humor, the sharing of the keyboard, and the promise in listening to others.

1

The Paradoxical Practice of *Zakhor:*

Memories of "What Has Never Been My Fault or My Deed"

Roger I. Simon

> Go catch the echoes of the ticks of time; Spy the interstices between its sands.
> —A. M. Klein, "Of Remembrance," *The Second Scroll*

Nearing the end of our catastrophic century, we live in the time of testimony. On talk shows, to journalists, at tribunals, in front of truth commissions, or video cameras documenting testimony for archival storage, never before has there been such recording of difficult memories, such speaking of disaster. When the clamor of these voices has become so persistent, who can bear the demand that we listen, that we take these memories into our lives and so live as though the lives of others matter? It is not just that the constant stories of human-inflicted debasement and death often leave one feeling powerless to respond to the needs of others. After the always insufficient "check-in-the-mail" to a local or international relief agency, one still needs to know "what am I do to with these stories," the memories of others? How and why would it matter if they were a part of my memorial landscape? My obsessions, at least for the last few years, have been addressed to such questions, questions I understand to concern the formation and consequences of historical memory.

A cultural practice, historical memory moves remembrance beyond the boundaries of the singular corporal body. Whereas autobiographical memory references the ability to recall previous states of consciousness (including thoughts, images, feelings, and experiences), historical memory is grounded in a public pedagogy of remembrance, a decidedly socially inflected repetition, or better, a rearticulation of past events through which I incur a responsibility in which I am "thrown back to-

ward what has never been my fault or my deed" (Levinas 1987, 111). On the terms of
such a responsibility, the very possibility of historical memory inheres in a response
to the question: What might it mean "to *remember* other people's memories" (Silverman 1996, 186)? This is an admittedly curious query. Is not the issue, what can
one can learn of other people's memories, casting the problem as one of knowledge acquisition, not remembrance? Should not the question be one of history, not
memory? The phrase "historical memory" may have a certain poetic resonance, but
is it not best to forgo metaphors and speak more explicitly of practices of writing,
reading, and teaching history? Does it make any sense at all to speak of a *remembrance* of "what has never been my fault or my deed"?

What must be signaled at the outset then, is that "historical memory" is not to
be conceived singularly as a practice of retention, as the recollection of expressed
experiences or grounded narrations of past events. Quite differently, historical
memory also includes the potential for a fertile commingling between present consciousness and the staging of evidentiary traces of past presence. Not merely historiographic documentation, such traces are ruins, remnants, disembodied semiotic
wounds neither decomposed nor forgotten. Following Kaja Silverman, I proceed
from the premise that to remember other people's memories is, in effect, "to provide a psychic locus for the foreclosed wounds of the past" (185). Critically, Silverman stresses that "if to remember is to provide the disembodied 'wound' with
a psychic residence, then to remember other people's memories is to be wounded
by their wounds. More precisely, to let the traces of other people's struggles, passions, pasts, resonate within one's own past and present, and destabilize them"
(185). As this chapter will argue, at stake in such a practice of remembrance is the
possibility of a "re-inventive resistance" (Boyarin 1994, 22) to the oblivion that
threatens to overcome all memories, a way of dwelling in history that keeps open
remembrance as a promise of hope. At stake is nothing short of the vigilance required for the practice of *zakhor*.

ZAKHOR AND THE PEDAGOGICAL
STRUCTURE OF REMEMBRANCE

In extending the referent of remembrance beyond personal recollection, I am
drawing on what, in Hebrew, is designated by the word *zakhor*. As an injunction
and responsibility, zakhor is a practice that has been central to Jewish life throughout its existence. In its most literal sense, zakhor is translated into English as both
an imperative and an obligation: "remember." However, I want here to broaden
and unfold the meaning of this term by invoking its specific and intertwined cultural and theological reference. Zakhor initiates the normative content of Jewish
memory. Within Torah, it is commanded by a Word that comes from without, that
is completely other. Taken up as a structured activity in response to this Word, zakhor is inherently pedagogical. Jewish existence has depended on this pedagogy of

remembrance as a practice that has brought previous generations into presence. Shattering conventional linkages of time and memory, zakhor presumes a transformation of time to something other than a precast continuum through which we move, or a spatialized rendering of "here" and "there." In this sense, the practice of zakhor does not measure time forming points "fixed in the past . . . which year after year, become increasingly past" (Rosenzweig 1972, 304), nor does it view the past as "a foreign country" (Lowenthal 1985), a place to visit and from which to bring back souvenirs. Within zakhor, time is reconstituted through relationships, through communicative practices that reinstantiate tradition—recognizing death while resisting the dissolution that is death (Gibbs 1992, Cohen 1994).

To grasp the sense of zakhor as relationship, as necessitating communicative practices, one needs to understand it as a component of a law that encumbers, obligates, yokes one to the specificities of promise. In his reading of the Talmud, Tractate Sotah 37a–37b, Emmanuel Levinas (1994,79) notes that there are four promises that adherence to the law entails: to learn it, to teach it, to keep/preserve it, and to do it. Applying these promises to the responsibility of zakhor, one must first note that zahkor is something one must do—it is not a passive undergoing of recollection or reminiscence. Furthermore, this "doing" is to be composed of practices of studying, teaching, and keeping, all practices implicating one in communicative relationships with others. In other words, remembrance as zakhor is composed of the activities of listening and reading (studying), of speaking and writing (teaching), and of repeating one's lessons, finding new questions to pursue, and hence not foreclosing one's relation to others (keeping/preserving). One may be considered as fulfilling the responsibility of zakhor when these activities are consolidated into a vigilant, interminable attentiveness to a "saying" that addresses one with its demand: remember. Thus zakhor implies both a deep commitment to attach oneself to a teaching that comes from without *and* the perpetual task of revitalizing this teaching so as to integrate it into the marrow of one's life. It is for this reason that the practice of zakhor can never be entirely unproblematic, embodied in a unified pedagogical form. Rather, zakhor must forever negotiate the tension between, on the one hand, providing a sense of continuity and confirmation, while, on the other hand, renewing the significance of memory through making evident a cited past's discontinuity with immediate existence. It is the negotiation of this tension that sets the terms for the practice of historical memory. To get a better sense of the tension at work here, I will briefly consider its polarities.

REMEMBRANCE AS CONTINUITY AND CONFIRMATION

As a practice that instantiates continuity and confirmation, historical memory obviously offers forms of learning central to life in human communities. Hence, it is no surprise that remembrance practices commonly attempt to stabilize memorialization through the repetition of established texts, sayings, and stories. This "telling again and again" is first and foremost a reminder and a warning of what threatens to be forgotten or has already been forgotten. This is no idle admonition, for the forgetting that remembrance acts against, if actualized, risks dissolving the very grounds on which notions of self and community are built. In this sense, remembrance's premise is the injunction, "one must not forget." Within such practices of remembrance, the desire for a manifest continuity is made apparent; oblivion refused. What has been or threatens to be lost must be brought into view not only so that one might "know" what happened but so that one might attach oneself to this remembrance. This is a moment of zakhor that carries the demand of allegiance. In such an allegiance, the attachments remembrance mobilizes are never neutral. They consist of emotionally charged identifications with narratives and symbols that reinforce the significance of specific memories for the identities and commitments of specific groups, be they families, communities, or nations.

On such terms, a concern for memories other than one's own is conditional on their incorporation within the memorial boundaries that circumscribe one's identifications. Clearly, one's attentiveness is heightened when one senses a "point of connection" between oneself and, say, a person who has spoken or written their memories. The more concrete and specific this connection, the more likely the memories of another will be drawn to one's attention. Hence, the memorial importance of making evident specific physical or cultural characteristics that may be "read" as shared elements between the other and oneself, calling one to an imaginative affinity. Additionally, this "connection" may also be elicited within the recognition that elements of another's memories have a familiar structure and context, as evoking forms of empathetic identification wherein one feels that which is being said by another is, in some ways, similar to elements of one's own experience.

Such points of connection substantiate a persisting sense of belonging to a "community of memory," of being claimed by a kinship of connections that have become central to one's self-definition. One's perceived membership in such communities of memories is often a powerful ground for the commitment to practices of remembrance. While this claim on one's memorial intensity is a psychic one, affiliation and identification should never be separated from their material and discursive grounds. Whose and what memories matter, not abstractly but viscerally, requiring my attention and vigilance, speaks volumes about the terms on which lives of others come into view.[1] While there is the risk in such practices of remembrance that what is of memorial importance serves and confirms current versions of self and community, to render such terms of connection with others as merely "narcissistic" is too gratuitous. While these connections are made on the basis of seeing some aspect of ourselves in others, such connections seem an inescapable element of sociality, something that cannot be—nor would we want it to be—completely wished away. However, one must not simply ignore the conservatism and potentially reductive violence in such memorial practices. Hence the necessity of rethinking what constitutes a "point of connection" for historical memory.

REMEMBRANCE AS DISCONTINUITY AND UNSETTLEMENT

If remembrance is collapsed entirely into the pedagogical project of continuity and confirmation, it suppresses the critical recognition that in order to renew the living force of memories handed down through remembrance, pedagogies that enable an approach to the past in relation to its absolute discontinuity from the time of the present are needed. This form of remembrance holds to historical memories as traces of another's time that may disrupt my own. On such terms, remembrance becomes a practice that supports a learning from "the past" that is a fresh cognizance or discovery that unsettles the very terms on which our understandings of ourselves and our world are based. In its most powerful form, such remembrance initiates forms of learning that shift and disrupt the present, opening one to new ways of perceiving, thinking, and acting.

Such an additional agenda for historical memory thus poses a difficult question: How can a remembrance of that which is an "absolute discontinuity from the time of the present" find a psychic locus, how might the memories of others be "remembered" as a wound that wounds me, that unsettles and destabilizes my own past and present? To explore possible responses to this question, we must rethink the very terms of the notion of "point of connection" offered previously. Rather than offering a logic of identification, it is evident that the tension required by a historical memory requires a much more dialectical and uncanny conception of what constitutes a "point of connection," one that initiates an ongoing attentiveness to identification and difference, to ordinariness and the shock of the un-ordinary.

To illustrate this reworking of the notion of a "point of connection," I provide a brief rendering of my viewing of a series of images taken by Canadian photographer Blake Fitzpatrick of the front porch and entranceway of a house in Port Hope, Ontario. This house was once the home of Marcel Pochon, who, in the 1930s, was hired by Eldorado Gold Mines Ltd. to set up a radium processing plant in the town. In contact with radioactive materials throughout his working day, Pochon inadvertently carried trace amounts of radium dust on this clothes, shoes, and hands, which were deposited on things he touched within his home. When Atomic Energy of Canada Ltd. (AECL) conducted a complete cleanup of the home in the summer of 1992, they discovered evidence of radioactive contamination on the surfaces and artifacts in Pochon's house. During the cleanup, many locations in the house were found to be radioactive. Fitzpatrick, who had been attempting to record a photographic history of radioactivity in Port Hope, was fortunate enough to be able to photograph the exterior and interior of the house, now filled with red dots left by AECL to mark contaminated household items and parts of the dwelling that had to be disposed of. When Fitzpatrick first arrived at this home, what he saw above its entranceway was a sign, "Muidar" (radium spelled backwards), the name the Pochon family had given to their home. Just to the right of this doorway were several empty spaces in the exterior wall of the house where single contaminated bricks had

MUIDAR: Overview, Port Hope, 1990
© Blake Fitzpatrick

been removed. It is Fitzpatrick's photographs of this doorway and its adjoining
exterior wall that concern me here.

   What I first noticed about these photographs was their ordinariness. It is simply
a front porch, doorway, and a puzzling, but quaint, personalized house sign that,
in its familiarity, is totally unremarkable. Yet then noticed are the gaps in the wall,
spaces where bricks used to be. Learning about Pochon and the AECL cleanup, I
renoticed the absence of these bricks . . . again. It is in this renoticing that what is
at once so familiar, now became strangely disconcerting. Attending to a sense of
anxiety provoked by the absent presence of those bricks, I wondered why were
just a few of them radioactive? Why was there one removed just about shoulder
height and a few others removed several feet lower and just off to the right? What
might Pochon have been doing on this porch that would have left his radioactive
dust singularly on just these few bricks? Indeed, it is this "study" of my discon-
certed response to the image and its denotative referents—these few gaps in the
front wall of a house, gaps where the bricks used to be—that opens this image as a
scene of historical memory. This memory is secured—but not definitively explained or understood—by the symbolic work it initiates. Thus, imaginatively, one

MUIDAR: Sign, Port Hope, 1992
© Blake Fitzpatrick

could picture Pochon coming home in inclement weather, leaning his left hand against the brick wall of his home and knocking the mud and snow off his boots before entering his house. Plausible? Perhaps. But most importantly, what registers here is how ordinary, how commonplace such a gesture would have been and how un-ordinary its implications. This is a memorial recognition that is deeply unsettling; indeed, Fitzpatrick has captured the wounds of the Pochon family that now wound me. For, not only can I now disturbingly imagine other places touched, perhaps caressed, by Pochon's hands, but this imaginative imagery implicates Fitzpatrick's photographs in the uncertainty of my own gestures, in an awareness of terror of a nuclear age where what is self-evident is never surety enough. My point here, of course, is not that there is one definitive way to "read" Fitzpatrick's photographs, but that, for me, the photographs have, through a dialectical, uncanny point of connection, become a memorial trace sedimented in my historical consciousness of the history of the Pochon family, the town of Port Hope, and the development of the nuclear industry in Canada. But, still nagging is a persistent functionalist sense of the pragmatic: Of what personal or communal importance are such forms of disturbing remembrance?

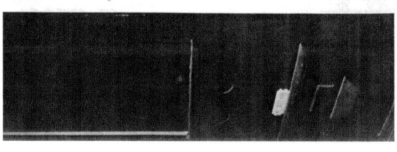

MUJDAR: Missing Bricks, 1992
© Blake Fitzpatrick

ZAKHOR AND OTHER PEOPLE'S MEMORIES

The fundamental importance of the doubled notion of zakhor, this necessary relation between continuity and unsettlement, is underscored by noting how this intricate practice of remembrance is bound up with the possibility of hope. Within zakhor, hope—that seemingly requisite mask of optimism worn by the present—is secured by the unresolvable tension, between a comforting prospect of immutable presence and a radical redemptive promise of a memory that breaks in on the present, enabling any given moment to bear a new beginning. Within this complex and perplexing formulation, hope depends on both connection and discontinuity. How and why this is so takes us back to the questions with which I began: What am I supposed to do with the stories of others, in particular stories of widespread suffering and trauma? How and why would it matter if accounts of systemic violence and its legacies were part of my memorial landscape? What I will argue is that the difficult stories of the suffering matter because the very possibility of hope depends on their memorial insistence. More precisely, the possibility of hope depends on our capacities for providing a psychic locus for such stories, a locus that requires we take up the stories of others within the pedagogical dynamics of zakhor. However, zakhor requires a particular mode of attendance, a particular embodied cognizance necessary to support its pedagogy. What is at issue here is the sensibility with which one engages the stories of others.

In North America, the range of painful historical memories we are asked to attend to surpasses those transmitted in gatherings of family and friends. In addition to what we absorb in such settings, we learn of other people's traumatic memories through reading texts, viewing images and narratives, and hearing stories of the lives of others, either secondhand or through autobiographical accounts. What I wish to emphasize about these practices—practices within which one becomes aware of the distinctive character of the lives of others—is that *how* one attends to such accounts constitutes and constrains much of the substance and character of one's historical memory. Thus, it is important to ask not only how selected stories are framed by existing social and technological systems of production and distribution but, as well, in what manner institutionalized discourses define what counts as successful and useful forms of attentiveness and learning in regard to such stories. Consider, for a moment, educative projects (e.g., in schools, media, and museums) that call on people to attend to such stories in ways that prefigure their importance and meaning. On such terms, the traumatic memories of others become object lessons meant to illustrate some significant historical moment, social process, or change and to provoke a compassionate and helpful response. Engaged in this way, stories are meant to fill in details and provide the human dimension of history through images that mobilize a complex of thought and feeling, making transparent an account's intertwined personal and historical significance.

As object lessons, however, such narratives and images run several risks. First of all, they risk becoming old news, redundant to that which a reader or viewer claims to already understand and have responded to. Second, the stories of others may become consumable, remembered but then forgotten, mattering only to the extent that one accepts the predefined importance of such stories and one's responsibility to reiterate that significance when asked, but only when asked. Third, as I previously argued, such stories may become the object of transferential obsession wherein they become the symbolic expression of one's own concerns, a position in which one grasps the stories of others on terms defined by one's own self-understanding. Even if indifference is overturned—and there is much to anticipate in such an overturning—the "object lesson" framing of the traumatic stories diminishes their power, in Silverman's terms, "to wound," "to resonate within one's own past and present, and destabilize them" (185). Thus, we are still left with the question, what might it mean to attend to the painful stories of others so as to experience the summons of another, to be consigned and challenged by the substance and substantiality of the one who, amid the practice of zakhor, now holds my regard? Can there be a more hopeful way to live historically?

TIME AND THE CHALLENGE OF TESTIMONY

Let us consider this question from within the perspective of the one called to witness a practice of traumatic testimony, of one called to read, view, or listen to an accounting of another's painful experience of being subjected to systemic violence. Whether within or across generations, testimony is always directed toward, indeed requires, witnesses: those prepared to accept the obligation of reading, viewing, listening, and subsequently responding to an embodied singular experience not recognizable as one's own. Thus, for the witness, testimony conveys not only a semblance of the historical substance and significance of prior events and experiences but, as well, something of the psychic shattering such violence initiates. On such terms, testimony is a multilayered communicative act, a performance intent on carrying forth memories through the conveyance of a fraught, fragile engagement between consciousness and history (Felman and Laub 1992). From this perspective, testimony demands remembrance, demands the responsiveness and responsibility of the paradoxical dynamics of zakhor. In other words, testimony necessitates a practice of remembrance in which one is required to draw near but yet remain distant, a memorial stance in which one is required to study, teach, and keep/preserve the memories of another, not in ossified form, but through a "handing down" whose substance lies in vitality, inventiveness, and renewal (Levinas 1994, 79). Attempting to fulfill the obligation of such a response to testimony, one must open oneself to uncanny points of connection, commanded by a persistent sense of belonging to something or someone that is other than the grounds on which one recognizes oneself. From this perspective, to witness testimony is to be claimed to another in ways that are not reducible to blood ties, geographically local or diasporic identities, or humanistic assertions of empathy. This is because, in a witnessing relation, one must become open to the possibility of unforeseen memory, the possibility of unfamiliar, unexpected connections that disrupt attempts to know what meaning a place or moment may hold.

Much more is at stake here than recognizing a vast imaginative space separating the ordeal of a witness from our capacity to comprehend it. Witnessing implicates my inexperience to hear the testimony that addresses me. What I encounter is not just the dramatic abundance of experience, or even the overflow of traumatic episodes, but the experience of my inexperience to hear and learn (Simon, Eppert, Clamen, and Beres 1999). What I learn in such an encounter are not just facts about another's life or even facts about my own, but that I can be challenged, awakened to an attending to my attending. It is this vigilance that may lead to new forms of living on after the event, new forms of bearing witness that initiate thought that has no rest, that can neither be completed nor end. While this disruption leaves one less secure in negotiating daily life with a managed history written in the present, it also brings forth the possibility of time, the possibility of futurity. Following Levinas on time, the future is *"what comes toward the self, ungraspable, outside its possibilities"* (Cohen 1994, 142, my italics). Given this, does not a world desirous of hope— banking on the very possibility of a future—need a practice of remembrance that is a witnessing of the "immemorial past," that is, that which is beyond my memory and which I had no implication in?

There is no future without uncanny memorial connections, without responsibilities to memories other than one's own, to memories you have no responsibility for but claim you to a memorial kinship. As Levinas (1987) suggests, in this responsibility "I am thrown back toward what has never been my fault or my deed, toward what has never been in my power or my freedom, toward what has never been my presence, and has never come into memory" (111). Hope and an ethical pragmatics mix in this responsibility "to a past that concerns me, that 'regards me', and is 'my business' outside of all reminiscence, re-tention, re-presentation, or reference to a remembered present" (111–112). This mix of hope and ethics depends on a responsiveness to another that recognizes that the meeting of testimony and witness does not take place "at the same time"; that one does not witness another as a contemporary. Witnessing is an event of two disjunctive temporalities, an event in which another's time disrupts mine. It is a new time, an interstitial time, neither mine nor yours; an extraordinary disjuncture of I and other, an experience of proximity that initiates an "infinite distance without distance" (Cohen 1994, 147). It is a moral time, a time of non-indifference of one person to another, of obligation and responsibility to and for the other (Cohen 1994, 149).

On these terms, testimony is not just the provision of information, but, as Walter Benjamin (1969) intimates, is also counsel for the witness. This "counsel is less an answer to a question than a proposal concerning the continuation of a story which is just unfolding" (86). But to seek and then hear this counsel, the witness would first have to be able to tell the story. Deborah Britzman (chapter 2, this volume) underscores this pedagogical dynamic of the testimony-witness relation when she suggests: "How one comes to find relevance for one's present world in events that are not one's own, but that have the capacity to say something more to the stories one already has, is . . . a central question of any pedagogy." To find relevance, to seek and then hear the counsel of a testimony shot through with the dynamics of traumatic remembrance is no small task. Such attentiveness requires a non-indifference in which not only is astonishment possible, but within which one risks being "alarmed," an "alarm" that itself risks being "smothered" by what one already knows, by the consolatory symbolic economy through which one's community has already tried to put-the-past-in-place (see Mario Di Paolantonio, chapter 8, this volume).

For this non-indifference of the witness to be a time of hope, it must receive its specificity in practices of zakhor. Every social unit (whether family, commune, community, or nation) is premised on the promise of its own continuity, of its futurity, that which is yet to come. Within an appreciation of their own historicity, such units can indeed anticipate their own narratives—the fulfillment of affiliative, spiritual, and material needs through the existence of a specific practice of sociality. However, this anticipation carries with it its own amnesic force. One experiences within such expectation the psychic and social necessity to forget that which may be unbearable, that which disrupts contemporary ego boundaries and their associative promise of a predictable sociality. But, in fact, without this disruption, without this wounding, this "abject manifestation (as a type of bleeding) [that] signals that this loss is not an ordinary loss . . . absorbed or stitched into the symbolic order" there is no provocation to think beyond present understanding (Di Paolantonio, chapter 8, this volume). Indeed, without remembrance practices that attempt to hold present that which is unbearable, practices through which we are "wounded by others' wounds," there is no future time, only more of the same. Such a proposition offers a radically different conception of the relation of time, memory, and hope than contemporary practices of remembrance whose function is reconciliation and social consolidation. In this more radical view, hope exists only when the present remains exposed, vulnerable, and hence incomplete. Remembrance as hope becomes "a way of naming the present's inherent incompleteness . . . functioning as a structural force . . . holding the present open and thus as being unfinished" (Benjamin 1997, 10). Thus, for remembrance to participate in "holding the present open" it must become a practice of unsettling the present; in particular unsettling the sufficiency of the terms on which the present recognizes the past as one of its own concerns. In this respect, remembrance is an opening, a learning, moving beyond that which is recognized as a concern of the present, because it is already known, and that which is of no concern, because it cannot be known.

Here, then is the paradoxical homecoming of zakhor. Human community relies on, indeed anticipates and depends on, continuity. But, for a true communal future to exist, required are practices that disrupt the promise of community through a remembrance of violences too difficult to publicly sustain as integral to communal history. Because the future requires something new (not a repeat of yesterday or today), without a relation to trauma, or at least without a relation to that which claims, calls, commands, interrupts, or troubles the subject, there would be no future, no hope. This is the importance of the task of remembrance of other people's painful memories. What then must be done?

BOUNDARIES AND BEGINNINGS

Zakhor requires the recognition of boundaries. To fulfill its ethical command requires the recognition of a boundary space as both limit and resource for one's actions. As I witness, I am confronted with a boundary that marks my distance from that undergone and spoken of by others. I am estranged from a past to which I always arrive too late (thus as I come close, I find myself moving away). Yet this boundary is not simply the limit of my social imagination condemning me to indifference, voyeurism, or an epistemological violence that renders the experience of others in terms I recognize or imagine as my own. This boundary rather initiates the terms for the reconstruction of my historical memory. It is the place from which to begin the practice of zakhor. That is, I begin to enact my memorial kinship to the memory of another with the recognition of my distance from these memories. And I accomplish this practice when, as a witness, I attempt to hear or see within this boundary space and re-say that which I have heard or seen, but in a way that takes cognizance of its strangeness, its foreignness, so that my rearticulation begins to touch, to interrupt my taken-for-granted performance of the present. What might it mean in practice to feel the disruptive touch of memories not mine?

Consider Dan Pagis's poem *Written in Pencil in a Sealed-Railway Car*. Pagis, a survivor of the Nazi genocide of European Jewry, has devoted a portion of his large and varied poetic writing to aspects of the experience of the Shoah. I present here Stephen Mitchell's English translation of Pagis's Hebrew text (Pagis 1981).

> here in this carload
> i am eve
> with abel my son
> if you see my other son
> cain son of man
> tell him I

This poem may be read as illustrative of the problem of witnessing. In his moving and fascinating book *Mother of the Wire Fence*, Karl Plank (1994) suggests the mother's message is addressed to a reader absent from the boxcar, who will always come to it too late. The reader always comes to these words "written in pencil in a sealed railway car," after and from afar (47). Yet it is insisted that the reader forge a connection on the boundary between Eve and her/himself and, in forging this connection, become open and responsive to being touched by the other side. The breaking off of Eve's speech enforces the distance between the boxcar and those who would hear her and subsequently speak of it. Still, the poem's address claims the reader. If Eve's silence muffles the pretext of language, her words, "tell [Cain]," afford no refuge, no escape from the claim of connection, the claim on responsibility of the reader-witness to repeat Eve's message in a different space/time. The poem's irony obliges the connection and continuity it renders so problematic. Insisted upon is a meeting between Eve and the reader that can only take place in the interstices that render the bond of testimony and witness so fragile and indeterminate.

In other words, the textual artifact makes available to some other time and place a vestige of a past, "creating a channel through which the reader, although 'not there,' *is yet touched by its presence*" (50) (my emphasis). Before any such connection allows the reader to claim a memory as his or her own, "it displaces the reader's world and subjects it to the incursion of [unforeseen and traumatic memories]. The reader does not claim, but is claimed by the profound difference, a connection forged from the other side" (51). To be able to tell Cain anything, the time of "the boxcar must be maintained in its difference. It must not be integrated into the reader's familiar world as if this world's categories had not been already cracked by Eve's silence. [Nor must it be] rendered as a cipher of an outsider's self-interest and projection" (52). The reader touched by, open to the touch of, the silence inside of the boxcar, will experience that trauma of unknowing that has as its complement the prospect of hope and the possibility of futurity.

In this moment the reader now commanded to zakhor is sent in search of a "said" that in its "saying" undoes its own certainty and makes its inadequacy and dissatisfaction present (Levinas 1991). This is a decisive break with notions of historical memory that render remembrance as recollection and reminiscence (see, for example, the often-cited work of Yosef Yerushalmi 1989). Rather a practice of zakhor adequate to the possibility of a communal futurity must paradoxically incorporate elements of trauma that disrupt the terms of sociality we have forgotten that we tolerate. This radical "unsatisfaction" provoked by difficult memories "is not simply a negative state, nor the denial of affirmation, [rather] it is the need to work through the problem of memory in reconstructing a 'sign' of history . . . not [as] a causal or deterministic narrative, [but as] . . . a powerful and poignant description . . . that pulls at us as we try and articulate, or enunciate" a renewed communal imaginary and its requisite subjectivities (Bhabha 1996, 204). A genuine tomorrow, not a repeat of yesterday or today, requires we reassess what we have learned and repressed; it is in this fundamental sense that zakhor becomes radically pedagogical.

THE NECESSITY OF TRANSLATION

Pagis's poem illustrates that the possibility of zakhor may depend on an exacerbation of what is culturally, historically incommensurable or strange, an exacerbation that allows an understanding of the "other" to emerge from an elision, an uncanny alien-ation, of one's own temporal priority (Bhabha 1993). At stake is a moving through and beyond this priority to an uncanny point of connection from which one returns to the present, in Bhabha's words, "to re-describe our cultural contemporaneity; to re-inscribe our human, historic commonality; to touch the future on its hither side." In this sense, the interstitial time of testimony-witnessing becomes a space of inter-vention in the here and now. To witness as an act of zakhor is to constitute this in-tervention as a realignment of memory and the present, as a practice of historical memory whose ethical importance "lies in its being at once a form of presence—an 'exposure'—and a technology of processing, remembering, repeating and working through" (Bhabha 1996, 203). Here, the practice of zakhor constructs the space of a psychic (and social) residence for the disembodied "wounds" that constitute other people's memories. Here is the interstitial time of testimony-witnessing where other people's struggles, passions, their pasts, may resonate within our own past and pre-sent, destabilizing the relationship between them.

In this light, the central project of remembrance is not contained in the melan-choly mimesis of the relation between an original text and its memorial translation, where performative problems are understood as ontological (I wasn't there) and epistemological (I cannot understand), in which every translation is in principle a failure, every remembrance a forgetting. Rather, the commemorative work I am exploring here opens in the interstitial boundary space, the intersubjective time of testimony-witnessing, in which one is called to zakhor and its practice of repeti-tion/reiteration through re-saying/rearticulation. This is a practice of dwelling in history, as recognizing the human as always in need of translation or mediation in order to accede to its historicity. Because a practice of historical memory must be, literally, a re-saying, a further bearing witness to one's own witness, this re-saying is not merely a recall, but always a renewal of the possibility of the past, which may innovate and interrupt the performance of the present.

I close then offering you my witness, re-saying here, Dan Pagis's poetic testimony.

> Re-Iteration
> in robarts library, section pj 5054
> a familiar voice, a woman's voice
> spoke to me from the leaves of a book
> saying
> > - here in this carload
> > - i am eve
> mother!
> > - with abel my son
> him, i knew
> > - if you see my other son
> > - cain, son of man
> in the shadows of the stacks
> she didn't recognize me

- tell him i
with disguised voice, i said
i will tell him you were asking

dan pagis said it wasn't mother
it was
     - written in pencil in a sealed railway car
he wasn't in the stacks

NOTES

1. How it is that other people's memories viscerally matter so as to require my attention and vigilance is an issue well worth extended consideration. In this regard it is worth contemplating on what terms images and stories of the suffering of others come into view within a media-saturated public sphere. What should be more widely known is that there exist public relations firms whose business it is to shape what constitutes one's public sphere, drawing the attention of specific groups to particular information. In this regard, consider the extract of French journalist Jacques Merlino interviewing James Harff, a former executive with the public relations firm Ruder Finn (for information on Ruder Finn, see their web site: www.ruderfinn.com/about/index.html). Merlino asked Harff what his proudest public relations endeavor was. Harff responded:

> To have managed to put Jewish opinion on our side. This was a sensitive matter, as the dossier was dangerous looked at from this angle. President Tudjman was very careless in his book, *Wastelands of Historical Reality*. Reading his writings one could accuse him of anti-Semitism. In Bosnia the situation was no better:
>
> President Izetbegovic strongly supported the creation of a fundamentalist Islamic state in his book, *The Islamic Declaration*.
>
> Besides, the Croatian and Bosnian past was marked by real and cruel anti-Semitism. Tens of thousands of Jews perished in Croatian camps, so there was every reason for intellectuals and Jewish organizations to be hostile toward the Croats and the Bosnians. Our challenge was to reverse this attitude and we succeeded masterfully.
>
> At the beginning of July 1992, New York *Newsday* came out with the article on Serb camps. We jumped at the opportunity immediately. We outwitted three big Jewish organizations, the B'nai B'rith Anti-Defamation League, the American Jewish Committee and the American Jewish Congress. In August, we suggested that they publish an advertisement in the *New York Times* and organize demonstrations outside the United Nations.
>
> That was a tremendous coup. When the Jewish organizations entered the game on the side of the [Muslim] Bosnians we could promptly equate the Serbs with the Nazis in the public mind. Nobody understood what was happening in Yugoslavia. The great majority of Americans were probably asking themselves in which African country Bosnia was situated.
>
> By a single move, we were able to present a simple story of good guys and bad guys which would hereafter play itself. We won by targeting the Jewish audience. Almost immediately there was a clear change of language in the press, with use of words with high emotional content such as ethnic cleansing, concentration camps, etc., which evoke images of Nazi Germany and the gas

chambers of Auschwitz. No one could go against it without being accused of revisionism. We really batted a thousand in full.

This interview excerpt appears in Merlino's book *Les vérités Yougosalves ne sont pas toutes bonnes à dire* (Paris, 1993). It has been translated into English on various web sites—not unsurprisingly by many posted by Serbian solidarity organizations—and was reported in the Canadian newspaper the *National Post* in an article by Isabel Vincent "International Media under Attack in Serbia," November 23, 1998.

Even when issues of media manipulation can be put aside by overwhelming evidence, the issues raised by how one articulates a "point of connection" between one's own past and the present realities of others are well illustrated by, at the time of this writing, current debates within Jewish communities regarding the identificatory connections between the images and stories of Kosovar refugees and Jewish memory. In Toronto, Rabbi John Moscowitz has written "we can't look at those who are crowding the Albanian border with few belongings; those who've fled Kosovo on foot, by train or stuffed into a truck; all those who've been uprooted by a well-organized assault to drive them out and away. . . . We can't look at them and not see grandparents, parents, or ourselves. . . . Although Kosovo is not Auschwitz and Milosevic is hardly Hitler, the Holocaust nonetheless resonates too loudly for us not to respond to those who find themselves in such dire straits." Yet other Jewish leaders decry this too easy equation of memories, criticizing the invocation of Holocaust imagery by parties to "Kosovo Crisis" and use of the Holocaust as "a metaphor to understand or manipulate the understanding of what is happening in Kosovo today." While those voicing this criticism are not indifferent to the terrible suffering of Kosovar refugees, they remind us that during the Shoah

> a refugee was a "privileged" status, a step ahead of death. In Kosovo, expulsions are to Albania or Macedonia; in the Holocaust the deportations were to Auschwitz. . . . To require of Kosovo to be a Holocaust in order to characterize it as radical evil is to deny its essential evil even when it is not a Holocaust. For while Kosovo is not a Holocaust, what is happening there—forced detentions, disappearances, expulsions, rape, murder—is evil enough. . . . Indeed, invoking the Holocaust to justify humanitarian intervention in Kosovo today results more from a failure of memory than from a parallel analogy. (Irwin Cotler, *Canadian Jewish News,* May 13, 1999, 1, 34)

2

If the Story Cannot End:

Deferred Action, Ambivalence, and Difficult Knowledge

Deborah P. Britzman

> In the middle of my life I fell into a trouble that was to grip, occupy, haunt, and all but devour me these twenty years. I've used the word "fall." It implies something accidental, a stumbling, but we also use the word in speaking of "falling in love" in which there is a sense of elevation and where a fatedness is implied, a feeling of being inevitably bound in through all the mysterious components of character to this expression in the life process, whether in the end beautifully gratifying or predominantly painful.
>
> —Meyer Levin, *The Obsession*

So begins Meyer Levin's postwar epic and lonely account of his unsuccessful thirty-year struggle with Hollywood moguls, lawyers, and Otto Frank over the rights to produce his own play based on Anne Frank's *Diary of a Young Girl*.[1] Frank chose the team of Goodrich and Hackett to write the 1956 Broadway play that subsequently won a Pulitzer Prize. Recently the play was adapted by Wendy Kesselman and directed by James Lapine and had another run on Broadway during the 1997–1998 season. Inevitably, the reviews of the revised play returned to Levin's earlier fights over the rights to make a play from the diary and to his profound dissatisfaction with the play Otto Frank chose. Levin was deeply pained over the first play's emphasis on family melodrama and its figure of relief, a comedic Anne. He argued that this structure downplayed Anne's Jewishness in order to make the play more palatable to what the producers thought of as the general Broadway public, and, in so doing, could not offer audiences insight into the devastating daily situations and the larger context European Jews confronted. Levin, of course, was not the only figure to be dissatisfied with the packaging of Anne Frank's diary,[2] but his

27

fight with Otto Frank, the father of Anne Frank, was so spectacular in affect, so scandalous in the trade of accusations, so traumatic in expression, that its belated force continues to be debated, retold, and even repeated. Indeed, the figure of Meyer Levin, the man who sued Otto Frank over the rights to Frank's daughter's diary and who attempted to mobilize Jewish leaders against what he saw as a Stalinist conspiracy to forget the Jewish loss,[3] now haunts the secondary history of Anne Frank's diary.

Levin was trying to respond to that first history—the near destruction of European Jewry—that called Anne Frank to rewrite her diary for others to read. But he could only encounter what Anne Frank left behind, and then everywhere he found traces of all that betrayed her, including the Broadway play that, in Levin's view, emphasized the uplifting and universal qualities of the diary to the detriment of grasping the magnitude of the disaster. From this belated meeting, he tried, not just in writing a script that would never be produced, but in his thirty-year public struggle with Otto Frank and his representatives, to craft from the diary both his own relation to the event of the *Shoah* (the Hebrew term widely used to reference the Nazi genocide of European Jewry) and what he hoped would be future understandings. This interminable work of making a relation to loss, the fragile work of mourning, is part of what troubles the history of Levin's troubles.

Levin's phrasing—whether his efforts to save the diary would be beautifully gratifying or predominantly painful—seems, at first glance, to be a part of contemporary pedagogical efforts brought to the question of what manifold forms attachment can mean for scenes of social recognition. We would do well to reconsider the poles of this wavering in our own attempts to work with the diary in school settings, through the terms of Levin's fall. Since the discovery and publication of the diary, profound arguments about the import of its use have also been a part of its reception. While we wish our students to make some insight from reading the diary, to identify with Anne Frank's struggles, to learn something about what it is like to confront one's own destruction, and to appreciate the power of narrating, indeed, of bearing witness to the relation one's life has to others—all forms that encourage the reader's attachment to the import of this text—we are just beginning to consider the psychic difficulty of learning from the traumatic experiences of others. Contemporary pedagogy and popular representations, however, seem to emphasize the idealized outcomes of learning; perhaps the most common concerns the inscription of hope. This approach assumes that the problem of making an attachment to the diary can be solved by the figure of Anne Frank, who has been used as a model of courage and as a child martyr. Perhaps educators believe these representations of Anne Frank can call their students to attention, provide suitable role models, and even speak to something desirable within the student. The problem with these appeals, however, and what this chapter is largely concerned with, is twofold. One dimension has to do with how pedagogy might consider the difficult qualities of approaching experiences of profound loss. Most generally, this chapter explores what the work of mourning means in learning. How might a psychoanalytically inflected theory of learning from the reception of difficult and traumatic events inform the ways teachers and students approach these events in relation to understanding profound loss? Another dimension is more specific and involves an exploration of whether the idealization of any figure, as a strategy of inciting identification, can allow insight into the conditions that invoke the urge and weight of idealization, the psychical needs that animate identification and its limits, and the intimate work, indeed the difficulties, of confronting what it means in the learner's present to respond to the questions of loss the diary continues to pose.

Perhaps this idealization of the figure of Anne Frank on the part of educators is a reaction formation, a defense mechanism used to ward off the significant anxieties that their students may not see any relation to the diary, see it as irrelevant to their own lives, and even deny that the text is authentic and truthful. Idealizing the figure of Anne Frank as the transitional object into school-based Holocaust studies, however, may work to inhibit any efforts on the part of students and teachers to understand not just what Anne Frank responded to but also how the diary has been used over the course of post-Holocaust years and the uses we make of it today. Certainly, idealization may be one way to avoid the painful dilemmas of confronting the traumatic residues of this devastating history. But these reactions and their attendant worries, themselves ego defense mechanisms that try to ward off the traumatic perception of helplessness and loss, can foreclose the very processes of what it means for contemporary students to attach to the diary: to make from the diary new meanings in their own lives; to become attentive to profound suffering and social injustices in their own time; to begin to understand the structures that sustain aggression and hatred; and to consider how the very questions of vulnerability, despair, and profound loss must become central to our own conceptualizations of who we each are, not just in terms of reading the diary as a text but also in allowing the diary to invoke the interest in the work of becoming an ethical subject.

If the question of ethicality does not begin with what is successful, ideal, or familiar about our actions and thoughts but rather with what becomes inaugurated when we notice the breakdown of meaning and the illusiveness of signification, then our pedagogical efforts must also begin with a study of the difficulty of making significance from the painful experiences of others, the confrontation with the recursive structure of trauma, and the ambivalence toward the very question of loss. To return to the arguments over the import of the diary may allow us to make some fragile insight into the difficulty within and defense against considering its reception. This is where the figure of Meyer Levin plays a role. However, to make some sense of what happened to Meyer Levin, to consider his painful dilemmas as more than a curious footnote in post-Holocaust history—indeed, to view his struggle as possessing the capacity to comment upon something difficult within our own contemporary efforts in pedagogy—one must bring something more to his story than his view of what went terribly wrong.

Hannah Arendt's discussion of what it is to learn from the remnants of another's life struggle suggests something about Levin's fall and his use of Anne Frank's diary. For this moment of learning from another's life and making from this learning a relation to a difficult history is also part of what structures the persistent use of the diary today. In her preface to *Between Past and Future,*[4] Arendt brings the question of biography closer to the problem of encountering the vicissitudes of thought:

> If one were to write the intellectual history of our century, not in the form of successive generations, where the historian must be literally true to the sequence of theories and attitudes, but in the form of the biography of a single person, aiming at no more than a metaphorical approximation to what actually happened in the minds of men, this person's mind would stand revealed as having been forced to turn full circle not once but twice, first when he escaped from thought into action, and then again when action, or rather having acted, forced him back into thought. (9)

We would do well to notice the trajectory Arendt traces: In taking an action, one cannot know in advance its effects on the self or its effects on others. This is certainly the dilemma with Anne Frank's diary and Meyer Levin's response to it. Arendt suggests it is thought that completes the signification of action or experience, but not in terms that necessarily affirm the intentions of the actor or even make closure for the action itself. It is not the case, at least in Arendt's view, that action is devoid of thought. But the thought that invokes action responds to what went before, and being forced back into thought after our actions allows for a revision of the time of experience, opening experience to something more than the immediacy of our needs, our capacity to disavow the ramification of traumatic events, and the obscurity of recognizing historical breakdowns in our own times.[5] This point is crucial in exploring questions of trauma as encompassing the time of deferred action. One could say, for example, that Meyer Levin's traumatic response to the diary opens a different awareness to Anne Frank's own traumatic contexts. While Anne Frank registered the force of traumatic events, our susceptibility to this force must, however precariously, exceed traumatic repetitions; new meanings of time must be developed. Freud named this dynamic *Nachträglichkeit,* as the revision of experiences, memories, and impressions are made to fit new circumstances. The force of experience undergoes a revision at a later time, but the qualities of the revision may lead to repetition or working through. If action is that first scene, it takes a secondary scene of thought to revise and even bring to the fore the ramifications of our actions. But, for the revision to affect the quality of thought, our present preoccupations, and how we come to understand what is past, action must be considered again, retrospectively. It is not experience that undergoes a change but rather how one perceives the aftermath of experience in relation to both previous experiences and those not yet made. This rather complex psychical dynamic is explored throughout this chapter, for even the criticism of contemporary pedagogical efforts constitutes a deferred action, a retranscription of how the diary's reception might be thought and encountered.

What, then, is it to be forced back into thought when the object of thought eludes comprehension, when the remnants of history cannot make coherent our present stories, and when thought itself is overwhelmed by profound emotions made from the psychic events of living with irrevocable loss, suffering, anxiety, and despair? We know that Anne Frank could not turn full circle twice. Meyer Levin tried, but his attempts in the end were predominantly painful. We are just coming to know that contemporary readers themselves must now accept this difficult obligation in ways that Meyer Levin and those who crafted the North American reception of the diary could not have imagined. This is because the infinite details of the Holocaust, details that continue to shock perceptions of our present and our past (for instance, the myth of neutrality in World War II, the Swiss banking scandal, the stolen art in museums, and so on) disturb the view that the past can be put to rest through declaring an event over. If there is to be a capacity to learn from the advent of social breakdown, then and now, can a reading of the historicity of the diary's reception begin to approximate some of this interminable work (a work that I will describe as the work of mourning) without foreclosing and forgetting not just the troubles made in history but that which should trouble us because of the history that becomes our lives? For someone like Meyer Levin, the sad conclusion must be no. In many ways, Meyer Levin's response to the diary suggests a reenactment of the fragments of the diary's traumatic context: a family in hiding that could not save itself, a young girl whose promise of life was betrayed by a profoundly violent and cruel social, a people whose subjectivity was cut off by legal design and its popularized sanctioned violence, and finally Levin's own view that he could not save his own version of the diary's crafting from falling into oblivion. And, in many ways, contemporary pedagogical attempts to teach the diary seem caught in Levin's dilemma of attempting to control how the diary will be received. Yet, even the consideration of these fragments is not the end of the story of the diary's reception and its fragile pedagogical yearnings in post-Holocaust North America. Something resists the force of thought.

This chapter, then, returns to the stakes of Levin's "fall," but not to settle what happened, not to tell a more adequate story in order to bring this drama to closure. The chronology at stake in this chapter is not a lineal progression but rather is recursive, akin to the transcriptions of Nachträglichkeit and transference, moving from present to past and back to our present. This is because the irremovable past sutures the present, but not in ways that make automatic our capacity for conscious apprehension of events that should call us to attention. But, as we will see throughout this chapter, to become susceptible to the forces of our own attention, to be called to attention and to make from this call a revision in one's own life, also invokes, at the level of the psychical, manifold forms of attachment and disassociation that signal some of the dilemmas of identification. My focus on the need for educators to consider a theory of attachment in learning stems from a consideration of the question of learning: of what it means for the learner to encounter and engage the experiences of another; to craft significance from how Anne Frank has been represented; and to consider in more general terms the question of learning from suffering and injustice. Over the course of the chapter I will signal very different forms of attachment, such as identification, idealization, clinging, splitting, incorporation, over-familiarity, numbing, uncanniness, and thinking, as some of the possible scenes that structure social recognition and mis-recognition. The model of attachment I believe to be the most helpful to the problem of learning to become an ethical subject is drawn from Sigmund Freud's essay "Mourning and Melancholia," for there experiences of loss invoke the contradictory desire to attach, to be touched and changed by a relation that is no longer. If there is to be an attachment to that which has gone but still exerts force upon our present experiences, and if the attachment is not to invoke rigid ego boundaries, mirror-like apprehension, the insistence upon familiarity, or profound modes of idealization and clinging that foreclose the ambivalent feelings that do accompany loss, then we are obligated to explore how what has been lost in the self and in the social affects the dynamics of learning.

If there can be a story of working through the repressions a story inaugurates, then that story of working through is closer to a consideration of a complex of stories and to an acknowledgment that part of this complex is made from the failure of imagination both at the level of the social and the individual. To settle these accounts through either discouragement or idealization, through the binary of what historian Saul Friedlander (1992, 42) names "catastrophe or redemption," is part of the trouble. The other part is equally troubling. It has to do with contemporary attempts to make from Levin's struggle over the import of Anne Frank's diary a final judgment on either Levin's efforts or the question of what it should mean in the learner's present life to attach to the diary's reception. What is it to attach to the arguments raised over the reception of Anne Frank's diary? Why study the secondary breakdown of meaning, the contemporary crisis of witnessing, which is also the crisis made from the diary's reception? To consider these large questions, each section of this chapter explores a play of fragments: those of thought, those of the unconscious, those of transference, and those of working through. I will suggest something unsettling about how the dynamics of the ways Anne Frank has been represented may say something about the limits of our own pedagogy, about how our pedagogical past presses into form that which is not yet. Indeed, while contentious discussions over the import of the diary's reception and over the loss that inaugurated its postwar crafting have not yet appeared to affect how the diary is encountered in schools, these very arguments seem to be repeated in educators' worries over the diary's pedagogical potential.[6]

APPEALS TO THOUGHT

For one to be forced back into thought may be just the beginning of one's attempt to break through the terrible confines of reenacting the transpositions of trauma. And, to be forced back into thought cannot be seen as either comparable to the insistence upon a facile and willed rationalism or the demand to make closure. Arendt suggests that thinking is a problem of ethicality; thinking may open the question of what conceptuality can mean for the working though of traumatic events. If trauma is the incapacity to respond adequately to a terrible and shattering event, the incapacity to think an afterward, and to make meaning from the ruins of experience, and if, as Cathy Caruth suggests, what makes trauma traumatic is the loss of the capacity to experience, trauma "does not simply serve as a record of the past but precisely registers the force of an experience that is not fully owned" (1995, 151). Part of the terror of the event can return and repeat as one attempts to make from loss a learning, a learning to live with an unresolved past. Within this difficult experience of what is not yet and, indeed, may never become fully experienced, a new subjectivity must be crafted from its traumatic ruins.

Sigmund Freud called this interminable work of living with loss "a working through." He used this term most poignantly in his important paper "Mourning and Melancholia."[7] Freud suggests there are infinite ramifications of what the painful experience of loss can mean and what loss does to the bereft, whether the experience of loss be the loss of an important ideal or the loss of an actual person. Contemporary pedagogical efforts that focus upon Anne Frank's diary must engage the working through of both kinds of loss: the loss of the idea of the social bond *and* the loss of actual individuals. These losses must be considered as intimately entwined, and thus any curriculum that invokes the difficulties and the sufferings of others must come to terms with both the events of loss and how these events are received and reworked. And, in considering both losses, the loss of an idea of the sanctity of the value of life and the loss of an individual, the appeal to thought must work against the sentimental consolation that the diary can somehow replace the loss that it signifies. Can a pedagogical encounter with the history of the diary, a history that is also our present, offer an insight into what learning means in relation to the work of mourning?

For Freud, the work of mourning is the work of memorializing the loss, of allowing the loss not just to become a part of one's memory, but of permitting its force to reconstitute the very transcription of memory. The mourner herself must change, and all that is familiar must be transformed. For a memory to become a memory, the first shock of reenacting the abandonment that loss invokes must be exceeded and the ambivalence that accompanies loss must be acknowledged. Otherwise, the memory can work as persecution and then must be defended against. Slowly, detail by detail, memory by memory, the grief made from loss must encounter the utter singularity of loss, and still, the griever must find a way to resume the obligations of learning to live, to risk new attachments in the world, and to demand something of the living. These new attachments are not substitutes for what has been lost. There can be no substitute for the singularity of loss, and this may be why Freud poses the question of crafting a memory from painful losses as a problem of ethical love.[8]

The work of mourning, of memory, requires that the mourner work through her or his own impulse to idealize the lost object, to split off the affect from the fact of loss, and hence attempt to bring back as unchanged and familiar what can no longer exist. Idealization inhibits the mourner's work of learning to come to terms with what has been lost in the self, what has been lost to the social, and to the working through of the ambivalence that such knowledge can bring. When idealization interrupts mourning, the lost object becomes incorporated and confused with the ego. The singularity of the other is thus displaced because, in incorporating the other, the other's singularity as a separate being is lost.[9] Freud called this displacement—when libidinality regresses back into the ego—melancholia, a profound loss of the self's capacity to be interested in the world and to work through the vicissitudes of what loss can signify. Melancholia is a form of narcissistic identification, where the ego confuses itself with the lost object, becomes split, and then attacks itself and the loss. One form narcissistic identification can take is idealization of the lost object, a form of controlling and judging the conflictive dynamics of loss. But what is actually idealized is not the object but the self, for in melancholia the object becomes the ego, or more accurately, the ego becomes split into absolute forms of good and bad that then wage for dominance. Neither the ego nor the object can become understood as vulnerable to forces other than good ones. Idealization then becomes a substitute for engagement and a mechanism of control that wards off the capacity to acknowledge the profundity of loss. It can neither restore the loss nor allow for the working through of the ambivalent feelings that accompany loss. Freud thus offers us two stories of psychical attachment, one bound to the nostalgia for an idealized and unchanged world that he calls melancholia, the other bound to an ethical struggle with reconstituting the self as subject to a relation that is no longer. Melancholia can be understood as a form of attachment called clinging, not to the object that is gone but to the ego that existed before the loss. Mourning is work because what is lost in the self and what is lost in the world become a part of the ego after the loss. In the work of mourning, it is the ego's own boundaries that are altered.

Because contemporary readers only encounter the textualizations of Anne Frank,[10] processes of idealization and attempts to restore as unchanged both the lost object and the ego who perceives the other may actually be invoked in the very design of the encounter, with the consequence that the relationship between reading and mourning is foreclosed. Saul Friedlander's discussion of "working through" in the context of encountering the inconsolable documents of living in and with the Shoah suggests this difficulty for historians and, we should add, for anyone encountering the documents of historians: "to keep some measure of balance between the emotion recurrently breaking through 'the protective shield' [of defense against trauma] and a numbness that protects this very shield. . . . 'Working through' means, first, being aware of both tendencies, allowing for a measure of balance between the two whenever possible"[11] (1994, 260–261). The difficulty, Friedlander suggests, is that at first, neither emotion nor numbness can be consciously apprehended and both of these responses are forms of identification and dis-identification that unconsciously serve to protect and defend against traumatic perception.

Whereas numbness is the incapacity to consider what has been lost in the self and what has been lost in sociality, the emotion that breaks through in identification obscures the historian's own statement of need and, hence, inhibits an analysis of the historian's transferential relation to the writing of history. These responses can be thought of as resistance to thought.

To understand the stakes of Friedlander's argument, it is useful to consider how emotion and numbness can work as transitory identifications in a common daily scene, elaborated by the analyst Rafael Moses (1986):

> Some years ago Joseph Sandler talked to me about how, when we see a stranger fal-
> tering a few meters from us, we feel, somehow, somewhere, in relation to our own
> body the "almost falling" of the other (Sandler and Joffee, 1967). Our ego boundaries
> will be momentarily inattentive and allow us to identify briefly with the stranger in this
> "almost falling." We will therefore try to counteract the hardly noticeable, momen-
> tarily unpleasant sensation. We do so either by the fantasy, acted out in a minute way,
> of righting our body so as not to fall; or by disidentifying with the person who stum-
> bles. Both mechanisms serve our need to be reassured that what happens to the other
> does not happen to us, that we are different from him. (137)

The only way out of this imaginary safety that, in fact, serves to make ego boundaries rigid, is, of course, to try to help the other who stumbles. But prior to this moment, a certain susceptibility to the other's action unconsciously plays itself out. Identification is precisely this susceptibility to the other but a susceptibility that is incomplete and subject to its own reversals into its opposite: disregard for the other. The sort of emotion and numbness also described by Moses suggests that fleeting identifications cannot, in themselves, allow for ethical thought. The em-barrassment that some may feel, the arrogance at not being the one who "almost falls," and the judgment of the stranger as somehow less than oneself suggest that emotion and numbness are not so much the opposite of each other but a to-and-fro movement, an attempt at sustaining one's illusory sense of stability and conti-nuity. Feeling the "almost fall" and then distancing oneself are symptoms of the incapacity to distinguish the time of trauma from, in the case of the historian, the trauma of time. To return to Friedlander's point, the difficulties of writing and reading history as a transferential problem, where what belongs to the historian and the reader and what belongs to history and the other cannot be distinguished, re-mind us of how the traumatic perception of encountering the remnants of the Shoah poses significant questions for what "working through" requires from each of us. For part of what must be worked though are the projective identifications that impede our capacity to make an ethical relation to the stranger, to encounter vulnerability as a relation and thus move beyond the impulse of repeating the trauma by placing helplessness and loss elsewhere.

Meyer Levin's view of his own fall suggests one sort of crisis made when one is forced back into thought. He cannot decide if his obsession with controlling the diary is worthy of either himself or the diary's meaning. This question, posed on the precipice of a fall, can be further elaborated within the qualities Arendt offers when she discusses what it is to undergo "an appeal to thought." The appeal can only be staged in a twilight time: the belatedness of a realization that a fall has already taken place.[12] Arendt (1993) described this moment of retrospection as "an interval of time which is altogether determined by things that are no longer and by things that are not yet"(9). Such an interval is precisely what circumscribes the work of mourning and the work of pedagogy. Levin's fall, his accidental stumbling, is made, I think, as an appeal to thought, but an appeal that has lost its address. Shoshana Felman's (1992) discussion of both the nature of accidents and the nature of a fall, in her chapters on literature and the Shoah, also suggests something about remorse, loss, and working through the demands this interval of time presses into form. Felman turns to the obligation such an appeal poses and suggests that what is required is: "the witness's readiness, precisely, to pursue the accident, to actively pursue its path and its direction through obscurity, through darkness, and through fragmentation, without quite grasping the full scope and meaning of its implications, without entirely foreseeing where the journey leads and what is the precise nature of its final destination" (24). But what is it to become ready? And, if pedagogy repeats the fall without pursuing its own accidents, without appealing to thought, what can we learn about learning to live a life?

UNCONSCIOUS PEDAGOGY

If one can enact the tensions of a history one may not have conscious knowledge of, this speculation suggests something about the unconscious play of pedagogy. While much of the writing in pedagogy considers questions of the curricular knowledge teachers and students engage, a significant feature also operative in the pedagogical exchange that requires our attention is the affective dynamics teachers and students enact in relation to the knowledge learned and in relation to anxieties over what resists learning. This transitional space is where manifold forms of attachment and disassociation, and where "almost falling," become reenacted. One of the most common experiences in teaching Anne Frank's diary is that school-structured encounters with the diary waiver between what Friedlander refers to as numbing and emotion. There is a profound idealization of adolescent yearning, where Anne Frank's voice is often taken as capable of transcending or even redeeming the very history that cut her life so short. To ward off the traumatic perception of what actually happened to Anne Frank, there is a comparable move toward the enactment of an unconscious rescue fantasy. This fantasy attempts to rescue Anne and her readers from the painful history that invokes the diary's writing, finding, and crafting. Transcendence and rescue, however, are two sides of the same coin. These imaginary actions are comparable to Friedlander's point that the historian may be caught between the poles of numbness and emotion, and to return to Moses' insight, repeat the phenomenon of "almost falling." The numbness of idealization and the illusionary satisfaction made from the emotion of rescue defend against the traumatic perception of loss and helplessness. In both responses, the actual event is taken over by the anxieties of its encounter and the chance to return to thoughtfulness may actually be felt as a threat to the integrity of pedagogy itself. This is because, to return to Felman's insight on pursuing the accident, one cannot know in advance where the pursuit will lead, and often the integrity of pedagogy is dependent upon a preordained goal.

While it may be strange to claim that pedagogy can also become a defense against thought and defend itself against its own capacity for ignorance, this view is meant to call attention to the fact that school curriculum does not have an adequate grasp of conflict in learning, either the conflict within the learner or the conflict within knowledge itself.[13] Mainstream discussions of curriculum, with their insistence on technical procedure and measurable outcomes, foreclose consideration of the conflict that inaugurates the very possibility of any knowledge and how the illusion of knowledge can work to dissolve the problem of ethics. Along with curricular efforts that tend to push the educator toward the valorization of technique and then toward the fear of its breakdown, another problem is foreclosed. This has to do with the limits of the educator's own education and her or his own forgetting that knowledge is interminable and hardly settled either in learning theories or in interpretive practices. This means that the limits of the teacher's own education persists unconsciously in pedagogical efforts. In drawing our attention to the unconscious qualities of education and to what educators must repress in order to stabilize knowledge, I mean to signal two meanings of the word *unconscious:* that knowledge does not structure action and that the wishes that structure the unconscious as a psychical event preclude a rigorous conceptualization of time and of history. The unconscious qualities of pedagogy can then reenact, as opposed to work through, the limits of the teacher's education.

Exquisitely thoughtful engagements with the difficulty the diary poses do exist, for example, in the work of Alvin Rosenfeld and Judith Doneson.[14] Yet this work remains shut out of pedagogical thought. The very structure of pedagogical engagement—the ways history is treated as if its narrative can somehow make restive the conflicts that remain unresolved and the wish that students should naturally find their own meaning in the text without teacher interference[15]—precludes the work of making insight into the experience of history, not as a progression or process that is made by individuals but rather, to return to Arendt's appeal, to approach history as an incomplete project of becoming an ethical subject in relation to other ethical subjects. For this work to even be considered, the teacher must become willing to explore not just her or his own relation to the diary's difficult knowledge but also how the students' experiences of the diary affect the teacher's own pedagogical actions and thoughts.

The project of becoming an ethical subject in relation to other ethical subjects is, perhaps, one of the most difficult problems opened when encountering representations of the Shoah. Those who were murdered in the Shoah were murdered precisely because they could not be considered, by their neighbors, fellow citizens, jurisprudence, and the pedagogical imaginary, as ethical subjects. This loss of ethical imagination is part of what must be confronted, mourned, and reconstituted. Many writers on the Shoah have pointed this out,[16] but perhaps one of the most urgent formulations is offered by analyst Dori Laub (1992), who considers survivor testimonies as an attempt to reconstruct, through the language of receiving their own testimony, a profoundly wounded subjectivity. Laub argues that the gift of testimony and its reception is an act of intersubjectivity, where the listener becomes willing to witness the painful inauguration of the testifier becoming an ethical subject. And yet receiving the testimony may well be precisely the place where the possibility of ethicality breaks down, for the receiving, as Laub and others have suggested, is belated, too late to prevent the trauma, too fragile to ensure that the trauma itself will not be repeated, albeit this time in the form of a feeling that cannot attach to what Ernst van Alphen (1997) calls "the urge to reconstruct an affective community" (176). Testimony must be received as a provocation of this urge and hence as a restoration of the capacity for subjectivity to be rebuilt from the ruins of destruction. And yet this work, as van Alphen suggests, is interminable: "Is it possible to get in touch with what cannot be understood?" (176).

Van Alphen's question is deeply disturbing to an education that presumes understanding. But there is something difficult about learning from history, particularly the history of a destruction. At the most intimate level, Derrida (1994) offers a view of the trouble: "What is most painful is that the painful is not painful for others, thereby risking the loss of its value"(263). And also, what perhaps is painful is that the singularity of the pain must be made relevant to those who, at first glance, feel beyond its reach and hence cannot accept—indeed, to return to Friedlander's point, defend themselves against—the reach of pain. Let us look more closely at the dynamic relations at stake when one confronts the pain of another but does not enact the unconscious identification of "almost falling." To study the difficulty of others is actually to study how one comes to relate to the conditions of difficulty expressed, as opposed to somehow attempt to reacquire the felt experience of the other. To be receptive to the difficulties of the other is not the same as feeling another's pain, itself impossible, because at first, when confronted with expressions of pain, one tries to attach by imagining how one would feel in similar conditions.[17] This imaginary move, sometimes mistaken as empathy, is closer to the reenactment of "almost falling" and, hence, still within the confines of the narcissistic impulse to control and judge. To make relevant experiences beyond one's own, indeed, even within one's own realm, means that one must work through the remittances that primary identifications put into place.

Van Alphen's own recollection of his high school days suggests some possible defensive measures. He recalls that, as a high school student in the 1960s in Amsterdam, Holocaust education bored him. The figure of Anne Frank haunted his boredom; he refused, until very recently, to read Anne Frank's published diary, a document written in the very city in which he now lives. This refusal was, at least initially, something that made van Alphen proud; as a youth he became the hero in his own drama of refusing to be affected. During his compulsory education, van Alphen could find no reason to make relevant the disclaimed pain of his parents and their actions, because in his education there was no pain or remorse, only stories of war heroism, emplotment, and redemption, all defenses that sustain what he now views as repressions of "Holocaust effects." These effects are not just symptoms of absence. They also haunt the question of how to obligate oneself to that which was destroyed but has not gone away. The material of his education did not reenact the past in a way that could give insight into the present question of what it is to encounter the Holocaust today. There was no obligation in van Alphen's education, and the congratulatory insistence that the present is better because the past made it so literally left van Alphen with nothing to do, nothing to think.

What then is it to learn from disclaimed history? Feeling pain, or refusing to recognize the pain of others, may be closer to trauma and to the incapacity to make sense of experience than it is to the complex question of making a relation to others by acknowledging or witnessing the incommensurability of pain. While one pedagogical wish may be that if we can learn from another's pain we can avoid doing more harm and another wish may be to avoid the dissonance that the difficulties of others can invoke, there is still a problem with what these conflictive desires can signify. The paradox is that because learning from another's pain requires noticing what one has not experienced and the capacity to be touched by what one has not noticed, identifying with pain requires a self capable of wounding her or his own ego boundaries, the very boundaries that serve as a defense against pain. The intimate problem is for the learner to notice how she or he is affected in the present because disclaimed history is being reconstructed. So, in actuality, it is not the pain that one can identify with but rather the secondary effects of distress, helplessness, and loss that the pain symbolizes. The line between trauma and its working through, however, becomes frayed when feelings of pain cannot become attached to conscious thought or when the pain and suffering of the other is viewed as an interruption of one's unconscious wishes for a life without conflict. This seems to be van Alphen's dilemma, where rather than confront the conditions of hiding and, indeed, what the Frank family was hiding from, which Anne Frank speaks of, he reverses the position and now hides from Anne Frank. His feelings of boredom repeat the very structure of his education, for there transcendence can only lead to becoming bored, to refusing to be touched. To learn from disclaimed history requires a willingness to confront one's own discomfort, one's own inadequacy, and the conditions and actions that coalesce to foreclose the possibilities of self and other as ethical subjects.

In pedagogical attempts to teach Anne Frank's diary, however, the profound ambivalence as to where to locate her pain prevents contemporary students from even considering who they can become because of what Anne Frank might offer. This ambivalence is not often admitted as part of the tension involved in thinking through the questions Anne Frank asks of her readers. Rather, situating the place of pain seems to speak more to educators' worries over how the diary can be made relevant to their students. Should, for example, Anne Frank be viewed as an adolescent struggling, like any adolescent, with growing up? Is it then easier for identification to occur if identification is with what is deemed universal? And, if Anne Frank can be encountered in all of her normality, would identification with her become easy? Should Anne Frank's pain be located solely in her growing awareness of a specific time of what it meant to be Jewish, of the family as trapped in anti-Semitic cruelty, and of the ways she noticed how the larger social denied herself as an ethical subject? If contemporary readers have never encountered the question of what it is to have one's subjectivity shattered, what would be the basis of this identification? How would those who encounter Anne Frank identify with what it is like to become so marginalized? Should Anne Frank's pain be associated with her wish for a magical healing, for her desire to make from hopelessness a hope for goodness? Would readers then identify with the command to have hope? In each of these speculations, what it might take to identify with Anne Frank depends upon which Anne Frank one is encouraged to meet. However, the problem with each formulation is that these desires for readerly identifications preclude the possibility of turning full circle twice and making from action a mode of thought that is ready to pursue the accident, without recourse to knowing in advance what might happen.

Within these choices, what tends to be emphasized is not the learning the diary provokes but the wishes it also offers. This is a different form of idealization in that wishes are on the side of fantasy. Our susceptibility to the wish suggests the force of the unconscious. For Freud the wish is a statement of both need and want and it is difficult to distinguish, once and for all, the difference between these two demands. The wish also defends against the anxiety that ego boundaries, so broken in trauma, will be further shattered. Van Alphen's boredom can also be considered a defense against the traumatic perception that there is no recovery or redemption in history and that stories of heroism may actually work to cover over the very painful questions of loss, helplessness, and even implication. Van Alphen wished that the history would just go away: His boredom, that there is nothing to learn, says as much. This secondary trauma, described earlier in this chapter as a deferred action, works to refuse what Derrida (1994) calls in his meditation on debts that cannot be repaid a learning "to learn to live *with* ghosts, in the upkeep, the conversation, the company, or the companionship, in the commerce without commerce of ghosts. To live otherwise, and better. No, not better, but more justly. But *with them*" (xviii). For van Alphen, the boredom he made from his education severed the possibility of even the thought of a debt.

As a high school student, van Alphen refused to identify with his country's capacity to shatter and with his country's wish for a heroic past. His schooling seemed to invoke this position of numbness through idealization, offering a closed narrative about World War II through endless details of battles fought and, then, in the congratulatory insistence that his country's present bears no traces of its past. But something else marks the experience of closure. It has to do with what is foreclosed in the act of closure, with what must literally be missed, or given over to loss, for experience to be experience at all. And, while Holocaust education must reply forcefully to revisionist accounts that negate the genocide, the questions of what happens to experiences, what happens to facts, when no conceptuality can order their shattering are also missed in an unconscious pedagogy. As the next section suggests, these dynamics are not outside of the history of the diary's popular crafting.

THE TRANSFERENCE

The skeletal details of the contentious history of the diary's reception can offer us insight into the difficulties of "learning to live more justly."[18] Many of these details conflate the question of representing and popularizing Anne Frank with the problem of identifying with her short life. While those who crafted her work for popular consumption did not pose this as a question of transference, one of the startling and uncontrollable effects of attempting to provoke identifications concerns the ways transference, or the capacity to bring new editions of old conflicts into present relationships, structures object relations as a question of static continuity[19] and perception as a return of internal conflicts. In this affective and imaginary relation, however, the transference is ambivalent, invoking both unresolved conflicts and profound desires for love. If the transference is to be the imaginary grounds of working through, ego boundaries as played through the structures of perception and mis-recognition must become a question. That is, the very act of finding continuity and making events familiar must become the new problem.

In 1956, Meyer Levin sued Otto Frank and the Broadway producer Kermit Bloomgarden over the rights to publish his play.[20] Levin's account of what he thought happened is aptly titled *The Obsession*. Even though the legal settlement that Levin won contained a clause that he was never to speak of the case, Levin could not keep quiet. Running over 300 pages, *The Obsession* tries to tell the story of what cannot be settled in a court of law and what cannot be settled in life. His worries concern not just the content of these stories and what the content must foreclose for the story to become a story; Levin also worries about aporia: the question of loss itself and whether a story has the capacity to work through—indeed, mourn—the story of loss. For the story of loss is also the story of the infinite details of loss, and these details are always specific details. The question that remains is: How can any reader come to identify with the diary's specificity if this specificity is forgotten and if these details cannot be those of the contemporary reader? Saul Friedlander puts this tension well: "Whether one considers the Shoah as an exceptional event or as belonging to a wider historical category does not affect the possibility of drawing from it a universally valid significance. The difficulty appears when this statement is reversed. No universal lesson seems to require reference to the Shoah to be fully comprehended" (1992, 54).

How one comes to find relevance for one's present world in events that are not one's own but that have the capacity to say something more to the stories one already has is, as many acknowledge, a central question of any pedagogy. Transferential processes, however, suggest that social recognition must first pass through complex psychical dynamics that can work to impede or inhibit the significance of the other's knowledge. The problems of transference become even more demanding within pedagogies that seek to restructure memory with the details one has not experienced but nonetheless must ethically confront. And yet, to make memory from the difficult and chaotic events of the past requires, on the one hand, a distancing of the impulse to reenact the traumatic knowledge through unconscious transferential relations. And, on the other hand, it requires an effort in crafting new desires to relate to what is now, at least in the beginning of encounter, a nonevent, something that has already occurred and can only be touched and touch in return through its representation. This doubling of space and time means that learning from such history is extremely difficult and demanding. Geoffrey Hartman (1996) suggests that a secondary trauma can be provoked: "The insemination of horror, or of horror and guilt, may produce terrible fantasies or else feelings of impotence. How does one teach a traumatic history without increasing inappropriate psychological defences?" (1997, 24). Van Alphen suggests the tension this way: "[T]here is a need to explore and develop manners and means of representation that preserve contact with this extreme history; means that continue to transmit knowledge of it, that simultaneously prevent forgetting *and* making familiar" (1997, 35). These are the psychical issues in any difficult knowledge: a knowledge that demands something of the learner; a knowledge of the working through of the defense and the resistance to reorganizing one's ego boundaries in such a way that the original defense against encountering the other is not reenacted.

Meyer Levin argued that the play first staged in 1956 neither addressed the horror nor prevented forgetting and familiarization. The play that was staged in 1956, and had its revival on Broadway, was authored by the Hollywood team of Francis Goodrich and Albert Hackett.[21] Structurally, the play repeated the familiar theatrical formula of melodrama, and as critic Vincent Canby noted, was written just ten years after World War II,[22] when Manichaean opposition, or the absolute splitting of good and evil and the evacuation of ambivalence was the rule.[23] However, that play seems to break unconsciously the decisive rule of melodrama with the last sentence, uttered by Anne: "I still believe in spite of everything that people are truly good at heart." The missing detail in this Broadway play is Anne's struggle with the question of belief, her terrible understanding that people are not good at heart.

A few years before this play, Meyer Levin wrote the first review of the English edition of the diary. He, too, offered a sentence of haunting force: "Anne Frank becomes the voice of six million." Both sentences are addressed to the heart: the first, conditional, "I still believe . . ." attempts repair; the other, "Anne Frank's voice . . ." is the sound meant to break the heart that believes. These directions—the making of belief and its shattering—are not outside contemporary pedagogical efforts, particularly those that attempt to understand the history we have become. And this appeal to the heart found in every field,[24] is one that structures the literary and empirical, one that perhaps can be refound in a certain humanistic longing and, more significantly, is made from the force of attachment (the desire to touch and to be touched) that inaugurates subjectivity and its ethical crafting. While this appeal to the heart is a part of our interminable pedagogical design, the appeal to the heart must also appeal to thought. If the heart can be broken, that which breaks the heart is the story of the heart that is broken.

Herein lies the pedagogical dilemma. Appeals to affect, whether they be affects of pain or those of identification, are, by definition, incomplete. If the affect is a wound to thought, how then is it possible to think the affect? Historian Michel de Certeau (1986) turns to fiction and notices that "psychoanalysis takes up the definition given to fiction as being a knowledge jeopardized and wounded by its otherness (the affect, etc.) or a statement that the speaking subject's utterance deprives of its '*serieux'* " (27). The discourse, he goes on to say, is "touched," i.e., something from within threatens its cohesiveness. This is the terrain of the troubling Freudian drive, the demand to work, the force within that is not bound by intention, but follows the rules of that other otherness, the unconscious: no time, no contradiction, no *"no."* This psychoanalytic turn to affect allows for a question typically foreclosed in educational efforts, namely, how do people attach to knowledge, specifically the knowledge of the other's suffering? Of what would such knowledge consist? What is the status of our susceptibility to histories we do not live, to stories that disturb one's sense of cohesiveness, to what I (1998) have called elsewhere "difficult knowledge"?

In psychoanalytic terms, the affect is a borderline concept, something in between the fault lines that suture thought, and yet something that also threatens thought from within.[25] The threat has something to do with the speculation that while affect is a statement of need, its force is prior to its representation. We feel before we know, and this uncertainty allows affect its strange movements: Affect must wander aimlessly; it arrives too soon; it is too encrypted with other scenes to count upon understanding. The affect that may propel identifications is subject to this flaw in that, without knowledge, identification can only depend upon the urge to make familiar what is, after all, outside the range of understanding. Curiously, identifications can work to sustain, rather than enlarge, ego boundaries. Affect, then, is precocious, it disrupts the thought's attention, its time is both too early and too late and, finally, its aim must be insufficient to its object. This is because affect seeks its representative and in settling on an object to express its force, there is still the question as to both the meaning of the affect and the adequacy of its attachment. Perhaps this is why Lyotard noted that thinking and suffering overlap.[26] But, if there is an overlapping, the combination, as Friedlander suggests, is also the space of resistance to working through.

This overlapping quality of thinking and suffering is part of the historicity of the crafting of Anne Frank's diary and of how its presumed structure of appeal was imagined. But the limits of imagination are also the limits of imagining the subjectivity of the other and, hence, the place where meanings of both the self and the other can shatter. Aspects of this overlapping are present in current debates over whether universality or particularity allow insight into knowledge, appeals for social justice, and appeals for the right to an everyday. One view suggests that if the other can be made familiar, understanding might be easier to invoke. This seems to be the dominant educational approach. But familiarity, as van Alphen suggests, can also lead to forgetting. To return to Moses' description of "almost falling," itself a familiar experience, the familiar can also be defended against, through narcissistic identification. These are not the only forms of identification. There are all kinds of identifications, such as the desire to make a relation, to create affective bonds, and to allow the scene of social recognition to include groups that may well challenge the more normotic defenses[27] against the other. Identification is also the imaginary site where individuals attempt to consider experiences outside of themselves and, if carefully thought about, attempt the fragile work of extending the self in relation to what is other to and beyond the self. One could say that identification is a relation to a nonevent but contains the material for the self to transform itself, provided that mental work reconsider affective impulses. The tension exists because identifications cannot work holistically—that is, because only fragments of the other's dynamic experience can be incorporated—and because identifications are, at least at first, unconscious, contradictory, and ambivalent. There is always a breach between the experience of actuality and the means of attachment, between social recognition and mis-recognition. Something must appeal to the self for there to be an identification. But also, there must be an appeal that is beyond the sympathetic bond identifications sometimes invoke. We are back to Arendt's appeal to thought, an appeal that requires one to make a new relation between thought and affect, precisely because of this subjective and unfinished experience.

Some of these tensions structured Anne Frank's own writing as well as the crafting of her diary.[28] Still, the story of the Anne Frank play, and indeed, the reception of this diary in our own pedagogy, has not settled the question of how readers make the diary relevant. The newly adapted play that had a recent run on Broadway enacts this ambivalence.[29] This play, too, continues the argument over how to present the diary and what this presentation might mean to contemporary audiences. In this version, previously edited out sections of the diary are restored and contemporary audiences now meet a Jewish Anne Frank, not just any refugee. The updated play invokes our present preoccupations with identity, with presenting role models, with questions of self-esteem, perhaps our own sort of sentimentality and familiarity. These contemporary preoccupations still require melodrama, the separation and splitting of good and bad, the idealization of the good subject, the appeal to affect as the means to make meaning from the other's suffering. Still, the "new" Anne on Broadway is no longer a comedic Anne, but someone who cares deeply about the possibility of living a life through acknowledging the ravages of destruction on the streets below. Ironically, this was Anne Frank's original dilemma, how to live in the attic with the knowledge of the despair and aggression on the streets below. And yet, no matter how much this new version tries to learn from the flaws of its predecessor, it cannot be separated from its shadow; the play still suffers from its traumatic origins. This may be why current discussions must also return to the difficult history of this play, an attempt, perhaps, to work through what the original production and those involved could not tolerate, at least according to Meyer Levin, namely the question of Jewishness, of the utter particularity of its suffering, and of what it is to confront, in the murder of one girl, the destruction of a people.

Levin insisted that only a Jew could identify with and convey Jewish suffering.[30] He was heartbroken that Otto Frank chose Christian writers over him. And, in this insistence, we have an early example of "epistemic privilege," the view that some identities understand events better because of their own experience in identity. However, what is foreclosed in this sort of argument is the difficult acknowledgment that there is never just one experience, one identity, particularly during times when both experience and identity are shattered. The debate that Levin could not quite reach concerns not whether there is one experience to know and to convey adequately, but rather, *what happened to experience?* This was certainly Anne Frank's question, as she grappled with not hiding her knowledge of the streets below. With this question, we might encounter the magnitude and the excess of suffering in ways that give insight into questions of how the idiomatic qualities of suffering can be ethically encountered and what such knowledge can mean to our present. What happens to our experience, when we ask what happened to Anne Frank?

One tension in the history of reframing Anne Frank's diary for popular circulation is that a great number of Jewish intellectuals were also involved, some of whom worried over whether a representation can be "too Jewish" to have any currency for those who are not Jewish. In many contemporary debates, this worry has been viewed as a question of assimilation versus the unambivalent claiming of religious and cultural identity. Otto Frank, for example, insisted that his daughter's diary was not first and foremost a Jewish story, but a story of adolescence. For Levin, the diary was a Jewish diary, and to preclude this from representation was, for him, a reenactment of the original destruction of European Jewry. The tension, in all of these debates, has to do, in part, with the worry over how the diary can retain its power of susceptibility, how contemporary readers become subject to the obligations of its call. And yet, if this tension can be viewed as a question of ethicality, the difficult acknowledgment is that the ethical is not a place of privilege but of obligation. The obligation, as Derrida put it, is one of "learning to live . . . more justly." And yet, if these worries are to have currency when encountering the diary, contemporary readers must also have the opportunity to encounter the history of such worries.

With the publication of the definitive edition of the diary, and now, with the new discussions of the finding and ownership of the missing pages of the diary, we know that Otto Frank edited out not only Anne's description of her sexual researches and passages that angrily denounced her mother and criticized her parent's marriage but also passages where Anne becomes attached to her Jewish obligations.

Otto Frank desired a universal message, and his way to this goal was to censor much that was particular to Anne Frank. This desire may well be a defense against the knowledge that it was the particularity—of being Jewish—that the Nazi imaginary and its sympathizers felt as intolerable, as rupture, and as persecution of its dream of no difference. Perhaps, for Otto Frank, a return to what was used to divide could only be a return of pain. If so, we might now consider Otto Frank's belated knowledge as more ambivalent than the choice between assimilation and roots. He, too, wondered what it would take for the larger social to identify with Anne's humanness when this identification was not a possibility during Anne's brief life. We are left with this wonder, that the restoration of one's humanness in contexts of profound dehumanization must be part of the work of reparation. We must also consider how this work proceeds bit by bit, how it has the capacity to reverse its content and become lost in disparagement, hatred, and aggressive returns that cannot be avoided merely in the appeal for humanity. The first Broadway play tried to close these questions by scripting, from the diary, something uplifting, a lesson, a story that could end. What they forgot, in their attempt to make Anne Frank something familiar, was that the return of the diary to Otto Frank, the return that opens the first act of the 1956 play, was not the ending of the diary.

This fight over the rights of Anne Frank's diary is now the subject of two book-length studies, academic commentary, and contemporary polemics.[31] Transferential relations seem to structure how each debate critiques the next, and many of the debates continue to repeat the painful dynamics of Meyer Levin's encounter with the diary. It seems almost impossible not to take a side in these debates, to transfer one's old conflicts and wishes onto new situations. The small reason has to do with the question of identification, for the sheer numbers of characters involved in the casting of the diary's reception offer us desires that are very familiar: the desire to be recognized, to have one's own story accepted, to refind the lost object, to be understood and to have understanding. The big reason, which is also at the heart of this history, resides in the attempt to answer the pedagogical question of what might constitute a "good enough" understanding if understanding itself eluded those who experienced the event and again eludes our own present. Both directions raise significant issues for the pedagogical. We desire others to attach to stories that cannot be their own but, in this attachment, we worry about what might also be foreclosed if these stories fit too closely or are too familiar with those we already know. We may forget that acknowledging the loss of understanding is also one of the obligations of witnessing the crisis of witnessing. But we also worry how this very desire to attach can destroy the otherness of object. What, then, is it to become susceptible to both the call of the diary and to the historicity of its reception? If identification, the capacity to attach passionately not just to the social but to the self's desire for a social, is the sine qua non of understanding, how do the arguments of history suture and undo our quest, our refinding of the lost object?

These questions must be placed in a troubling dialogue with the event of the Shoah. And it is precisely in this difficult relation that universality becomes an empty signifier, a normotic defense. What troubles is the contemporary insistence that the Shoah has moved from the inconceivable to the unrepresentable, from the question of address to the crisis of witnessing, from the specificity of the absolute horror and mass murder of Jewish individuals to what Lawrence Langer (1998) calls the desire for finding universal redemption, the consequence of which pre-empts the Holocaust. Alongside these difficult and conflictive conceptualizations, there remains the question of identification itself and the problem of what impedes or propels our capacity to notice the vantage of the other and to make from this notice an obligation for our own implication with the other. What many of these arguments suggest is that the very act of noticing can also instigate ego defenses that work against noticing the utter horror of mass murder.

For van Alphen, the act of noticing concerns movements from continuity to difference, or what he describes as wavering between feelings of the uncanny to what is sublime in thought. The example that he offers for this claim startles. It begins in his own house, when he decides to learn who owned the house in Amsterdam before he took occupancy. The house was owned by a Jewish architect who was arrested and died in the Theresienstadt camp. This knowledge, so entangled in van Alphen's disavowal, provoked for him profound anxiety, the worry that somehow the original owner's family would return to reclaim their home and push him out. His anxieties defended against his capacity to even notice what it was like for the original owners to lose their possessions and resided instead with his own shame in repossession. Van Alphen names this as the uncanny affect, where one is worried about being mistaken for the perpetrator and, hence, defends against this thought by feeling persecuted. In the uncanny, something is not strange but terribly familiar, and this familiarity is what must be repressed. For the uncanny affect to become sublime in thought, van Alphen must become obligated to this knowledge and notice that nothing about his house and his present life can be the same. Continuity with the ignored past must become broken. "The uncanny," writes van Alphen, "is threatening because one's ego boundaries become lost. One's self-experience is at stake and must be defended. The question I must ask, then, is: How can the return of the idea of somebody who died in the Holocaust threaten my experience of self? And why do I need to repress this person . . . or memory or awareness of his dying in the Holocaust, in order to feel at home?" (1997, 202).[32] To bear this question, van Alphen suggests that the uncanny is not so much the opposite of the sublime but part of its process. To work through defenses against the inconceivable, without transferring his own aggression onto the other, he must refind, not the ego's boundaries, but the capacity to live without the boundaries that preclude the experience of the other.

WORKING THROUGH

The personal implications of reading the diary—of how the reader's conceptualization of her present life might be altered—is perhaps the most stressed pedagogical issue. But the diary looms larger than the reader's regard for the personal, and it has to do with the troubling question of evil itself. For Cynthia Ozick (1997), the various castings of the diary are not meant to come to grips with the profound evil that engulfed Anne Frank, for the representations are still stuck in uncanny time, even if Anne Frank's diary should invoke its own otherness. Writes Ozick, "A story may not be said to be a story if the end is missing. And because the end is missing, the story of Anne Frank in the fifty years since *The Diary of a Young Girl* was first published has been bowdlerized, distorted, transmuted, traduced, reduced; it has been infantilised, Americanized, homogenized, sentimentalized; falsified, kitchified, and in fact, blatantly and arrogantly denied" (78). No one is innocent in Ozick's account: She accuses dramatists, theatergoers, translators, educators, and even Otto Frank. "Almost every hand that has approached the diary with the well-meaning intention of publicizing it," writes Ozick, "has contributed to the sub-version of history" (78). This may even be the case for the writing about the last fifty years of the diary's reception: the history of its refinding and public circula-tion—of Anne Frank's lonely death, of Otto Frank's censorship, of the House Unamerican Activities Committee hearings that formed the backdrop to the play's production, of the Nazi actress given the part of Mrs. Frank in the first Broadway production, of Eleanor Roosevelt's attempt at intervening between Meyer Levin and Otto Frank, of Carson McCuller's interest in trying to write the play but hav-ing to excuse herself, of Lillian Hellman's hand in the writing, of intellectuals such as Bruno Bettelheim, Hannah Arendt, and Martin Buber's commentary on the treatment of the diary, and finally, of our own contemporary debates on its sym-bolic reach and pedagogical value.

In all this crowded and contradictory history, the "subversion of history" is still a difficult learning, wavering, perhaps like the question of love, between the beau-tiful and the painful. What remains are questions of what it is to subvert history, to live in deferred actions, to attempt to make a lesson from the incommensurable na-ture of cruelty, genocide, and even one's own desire for reparation. Meyer Levin suggested as much in his poetic insight into the fall and his own troubles. But the suggestion could not help him live with what he believed was lost.

This fall is not yet over; we are still falling. Here is how Cynthia Ozick offers her own horrid fall: "It may be shocking to think this (I am shocked as I think it), but one can imagine a still more salvational outcome: Anne Frank's diary burned, vanished, lost—saved from a world that made of it all things, some of them true, while floating lightly over the heavier truth of named and inhabited evil" (87). But should one even imagine salvation in the context of profound evil? And should we expect that the representations and reception of Anne Frank can ex-ceed the reach of the traumatic events that, in the first instance, gave us the diary? The desire to save the diary, this time from a history of its own usages, has come full circle, but not yet twice. There is something understandable about Ozick's fantasy, particularly if we can think metaphorically, for the crafting of the diary is not outside of the reenactment of its traumatic fragments, the force of Nachträglichkeit, the infinite traces of Holocaust effects in our own time. And, yet, even this fantasy, because it is still inside the traumatic encounter, still possessed in the time of deferred action, cannot transcend the wish to rescue Anne Frank, this time from commercialization, from banality, and from a circus of affects that cannot attach to thought. These responses, as Ozick rightly suggests, are defenses against encountering evil, and they also sustain rigid ego boundaries in such a way that what is foreclosed is the capacity to recognize the social actions that induced the suffering of others. This is the secondary evil. Such missed encounters, made from the mix of projections, wishes, and identifications defend against the traumatic perception of a lost social. What is missed, and Ozick's response centers the problem, is the difficult knowledge that a social can destroy itself through destroying the desires for what van Alphen describes as "the urge to reconstruct an affective community," a community of ethical subjects. We might consider Ozick's polemic as an attempt to restore two kinds of loss: the loss of the idea of ethical conduct or the ethical capacity for the social to do less harm, and how this incapacity leads to the loss of individual lives. In bringing these two experiences together, in naming such destruction evil, Ozick offers us the most stunning argument against the idealization that structures popularized accounts. In doing so, she may well inaugurate the work of mourning a pedagogy that cannot address and work through its own limits, its own passion to ignore.

If pedagogy is to create the conditions for the idiomatic urge to reconstruct an affective community, it must begin with how communities can also be destroyed. This is an appeal to thought and, in doing so, thought must touch what is both uncanny and sublime. And yet, all of these falls, these flaws that make the engagement with the diary so difficult must, however painfully, be considered as the beginning and not the end of pedagogy. For if we are to make something from the diary, we must learn to work through our own defenses against learning from the complex and unfinished history of the diary's reception. If something must break for the heart to break, when the heart breaks, there must be made, from this loss, a work of mourning. Anne Frank must not, indeed cannot, be rescued from history. But to encounter her writing in all of its historicity requires a great deal of thought on the part of students and teachers, a willingness to bring the diary into the present, not as repetition or as overfamiliar, but as a means to work through what the diary might offer to our own contemporary understandings.

The teacher's own engagement must begin with enlarging her knowledge of contemporary debates on the uses of Anne Frank, on the changing structures of engagement for each generation of readers, on the popularization of the figure of Anne Frank, and on how a study of Anne Frank—the Anne Frank that is no longer but who still seems to give life to her diary—can say something about our own capacity to mourn and to make part of our everyday lives our urges for an affective community. Such knowledge is no longer a knowledge of closure but rather a knowledge that appeals to the thought of ethical urges and that can work through the urge to close down knowledge through idealization. Teachers must also become open to learning something about the confines of trauma, for the urge with-

out the thought is subject to unconscious reversals and displacements. Symptoms
of these dynamics can be located in the desire for rescue, in the idealization of the
lost object, and in the numbness of disassociation. If contemporary students are to
do more than be subject to the traumatic combination of the unconscious of both
their teachers' and their own anxieties, then teachers will have to grapple with questions of transference and countertransference in pedagogy.

The lesson of Anne Frank's diary may be the history of how there is no salvation in history, only difficult knowledge, fragile attempts to make, from the diary,
a lesson. A story that has no ending is, after all, a story that has lost something. And
this loss agitates the efforts at restoration, at refinding the lost object, at reconstructing a subjectivity that can encounter loss without becoming lost in traumatic
reenactments. Here, gone. The story is not yet over, for we have not yet faced what
is persistent and evil in our own time. We might ask, why return again to Anne
Frank? Are there not better texts that can exceed such dilemmas? And yet, even
this question forecloses the work readers must commit themselves to when reading about the difficulties of others. Perhaps, like Meyer Levin, we have never left
Anne Frank. She has left us. We cannot be done with Anne Frank because, at least
in what she left behind, her diary, we might learn from her own broken urges for
affective bonds.

This unfinished story is the story pedagogy must learn to tolerate. It is the story
of the breakdown of meanings and, in this difficulty, attempting to learn from others, learning to tolerate and accept the ethical obligations the other offers. That first
obligation, another story that has no ending, is learning to become an ethical subject as one witnesses the crisis of witnessing. The tension such an obligation opens
is that one cannot know in advance what the ethical demands; one can only be
open to the twists and difficulties of its content and trajectories, of its breakdowns
and broken hearts. Becoming willing to take on such obligations means turning full
circle twice, moving from the thought that invokes action back to the capacity to
think. If knowing others is limited by the way one imagines how one is known—
if transitory identifications without recourse to examining the desires that structure
modes of social recognition and mis-recognition and thus repeat the syndrome of
"almost falling" seem to complete the story—we may be trapped in an uncanny
time, where repression, forgetting, and familiarization precariously defend the
boundaries of the ego. When education mistakes the question of subjectivity and
turns it into a familiar answer, it does so at the risk of losing the interminable question of understanding itself. But understanding itself can offer no consolation, and
if it is treated as if understanding settles anything, all we are left with are repetitions of the suffering, a suffering unattached to thought, a suffering whose value
has shattered, a suffering that cannot become the transference that is also crucial for
the work of mourning.[33] For what is transferred in the work of mourning is not
the ego's boundaries onto the lost object, but the ego's capacity to exceed those
first protective gestures that require the ego to defend itself against acknowledging
the loss of boundary. Yes, it is important to think. But then, we are no longer in

the realm of interpretation, where if we have the proper story all will be settled. Learning to live with ghosts means learning to understand what has been lost in the self and what has been lost in the social. This is a question of becoming an ethical subject in relation to other ethical subjects, a question Freud called "the work of mourning." The loss must be made into a memory, which in itself requires a distance called thought. And, in thinking the thought of loss and the loss of thought, we may also begin the interminable work of making more generous, more righteous, more just, the urge for affective community.

NOTES

I would like to thank Roger Simon, Sharon Rosenberg, and Claudia Eppert for their thoughtful comments on earlier drafts. This chapter was also written with the support of the Social Science and Humanities Research Council of Canada, grant #410-98-1028, "Difficult Knowledge in Teaching and Learning: A Psychoanalytic Inquiry." The views expressed here do not necessarily represent the council.

　　1.　By 1974, still hoping for vindication and sympathetic acceptance, Levin had published his own story of what he felt had gone terribly wrong. After all, Levin had sued Otto Frank for the rights to publish a play based on the diary, and this legal action was scandalous. Much of Levin's book, *The Obsession,* is a struggle to understand his three engagements in psychoanalysis where he tried to confront his own compulsion to control the reception of the diary. His second analyst asked, "The enemies you tell of are undoubtedly real. The question is, are they worth all the trouble you give yourself over them?" (19). The question cannot be answered, for a larger struggle preoccupies him. Levin cannot decide whether some obsessions are worthy, even as the cost in his life is misery.

　　2.　One of the most commented upon critiques on the worldwide acclimation of the diaries was made by Bruno Bettelheim in his controversial essay "The Ignored Lesson of Anne Frank." Although by the end of his life Bettelheim did soften his views on the family in hiding (admitting that while the Frank family was in denial over the profound danger they faced, the expectation that they should have known in advance their fate is too harsh a judgment), the essay does offer a significant overview on the problems of learning about the Holocaust in the postwar years. Bettelheim suggests three reactions on the part of people to the knowledge of concentration camps: (1) that the actions were done by only a small group of people; (2) that the reports were exaggerated (and this reaction originated with the German government); and (3) that the reports were believed but the knowledge of horror was repressed. It is largely this last reaction that Bettelheim attributes to the popularity of Anne Frank's diary. Writes Bettelheim:

> What is at issue is the universal and uncritical response to her diary and to the play and movie based on it, and what this reaction tells about our attempts to cope with the feelings her fate—used by us to serve as a symbol of the most human reaction to Nazi terror—arouses in us. I believe that the world-wide acclaim given her story cannot be explained unless we recognize in it our wish to forget the gas chambers, and our effort to do so by glorifying the ability to retreat into

an extremely private, gentle, sensitive world, and there to cling as much as possible to what have been one's usual daily attitudes and activities, although surrounded by a maelstrom apt to engulf one at any moment. (246)

Adorno (1998) also commented upon, albeit with ambivalence, the problem of what individuals are identifying with when they encounter Anne Frank. He recalled a story about one woman's becoming upset at seeing the play: "To be sure even that was good as a first step toward understanding. But the individual case, which should stand for and raise awareness about the terrifying totality, by its very individuation became an alibi for the totality the woman forgot" (101).

3. Ralph Melnick's *The Stolen Legacy of Anne Frank: Meyer Levin, Lillian Hellman, and the Staging of the Diary* is structured around the view that Lillian Hellman had a great deal of behind the scene responsibility in writing with the team of Goodrich and Hackett. He argues that Hellman's Stalinist sympathy for an uplifting and universalized art ensured that Anne's Jewishness would become erased.

4. Arendt's (1993) collection of essays can be read as a response to the bitter battles inaugurated in her reportage of the Eichmann trials in Jerusalem. In a recent study of Arendt, Jennifer Ring (1997) argues: "It has been obvious from Arendt's notes, in nearly everything she wrote after *Eichmann in Jerusalem,* that Eichmann impressed upon her the importance of articulating a worldly way of thinking in order to prevent the recurrence of thoughtless evil" (21–22).

5. The refusal to believe that one will be affected by social violence is one possible way an individual might rationalize her or his wish for safety. For a discussion of the ways disavowal works to impede the recognition of one's own danger in repressive military regimes, see Hollander 1997.

6. I am indebted to Roger Simon for this insight. Judith Doneson (1987), for example, suggests that contemporary students are meeting a 1950s version of Anne Frank, a criticism that still plagues the newly revised play, according to Vincent Canby (1997). We might also observe how reading theories that are dominant in English education are also a throwback to the 1950s and 1960s literary theory school of close textual readings. In this theory, historical and authorial biography are kept separate from the act of textual interpretation.

7. The title of Freud's 1917 [1915] paper conveys the difficulty of experiencing loss, for at first there is no distinction between mourning and melancholia. The question Freud grapples with concerns what it is to identify, or what are the means of identification with loss. For Freud, identification comes before and can replace an awareness of the separateness of the object. Freud offers the following speculation: "[O]ne feels justified in maintaining the belief that a loss of this kind has occurred, but one cannot see clearly what it is that has been lost . . . cannot consciously perceive what he has lost either. This indeed, might be so even if the patient is aware of the loss which has given rise to his melancholia, but only in the sense that he knows *whom* he has lost but not *what* he has lost in him" (245). In melancholia, the loss is unconscious, in mourning, the loss is made conscious. This is because the identification that grounds melancholia is not with the object but with the ego that has become an object. Freud notes three preconditions of melancholia: "loss of the object, ambivalence, and regression of libido into the ego" (258). It is the third condition, where the object unconsciously becomes fused with the ego, that interrupts, in Freud's view, the coming to terms with what has been lost on the outside and inside.

8. For a discussion of Freud's acknowledgment of the limits of mourning, see Caruana 1996. For a discussion of what Freud could not admit in his thinking about mourning, see Haver 1996.

9. Freud's view of the workings of ambivalence in love are complex and dynamic. Ambivalence is a borderline concept, figuring somewhere between the desire for love and the fear of the loss of love. Whereas in the desire for love, the ego is willing to make more flexible its own boundary maintenance, the fear of the loss of love renders the ego rigid and incorporative.

> In melancholia the relation to the object is no simple one; it is complicated by the conflict due to ambivalence. The ambivalence is either constitutional, i.e., is an element of every love-relation formed by this particular ego, or else it proceeds precisely from those experiences that involved the threat of losing the object. . . . In melancholia, accordingly, countless separate struggles are carried on over the object, in which hate and love contend with each other; the one seeks to detach the libido from the object, the other to maintain this position of the libido against the assault. ("Mourning and Melancholia" 256)

In mourning, the ego must de-cathect libido memory by memory. That is, the ego must stop demanding satisfaction from the lost object and begin demanding something from itself and from others in the world.

10. James Young's (1998) reconsideration of Art Spiegelman's two-volume graphic novel, *Maus*, suggests some of the stakes in learning from textualized representations of the Holocaust. Young suggests that Spiegelman's work offers readers the means to conceptualize the difficulty of understanding the event, even as the event is graphically drawn. This difficulty of understanding is a generational question, where the children of survivors have memories of their parent's stories as a "vicarious past." Young suggests: "What distinguishes many of these artists from their parents' generation of survivors is their single-minded knack for representing just this sense of vicariousness, for measuring the distance between history-as-it-happened and their own postmemory of it" (670). The story of how Art came to know the history of his father's experience as a survivor is now a part of the history of the handing down of the event. Comparing this view to contemporary school study of Anne Frank's diary, one gets a sense of how learning the historicity of its reception might allow students the distance to consider their own "vicarious pasts."

11. In an earlier essay, "Trauma, Transference and 'Working Through,'" Friedlander (1992) focuses on the difficulties that writing requires of the historian. He observed a split between the historical discourse and testimony that resulted in a catch between stories of catastrophe and stories of redemption. Both directions, Friedlander argues, are symptoms of a desire for a closure that is not yet conscious and actually is a defense against the excess of the Shoah, or that which cannot be symbolized yet remains. For Friedlander, the sheer geometry of human loss has not yet been integrated with the singularity of each particular loss, each particular voice. Friedlander defines working through as "*confronting the individual voice* in a field dominated by political decisions and administrative decrees which neutralize the concreteness of despair and death" (53). This confrontation is also just the beginning: "Working through ultimately means testing the limits of necessary and ever-defeated imagination" (54).

12. Shoshana Felman's (1992) discussion of Camus' novel *The Fall* suggests the traumatic consequences of "the lost chance of encounter with the *possibility of rescue*" (177). Her discussion of this novel is a way to consider two views of history enacted in the disputes between Camus and Sartre, where Sartre accuses Camus of failing to see the progress of history and Camus views Sartre as refusing the implications of an unresolved past that persists in the present. Sartre accuses Camus of not making history. Camus accuses Sartre of being

unable to contemplate or look upon, and hence witness, history. This tension between viewing history as something to make and thus centering human rationality and its capacity to shape the world in its own image verses looking at history as that which exceeds human intention, objective patterns, and totalizing conceptualization because history is not a grand plan that can be known in advance is a central distinction also made by Arendt (1993) in her essay "The Concept of History." Arendt argues that the view that centers making history over the singular actions that constitute what we now look back upon as history is the basis of political totalitarianism.

13. I explore education's capacity to shut out as well as shut down conflict in Britzman 1998.

14. Rosenfeld's (1991, 1993) work has been quite central to my own thinking about the diary and has been central to recent scholarship on the Levin-Frank disputes. His work focuses on the profound idealization of Anne Frank and the ways such idealization works as disavowal in translations of the diary, in the censorship of the diary, and in the reworking of the diary for Broadway and Hollywood.

15. The view that teachers interfere with the ways students read fiction is debated in discussions of student-centered language arts pedagogy. At times, romantic applications of whole language and student-centered pedagogy stress the need for student discovery of meanings without teacher intervention. The view is that personal relevance will naturally aid the student in their textual attachments and interpretations. Such an orientation cannot consider a theory of knowledge that can grapple with times where personal relevance itself becomes fractured and broken and when personal relevance cannot offer insight into new encounters. This is certainly the case with representations of the Holocaust and representations of war, genocide, and social breakdown. But it may also be the case in everyday encounters with strangers. While personal relevance seems to be one answer to the interminable question of how can students attach to the curriculum, the problem of narcissism in personal relevancy theories is ignored.

16. Here, I am thinking both of writers who raise the question of representing the Holocaust in such a way that the dynamics that allowed the Holocaust to shatter the social are not repeated in the representation and of those literary engagements that focus upon the question of what happened to experience in and after the Holocaust. For examples of the former, see Young 1988 and van Alphen 1997. For examples of the latter, see Fink 1997, Becker 1996, and Singer 1998.

17. Sigmund Freud's *Civilization and Its Discontents* makes this point: "We shall always tend to consider [we can imagine] people's distress objectively—that is, to place ourselves, with our own wants and sensibilities, in their conditions, and then to examine what occasions we should find in them for experiencing happiness or unhappiness" (89).

18. Although the diary was first published in English in 1952, its popularization in pedagogy began with the advent of the Broadway play and then the 1957 Hollywood film and its teaching guides. For a longer mediation on the historicity of the diary's reception in pedagogy, see Britzman 1998.

19. Hannah Segal's (1997) discussion of transference as a conflict between fantasy and reality, is useful to this discussion for she thinks of transference as a conflict between perception and misperception. And while classical accounts of the transference focus on the question of the exchange of authority, rooted in the analysand's earliest experience with parents, Segal also maintains that present preoccupations are also transferred as the basis for social mis-recognition. Here is Segal's view:

Reacting to the analyst as though he or she were a figure of the past is a misperception of the current relationship and, when this is corrected, the past is also revised. In this way the misperceptions in relation to the original figure can also be corrected, because, as we have discovered, transference is not a simple phenomenon of projecting the figures of the parents onto the analyst. It is internal figures, sometimes part-objects, which are projected, and these internal objects have themselves a history in which the conflict between phantasy and reality has led to distortions. In fact, the internal models on which we base our attitudes to one another not only fail to correspond to current reality; they are also, to a varying extent, a misrepresentation of past reality. (27–28)

20. One of Levin's charges was that the Goodrich and Hackett play plagiarized his own. This charge of plagiarism returns to haunt Steven Spielberg's film *Amistad,* presently under consideration in the courts. In making this association, I am not suggesting that these two representations of history (one in the form of a play and one in the form of a popular film) are comparable, even if in the popular press there is the push to compare this film with Spielberg's *Schindler's List* and even as debates over the applicability of the term *Holocaust* are central to these representations as well. However, given that both representations attempt to portray profound dislocation, the dynamics of the event do seem to structure the history of its reception.

21. Goodrich and Hackett are best known for their writing of Frank Capra's film *It's a Wonderful Life.* Otto Frank selected this team over Meyer Levin's script that was based on the diary.

22. Canby (1997) makes the important point in his review of the new production of the diary currently running on Broadway that the 1957 play was one of the first popular representations of the diary, before Eichmann's trial and Hannah Arendt's report on the banality of evil, before the publications of Elie Wiesel and seven years into the establishment of the State of Israel.

23. While it is well beyond the scope of this chapter to sketch out the psychical complexities made from the splitting of good and bad into absolute categories, a few observations on the dynamic of splitting may be useful. Brooks (1992) identified three kinds of representations that are split: "representations of objects, representations of affects, and representations of the self" (335). While all of these splittings occur through this chapter, it is the second kind, the splitting of affects, that I stress. Very briefly, here is the dynamic trajectory splitting enacts: When the good and bad of representations are separated, both can then be displaced to the outside. Then, these forces seem to come back at the self who splits. Splitting is an early mode of perception that inaugurates judgment as it returns to structure the ego. This splitting is also, according to Melanie Klein, the basis for the possibility of guilt to allow for "the work of reparation." See Klein 1994.

24. For example, see Behar 1996, Clark 1997, and Spelman 1997.

25. André Green (1986) offers a way into the problem of why affect so disturbs thought when he distinguishes affect from desire: "However, what must be remembered is that affect is not a direct emotional expression, but a *trace,* a *residue,* awoken by a repetition" (179).

26. Lyotard (1991) writes: "The pain of thinking isn't a symptom coming from outside to inscribe itself on the mind instead of in its true place. It is thought itself resolving to be irresolute, deciding to be patient, wanting not to want, wanting, precisely, not to produce a meaning in place of what must be signified. This is a tip of the hat to a duty that hasn't been named" (19).

27. The term *normotic defense* is borrowed from Bollas (1987), who considers the "drive to be normal [as] . . . typified by the numbing and eventual erasure of subjectivity in favour

of a self that is conceived as a material object among other man-made projects in the objective world" (134). A normotic defense works against the unknown of subjectivity by exaggerating the ego's own stability and capacity to remain untouched by others. Bollas also offers the example of an individual who, while having season tickets to the theater, refuses to discuss the content of the plays or even acknowledge the work as "a sophisticated mental accomplishment" (138) that requires something of the viewer. I bring Bollas's insight to van Alphen's early denial of the diary's power.

28. The notion of "crafting" is meant to suggest that Anne Frank's diary went through a series of revisions. The second crafting of the diary begins after Anne Frank's death in the Bergen Belsen camp, when Otto Frank, the only survivor of the family, returns to Amsterdam upon his liberation from Auschwitz. He made from the documents he was handed an edited diary that was published.

29. All of the recent writing addressing the revised play returns to the painful debates over the uses and currency of the earlier play and of Meyer Levin's critique of the trivialization of Anne Frank's identity in that first play. Bernard Hammelburg's "A Fresh Look at 'Anne Frank': In Search of the Historical One" argues that the recent play revised by Wendy Kesselman and directed by James Lapine was an attempt to rethink the "superchild" and present Anne as more human. Frank Rich's "Anne Frank Now" recounts the diary's history but is also struck by the thirteen-year-old boy's response who had accompanied him: "But maybe adults' reactions don't matter as much as those of children who are seeing it for the first time and carry none of their parents' baggage. A 13-year-old bar mitzvah boy who came with me was shaken by the experience—and was incredulous when I told him afterward how the version I saw as a child ended with Anne's cheery testimonial to people's goodness of heart" (A 21). And finally, in the review of the new play, Ben Brantley notes, "This version . . . offers no teacherly consolations about the triumph of the spirit. . . . An uncompromising steadiness of gaze, embedded in a bleak sense of historical context, is the strongest element in a production more notable for its moral conscientiousness than for theatrical inspiration" (B 1).

30. Even this insistence is not without qualification, for within Jewish communities there is still the debate on who qualifies as "a Jew." The question of belonging is, of course, a question of any culture and its capacities not just to distinguish the inside from the outside but also to constitute, in this process, the qualities of the inside. However, Levin's insistence also raises a different question than the one implied in "who can know?" And this is the question of identification with the loss that is the Shoah. Levin, for example, was well aware of the larger social's woeful disregard of the destruction and murder of European Jewry. He was a reporter in Europe at the end of World War II and was present when Polish camps were liberated. His assumption was that the articulation of the profundity of the loss must emerge from the loss itself. And therefore, the narrator must have already been attached to the event to convey its magnitude. But while this proximity may implicate one's identity, there is still a question as to whether it is identity that allows proximity. This is the dilemma I am attempting to consider.

31. For example, Graver 1995; Melnick 1997; Doneson 1987; and Rosenfeld 1991, 1993. In a recent review of the Graver and Melnick studies, Buruma (1998) reviews the arguments over the crafting of the first Broadway production but comes to the conclusion that while this first play was a compromise, its popularization did allow for an identification of sorts with the play's characters. Buruma writes: "Hollywood's international appeal always has been its stress on character rather than milieu. Cultural and historical accuracy suffers.

But making German audiences identify with Jewish victims is better, it seems to me, than teaching them lessons on how to be a good Jew. Such identification can result in sentimental self-pity, but it is more likely to give people at least some idea that evil was done" (7).

Hoagland's (1998) discussion of Anne Frank suggests the need to separate the play from the writer of the diary. She argues, "Anne Frank has always spoken for herself" (63). And yet, there is still the question of how to receive her thoughts, particularly given the recent public discussions on the "missing pages" of the diary. Blumenthal's (1998) reportage on the newly found five missing pages of Anne's diary suggests how old battles are replayed as new conflicts. These pages were given to Cornelis Suijk by Otto Frank with the instruction not to publicize them until his death. In these five pages, Anne discusses her parents' marriage and insists that the diary is not to be read by her family. Along with questions as to how to interpret these pages in relation to the history of the diary's crafting by Otto Frank and others, and now to the definitive edition, there are now disputes over who owns these pages.

32. The term *uncanny* is the English translation of Freud's term *unheimlech*. In Freud's essay, "The 'Uncanny'" (1919) he considers the etymology of this German word that depends upon the meaning of home. The home is a place of secrets, and it becomes unhomely when the secrets threaten to erupt. Freud also suggests that another person can be viewed as uncanny "when we ascribe evil intentions to him. But that is not all; in addition to this we must feel that his intentions to harm us are going to be carried out with the help of special powers. . . . The layman sees in them the working forces hitherto unsuspected in his fellow-men, but at the same time he is dimly aware of them in remote corners of his own being" (243). The uncanny is thus a relationship that cannot be made even if its force is felt.

33. This notion of the transference is borrowed from Derrida's reading of Freud (1987), where Derrida marks the place that Freud acknowledged the limits of interpretation:

> 1. *Failure of a purely interpretive psychoanalysis,* its time is over. Psychoanalysis is no longer what it was, "an art of interpretation" . . . an interpretation the consciousness of which in reality had no therapeutic effect for the patient. At the moment of this practical failure another means has to be found. . . . It is through the "transference" (*Ubertragung*) that one will attempt to reduce the "resistances" of the patient, who cannot be reached by simply becoming conscious of a *Deutung.* Transference itself displaces, but it only displaces the resistance. (339)

3

Anxiety and Contact in Attending to a Play about Land Mines

Julie Salverson

I was recently invited to see a short play at a local community college. Student actors and their director had drawn on stories from Bosnian children to create a twenty-minute performance about land mines. The piece opened with the actors lying on the floor doing breathing exercises and inviting the audience to call out thoughts evoked by the idea of land mines. Phrases such as "incomprehensible," "stop it," and "dead, dead" were grimly and vigorously taken up by groups of young performers and turned into tableaus of disaster, which segued into first person narratives declaring stories of loss and dismemberment tempered with heroics. My disenchantment with this play is not at the expense of the student actors, who no doubt approached the project with sensitivity and the preliminary skills their level of training would allow. What disturbed me was a sense that the students were not present in the performance; that they were not seeing themselves in the picture; and, consequently, that we as audience members were neither asked nor able to implicate ourselves. Audience and actors together were looking *out* at some exoticized and deliberately tragic *other*. Even more discomforting than the voyeurism in which I felt to be a participant was the almost erotic quality of the manner in which the actors performed pain. There was pleasure in it. Perhaps this is not as surprising as it might seem. Depths of feeling participated in without cost provide a kind of pleasure. Several audience members expressed being extremely moved by the whole thing. But what, I wondered, was our obligation as witnesses to this story, to this unacknowledged pleasure? Yes, the audience was moved, but by and toward what?

THE CONTEXT OF THE EVENT

The problem of how to tell stories of violence through the medium of theater is not an abstract one for me. In June 1997, I was commissioned by the Canadian

Red Cross to write a play about antipersonnel land mines to be performed by schools and youth groups across Canada. The play was created in two stages. First, ideas were developed with student teachers in a summer course on theater across the curriculum that I taught at the University of British Columbia (U.B.C.). Fellow playwright Patti Fraser and I then wrote the one-act play *BOOM* to be premiered the following December by Ontario secondary school students. The occasion of the performance was a conference in Ottawa where the first international treaty banning the production and implementation of mines was signed. The task of creating and performing this play confronted me in extremely practical terms with what it means ethically to attend and bear witness to testimony.

Director Peter Brook writes that the theater audience is a third eye whose presence must always be felt as a positive challenge, an accomplice to the action, "a constant participant through its awakened presence" (1993, 18). The challenge Brook poses to those of us who make theater is to consider all of our actions public, communal, and witnessed and subject to judgment and consequence. Implicit in his statements about the audience is the need for ourselves as artists to be awakened. This chapter considers what it meant for the playwrights and student actors who wrote and performed *BOOM* to *wake up*. Ora Avni has written that we need to take seriously what it means to speak and listen to accounts of violence, particularly systemic violence perpetrated on a state-sanctioned scale (1995). The risk for the listener—a risk present from the first moment of the encounter with testimony—is a complete reimagining of oneself in relation to one's community in a way "that defies storytelling, 'lifting to consciousness,' or literalized metaphors" (Avni 1995, 213). My focus—in this chapter and in the play—is on the potential witness to testimony, the listener who may be changed by what he or she hears, who may enter a relationship of significance with the story, and who may pass that story on. I will discuss this in terms of *presence for* and *meeting* as dimensions of witnessing the story of land mines.

The facts and figures about mines, the cost to human life, land, and communities, all of this, suggested consequences beyond what any of us imagined, or imagined we could imagine. In the opening scene of the play, the character of The Teacher tells the class:

> There are an estimated 110 million active land mines scattered over 70 countries, one for every 52 people in the world. A further 110 million have been stockpiled. 2,000 people are involved in accidents every month. Mines are left from really old wars and set every day in new ones. A mine goes off every twenty minutes. Doctors say the injuries are more horrible than anything. Most people hurt are too poor to pay for medical help, artificial limbs or even anesthetic. (HOLDS UP PICTURES) These are the pictures I will not show you because you would not sleep at night.

Roger, the fictional Canadian teenager who became *BOOM*'s central character, responds to the teacher's words by asking: "Why should I listen to this? I'm not even finished grade twelve. I didn't put them there. I have enough to worry about."

What does it really mean for Canadian-born teenagers, artists, and teachers to meet the story of land mines? What are the stages to this encounter, the characteristics of approach, understanding, or refusal? What are the advantages and dangers inherent in an encounter based in identification? What is involved in preparing to be a witness, to meet with testimony? These questions emerged as the focus of both the pedagogical process and the play.

MEETING IN THE CONTEXT OF WITNESSING

What is the nature of the call to witness? According to philosopher Emmanuel Levinas, the call by the other, from what he calls "the face," is the encounter through which, in allowing myself *to open*, I *am opened* and am taken beyond myself. The face is not a content of my thought, not knowledge; rather, "it is uncontainable, it leads you beyond" (1985, 87). This encounter with and call by the other is a surprise, a deformalization of what's assured, an infinitude of the other that requires attentiveness to hear beyond my conceptions. The curious paradox in Levinas's structure of the call is the combination of inevitability and freedom in the encounter. My fundamental subjectivity exists precisely in my response-ability to the face: "I am he who finds the resources to respond to the call" (1985, 89). At the same time, the call urges without insisting. It is a compelling invitation but an invitation nevertheless. The meeting is not about intentionality. It is a "for the other . . . whether accepted or refused, whether knowing or not knowing how to assume it, whether able or unable to do something concrete for the Other" (1985, 98–99).

Within this encounter with the face, I speak to and not of my friend. I announce myself publicly as a witness, and I commit myself to the consequence of response. Again, this is not about a consequence of intended action—this would make the encounter into a prescription, a knowledge of moral content—but the fact of response as inevitable once the face of the other is met. Within these terms, all involved in performing testimony are asked to become a "Here I am . . . a witness that does not thematize what it bears witness of, and whose truth is not the truth of representation, is not evidence" (Levinas 1978/1991, 146). These are the elements I felt were missing in the college play described earlier: The students spoke "of" and not "to" the Bosnian children behind the stories; the characters were presented as familiar thematic portrayals that collapsed them into interchangeable victim portraits and did not surprise or unsettle our expectations as audience members; and, finally, we were not offered an encounter in which to respond but presented with only a narrowly prescribed obligation—to feel *bad* in terms tightly structured by the play.

When the teenager Roger in *BOOM* asks, "Should I listen to this?" there is a subtext to his question: "Will listening to testimony be a listening to the horrific, to catastrophe? Will it be only that? Will I forever lose who I am in the encounter, will it drive me mad?" Levinas offers a way through what he calls the horror of the confrontation with being in this encounter with the other person, which he calls not only the face but "the neighbour," who "already claims me and demands me" (1994, 166–167). The imperative to refuse a despairing response to horror—including being overwhelmed by feeling, sentimental or otherwise—and to attempt instead the initiative to act justly is a matter of ethics. But within this ethics is not only loss. Together with the element of horror in the nature of testimony's story is the element of vitality, perhaps even joy, in the contact with another and the experience of being opened, of opening, of response. Perhaps this is what is most paradoxical in the structure of the meeting with another: the existing together of joy and horror, the Infinite within the finite that Levinas says "is not a knowledge but a Desire (which) cannot be satisfied (and) in some way nourishes itself on its own hunger" (1985, 92).

A significant element in the encounter with testimony is the unexpectedness, the shock of the collision between the world of the listener and the world of the event. In the case of our project, this does not simply mean that the students who performed *BOOM* had no idea they would be spending the fall of 1998 learning about land mines. Even those of us who chose the project voluntarily had no way of imagining what we were about to encounter. We were inevitably, in Levinas's terms, *surprised* by testimony and challenged to listen beyond how we had previously understood. Yet Levinas says that the call from the other comes as an invitation and that refusal must be possible. How is this a real choice? Faced with the actuality of the request to attend to the vast destruction caused by land mines, what does refusal mean? When I accepted the Red Cross commission to meet and in some way pass on the story of land mines, I decided that this matter of the right to refuse a story was critical. Deborah Britzman reminds us that when education engages with the right of refusal, what gets opened up is the territory of psychic trauma and the internal conflicts the listener brings to testimony (1998, 117). The possibility of meeting and bearing witness to the story of land mines demands a prior question: What is needed in order to approach the other?

ATTENDING AND PRESENCE IN THE
CONTEXT OF WITNESSING

> The listener . . . will experience hazards and troubles of his own. . . . While overlapping to a degree with the experience of the victim, he does not become the victim—he preserves his own separate place, position and perspective; a battleground for forces raging in himself, to which he has to pay attention and respect if he is to properly carry out his task. (Laub 1992, 58)

Performance forms that might enact possibilities of ethically meeting testimony may be thought through and developed in terms of an implicatedness that stays conscious of its difference from the other, and so becomes a presence for the other.

To explain this I will apply psychoanalytic concepts—in particular, notions of mourning, melancholia, and working through—and extend them to the social context of the classroom and the theater. In "Mourning and Melancholia," Freud (1917/1915) distinguishes between mourning, as a psychic response to loss that maintains the integrity of the other, and melancholia, as a narcissistic response that subsumes the lost other into the self. Whereas in mourning the lost object is distinct from the self and eventually becomes replaced by something else out in the world, melancholia proceeds through identification with what has been lost. What is lost is internalized and becomes the focus of one's own psychic pain. In a sense, the melancholic replaces the lost object with the experience of loss itself. The person lives continually with an indefinable and interminable yearning for something for which no substitute is possible.

Encounters with what Britzman calls the *difficult knowledge* of trauma (1998) have the potential to set in motion dynamics of identification and defense that play out the uneasy negotiation between one's own experience of loss and another's account. There is an evident connection between the ability to distinguish oneself from the object of loss constituted within the act of mourning and the need to make the distinction between one's own pain and that of another, a distinction necessary if the student actor, or the character Roger, is to become available to the *saying* of testimony. This suggests that as playwrights and student actors approaching the story of land mines, we must notice how our identifications are characterized, what versions of the story they emphasize, and what futures they permit.

The writing and performance of *BOOM* can be understood as an attempt to intervene in a melancholic approach to testimony. Both our classroom practice and the structure of the script and performance tried to put in place mechanisms that invited—for the playwrights and the student actors—a collective engagement with what Freud called a *working through* of loss. Working through is an essential component to learning *from* and not merely *about* (Britzman 1998, 119). It requires naming and experiencing (but not repetitively recycling) the shock of the encounter: anxiety, pain, resistance. Working through is by no means a simple task, and, it may be argued, the task itself is never completed, nor is mourning completely distinguishable from melancholy. Attention to and consciousness of the task of working through, however, may make possible, or at least imaginable, an eventual surrender to the fact of loss; and, paradoxically, make equally possible movement toward a regaining of contact between the story (or storyteller) and the listener, a contact that was previously made impossible by the preoccupation with the constitutional element that began the encounter—that of loss itself.

Working through, or the work of mourning, possesses a number of characteristics necessary to attending and becoming present for. First, it requires the presence of anxiety and resistance, understood as a necessary precondition to learning. Second, it requires the presence of a listener, an *"addressable other"* (Laub 1992, 68) that moves the story from the individual to the social realm. Third, it requires a naming of both the event and the illusion of naming itself, the impossibility of representation, what Shoshana Felman calls the impossibility of witnessing (1992, 160). I will now move to a discussion of the stages of creating and performing *BOOM* and negotiating the complex terrain of approaching testimony and working through.

THE SHOCK OF THE ENCOUNTER: PREPARING THE PLAY

Teacher: "What would you do if I told you something you don't want to hear?"
Clown #1: "Is this about what happened in the newspaper yesterday?"
Clown #2: "Which things? The horrible made up ones, or the ones that are true?"
Clown #1: "I guess it depends what happens after you hear a bad story. I mean, does it mean you have to feel BAD about it?"
Clown Queen: "Oh, you'll feel bad when you hear this!"

Approaching testimony given from firsthand accounts, or speaking of one's own encounter with extremity, poses difficulties. Poet Carolyn Forché writes, "[E]ven if one has witnessed atrocity, one cannot necessarily speak *about* it, let alone *for* it" (1993, 37). In our case, all of our information came from mediated accounts: visits from Red Cross staff who had encountered land mine survivors, print and television news media, video documentaries. The enormity of the destruction caused by land mines was complicated by the nature of this peculiar distance across which the stories came to us. Yet the shock of impact registered almost immediately. During the first days at U.B.C., the student teachers made sculpted images of their initial responses to land mines. The images included: dread, horror, pushing away, isolated figures switching TV channels. In a paper written at the end of the course, one student teacher wrote: "As the presentation continues, I notice an intense feeling of nausea washing over my body. I feel weak and full of despair, unable to watch the video. I was sick to hear that mines have killed more people than chemical and nuclear weapons put together." The shock of the encounter is evident in a poem written by one of the student teachers:

> A stab at poetry:
> I knew I was ignorant
> But they say that's bliss
> I believe them
> Knowing is hard
> The damage is done
> Now i know
> You got me
> So what?

Current literature about what is involved in listening and responding to accounts of trauma stresses how important it is for a potential witness to first be able to bear witness to oneself. This means understanding one's own relationship to violence and loss and the trickiness of navigating trauma's known and unknowable hazards. The listener needs to appreciate what Dori Laub calls "the lay of the land . . . the landmarks, the undercurrents and the pitfalls both in the trauma witness and in himself" (Felman and Laub 1992, 58). An integral step in becoming present to testimony is admitting one's own often conflicted initial responses. In efforts to take seriously the response of the teachers—even, or indeed particularly, when that response was in no way heroic—it was important for the class to honor the presence of fear, dismay, and reluctance by including those discomforts in both the theatrical images and the conversations we developed.

Felman has written that knowledge "is not a substance but a structural dynamic; it is irreducibly dialogic" (1987, 83). What she is discussing here is a pedagogy that is always prepared to be taken by surprise, proceeding not in a direct line from ignorance to knowledge but "through breakthroughs, leaps, discontinuities, regressions and deferred action" (76). With this in mind, I tried to make sense of what the students were saying and feeling. One wrote: "Will I be perceived as an uncaring individual because I ask this question: Don't we have enough problems here at home?" Was there an explanation for this resistance beyond the dismissive pronouncement of "privilege" or "middle-class guilt"? I suggest that some of these student teachers were exercising a form of refusal, an unwillingness to approach until they could do so without what I would term *disappearing themselves* in the encounter; refusing to approach until they had at least registered their own relationships with another's pain. They also may be resisting not only the enormity of the task they suspect is before them but the impossibility of that task, the inevitability of their complicit failure before it. All of these are steps of negotiation in bringing the "I" to the encounter. Drawing near, to become myself approached. "I" accepting my designation as called upon.

IDENTIFICATION, MOURNING, AND PERFORMANCE STYLE

It seems to me that, in the class, we were grappling with our various identifications with both experiences of loss and the event of land mines. Analysts Nicolas Abraham and Maria Torok (1994) have clarified two aspects of identifying that function differently in mourning and melancholia. *Introjection* is a term used to describe a child's learning to fill the emptiness of the mouth—searching around for replacements of what's lost, in a primal sense the lost breast—with words. It is a form that allows the child to express through slow difficult work like that of mourning. It is a process mediated by language: "True to its spirit, introjection works entirely in the open by dint of its privileged instrument, naming" (Abraham and Torok 1994, 114). For introjection to occur throughout life (the continual process of experiencing loss and the psychic dimensions surrounding that loss, expressing grief through language, and moving out again into the world to attach one's love to another), one's suffering must be recognized by others, listened to. This process is about contact with others in the presence of interminable pain, about reestablishing contact with ourselves, the world, and others.

Incorporation, on the other hand, is a fantasy that engulfs the object in a way unmediated by language. Unlike the slow work of introjection, incorporation is "instantaneous and magical. The object of pleasure being absent . . . the incorporated object is settled into the ego in order to compensate for the lost pleasure and the failed incorporation" (Abraham and Torok 1994, 113). Whereas the process of introjection is visible, incorporation acts in secret, the ego has taken another's death and disappearance as its own but has no knowledge of this self-imposed exile, this double robbery. John Caruana, writing of mourning and mimesis, says that what is at stake is the ego's ability to differentiate, to not completely mirror the object, to name the illusion of identification (1996, 96). Theories of performance aligned with classical traditions of narrative closure that make no ontological distinction between object and image sound curiously like this description of incorporation; for example, "theater ingests the world of objects and signs only to bring images to life" (Bert O. States, quoted in Elin Diamond 1992, 394). A pedagogy that intervenes in melancholy, that attends to introjection, could pay particular attention to the voicing of secrets, the naming of the unsayable (including marking the limits of such naming).

Operating within the fantasy of the melancholic is the paradoxical inability to accept, and thus name, loss. Approaching as writers, Patti and I realized that we had our own fears that needed to be named, made present to each other. To articulate these was difficult, sometimes embarrassing. For example, we did not want to look like clumsy Canadians tramping through the territory of people's pain and so were reluctant to state material facts that could too easily reduce lives to terms of guilt and innocence. We became terribly aware that this fear of being accused could restrict our opportunity to tell people that thousands of mines so tiny they would fit into your child's hand fall from helicopters in the shape of butterflies. A sea of brilliant colors attracting curiosity, tiny mines that do not know the war is over.

The students, who were being asked to generate material that they acted out in various theatrical ways, were faced with the difficulty of how to name and make present what they were hearing and feeling. A situation that arose midway into the class made visible for many of us the complexity of the relationship between identification and performance. Anita, one of the teachers in the course, was visibly upset by what she was learning and took home a book about Bosnia to read. She returned with a monologue she had prepared about a woman who had lost several members of her family. When Anita performed this monologue to the class, she spoke in a low, hushed voice filled with sadness. The performance had an air of falseness. Anita, with the best of intentions, could imagine nothing of the Bosnian woman's strength, her possible humor, even her courage, caught as Anita was in her almost romantic identification with what the woman had lost. Anita performed as if she was waiting to be confirmed, by the class/audience, as wearing the nobility of the victim. The class described how they felt sympathy, guilt, and horror while watching this speech, but also a complete inability to respond. This student, with the best of intentions, was herself completely invisible in the presentation of the unknown woman's story. There is a problem with how an audience may identify with a character like that of the Bosnian woman as performed by Anita. If we write a play that presents an uncomplicated portrayal of victims, villains, and heroes, what choices do we give an audience as to how to relate? What are the connections between the individual audience members' relationships to land mines (as Canadians, as war veterans, or perhaps as immigrants or refugees?) and questions of identification and even victimization? If making contact with characters in the play slips too easily into substituting myself for them—putting myself in their shoes—will I want to identify with a victim? This is a serious question for a theater that desires to have an educational component. If understanding what it means for land mines to exist means I must substitute myself for either the victim or the soldier who put them in the ground, is it any wonder I will resist this knowledge? Might a student *refuse* to approach testimony presented in this way on the grounds that it assumes too narrow a definition of the listener?

The above response to the problem of performing testimony is reminiscent of the play described at the beginning of this chapter, and raises the question of how performance style contributes to the ability to be present to testimony. The play I saw at the local college emerges from a tradition in Canadian theater that privileges dramatic realism, a theatrical form very much influenced in North America by interest in personal psychology and in representing life *as it is lived*. As one significant example, many exercises taught in Canadian theater classrooms are adapted from Russian acting teacher Constantin Stanislavski in such a way as to emphasize the internal, psychological aspects of the craft to the exclusion of Stanislavski's work on theatricality, historicization, and the external (Mann 1998). The goal of such exercises is to help students identify with the roles they are playing and to discover the emotionality and intention in themselves that is similar to that of their characters. This approach looks for empathy and connection and encourages a *standing in* for another. People who are only exposed to a taste of theater training in this way (for example, the student teachers in my class) tend to play the emotion, believing that putting across strong feeling displays (to themselves and listeners) their compassion and depth of commitment to a role or a story.

The tendency of dramatic realism to be a performance style that encourages a standing in for another proves more disturbing when the question is asked, what does the event being testified to mean to the potential witness? Britzman (1998) has suggested that in our desire to exhibit loyalty to the dead, pedagogy resides in the fault lines of melancholia. Speaking of the conflicts and ambivalences that are part of the work of mourning, she says that loyalty to and identification with the fate of another are not the same thing. We desire to empathize and understand the pain

of another but end up making our own selves the focus of the inquiry. Such identification is not only voyeuristic, not only does it distort my ability to listen and respond, it is also too great a burden. If our project is to attempt a pedagogy that interrupts a process of identification that can't distinguish between one's own loss
and that of another, the project and the play must ask the following questions: How
can I accept obligation without having to stand in the shoes of those to whom I
am obliged? How might I consciously and responsibly include myself in the inquiry? How might all involved in this play understand the difference between honoring the pain of others, working toward diminishing future losses, and mourning
the distinct ways in which we and others have been violated?

A MEETING WITH TESTIMONY: PERFORMING THE PLAY

When the U.B.C. class was over, Patti and I took two months to write the play
and then rehearsed it with director Toni Wilson and high school students from
southern Ontario. *BOOM* is a story of approach. It is a play where two realistic
characters—a teenage Canadian boy and a Croatian girl—try to become friends.
Roger is a grade twelve student who doesn't really want to know or care about
land mines. Ana is a Croatian girl in his class who wants to be Canadian, to be a
scientist, who doesn't want to talk about her homeland and tries to control her
trauma through designing a land clearance device that will rid the earth of land
mines. When their teacher comes in one morning and talks to the class about mines,
Roger realizes that Ana might know about this because she is from Bosnia. He begins to question her and pursues the friendship further than he had intended, approaching her world. As he does so, he finds his own becoming disrupted.

The complexity and urgency of becoming present to and meeting testimony had
convinced Patti and I that we needed a character who represented all potential listeners to the play who faced the task of witnessing. The character of Roger became the structural device through which the play could raise many of the questions voiced in this chapter. Roger begins in the same place as the Ontario student
who played him: As soon as Roger hears that Ana has experienced land mines, he
is filled with assumptions about her. His question becomes, how do I approach Ana,
how do I speak to her, how do I ask her to speak?

The question of representation is posed in *BOOM* in a number of explicit ways.
The character of the teacher wonders how to teach about land mines. Roger wonders how to tell his friends about Ana. Ana tries to translate her experience of land
mines into the language of science. The set (by designer Ruth Howard) is composed
of a shadow screen, a series of blocks covered with a painted landscape, and a com-
puter. All direct testimony—including Ana's story of leaving her country—happens
behind the screen and is only partially available to the audience, to the clown chorus
and Roger (who in the play are students in a class), and even to Ana in her present life
in Canada. The set blocks, covered with the painting of a rural landscape, are gradu-

ally taken apart during the performance, so that the world of the play is increasingly dismembered and disrupted, actually coming apart before the eyes of the audience. Our decision to dismember the wholeness of the design picture was an attempt to suggest what Simon and Eppert describe as the "surreal" quality of many testimonial accounts and to provoke in the audience "a dis-orientation that displaces the terms upon which we seek to define ourselves and our relationship with others" (1997, 185).

Elin Diamond tells us that mimesis is both the doing and the undoing of representation, "impossibly double, both the stake and the shifting sand: order and potential disorder, reason and madness" (1997, v). There are significant resemblances between melancholia, incorporation, and the function of mimesis as a standing in for the object, just as links can be made between mourning, introjection, and the function of mimesis as an operation that destabilizes identity and lets the object be. John Caruana relates Freud's concept of mourning to Adorno: "If Freud offers mourning as an alternative to the retentive compulsion of the subject, Adorno names mimesis as the appropriate antidote" (1998, 103). According to Caruana's reading, Adorno accepts that an ego/subject will believe itself to have mirrored the object, but must at the same time remember and *name the illusion* of this very mirroring. Failure to do so is not only voyeuristic, a failure to honor another's difference, it also robs the subject of what Adorno calls *happiness*, which he characterizes as the ability of the world to speak back to us. Caruana suggests that Adorno and this concept of mimesis radicalizes Freud's concept of mourning, moving it from a process that can be completed to an ongoing and interminable one: "For Adorno, a letting go or relinquishing that does not preserve a pain or distance would not respect the other" (104). The paradox here is that by naming the loss and accepting its burden, it is possible for the subject to reenter the world.

PERFORMING *BOOM* AND WORKING THROUGH

Clowns: "Mines are the stars of this show
they don't sleep, and they never go
they wait forever, and ever, they never let you know
just when the whole thing will blow"
Clown 1: "How long is forever?"
Clown 2: "As long as it takes!"

Saul Friedlander writes that a main aspect of working through for the historian is to render as truthful an account as possible *"without giving in to the temptation of closure . . . to face the dilemma"* (1992, 52). He describes the self-awareness necessary through which "the commentator must be clearly heard. The commentary should disrupt the facile linear progression of the narration, introduce alternative interpretations. . . . Working through ultimately means testing the limits of necessary and ever-defeated imagination" (1992, 53–54). For a student actor performing a character in *BOOM* to name mourning as an ongoing process, that student must grapple simultaneously with the worlds of Roger and Ana, the world of the clowns, and the student actor's own multiple identifications with the event—of land mines, of trauma, and of loss. Diamond writes of the potential of mimesis to make of the mirror of representation a trick mirror, through a politics of identification that places "identity in an unstable and contingent relation to identification . . . that works close to the nerves that divide/connect the psychic and the social" (1992, 397). *BOOM* makes an explicit attempt to activate this destabilizing of the nerves through the design of the show, through its structure, and most particularly with the function of deliberately nonrealistic characters—a clown chorus that continually pulls the story out of its narrative, contests it, defies it, names the slipperiness of identification.

> *Clowns:* "This is a play from beginning to end
> So don't take things too seriously."

Levinas names the call to responsibility he offers us in the face of the neighbor, "the impossibility of letting the other alone faced with the mystery of death" (1996, 167). What he describes as "the gravity of this love . . . is not a matter of peace as pure rest that confirms one's identity, but of always placing in question this very identity" (167). This disorienting notion of contact together with the suggestion of mourning as continuous is most consciously embedded in both the structure of the play and the pedagogy of performing it through the presence of the clowns. For both the teachers at U.B.C. (who had taken an intensive clown workshop) and the young people trying to figure out how to perform this story, the clowns provided obstacles to any easy identifications they wanted to make with *BOOM* as a simple or linear story of victims and pain. The clowns play a number of different roles: the classroom teacher presenting a workshop on land mines, a tour guide taking Roger to visit Croatia, a clown Queen who prods Roger along in his attempt to meet Ana. Together they mimic and subvert the secret and voyeuristic pleasure of melancholy.

> *Clowns:* "Roger's a hero, grab a camera
> put him on the evening news
> our man on the spot
> boy is he ever on the spot
> how's it feel, Roger? what'ja gonna do?"

On the first day of rehearsals, one high school student asked: "Why are there clowns? Isn't the play just supposed to tell people how terrible land mines are?" For many in the cast, tackling the problem of performing the clowns engaged the students in the conscious work of sorting out and recognizing their many and sometimes contradictory responses to the story they were telling. Central to this was the issue of laughter. How, many asked, was it possible to laugh at a play about land mines? "Clowns," said Steve Hill (the professional clown who worked with our class at U.B.C.), "always live in the shit. They want to be loved, they want to fix things, and they can't. But they continue, courageously, to try." *BOOM* follows Roger's journey of coming to know Ana beyond his assumptions about what being a victim of land mines has made of her. He presses her to talk. She keeps trying to speak through her experiment and the language of science, which is her way of telling. This is a play about difficult friendship: Across different losses. Across land mines. Across the impossibility of a completed mourning. Across the failure of witnessing. As one of the student teachers wrote, "clowns succeed at failure." Working with clown techniques in the class allowed the magnitude of the issue to be named and embodied in a way that was large enough to encompass not only what individuals felt and thought but what they could not reach in their attempts at expression.

The function of the clowns in *BOOM* is to name both the limits of identification and the trick mirror of representation. Roger must reach Ana through the clowns who tease him, confront him, but who also listen. In a sense, the clowns are Roger's witnesses. In mocking his ambivalence, they also claim it for themselves and the audience, at the same time encouraging him to keep going, never allowing it to be a reason to withdraw from Ana. The problem of the clowns in the play both frustrates and challenges the student actors, who are forced to make their way through the rupture the clowns make in their preconceptions of how testimony should look and sound. They must tackle this problem in order to figure out, quite literally, how to play the play. All the time remembering it is a story of urgency, a dangerous story. You are free to choose Roger, but remember—as Levinas reminds us—freedom is for the other person, my freedom "is only to do what no other person can do in my place" (cited in Handelman 1991, 249).

According to Robert Gibbs, the saying in Levinas is the drawing near, my exposure as a kind of giving. Saying arises from suffering, a letting down of defense and control (1995, 4). Approach, the clowns tell Roger, but know that you may be wounded. Enter, engage, risk, but understand that the narrative can be pulled from beneath you at any point, disrupted by any number of things: the structures of trauma and the roles and hiding places where in our vulnerability we seek safety, the shock of material realities that break continuities and disrupt our understanding of who we are in the world. The narrative is broken, our sense of who we are in the world is shaken, and what will we do? Will we still risk friendship? Will we risk contact? Will we risk witnessing?

ANXIETY, CONTACT, AND A RADICAL MOURNING

Roger: "What the hell are you doing? What do you want, to totally confuse me? Scare me? Guilt me out? I'm doing everything I can to try and understand you,

Ana, and you push me away every single time. I can't do anything about your war, or your silence, or your family or any of it. I don't know what happened to you, cause you won't bloody tell me. I wish you would. I like you, I want to be friends. But you've gotta tell me something. You've gotta give a little."

I want to return to the integral role that risk—and the anxiety that accompanies it—brings to the possibility of meeting testimony. If I take seriously the notion that encounters with difficult knowledge will require working through of our own relationships with loss, I will need to consider resistance, defensiveness, and anxiety as steps of approach, as signs of potential rather than evidence of pathology. Dorothy Soelle, a Christian theologian committed to an active nonviolence, has written about Kierkegaard's concept of anxiety as a pathway from guilt to freedom, a moment that can change us and move us to conversion. Kierkegaard located *anxiety* at a point of transition from what he terms an ethical state of existence to one that he calls *religious*: "Those who are spiritless enough not to be afraid can settle down in the ethical stage and live in a kind of social democratic reductionism. A radical ethic, on the other hand, exposes itself to anxiety, to loss of life" (Soelle 1990, 118–119).

This idea of a radical ethic exposed to anxiety suggests the notion of a radical mourning, which reveals the anxiety of loss for what it is. This is the radical mourning that exposes the content of loss's secret, the secret that, as Freud says, the world has become poor and empty. If we delay the job of witnessing ourselves, of facing our own losses, in the hopes that loss will disappear and that mourning will end, it will be a long wait. Loss exists. Without this acceptance, this naming, we remain trapped in what Torok calls "the illness of mourning," forever invested in loss itself, not realizing that it is our own and not the others' that possesses us. There was a certain personal urgency in how some of the students took on the issue of land mines, in some cases calling anyone who asks the questions that Roger asks "ignorant." The students' refusing the right of refusal displayed an almost libidinal satisfaction, an "exquisite pain of mourning" (Abraham and Torok 1994, 121), that resembles the manic behavior Freud says is another characteristic of melancholia. But in the encounter with *other,* what is the source of our deepest anxiety? Is it that we will subsume the other? Could it rather be the fear that we will not be able to be present, and thus not able to consciously meet with testimony, to be *ourselves witnessing?*

Anxiety is conceptualized by Kierkegaard as a moment that drives us to our limits where we dare a leap of faith—in his terms, beyond an *ethical stage* to a *radical ethic*. Only by becoming spiritless and unfree can we avoid anxiety—and, perhaps, avoid an encounter with mourning. Only by admitting anxiety, considering it a creative moment of change, can we move beyond guilt. Guilt—like melancholia and incorporation—represses anxiety, makes it an unmentionable, something to be hidden or confessed. Kierkegaard posits anxiety as not a pathology to be cured but a human condition to be entered, navigated, worked through, and called upon for the best or worst of what we are capable. Holding the tension between trauma and the desire to witness means not only admitting but inviting anxiety into the process of performance and pedagogy.

> *Roger:* "I know I'm no one special, but maybe I could listen.
> Maybe you could trust me, maybe I could know you.
> I wish I could be bending to pick for you a flower
> cause everybody has to leave the darkness sometime."

Meeting with and witnessing testimony requires an actual desire to go somewhere you may be hurt and stay there. It may be that this is easier to explain in terms of obligation than it is in terms of pleasure. If the pleasure of engagement with testimony—Roger's engagement with Ana, for example—is not the erotic pleasure I described at the opening of this chapter, if Roger and the student actors can work through voyeuristic and heroic impulses and responses, what else might fuel the energy that draws, rather than forces, a person forward? If we are able to hold the tension between our anxiety and the call of the face before us, what might lie beyond the shocking encounter that seduces so much of our attention, both in literature and in life?

Roger's question—and perhaps it is not his alone—is how to hold the distinction between himself and another and still engage the role of contact, feeling, disruption, and pleasure in the touching of worlds that is testimony. The trick, perhaps, is to endure anxiety while distinguishing from the trauma of the other and still holding her in mind. What kind of meeting does this describe? What does it mean to articulate and live a responsibility to another that is not rooted in guilt, pity, or a facile empathy, but that still allows contact? What the work of mourning offers is the possibility of connection and detachment, the generosity of approach that does not recycle in melancholic repetition, does not ask for returns.

Is there a point to friendship if there is no assurance? What is the purpose of a play about land mines if there is no guarantee it will teach me something, change a student's behavior in the world, give an audience enough information? Perhaps friendship and pedagogy are not about outcomes. What if the passing on of stories is not to produce meaning or truth but simply, but not at all easily, to attend: to engage in a relationship of attention. There is a risk, a stake, attention is not neutral, it is paid. The students in the process of doing this play talked about a feeling of being off balance, of not quite getting the whole picture. Just when they thought they did, it shifted, like a trick mirror. And yet the group, as a whole, became strongly committed to the project, and, in a way, became friends with the story of land mines. By which I mean they entered an engaged, invested relationship with it.

Caruana says that melancholy and incorporation—identification with instead of identification of—arise from the inability to expect, foreclosing the possibility of receiving back from the world something different (1996, 97). What a play can perhaps do is engage the question: How can Roger and Ana meet? What are the possibilities for the nature of this meeting? What might a relationship with testimony look like where loss exists, mourning does not end, and yet contact is maintained? We will only find answers in the lived relation, in the step toward the other person, in receiving the invitation. As Ana says to Roger about her scientific invention, the project through which she faces Roger: "See this? The molecules have to be balanced perfectly. Think of the crystals under the light. It's like they're dancing. Responsibility. The ability to respond. We are innately free to respond however we want. Depending. You want to take a look?"

4

Standing in a Circle of Stone:

Rupturing the Binds of Emblematic Memory

Sharon Rosenberg

> This week, the unimaginable happened. A 25-year-old man . . . strode into the University of Montreal and opened fire on innocent students. . . . The shock, horror and grief reverberating throughout the country are all prefaced with the question, "why?" Why Lepine? Why female victims? Why now? Why Canada?
> —*Toronto Star,* December 9, 1989

> You're 30, you're 43, you're 50, you're reading the paper, or someone calls you, you can't believe it, you're numb or you feel angry. You're a feminist. You've spent five, or 10, or 15 years going to meetings, organizing demos, publishing / writing / fundraising / speaking / marching. Suddenly, you're tired, or you're burnt out, or you're demoralized, and you cry for the deaths of 14 young women you've never met. You grieve also for the literal expression of a hatred for feminism that you know to be embedded in your culture. You feel targeted. Your heart feels cold.
> —Marusia Bociurkiw, "Je me Souviens"

It has been almost a decade since a gunman entered l'École polytechnique (the School of Engineering) at the University of Montreal in Quebec, murdering fourteen women. For those who lived in proximity to these murders, it is likely that the details do not need to be recalled, for their imprint is not easily forgotten. For others, this brief recollection alone will be insufficient to the substance of memory. So, to recall: In the early evening of December 6, 1989, Marc Lepine, a twenty-five-year-old white man, entered a university building in the city of Montreal armed with a semiautomatic rifle. He walked into an engineering classroom, told the men to leave—which they all did—and shot six women to death, accusing them of being a "bunch of feminists." He then walked through hallways and entered other classrooms, murdering eight more women and injuring thirteen others (nine women and four men, men who were shot presumably because they attempted to impede his rampage). Then he killed himself. In the three-page note found on his body, but not released into public circulation for a year, he described the murders as a political act and blamed feminism for ruining his life.[1]

Since their immediate aftermath, these murders on December 6, 1989, have been marked off, delineated, as an event in and for living memory in Canada. Such delineation has been established, in part, through ordering the murders under a distinct name—the Montreal Massacre, a naming that began to take hold within hours of the bloodshed—and has continued through the enactment of memorial activities each anniversary. Such marking off of the killings at l'École polytechnique has had, I suggest, a dual and contradictory effect. On the one hand, it has allowed for, perhaps encouraged, interpretations of the murders as "incomprehensible" (in Lakeman 1992, 94), "one man's act of madness" (in Nelson-McDermott 1991, 125), an act that "many argued . . . had nothing to do with women and everything to do with psychosis" (Scanlon 1994, 77). On the other hand, and in contradistinction, the delineation of the Massacre as a distinct, separate "event" has made possible its interpretation as emblematic.[2] In this interpretation, the killings are understood not as aberrant breaks in the everyday, but as intimately bound to, indeed symbolic of, mass systemic violences against women in Canada. As Julie Brickman has argued: "The nature and circumstances of their deaths has shaped the meaning of their individual lives, transforming these fourteen women into symbols, tragic representatives of the injustice against women that has been built into the fabric of the society in which we live" (1992, 129).

While initially put forward as a counter-dominant stance (to contest the individualizing and pathologizing interpretation that circulated in mainstream media), within a couple of years, emblemization began to take hold as the more commonplace reading. This is not to argue that emblematic memory has been produced unproblematically. Certainly, the manner in which the remembrance of the Massacre has been contested revolves around issues of emblemization, issues to which I will return. That noted, however, it must also be recognized that emblemizing the Massacre has put violences against women *as a social and political issue* in the domain of public discussion, in a manner unprecedented in Canada. Indeed, I would argue, the force of the memorial legacy of the Massacre has come to depend upon its being read as symbolic of a "larger problem" that requires social and political address. Thus, remembrance has become attached to strategic efforts to intervene in politics of the now, linking memorialization, however obliquely, to projects of change. From the resolution "never again" that has echoed through vigils held across the country, to calls for stricter gun control legislation, to the feminist rallying cry, "first mourn, then work for change," to the 1991 state declaration of December 6 as a National Day of Remembrance and Action on Violence Against Women, there has been an iterative registration of the binding between remembrance and change, memory and social justice.

While such bindings have no doubt been, and will continue to be, necessary, what concerns me—forms a deep impulse for this writing—is their orientation and substance. It is a central argument of this chapter that accepting the structure of emblemization—as *the* organizing structure for remembering the event of the Montreal Massacre—has foreclosed much needed consideration of the very relations between remembrance and change, the living and the dead, loss and hope. In particular, I suggest that what is foreclosed in this "strategic remembrance practice" (see Introduction, this volume) is the possibility of encountering and facing the very shock of the murders: a shock at the profound piercing of the skin of civil humanity that was palpable in the hours and days following December 6, 1989.

As Colette Guillaumin describes it, this shock must be understood not as one of incomprehension, but of *resemblance,* of recognition. She states:

> [o]ne cannot regard the slaughter in Montreal as an act devoid of meaning, a *senseless* act, just a break in the normal course of events, an unpredictable event that is limited to creating a "shock." Yes, it is a shock, but it is not a shock of the unknown, it is a shock of pain, of anger. In fact, it is a shock of the known, the "I can't believe it" of the known that is not acknowledged—of *unbearable* reality. (1991, 12–13, original emphases)

The shock that Guillaumin directs us to is the shock of the known that cannot be borne, a shock forged through a decisive linkage between the traumatic impact of two distinct ruptures initiated by the murders in Montreal. The first of these was the rupture of what was expected and anticipated for women attending an institution of higher learning in late twentieth-century North America; that is, that they (we) were (are) safe, welcome, and therefore could attend classes without the threat of violence and violation. The second was a rupture of the necessary and everyday systemic refusals to attend to the horrors of oppression that pass as normal. The Massacre may be considered "emblematic," from this understanding, in that it enacts a return of the repressed, in which we are confronted with horrors revealed in the realization that "I can't believe it" is a veneer, a skin against the unbearable that is so profoundly difficult to know.

I do not dispute this difficulty, more than that, am profoundly familiar with its weight, but I am drawn to consider how (our) memorial pedagogies might be engaged, deepened, rethought, altered . . . *to make possible* encounters with this traumatic inheritance, with "the shock of the [unbearable] known." In thinking about this imperative, I am drawn to these words from Judith Butler, who argues, in another context, "[t]he emergence of collective institutions for grieving are . . . crucial to survival, to reassembling community, to rearticulating kinship, to reweaving sustaining relations. . . . [T]here are dire psychic consequences of a grieving process culturally thwarted and proscribed" (1997, 148). If we replace "institutions" with memorial practices, then Butler offers what I find to be compelling terms for a remembrance/pedagogy in response to the Montreal Massacre. That is, a pedagogy that stages encounters—individual and collective—with the loss, grief, horror, the ruptures that the murders initiated. These ruptures are severely constrained, I will argue, by emblematic memorial practices, which seek to stabilize *resemblance* (between the fourteen women murdered and all women subject to violences at the hands of men), *continuity* (between the past, present, and future), and *a definitive separation between grieving and activism* (first mourn, then work for change). While such strategic containment is understandable, even necessary, in current political climates, it risks occluding the "difficult return" of the Massacre in Montreal—a return of the event of the killings *and* of the shock of the (unbearable) known. To give some texture as to why I feel it is imperative to argue this point and to offer some sense of producing our memorial practices in ways that might approach and tolerate this return, I will move now to considerations of the first national permanent monument dedicated to the women murdered in Montreal and "all the women who have been murdered by men" (Women's Monument, Vancouver).

Geneviève Bergeron
Hélène Colgan
Nathalie Croteau
Barbara Daigneault
Anne-Marie Edward
Maud Haviernick
Barbara Maria Klucznik
Maryse Laganière
Maryse LeClair
Anne-Marie Lemay
Sonia Pelletier
Michèle Richard
Annie St.Arneault
Annie Turcotte
Murdered December 6, 1989
l'École polytechnique, Montreal

THE WOMEN'S MONUMENT AND THE
TROUBLE WITH EMBLEMIZATION

Initiated in the winter of 1990–1991, through the Women's Centre Steering Committee at Capilano College in Vancouver, British Columbia, the Women's Monument was a seven-year project that came to completion in the summer of 1998, with a ceremonial unveiling at Thornton Park in downtown Vancouver. My interest in this chapter is to explore how the monument was constituted through the framing of emblematic memory and how it may be rethought through a remembrance/pedagogy attentive to the dynamics of traumatic rupture. Before moving to the substance of these contemplations, however, there are two points of note that I want to offer, notes that feel particularly pressing to articulate, given that I am writing at a time coincident with the time of completion of the Monument Project. First, I acknowledge that aspects of my argument may not rest well with those who have invested years of time, energy, creativity, funds, and political vision into the development of the Women's Monument. My comments are not born from a disrespect of that work, far from it, but from a sense that there is an urgency to confront the limits of strategic, emblematic memorial practices, now, a decade after the killings in Montreal. Second, since my comments are oriented by this critique, there is a risk that my "readings" of the monument may at times foreclose the indeterminate ways in which it may be(come) individually meaningful. I do not intend this. Rather, what I am attempting is an analysis that begins from two paradoxical assertions: first, that the monument, in its materiality and visual openness, can be understood to invite a diversity of engagements, the content of which cannot be determined in advance; second, that such engagements cannot be understood as simply idiosyncratic, but are structured by *how* the completed monument binds women to women, women to men, past to present, remembrance to change. It is this particular set of bindings—and how they may be rearticulated— that predominantly concerns me here. In this, I am arguing not for turning away from the monument, but for turning toward it anew.

Given a focus on remembrance/pedagogy, my analytic interest with the Monument Project begins with the design competition guidelines (henceforth, the guidelines) that women artists and architects were required to follow in their submissions.[3] A useful orienting point for this discussion is the summary section, which opens with the following question: "Given the opportunity to permanently mark our grief and outrage over the murder of women, how do you envision a monument dedicated to their memory?"[4] Although this question clearly locates a remembrance politic in grief, rage, and a commitment to honoring the dead, these affective responses are minimally translated in the directions to artists.

Thus, the guidelines note, first, that the Women's Monument "must include the dedication," which lists the full names of the fourteen women murdered in Montreal. This is followed by the line: "murdered December 6, 1989, Université de Montréal," and, then, "[w]e, their sisters and brothers, remember, and work for a better world. In memory and in grief for all the women who have been murdered by men. For women of all countries, all classes, all ages, all colours" (14–15). Secondly, the monument itself or the site "must include the names of [financial] contributors," which in the guidelines is estimated at 5,000 (15) and upon completion was closer to 6,000 (Millar et al. 1998).

What is effectively displaced in this singular emphasis on a fixed textual inscription is how experiences of loss, grief, and rage may be translated into the *memorial design*. This displacement is reinforced by the deflection of design considerations into the restrictions that are attached to placement of the monument in a public space.

Artists are broadly directed to "recognize [the] contextual issues of the site such as climate, view, the surrounding trees, buildings and neighbourhoods, some of which have a Heritage designation" (15). Specifically, they are asked to consider how a monument may "respond to the challenge" of being "accessible 24 hours a day . . . be permanent and not subject to deterioration due to weather, pollution, or vandalism." The monument design should, further, be "accessible to persons with disabilities," have "no sharp or jagged edges," and consider issues of "light-ing and visibility." Although these restrictions are not surprising (especially given that the committee was reliant on the Vancouver Parks Board for access to and maintenance of the site), they do not readily correspond with remembrance of the Massacre as a difficult, rupturing return—in which permanency, smooth surfaces, and avoiding deterioration/vandalism may be taken not as unproblematized givens, but open to inquiry. What this lack of correspondence begins to gesture toward is a larger set of questions in regard to how the public space of Thornton Park—*as a site of memorialization*—has been conceived, questions to which I will return.

But to continue: Beth Alber's winning design is clearly constituted on the terms of the remembrance/pedagogy articulated in the guidelines, a pedagogy that is re-peated and recalled both in her proposal to the Momument Committee [5] and in subsequent discussions of the proposed monument in fund-raising publications.[6] The key design element of Alber's "Marker of Change" are fourteen pink granite slabs (interpreted either as benches or sarcophagi[7]), equally spaced around a 300-foot circle. The stone circle is intended to recall "the great stone circles of the ma-triarchal societies of the iron age in England [which] still stand today and have col-lected a patina of time which reflects their place and history." Each granite form is "raised six inches off the ground on two plinths of the same material." Horizon-tal, rather than vertical forms, each "solid mass of stone," cut at lengths of "five and a half feet," is designed to reference "fallen female bodies." "A shallow, sub-tle and textured oval" is carved into the top surface of each stone form, to "serve as a reservoir for collected water and a vessel of memory—a collection of tears." Each of the granite slabs stands distinct and separate from the others, a distinction that is marked in part through an incising of the name of one of the women mur-dered in Montreal into the surface facing the circle. And, yet, each may be read as substitutable for another in their similitude of size and form.

This minimal, abstract design lends itself, I propose, to assertions of an emblem-atic memory. This is put into place, first, by the fourteen congruous granite forms (referencing a/the fallen female body), grouped into the collective shape of the monument. Viewed as a composite, definitive distinctions between the forms fade (the incised names become indistinguishable) and one becomes (like) another. It is this blurring of individual distinctions that sets the terms for the second layer of emblemization, in which the granite forms are distanced from the individual dead and come to reference, instead, "tragic representatives" (of murdered women, an-tifeminism, misogyny). This collective symbolization may be read, then, as beck-oning the living—specifically women—into a binding relation to the dead through identification. On these terms, identification is formed through substitution, or, in the words of the Wyrd Sister's memorial song, "it could have been you / just as easily / . . . it could have been . . . me" (1992). In this remembrance/pedagogy, the living are aligned with the dead, perhaps to "rest" with them at the site of symbolic burial. For, as benches, the fourteen granite forms can be understood to provide the living with a site of rest, contemplation, reflection; as sarcophagi, they are tombs for the dead, a place of permanent rest.

Such issues begin to gesture to the trouble with an emblematic pedagogy as it takes form through the monument, troubles that are amplified and made explicit through the assertion of the memorial dedication that artists were required to include. To recall, this dedication consists of the full names of the fourteen women killed in Montreal, followed by the line: "murdered December 6, 1989, Université de Montréal," and then, "We, their sisters and brothers, remember, and work for a better world. In memory and in grief for all the women who have been murdered by men. For women of all countries, all classes, all ages, all colours." In this inscription, the fourteen women murdered at l'École polytechnique are first delineated by name as distinct individuals and then bound in remembrance as a collective, symbolic of the murder of "all women by men." It is noteworthy that it is this inscribed dedication—and particularly its emblematic phrasing—that has marked the terms of controversy in regard to the monument.

This controversy has surfaced through how "women" and "men" are figured as singular memorial constellations. Once the Momument Committee began seeking public and financial support for their project, the central emblematic phrase became the focus of significant dispute, particularly in its condensed form: "murdered by men." These comments, cited in mainstream media, were typical: "The monument's purpose is not to honour slain women but to dishonour living men" (Vancouver columnist in Dafoe, 1994: C16). "The monument singles out men [and] that's the problem." (Ted White, Reform MP-North Vancouver, 1994). "With the phrase, 'by men' I felt attacked and I felt as though it was my fault that [the killer] did this incredibly awful act. I feel as though I have been assaulted as much as if I had been in the room with those women [who were murdered]" (CBC listener on the talkback portion of *As It Happens,* 1994).[8] While I/we may be suspicious of efforts on the part of men to gain a position in which they can be identified (and identify themselves) as distinct from Lepine—efforts evidenced in these comments—I propose that such moments are instantiated by the *very terms* of the emblematic dedication. That is, in an equation in which Lepine comes to stand for all men, and "all men" become equated with killers (of women), it is not surprising that "men" would refuse this symbolic identity.

In the face of such obvious limitation, the Monument Committee, urged in part by the Vancouver Parks Board, endeavored to rework the dedication to include men on other terms—without diminishing the imperative of drawing attention to the social-political issue of men's violences against women (one central reason for the monument itself). The resulting dedication (as cited previously) contains a reordering of the memorial phrasing, so that the sentence that includes the phrase "murdered by men" is now prefaced (rather than followed) by one that offers men the positioning of "brothers" who "remember, and work for a better world" (Millar et al. 1998). While this strategy establishes a discursive ordering of identificatory space in which men can first identify as brothers (in solidarity with sisters), potentially displacing or at least mediating the subsequent positioning of men (who murder women), it continues to depend upon identification as *the binding mechanism* of remembrance/pedagogy. Further, these identificatory terms are formed on the basis of exclusions—brothers are separated from men who murder—a structure that elides the possibility of a memorial positioning for men who may be "brothers" *and* have enacted deathly violence against their "sisters."

Issues instantiated by the imbrication of identification and remembrance have further surfaced in regard to the memorial positioning of "women" by "Marker of Change," specifically in regard to the placement of the monument in Thornton Park. A city park in the downtown east side of Vancouver, Thornton Park is in an area marked by poverty and violence, particularly against the bodies of Aboriginal women. As Caffyn Kelley argues:

> the names inscribed on the monument will not be the First Nations women of the neighbourhood who have been murdered in back alleys and beer parlours, left to die in garbage dumpsters or thrown out of hotel windows. In this neighbourhood where women are six times more likely to be murdered than in the city overall—10 to 20 times more likely if they are between the ages of 20 and 45—the monument will be inscribed with the names of fourteen, white, middle-class women from four thousand miles away. (1995, 8)

What Kelly incisively identifies here are the limits of the emblematic dedication in regard to how the gap between women (living and dead) is being memorialized. Bound by its strictures, the monument can *only gesture to* "the loss [of women in Montreal] in the context of the many women lost" (guidelines, 7), it cannot make explicit the presence—in name—of those women whose slain bodies mark the grounds (the context) of Thornton Park. On these terms, it should be of little surprise, although of ongoing concern, that Aboriginal activists of the neighborhood and Monument Committee members could not arrive at a consensus about how to "include" women murdered in the downtown east side (Kelley, 10–11).

What this instance must alert us to is the very instability of identity categories in memorial pedagogy. One response to this instability has been an attempt to make memory more precise by qualifying and, hence delimiting, the terms of *symbolic* reference. This has been made evident in feminist efforts to assert, in remembrance, that the women who were massacred in Montreal were targeted as women in a school of engineering—with the privileges of race and class that tend to accompany this location (see, for example, Bociurkiw 1990; Kelley 1995; Kohli 1991). While this remembrance stance has been important for how it complicates assumptions of a binding commonality among women (and feminists), it founders on an irresolvable contradiction. That is, it attempts a simultaneous acceptance *and* refusal of the Massacre as symbolic of, substitutable for, all the murders of women by men. As indicated by the controversies cited previously, when this is recognized as a fragile substitutability, the implications are far reaching—not only for the remembrance of the dead but also for the struggles of the living, for whom "substitution" may be experienced as more barbarity.

What is made evident in these struggles over identity positionings—for women and men—is the inherent limit of a pedagogy enacted by the emblematic dedication of the Women's Monument. As I have endeavored to show, this limitation is figured, in part, through how the dead are remembered, a memory that is circumscribed by the names of fourteen women "from four thousand miles away," names that have become symbolic substitutes for "all the women who have been murdered by men." Limitation also figures in how the living are positioned *in relation to those dead,* in a gendered dichotomy of memorialization that singularizes "women" and "men" into already-secured identificatory bindings with the murdered *or* the murderer. The controversies instantiated by the Monument dedication suggest that these are regulatory bindings, occluding the very unsettledness that is required by the difficult return of the Massacre and what it may mean, on these terms, to work toward a "better world." What is left open to question—and where I will now turn—is what it might mean to *re*figure these bindings between remembrance and change, and, more broadly, between the living and the dead. To return to my opening arguments, how might the remembrance of the Montreal Massacre—as it takes form through "Marker of Change"—be rethought, now: not on the terms of identity/substitutability, but as a "shock of the known," as a traumatic rupture of the regimes of social power? How might this memorial pedagogy ready women and men to "remember," not as an act of moral vigilance for a different future, but as an opening to the Massacre as a difficult return—a return of what is repressed by the very strategies of distancing mourning from change, grief from the site of memory?

FROM BENCHES TO SARCOPHAGI

As I contemplate these questions, I return to the design element of "Marker of Change." In particular, I am interested in working with the ambiguity of the meaning of the granite forms, an ambiguity that is foreclosed by the effects of the emblematic dedication, but, can, I want to suggest, be recuperated. To recall, in her design proposal, Alber offered that these forms may be understood as sarcophagi (tombs) or benches; it was the Monument Committee who distilled their meaning to the latter. It is perhaps not surprising that this interpretation was secured in fund-raising materials, particularly given the controversies over the emblematic dedication. However, this is an interpretation that risks a slippage from memorial bench to park bench and in this may offer little in the way of staging an encounter with the loss and grief instantiated by the rupturing effect and legacy of the Massacre. For, where benches are reasonably places where one may rest, contemplate, even quietly remember and honor the dead, they are unlikely to prompt a viewer/visitor to, in the words of James Young, "grasp their own life and surroundings anew in light of a memorialized past" (1993, 128). The risk here lies in the detachment of "memorial" from "bench," such that the monument becomes integrated into the landscape, rather than drawing attention to that very landscape as an aspect of its remembrance/pedagogy.

Young's conceptualization of a "countermonument" offers a set of terms for addressing this concern. He argues,

> with audacious simplicity, the countermonument . . . flouts any number of cherished memorial conventions: its aim is not to console but to provoke; not to remain fixed but to change; not to be everlasting but to disappear; not to be ignored by passersby but to demand interaction; not to remain pristine but to invite its own violation and desanctification; not to accept graciously the burden of memory but to throw it back at the town's feet. (1993, 30)

This is a conception of memorial practice that corresponds more readily with remembrance of the Massacre as a difficult return, wherein what needs to be encountered is the shock of the unbearable known. Contrary to the Monument Committee's limiting translation of grief and outrage into the phrasing of the dedication (a more conventional memorial practice), the pedagogy of a *counter*monument stresses the provocation of uncertainty, anxiety, and self-interrogation as matters of design.

As I contemplate what it may mean to rethink "Marker of Change" through this pedagogy, I have in mind another project, also in Vancouver, conceived by local artists as an attempt to "create thought provoking commentary for the travelling public," by intervening in the commercial use of public benches (Edelstein 1994, 2). There is one design in particular that draws my attention and interest. Designed by Margot Leigh Butler and Karen Tee, this transit bench was conceived in relation to the Women's Monument Project and installed at the corner of Main and Terminal Streets (at the same location as Thornton Park) from February to April 1994 (Larson 1994, 5). A computer-manipulated photograph of a tombstone, this design read:

> I remember when we walked in fear of men's violence, she said.
> SKIN MEMORY   We were drenched in vigilance
> KIN MEMORY   We have been learning by heart
> IN MEMORY   We are still shredding forgetting
> IN LIVING MEMORY
> (in Larson, 5)

Butler and Tee's tombstone design interestingly evokes the conventions of a countermonument with its emphasis on unsettlement, an unsettlement that calls on passersby to attend to the practice of memory. In contrast to the Monument Project's specification of an immutable text (which works on the assumption that the names and the dedication are fixed, will always mean the same), Butler and Tee's shifting SKIN—KIN—IN—KIN—SKIN configuration points to the displacing effect of traumatic memory, breaking in on the terms of comprehension. Further, the reference to "in living memory" calls attention to the relation between the one who passes by, stopping to read, and those (presumably dead) who are being remembered. This is in contrast to the Women's Monument, where memory inscribed into stone may be presumed to be held there, a presumption that encourages an amnesiac distancing between present and past. As James Young remarks: "Under the illusion that our [modernist] memorial edifices will always be there to remind us, we take leave of them and return only at our convenience. To the extent that we encourage monuments to do our memory-work for us, we become that much more forgetful" (1993, 5).

Young's statements also bring to mind an additional appeal of the tombstone inscription: the interpellation of a "we" who has walked in fear, been drenched in vigilance, is learning by heart, shredding forgetting. The "we" may be understood as a direct call to "women" to engage in what Andreas Huyssen refers to as "the slow and persistent labor of remembrance" (1993, 259), a labor that, based on the terms associated with it in the inscription, is as bodily as it is mindful. This is positioned quite differently to the inscriptions on Alber's "Marker of Change," as directed by the Monument Committee, where the interpellated we is "sisters and brothers [who] remember, and work for a better world." What Butler and Tee's inscription does, perhaps, is offer some sense of the substance of that remembrance work, a learning to "awaken to" (Rosenberg and Simon, 1999) the fear, the vigilance, and the forgetting that is required (albeit to different degrees) in a social regime of power in which everyday horrors pass as normal. The hope here is attached to the possibility of this awakening and the learning (by heart) that it might instantiate, so that walking "in the fear of men's violences [she said]" may become a memory.

In contrast, then, to a modernist conception of a monument (a conception that is broadly consistent with that of the Women's Monument), Butler and Tee's design, read alongside Young's conceptualization of a countermonument, suggests a pedagogy of remembrance that may begin to engage visitors in the memory of the Massacre in Montreal as an anxious and difficult return. This is a pedagogical possibility that is far extended if the forms of Alber's design are read not as benches, but through her reference to sarcophagi—coffins or tombs that bear inscriptions to the dead. While this reference is broadly suggestive of a memorial practice responsive to loss and mourning, it becomes particularly so when the design is considered in its setting. Unlike monuments built to mark the history of atrocities on a particular site, the Women's Monument was not planned to mark the specific grounds of Thornton Park; indeed these grounds are thousands of miles away from the site of the Massacre. However, I will argue, that, in actuality, "Marker of

Change" is not separate from this land. Thornton Park is not a benign landscape, but—now—a public memorial space and, thus, is part of what constitutes the Women's Monument in downtown Vancouver.

To understand the site on these terms is to suggest a radical shift, not only in terms of what constitutes the monument but also, and as importantly, in terms of how the landscape of Thornton Park is to be "read." Jonathan Smith argues for the analogy of a "landscape as a text" (1993, 88) and advances the central, corresponding question, "how, or by whose authority, is it able to mean what it does?" (89). To pose this question in regard to the landscape or the site of Thornton Park is to ask: By whose authority has the park come to mean what it does, and in what ways may these meanings be destabilized by a conceptualization of the site as memorial ground?

"History of the Site":
"Thornton Park was built during the Edwardian Period . . . in an Edwardian style. This style is characterized by a formal and balanced geometry, with walkways that intersect the site creating square components and circular features. Often used in 'railway parks,' the Edwardian style of park design has been used in several Canadian cities.

Over time, some walkways in Thornton Park have been replaced or installed in such a way that the original geometry has been compromised. The Park Board would like to re-establish the original symmetry of the design so any walkways planned as part of the monument should bear this in mind. The monument design should take into consideration the original design philosophy of the park."

(guidelines, 5)

Another history of the site:
"I have lived in Vancouver now for twenty-five years, but I never knew the city was a gravestone marking the internment of a vast estuarial habitat until I began working on the Women's Monument. Thornton Park, where the monument [has been] built, was once a salt marsh where gooey mudflats supported an intricate web of life. Now it is a flat, square patch of green, made to stand for nature where there was once all that chaotic life and stink. The city gave away the wetland to the Canadian Northern Pacific Railway. By 1917, the swamp was buried.

The underground rivers and the buried landscape are the unconscious image of this city, testimony to a violent culture. . . . What form of forgetting would not remember this?"

(Caffyn Kelley 1995, 9–10)

Thornton Park, as described by the design competition guidelines, is, in Smith's terms, "an aestheticized landscape" (1993, 80). Presented as "scenery," this is a landscape that transforms the visitor "into a species of voyeur . . . [imbued] . . . with a sense of detachment and [a] luxury of indifference" (79). How different this description from the one presented by Kelley, in which detachment and indifference are displaced by the force of her recognition: of the buried history that is *covered over* by the Edwardian design of Thornton Park, of what was forgotten (literally forced underground) as part of the colonial enterprise. I wonder, how might the monument be different if *this* history of the site had been "remembered" in the specificities of the guidelines?

I am not implying by this question that the authors of the guidelines intentionally did not remember the buried, colonial history of the site. Rather I suggest that this is an instance of how dominant social regimes are read as separate and distinct from each other, a separateness that is itself a form of amnesia inherited over generations. In orienting artists toward designing monuments that considered only the "original" design philosophy of the park, the guidelines favored designs that maintained the landscape, and its history, as unproblematic. Thus, Alber's "Marker of Change" translates the philosophy of the site as rendered in the above citation: the granite slabs are of equal size and shape, placed in the symmetrical form of a circle, balanced in relation to each other and a larger sense of the park space; the ceramic tiles detailing contributors' names (placed in a continuous ring on the ground around the stone circle) are consistent with this form. This is a remembrance/pedagogy that maintains the conception of Thornton Park as benign, simply *a setting* for the Women's Monument. What cannot be reckoned with in this conception is the absent presence of the buried landscape, "testimony to a violent culture," that is, ironically, "forgotten" in the very attempt to remember another violent act from thousands of miles away.

Far from distracting me/us from remembrance of the Massacre in Montreal, I offer that such meditations on the landscape of Thornton Park point toward the possibilities generated by Alber's reference to the pink granite forms as sarcophagi. If the forms were positioned to be read not only in the site, *but of it,* then they may direct visitors' attention to the "second rupture" of the Massacre in Montreal, a breaking in on the present through the unbearable shock of the known. On these terms, the granite tombs may mark the landscape of Thornton Park as a site of loss and mourning, encompassing, but not restricted to, the women massacred in Montreal. In this interpretation, recollections of the names of Aboriginal women murdered in the neighborhood would not be placed outside of who and what the Women's Monument was designed to mark, but as situated within a legacy of violence—colonial and misogynist.

That is, as sarcophagi, the fourteen granite forms may not only bear inscriptions to the massacred women (each one inscribed with her name), but also be positioned to be read as witness to the buried landscape, tombs to the site. From this perspective, the monument may at least point to, rather than simply absorb, that which has (already) been made invisible—both in the Edwardian style design of Thornton Park *and* in the emblematic dedication of the monument. I imagine myself in the circle of these stones, and I wonder . . . might the shallow, curved depressions on the surface of each form serve as gestures to the (un)knowable beneath the surface? May memory's skin begin to thin, give way, as tomb after tomb comes into vision, as I stand surrounded by stones to the dead? And if the "skin of memory" (Delbo in Langer 1991, 7) does rupture, what may become of the memories spilled there? Buried in the tombs? In the landscape? More dead to forget?

I pose these questions, not in a search for definitive answers, but as gestures toward a form of learning that might be occasioned by reading "Marker of Change" as a *situated* memorial practice, designed to reckon with the event of the Massacre— and its legacy—as a rupture of comprehension. For, while the monument was conceived as a way to permanently mark a *collective grief* that emanated from this slaughter of fourteen women in Montreal on December 6, 1989, it has been the argument of this chapter that it was too quickly caught within the terms of remembrance as a strategic, emblematic practice and response. Oriented by this pedagogy, the living who visit the monument (as it currently stands) are unlikely to be confronted by an anxious, difficult memory of the loss of the fourteen women in Montreal and "all the women murdered by men." Although (some of) the dead are honored by name, their absent presence is not fully held in an emblemized memory that glosses over differences in how women ("of all countries, all classes, all ages, all colours") are subject to violences in their living and at their deaths. What is obscured in this call is the very insufficiency of the terms of an emblematic response for ending violences against women, terms that were ruptured by the event of the killings and continue to trouble what it may mean to understand these deaths and to live with hope for a better world. While not suggesting that a revised positioning and reading of the Women's Monument could fully address this insufficiency, I am offering that such an address cannot ensue without encountering the loss and rupture instantiated by the Massacre—an encounter with the dead and with what their absent presence means for "our" living, now.

NOTES

A much earlier version of this chapter was included in my dissertation (Rosenberg 1997). For financial support toward and during the development of that text, I am grateful for fellowships from SSHRC, OGS, and OISE/UT. My thanks also to Roger I. Simon, Claudia Eppert, and Marlene Kadar for conversations that continue to kindle my passion for questions of loss, remembrance, and learning. For their nurturance of hope, I am indebted, in particular, to Susan Heald, Tanya Lewis, Kate McKenna, Diane Naugler, and Lorie Rotenberg.

1. The letter, detailing antifeminist sentiments and a "hit list" of prominent Quebec women, was released by authorities a few weeks prior to the first anniversary of the murders. It was first printed in *La Presse,* a French-language daily newspaper in Montreal, in the November 24, 1990, edition. It is reprinted in English translation in Malette and Chalouh, eds. (1991).

2. The understanding of emblemization discussed here relies upon work developed by myself and Roger I. Simon (see Rosenberg and Simon, 1999). I thank him for his permission to borrow from that work.

3. One of the Monument Committee's positions was that only women were eligible to enter the design competition. They cite two key reasons for this decision: the history of

women's exclusion from the creation of public art in Canada, and the topic of the monument—violence against women (guidelines, 9).

4. This citation is from the guidelines, page 14; all subsequent references in this section are from this page in the guidelines, unless otherwise indicated.

5. My thanks to Beth Alber for providing me with a copy of her proposal to the Monument Committee. It has been an invaluable resource for developing the nuances of the analysis presented in this paper. Since the copy I have is neither dated nor paginated, all references to Alber's proposal are merely cited to the document. To avoid cumbersome referencing in the text, descriptions in this section are from the proposal, unless stated otherwise.

6. Over the years, the Monument Project has produced a series of fund-raising brochures. The one I am referencing here was circulated after the jury had chosen Alber's design.

7. I want to draw attention here to a distinction between Alber's language and the language that has been put into place through literature developed by the Monument Committee. In her proposal, Alber uses the language of slab and form, suggesting "benches" or "sarcophagi" as plausible interpretations. However, the brochure, detailing "Marker of Change," does not mention the latter interpretation, describing the forms only *as* benches. I suggest that this is not an insignificant displacement of meaning, a point to which I will return.

8. Such comments have mobilized and helped to sediment arguments against fund-raising efforts on the part of the Monument Project. Ted White, a Reform Party MP for North Vancouver, was particularly vocal on this matter, describing the monument as "strongly anti-male" and "openly offensive" (in Dafoe 1994, C16). He effectively ensured that at least one source of state financial support was denied (Gale 1994, A24).

5

Never to Forget:

Pedagogical Memory and Second-Generation Witness

Rachel N. Baum

I know that whoever listens to a witness becomes one in turn; you told me that more than once. But we are not witnessing the same events. All I can say is, I have heard the witness.

—Malkiel, son of Elhanan, in Elie Wiesel's *The Forgotten*

Elhanan Rosenbaum, survivor of the Holocaust, former partisan, well-known psychotherapist, forgets. A protagonist of Elie Wiesel's novel, *The Forgotten* (1992), Elhanan suffers from an illness that steals his memory. To lose one's memory and sense of self is always horrifying, but particularly so for Elhanan, for whom memory is a tie to his people, to his God. The book begins with Elhanan's prayer, beseeching God not to sever him from the people of Israel: "You well know, You, source of all memory, that to forget is to abandon, to forget is to repudiate. Do not abandon me, God of my fathers, for I have never repudiated You" (11). For Elhanan, the loss of his own memory is a sign that he is disappearing from God's memory. In this post-Auschwitz novel, God is represented not as One who ignores His children, but One who, like an aged parent weary with senility, has simply forgotten them.

In the face of a God who has forgotten, survivors such as Elhanan must turn to others to remember. In this way, Elhanan's prayer reflects the concerns of an entire generation of Holocaust survivors, losing their memories not necessarily as individuals, but as a group. As each Holocaust survivor dies, a part of Holocaust memory is lost, reduced to what the survivor was able to record and share before death. In the place of the eternal life traditionally offered by God, survivors ask to live through memory, which becomes the responsibility of the next generation, their only means of keeping their parents alive. If children continue to tell the stories of their parents, perhaps Holocaust memory can be maintained, perhaps the dead can be kept alive. This is the redemptive promise of memory—that one will, through the story, survive even death.

Redemption must be earned, however. Elhanan believes that he is being punished by God for the moral failure of having failed to act, of standing by while his friend raped a German woman. "I forgot," he says, "that we can never simply remain spectators, we have no right to stand aside, to keep silent, to let the victim fight the aggressor alone. I forgot so many things that day. . . . That is why I am forgetting other things now" (43). Yet, if his son Malkiel can take on his memory, Elhanan believes, perhaps not only the present can be redeemed, but the past as well. Perhaps his son can make right what was so wrong long ago. And while it is impossible to "make right" the Holocaust, post-Holocaust generations are invested with this kind of dream, that perhaps through their memory, the dead might find some kind of solace.

Yet memory is not easily transmitted between generations, as *The Forgotten* warns. Losing his memory, Elhanan knows that his only chance is to pass his story onto his son, Malkiel, before it is too late. He begs Malkiel to take down every detail, however insignificant, however unpleasant, worrying that time will run out before he has finished. Malkiel initially resists bearing the burden of his father's memory, but as Elhanan worsens Malkiel comes to see a "memory transfusion" as the key to keeping his father alive. He speaks to his dead grandfather, for whom he is named, and promises to keep Elhanan alive through memory: "Grandfather Malkiel: I, Malkiel, your grandson, will fulfill his wishes, I promise you. What he has buried within himself, what he has entrusted to his extinguished memory, I will disclose. I will bear witness in his place; I will speak for him. It is the son's duty not to let his father die" (232). Yet the "memory transfusion" is unsuccessful. Malkiel realizes that however much he wants to fulfill his promise to remember, he cannot stand in for his father, cannot inhabit his memories:

> I promised to remember, in your name and in your place. But I cannot. I cannot relive your life, see again the child and adolescent that you were, find traces of you in these walls that saw your birth and your childhood. I can live after you and even for you, but not as you. What you felt here when you explored the mystery of daybreak, I shall never feel. What you felt when you welcomed the Queen of Shabbat, I shall never feel. (147)

Even were Malkiel to take down his father's story faithfully, to carry the story within him as his own, he could not dwell in the feelings of his father. Looking back on the world that was destroyed, Malkiel will never be able to know it, with love and with the certainty of home, as his father did.

Through this narrative, Wiesel reminds the reader that while memory is given shape through stories, it is never fully contained within them. Malkiel can share in his father's stories, can remember them faithfully and carry them to the next generation, yet there remains something that is Elhanan's alone, something that will die with him. Even sharing his father's story, name, and history, Malkiel is unable to share completely his father's feelings. In the poignant passage above, one can hear a new resonance of loss: What the Holocaust destroyed was not only a way of life but an emotional universe.

RESPONSIBILITY OF HOLOCAUST REMEMBRANCE

I begin this chapter with a meditation on Malkiel and *The Forgotten* because Malkiel's story is, in many ways, not only his story—it is our story, all of our stories. As Holocaust survivors die, the memorial burden increases on those who remain. Museums, memorials, films, and books implore their audiences to remember, but a complete "memory transfusion" is impossible, even for history. Although the imperfection of memory is always a matter of historical concern, Holocaust memory bears a particularly strong ethical responsibility. Those who live after the Holocaust are commanded not only to remember, but also to remember *well*. Remembering the Holocaust, we are told, should make us more sensitive people, people who will prevent such horror from happening again. In this way, memory is understood as a relationship not only to the past but to one's self and the present as well.

Yet, as I will argue throughout this chapter, we, like Malkiel, are not sure what it means to remember in this way. As a teacher of the Holocaust, I hope that my students come to see themselves as guardians of memory, as I do. Yet even I cannot easily define the boundaries of such guardianship. Of course I want my students to be more sensitive to the pain of others; I want them to learn from history how to set their own moral compasses. Yet students' reactions to Holocaust texts are usually much more complicated, and their relationships to the horrifying past much more vexed. Students may spend hours imagining themselves in a concentration camp or as a German soldier; some of their comments can be disturbing and difficult to answer. Anyone who has been immersed in Holocaust memory, as a student or a teacher, knows this essential fact: It is difficult, if not impossible, to draw clean-cut boundaries around Holocaust memory. Indeed, Holocaust memory presses against everyday life, insistent on being recognized. Learning about the Holocaust may indeed make one a better person, but it may also—even at the same time—give one nightmares, make ordinary conversation nearly impossible, and alienate one from friends and family.

Ultimately, then, what I want for my students—and for myself—is to develop a moral and healthy relationship to the past. I will argue throughout this chapter that such a relationship cannot develop from simply taking on the stories of the past. What is crucial, I will argue, is not for present-day men and women to take *on* the stories of the survivors, but rather, to take *in* those stories and to weave them into their own lives. Holocaust education must therefore attend to the complex ways in which students hear Holocaust stories and offer students paths by which they can appropriately tell these stories, with a recognition that they both are and are not *their* stories.

It is the narratives of the second generation that throw these pedagogical issues into stark relief for me. Here are the stories of those who have, for better or worse, absorbed the lessons of Holocaust education, who know too well what it means to be responsible for the dead. These narratives emerge from the tension between the imperative to remember and the impossibility of ever remembering enough, from the burden of a pedagogical memory that imparts unrealizable lessons. They are the narratives of men and women who grew up surrounded by tales of the Holocaust and who struggle to find their own places in that massive history.

Second-generation texts reveal the tension between the redemptive claims of memory, that memory can honor the dead and teach the living, and the experience of an unredeemed memory, which perpetuates the horror of the past. Although it may be clear that the memory of survivors lies as an open wound, there is a common belief that such tainted memory can be cleansed in the next generation, particularly through education. "Remember!" students are told, as if remembering were only a question of moral choice. Yet narratives of the second generation reveal the limitations of such a view. Books such as Carl Friedman's *Nightfather* (1994), J. J. Steinfeld's *Dancing at the Club Holocaust* (1993), and Thane Rosenbaum's *Elijah Visible* (1996) offer a glimpse into what can happen to men and women who want so much to honor the dead that they assume too great a burden, taking on their parents' experiences as their own. In trying, like Malkiel, to feel what their parents felt, the protagonists of these stories often appear like actors stuck in the wrong scene—not because they fail to deliver their lines with conviction, but because the scene itself is wrong, the film stuck on a single frame.

In their poignant recounting, these narratives speak with the inflection of autobiographies, yet are not strictly memoir, sometimes taking shape as a novel or a fictional short story. This blending of genre, of fact and imagination, reflects the complexity of the term *second generation*. The truths of these texts extend beyond the purely familial; their power, I would argue, stems in part from their embodiment of the existential and theological issues that face many young Jews in North America: how to embrace a Judaism of both memory and joy, how to define one's own relationship to the destruction, how to be shaped by history without being destroyed by it—in other words, *how to remember*.

Thus, I would argue that the term *second generation* marks a space that is as much pedagogical as it is familial. Although I do not want to make the term *second generation* so broad as to have no meaning, my interest is in exploring the ways in which the texts of the children of Holocaust survivors throw into relief broader cultural concerns. Specifically, second-generation narratives point to the complexities of growing up among the imperatives to remember the Holocaust and to learn the lessons of the Holocaust. While these issues are especially vivid within the Jewish community, they are increasingly relevant to non-Jews, who continue to visit the Holocaust museum in Washington, to take courses on the Holocaust, and to see Holocaust films such as Steven Spielberg's *Schindler's List.*

Indeed, I will argue that second-generation narratives must be written into the Holocaust story because they provide models, however dystopic, of how to live after Auschwitz. Against the constant appeal to memory, to return to the site of the trauma, the event itself, I suggest that a fuller understanding of post-Holocaust responsibility may require turning away from an exclusive attention to the stories of survivors, to search for their traces in the stories of the second generation. While some fear that survivor's stories will be forgotten, I fear the other extreme—that future generations will see survivor testimony as utterly distinct from their own narratives. If memory of the Holocaust is to be preserved and handed down, each generation must articulate its own particular relationship to the event. This suggests that those of us concerned with education must carefully attend to the ways in which Holocaust pedagogy changes, and should change. The current generation bears an entirely different pedagogical relationship to the Holocaust than did earlier generations. The proliferation of museums, monuments, videos, and books has only increased the pedagogical burden to learn the lessons of the *Shoah*—hardly an easy or obvious task.

It is ultimately, then, as a teacher that these texts of the children of survivors speak to me. They are not overtly pedagogical texts; in many ways, they press against our assumptions that learning about the Holocaust makes one a better person—more moral, more compassionate. It is not that the protagonists of these works are not moral—quite to the contrary, they are often burdened with an intense desire to be good, and to remember well enough. But in their pathos, these stories reveal the impossibility of the task and the complexity of shaping a life out of the ashes of Auschwitz.

This is why second-generation texts must be included in courses on the Holocaust and why each generation must add yet another layer to an ever-expanding legacy of the Holocaust. Survivor stories are irreplaceable in their witness of the event, but they do not provide models of remembrance for those who did not experience the destruction firsthand. Without detracting from the specificity of the experiences of children of survivors, I want to take seriously that second-generation narratives have something to say to post-Holocaust generations about what it means to live after the Holocaust, and of how to create an identity in relation to the past. Those committed to learning about the Holocaust must read these texts too as testimony, as they bear witness to the struggle of living within the shadow of the destruction. The protagonists of these stories are burdened, oftentimes intensely, with the responsibility of memory, precariously balanced between the past and the present. Those of us who read these stories where memories lie like shards of glass under the skin can no longer take refuge in the imperative to remember. For survivors and those who really hear their stories, the call of "Remember!" may seem not the door to redemption, but an eternal curse.

THE SHADOWS OF MEMORY

In the preface to *Holocaust Testimonies: The Ruins of Memory* (1991), Lawrence Langer recounts one of his first experiences watching videotaped testimonies of survivors. In a videotape, Mr. and Mrs. B. are being interviewed in the presence of their son and daughter. Surrounded by their children, both Mr. and Mrs. B. speak of an unbearable loneliness. "Nothing to say. Sad," Mr. B. whispers, weeping (ix). Describing her children's upbringing, Mrs. B. speaks of how deprived they were of relatives and the special kind of attention they offer. When the interviewer turns to the daughter and asks her how she feels about her parents' experience, the daughter speaks an entirely different language:

> First of all, I think I'm left with a lot of strength, because you can't have parents like this who survived some very, very ugly experiences and managed to build a life afterwards and still have some hope. You can't grow up in a household like that without having many, many strengths, first of all.
>
> And second of all, something I have as a child of survivors which second and third generation American people don't have is still some connection with the rich Jewish cultural heritage which is gone now. That is my connection. (x)

Langer is initially confused by the different tone of the daughter's speech, her "vocabulary of chronology and conjunction" (xi). Although he says that he came to realize that each member of the B. family spoke from his or her version of truth, in the very next paragraph he adds, "Nevertheless, the longing for connection continues to echo in our needful ears," thereby suggesting that the woman's narration comes out of a psychological need for security that the reader would do well to hold suspect.

Langer develops his suspicion of this kind of "connected" narrative throughout the rest of the text, continuing into his 1995 volume of essays, *Admitting the Holocaust*. Langer's central thesis in that text is that because we cannot admit the true horror of the Holocaust, we comfort ourselves with narratives of redemption. Thus, rather than focusing on the men and women who threw stones at their Jewish neighbors, we look at the handful who risked their lives to save Jews. Even survivors may seek refuge in redemptive thinking, searching for some higher good that will explain why they survived when so many died. Langer particularly takes Victor Frankl to task for trying to redeem suffering as part of "Man's Search for Meaning," for suggesting that the literary, Christian tradition of redemptive suffering, exemplified in the writings of Tolstoy and Dostoyevsky, "is somehow relevant to the Jewish victims of Auschwitz" (90).

To distinguish between the kind of memory that acts as a salve and the kind of memory that forces us to face the horror, Langer evokes Charlotte Delbo's distinction between common and deep memory. A member of the French resistance during the war, Delbo was arrested with her husband, Georges Dudach, in March 1942, and sent first to Auschwitz in January 1943, and later to Ravensbrück. Delbo, who died in

1985, wrote movingly about her experiences in haunting prose, poetry, and plays, often interweaving genres within a single text. Delbo used the terms *common memory* and *deep memory* to distinguish between the part of her that was able to speak about her Auschwitz experiences as if they were over and the part of her that lived always with Auschwitz. "Auschwitz is so deeply etched on my memory that I cannot forget one moment of it," she wrote. "So you are living with Auschwitz? No, I live next to it. Auschwitz is there, unalterable, precise, but enveloped in the skin of memory, an impermeable skin that isolates it from my present self" (quoted in Langer 1995, xi).

Langer argues that while common memory "urges us to regard the Auschwitz ordeal as part of a chronology, a dismal event in the past that the very fact of survival helps to redeem," deep memory "reminds us that the Auschwitz past is not really past and never will be" (1995, xi). For Langer, common memory is the means by which people avoid admitting the Holocaust, through a "persisting myth about the triumph of the spirit that colors the disaster with a rosy tinge and helps us to manage the unimaginable" (1995, 3).

In essay after essay, Langer points out ways in which authors and readers fail to confront the central horror of the Holocaust, which, he believes, holds no lesson about the triumph of the human spirit, no redemption that can give it meaning. Langer links common memory to chronology and deep memory to duration, seeing chronological time as a seductive tendency that "entreats and *enables* us to forget the unforgettable," while durational time "relentlessly stalks the memory of the witness" (1995, 22). Chronological narrative, according to Langer, is an accomplice to amnesia in that it sutures the Holocaust into a narrative of before, during, and after, each moment tucked inside its own temporal box. In truth, Langer argues, the Holocaust bleeds into other moments, drowning chronological expectation in a sea of inconsolable loss.

Thus, while survivors experience both common memory and deep memory, Langer speaks about them in value-laden terms, not acknowledging the extent to which they are interdependent. In part, this is because he fails to distinguish the memory of survivors from the memory of those who came after, thereby avoiding the difficult issue of how post-Holocaust generations can respond to the deep memory of survivors. Langer might say that the very point of deep memory is that it allows for no response other than witness, yet those raised within the knowledge of the Holocaust have been taught that memory does indeed demand a response. To return to the initial example of Mr. and Mrs. B. and their children, Langer does not consider to what extent the daughter's response is generational and possibly gendered. He fails to acknowledge that perhaps the daughter is all too familiar with her parents' pain and has already stepped into (or been placed into) the role of redeemer, offering herself as the one who will give meaning to her parents' existence. In other words, Langer never considers that it may not be only *herself* whom the woman is trying to comfort.

Langer certainly points to an important tendency in Holocaust writing to soften the absolute horror of the experience. Yet in neglecting the specificity of the second generation, Langer fails to consider the role of education in shaping memory, storytelling, and the emotions. To Langer's use of "common memory" and "deep memory," I would add "pedagogical memory," which infuses both. Whether responding to deep memory or common memory, post-Holocaust generations are asked to learn from the testimony of survivors. Whereas for Langer, redemptive narratives are inherently suspect, the values of Holocaust education push against that claim, embracing the possibility of optimism for the future at the same time that they acknowledge the impossibility of salvation. The second generation therefore bears a pedagogical burden that is quite different from the burden shouldered by the survivors. Those that follow the generation of survivors are asked not only to hear their testimony but to become themselves narrators of the story, to take the place of the survivors when they are gone. While this need not be a project of redemption, it insists upon common memory. I share Langer's concern that any narration of the Holocaust needs to face its utter incommensurability with normal life, but in contrast to Langer, I offer that chronological time is essential to this process.

Chronological time is important for a generation that literally *comes after* the Holocaust. The effort at chronology here is nothing less than a grasp at self-identity—not as a victory over Hitler, or a redemption of the dead, but as an attempt to make sense of how one is living when so many are not. Chronological narrative comes with difficulty to the men and women of this generation, trying to make sense of their place in the Holocaust story, and in its stead, they are left too often with the wounds of deep memory. For such a generation, chronological time may not be a salve, but a path out of madness.

While Langer's greatest fear is that the Holocaust will be forgotten because of the seduction of common memory, deep memory has its risks as well: the risk of absorbing the story too well, of losing oneself to the dead, of being overcome with guilt and sorrow. I want to ask what happens to those who inhabit deep memory, who try to live through durational time. I want to ask not about those who soothe themselves with platitudes about the perseverance of the human spirit, but about those who have taken into themselves the knowledge of what is possible on earth. Against the easy narrative of a story passed down between generations, memory redemptive, the dead honored, here are stories of what it means to truly "admit the Holocaust," to admit it entry into your soul and to agree, perhaps against your will, to have it live beside you. I want to ask where the line falls between honesty and madness, between admitting the Holocaust and being consumed by it.

The second-generation texts I will discuss exude their own deep memory—rarely explicitly about the character's own history, a history of being the child of Holocaust survivors, but about the Holocaust itself, a memory of an experience the child did not have. In contrast to Langer's concern that the Holocaust will become so narrativized as to be forgotten, the characters of these texts are often too intimate with the event, unable to narrativize their pain. Just as Holocaust survivors have difficulty sharing their deep memory with others, the second generation too bears a deep memory that is difficult to share, a memory that is not quite their parents' and yet is not solely their own. This deep memory remembers their obsessions and nightmares, the ways in which their lives have been changed forever by the Holocaust.

In reading these stories, the reader is asked to confront the possibility that the Shoah has claimed another generation, young people not dead, yet not fully living either. The narratives that concern Langer are narratives of redemption, but there are antiredemption narratives as well, narratives where parents ask their children, "For this I survived the camps?," narratives that demand a high price from a generation asked to heal unstanchable wounds, fulfill impossible dreams, narratives that may impart an enormous guilt to those who not only survived, but prospered, living the comfortable middle-class lives stolen from the rest of the family. As psychologist Aaron Haas, a child of survivors, writes: "'For this I survived the Nazis? For this I survived the camps?' This was my parents' frequent anguished refrain— if I talked back to them or if I came home later than I said I would without telephoning to report my delay. . . . It was as if they had injected guilt directly into my heart" (1990, 51).

Although the children of Holocaust survivors have experiences that are theirs alone, the experience of shame and guilt is often shared by others who struggle with the responsibility of Holocaust memory, who try to listen well enough. I have seen this in students who do not know how to balance their responsibility to the past with their engagement with the present. It seems to me that my students who speak of picturing themselves in the death camps are trying through the imagination to *place themselves* in relation to the Holocaust. Teaching such students demands that we help them find their own places in relation to the past, in such a way that encourages their engagement in present-day life. It is only through narrative and common memory that such students can acknowledge their own deep memory— not the deep memory of the survivors, but their own deep memory of encountering the Holocaust.

While Langer appreciates the brutal honesty of first-generation writers such as Delbo and Primo Levi, their words may contribute to the shame of the second generation, the shame of the living. Like Levi's "Shema,"[1] Delbo's "Prayer for the Living to Forgive Them for Being Alive" (1995, 229–230) is addressed to "You":

. . . .
You who are passing by
well dressed in all your muscles
clothing which suits you well
or badly
or just about
you who are passing by
full of tumultuous life within your arteries
glued to your skeleton . . . how can we forgive you
that all are dead
You are walking by and drinking in cafés

you are happy she loves you
or moody worried about money
how how
will you ever be forgiven
by those who died
so that you may walk by
dressed in all your muscles
so that you may drink in cafés
be younger every spring
I beg you
do something
learn a dance step
something to justify your existence
something that gives you a right
to be dressed in your skin in your body hair
learn to walk and to laugh
because it would be too senseless
after all
for so many to have died
while you live
doing nothing with your life . . .

Delbo's words not only help the reader to admit the Holocaust, but place an enormous burden on her for having survived. What would it mean to live on top of a pile of corpses, young children extinguished in Europe, and to do nothing with one's life? What, in this context, could it possibly mean to "do something with one's life"? If there is an impulse to turn away from the horror of the Holocaust, perhaps it is because it is so difficult to articulate how to live in its shadow, what the Holocaust means today, to those born after the destruction.

It is possible, I hold, to walk the line between horror and redemption, between the fear and hope evoked in Israeli psychologist Daniel Bar-On's 1995 book, *Fear and Hope: Three Generations of the Holocaust.* The characters of second-generation texts are often not successful at walking this line, because they are only beginning to develop the narrative frame that can hold their stories. They need witnesses to bring their stories to light, to acknowledge that they have their own stories to tell. Second-generation texts offer the reader the possibility of being such a witness—and in turn, they offer the reader the possibility of developing her own narrative.

TRANSLATING MEMORY

While the importance of passing on the story is a recurrent motif in Holocaust education, second-generation texts often foreground the impossibility of the child taking on the story of the parents. The survivor speaks an entirely different language, creating distance between parent and child. This question of language is at the heart of Carl Friedman's 1994 novel, *Nightfather,* translated from the original Dutch. Friedman, herself the daughter of a survivor, tells the story of a young girl and her brothers who try with difficulty to understand their father's world. The forty brief chapters are each headed with ordinary words or phrases such as *Camp, Animal,* and *Woods* that emphasize the children's distance from their father's experiences. For the children, these are everyday words, but the father is no longer able to see them benignly. Always there is the effort of translation, as the children try to understand their father's definitions of familiar words. The girl explains: "Camp is not so much a place as a condition. 'I've had camp,' he says. That makes him different from us. We've had chicken pox and German measles. And after Simon fell out of a tree, he got a concussion and had to stay in bed for weeks. But we've never had camp" (22). *Nightfather* makes clear that camp is incurable; those who have it will always be different from those who do not.

The more the children try to speak the father's language, the more uncomfortable the words appear. They cannot fully take on the father's story, for even their words resonate differently, in ways the children cannot fully understand. After the Holocaust, everything is different, and those who have come after are left trying futilely to understand, to hear the story, to remember well enough. Yet the poignant lesson of *Nightfather* is that there is more than one way to get "camp." The children do not have their father's "camp," and yet they have come to exhibit some of his symptoms, taking on his obsessions as their own.

By creating her characters as children, just beginning to take on language themselves, Friedman emphasizes the difficulty of mediating between the world of the past and the world of the present. Unlike Langer, who judges Mr. and Mrs. B's daughter for not speaking the same language as her parents, Friedman explores the poignancy and complexity of the parent-child relationship. The children of survivors cannot take on the language of their parents, yet their own language has been forever changed by the echo of history.

While the children are not like the father, neither are they like other children. In school, the protagonist draws a picture of a prisoner being hanged, while other prisoners, including her father, starve, waiting for soup (5). When her friend Nellie tells her what a funny father she has, the girl avoids Nellie's eyes. "She knows nothing about hunger or about the SS," she thinks. "Words like *barracks, latrine,* or *crematorium* mean nothing to her. She speaks a different language" (21). The children are translators between their father's world and the outside world, yet they are uncomfortable translators, at home in neither world. Their efforts at translating their father's experiences always fail because "camp" is a language unto itself, specific to that world. That the family refers to the father's "condition" as "camp" emphasizes the significance of location—outside the *Lager,* "camp" is unintelligible. Trying to assimilate their father's "camp" to their own world creates fear in the children. They prepare for the time when the SS will come for them and when they will be forced on a death march. Their efforts at translation cannot work, because the scene has changed. The children have inherited the emotional legacy, but they have failed to recognize that their father's story is not theirs.

The children try to take on the father's story, but his story is incommensurable with their world. The child's familiar cry, "Tell me a story," elicits not "Little Red Riding Hood," as one chapter title promises, but the father's variation, a story of the dogs that guarded the camp and the food they received, better than that of the prisoners. He tells the children how he and other prisoners would steal scraps of the dog food, boiling it into a vile stew. The narrator ends the chapter with her brother's disappointment:

> "That isn't a story," Simon grumbles with disappointment. "That really happened."
> "Do you want a story then? Okay, have it your way!" says my father. "Little Red Riding Hood is walking with her basket through the woods. Suddenly a vicious dog jumps out of the *Hundezwinger.* 'Hello, Little Red Riding Hood, where are you going?' 'I'm going to see my grandmother,' says Little Red Riding Hood. 'She's in the hospital block with typhus.'"
> "No," says Simon, "that's not how it goes." (33–34)

The father may be led by a desire to share his story with his children, to warn them against the world, but they hear the story, as we all do, through their own contexts, drawing on what they know to make sense of what they do not know. The children live in a world of dailyness, where hunger means a growling belly and the one killed at the end of a story is a big, bad wolf. The father inhabits a world too horrible for children to make sense of. At the meeting of these two worlds, out of the inability of parent and child to share a single language, grows something utterly heartrending.

Nightfather reveals the difficulty of taking on the story of another. Holocaust education tells us to remember the story of the Holocaust and to pass it on to our children and our children's children, but telling the story of another in one's own language can be difficult, particularly when one is deeply connected emotionally to the story. One tries to speak the words one knows, yet like the children of *Nightfather,* one is always in danger of taking the scene out of context.

After reading *Nightfather,* the reader can only take with bitter irony the words of Elie Wiesel, which grace its dust jacket: "Yours is a privileged generation: you remember things that you have not lived; but you remember them so well, so profoundly, that every one of your stories . . . comes to bear on our own. You are our justification." The attempt to redeem the memory of the second generation falls dully on ears that have read Friedman's novel, which so poignantly reveals the difficulty of living as justification for someone else's survival.

INHABITING MEMORY

Like Malkiel from *The Forgotten,* the characters of *Dancing at the Club Holocaust,* J. J. Steinfeld's collection of short stories, seek to inhabit the past, to create a kind of "memory transfusion"; yet unlike Malkiel, they do not entirely recognize the futility of their efforts, moving toward increasingly terrible ways of inhabiting their parents' stories. They are, perhaps, the children of *Nightfather* grown up, groping toward adulthood in the shadow of their parents' lives. That the stories take place in Canadian provinces with few Jews emphasizes the extent to which the characters bear their burdens alone, unable to share their experiences with those around them.

In one of the stories, "Ida Solomon's Play," an actress performs a one-woman play about her mother, Ida Solomon, "born Radom, Poland, 1921, died Toronto, Ontario, Canada, 1977" (67). Each night, the daughter relives her mother's life through eight stages that she has selected "as the most dramatically important to tell Ida's story": "I go," she says, "from sixteen in 1937 through age fifty-six in 1977, forty years of a woman's life, the transformation from the dancing, joyous teenager to the wailing, sad woman seeking a solitary death" (67). Yet spinning Ida Solomon's life into eight stages seems to avoid what is the daughter's central truth: that only Ida Solomon's identity as a survivor of the Holocaust can explain her death. The "solitary death" the woman tells of is the only suggestion that Ida Solomon killed herself.

The daughter believes that she has found a key to her own identity in her mother's story. Before her mother's death, the protagonist was a writer, but she wrote "the most abominable rubbish" whereas now she is "a writer, and an actress to boot" (70). More pointedly, the actress sees knowing her parents' experiences as a way to test the boundaries of her own self: "I wanted to know their secrets. . . . What had they thought during those days and hours and minutes of hell? How had they survived the concentration camps? I wanted to know if I could have survived. Every night on stage I tried to find out" (69). Writing the play, the woman recounts, was a way to keep sane, to keep from jumping off the balcony. She had thought that another actress could perform the part, but in the end, it was up to her to bring her mother to life. She begins to take her performance beyond the stage, leaving the theater as her mother, going to bars as her mother, even fighting an intended rapist as her mother. Yet the performance brings the woman no closer to understanding either her mother or herself; instead, Ida Solomon becomes simply a dramatic persona of her daughter, the one who can hold a man's attention at a bar.

What breaks Ida Solomon's spell over her daughter is the actress's final barroom encounter. As she tells her mother's stories about life in Poland before and during the war, the man beside her seems interested, but numbed. In an effort to draw him out, the woman asks what he thought of her story and, getting no response, shows him the number carefully painted onto her arm each night. Gripping her arm to the point of pain, the old man pushes up his own shirtsleeve, showing her his concentration camp number, his, of course, real:

> "I'm so sorry," I said; Ida had disappeared. I embraced the old man and searched for Ida.
> I no longer want to be my mother in the play, to go through the eight stages of her life I selected in some madly punishing and creative attempt to make sense of the past,

to counteract my guilt, to justify remaining alive. I want the play to end, but I cannot under any circumstances allow my mother to die and remain lost to me, not again, ever again. (74)

In taking on the story of her mother, the protagonist of "Ida Solomon's Play" hopes to keep her mother alive, but in the end, she ends up only emphasizing the distance between her mother's life and her own. Like Malkiel of *The Forgotten,* she cannot fully inhabit her parent's experiences, however faithful she is to the story. The daughter believes that inhabiting her mother's story will give meaning to her life, will justify her survival, but in the end, the story she has surrounded herself in falls away, because it is not her story.

That Ida Solomon's daughter has her vision changed by an encounter with a Holocaust survivor foregrounds the difference in their narration. It is not simply that the survivor bears deep memory that the actress only performs; rather, I read "Ida Solomon's Play" as a story about the extent to which deep memory inheres in common memory. Meeting the survivor in the bar forces the actress to realize that she cannot carry her mother's deep memory as her own. That the woman is a writer suggests that perhaps she will be able to narrate her own relationship to the Holocaust rather than reenacting her mother's, giving shape to her own deep memory rather than carrying her mother's.

Steinfeld's book is filled with images of children who try to honor the past by re-living it, often by taking on a more Yiddish name or the concentration camp tattoo of the parent. These stories are second-generation stories not only because of the identity of their characters, but because they grapple with what it means to re-member the past and live in the present, a present where Germans are not all Nazis and Jews are not all slated for death. One story, "The Heart," tells of Isaac, a thirty-five-year-old child of a Holocaust survivor, who had died "twenty years before the actuaries promised, the concentration camp number unerased, leaving [him] the last male in his family" (91). Isaac becomes obsessed with a German patron of a bar who sits in the corner with a small box. Isaac asks repeatedly to see what is in the box, saying that the bartender has told him it contains the petrified heart of a Jew, "a souvenir from the War" (90). The use of the word *souvenir,* from the French verb *to remember,* foregrounds the extent to which Isaac's struggle is a struggle of memory. Remembering the dead, he does not know how to respond to the living. He has made himself into a living monument to the dead, tattooing a number across his own arm. Isaac explains to the German that he had "paid fifteen dollars and a small oil painting to bridge the gap between dead relatives, tormented parents, and his privileged, sheltered self," but that after getting the tattoo his demons grew only stronger. "I'd need a million tattoos," he realizes. "'Six million, perhaps,' the German said with satisfaction." (90). At the end of the story, Isaac attacks the German and grabs the box, but finds it locked. Smashing the box against his own chest, Isaac finally opens it, only to find it empty. At the "heart" of his memory, his "souvenir," the box forever locked to him, there is only air. "Well," Isaac reflects, now utterly calm, "you can never be too careful. If not a petrified heart, you could have had a dangerous device for forgetfulness" (94). Although there is nothing inside the German's box, the performance between the two men has ironically kept memory alive.

Steinfeld's contemporary Jews struggle with what it means to be a privileged North American Jew in the shadow of the destruction of millions of one's people. Steinfeld's characters pick up Delbo's charge to "make something of your life" but as monuments to a dead past, they are out of sync with the present. "The Apostate's Tattoo" tells of Sam Morgan who has changed his name to Shlomo Markovitz and set off for a tattoo parlor to honor his dead mother, a survivor of the camps. He has been acting strangely, possessed by demons his wife, Sylvie, does not understand, but after the tattoo, he knows he will be better. Yet after the tattoo is completed, six numbers engraved in blue on his arm, as Sam looks happily at his wife for approval, he has a crushing realization: He told the tattooist the wrong arm. In the final scene, Sam is immobilized on the ground, his wife cradling his head in her lap, "a hand clutching his forearm, attempting to cover the blue tattoo" (19). As in "Ida Solomon's Play," there is an attempt to reexperience the past, yet the attempt is doomed to fail, because the historical moment has changed. It is, as Nadine Fresco notes in her study of children of survivors, "[a]s if the dead had carried off with them the sense of life and identity, as if those who were born afterwards could no longer do any more than wander about, prey to a nostalgia that has no legitimacy" (1984, 421).

The language of Steinfeld's stories resists easy moralizing, yet reveals an intense ethical force. The weight of the stories comes in part from the struggles of children trying to do the right thing, trying to be guardians of memory. In "The Fuhrer's Halloween," Muni, the child of Holocaust victims, attacks a couple who has come to a Halloween party dressed as Adolf Hitler and Eva Braun. That the story takes place on Prince Edward Island, a place with few Jews, heightens the tension between Muni and the costumed couple, who do not understand why he is offended. "I happen to be Jewish," Muni shouts, but the couple only responds with fascination, the man "genuinely pleased—and surprised—to meet a Jew on the Island" (102). Muni is alone in his obsession, alone in his desire to create an ethical relationship to the past.

THE TRAUMA OF PEDAGOGICAL MEMORY

Unlike Steinfeld's Canadian stories, Thane Rosenbaum's *Elijah Visible* revolves around the world of a New York Jew, trying to find himself in history as well as in contemporary, urban Judaism. Rosenbaum's volume is a book of short stories with the same protagonist, Adam Posner, although the stories are not continuous. By changing Adam's character from story to story (in one he is a lawyer, in another a college professor), Rosenbaum's volume explores through its very form the difficulty of creating an identity.

Elijah Visible opens with a story about torturous memory. Leaving his high-rise office, Adam, here a lawyer, gets stuck in the elevator; in his mind, he becomes trapped in a cattle car, suffocating, waiting to be killed. The story might have a particular resonance were Adam Posner a Holocaust survivor, but Adam has received his nightmares not through his own experience, but through his parents, survivors of the camps: "Their own terrible visions from a haunted past became his. He had inherited their perceptions of space, and the knowledge of how much one needs to live, to hide, how to breathe where there is no air" (5). Rosenbaum refers to this connection as "the umbilical connection between the unmurdered and the long buried" (6).

Adam Posner has been educated not only in memory but in fear. The world in which he moves has been forever altered by the stories of his parents. And yet, ironically, disturbingly, is not this the goal of Holocaust education—that the lessons of the Shoah seep into our waking lives, change the shape of our nightmares? Yet if humanity owes a debt to the survivors, as I believe it does, it owes something as well to the Adam Posners, to the men and women who have absorbed the terror of the story long after the scene has changed.

What we owe to these men and women, I am arguing, is witness, the acknowledgment that they too are survivors—not in the same way as their parents, but in their own ways. The witness in Rosenbaum's text comes in the figure of the prophet Elijah, who, according to Jewish tradition, will return to Earth to announce the coming of the Messiah. At the Passover Seder, Jews set out a cup of wine for Elijah and open the door for him, welcoming the invisible guest and the possibility of redemption. The story of Elijah is often told particularly for the children, who wait expectantly for him to drink the wine they have set out for him, as Christian children look for bites out of the cookies left for Santa by the Christmas stockings. In a sense, the title *Elijah Visible* is a taunt, or perhaps a fervent wish, but it also reflects the thread of redemption that runs throughout the volume.

Significantly, it is Adam who is in such dire need of redemption, who needs salve for his torment. In "An Act of Defiance," the fourth story of the volume, that redemption arrives in the shape of Haskell, Adam's uncle who comes from Belgium. "I come to New York in three weeks. I stay by you, no? We get to know each other. I fix your life," Haskell proclaims in the first phone call (57). In this story, Adam is a college professor, teaching a Holocaust course whose enrollments have steadily plummeted. He sees Haskell's visit as a burden, an opportunity perhaps, but one, he thinks, that would only "feed my guilt, replenish my craving for the soul of survivors" (59).

Having never met his uncle, Adam Posner can only visualize him as a living corpse, a monument to a dead past: "The Holocaust survivor as myth, as fairy tale, as bedtime story. I had created my own ghosts from memories that were not mine. I wasn't there, in Poland, among the true martyrs. Everything about my rage was borrowed. My imagination had done all the work—invented suffering, without the physical scars, the incontestable proof" (59). Yet when Haskell comes, he does not conform to Adam's imagination. Adam has written the script of Haskell's arrival, imagining him harassed by border guards for being a Jew, fumbling nervously for his papers. Arriving at the airport, Adam finds evidence of his fears confirmed—a stretcher being led out of the gates, a man hurt, rubber tubes coming out of his nose. Rushing to the door, Adam hears behind him, "Adam, this is you?" Haskell is healthy, unharmed, looking nothing like the survivor of Adam's mind. Sporting both toupee and colostomy bag, Haskell loves women, gambling and Manhattan. While Adam nervously tries to keep Haskell safe from all the dangers of New York, Haskell, unlike his nephew, knows the difference between fears real and imagined. What Haskell really worries about is his too serious nephew. Looking around Adam's library of Holocaust tomes, Haskell remarks, "I see that you have dedicated yourself well to the study of what happened to us. But what has this all done to you?" (45).

Haskell sees his own good living as an "act of defiance" against the Nazis. "To be like you, marchers in the army of the living dead, is a victory for the Nazis," he warns Adam (66). Yet even Haskell's spirit cannot keep death away, and he dies while in New York, a heart attack. The story ends, Haskell gone, yet on the next page, the title story "Elijah Visible," suggests his return.

In the title story, Adam Posner celebrates Passover with his Americanized, secular cousins for whom Passover is an opportunity to hear Elvis Costello sing, "Everyday I Write the Book." When the parents were alive, the Seder was a ritualized, solemn occasion, but in the ten years since their death, the Posner Seder has been reduced to a carnival, much to Adam's disgust. It is clear that Adam bears the burden of their murdered family in a way that the others do not. Although he has been attending the modernized, profane Seders for ten years, a letter from a cousin Artur, from Antwerp, has changed his relation to the present. Artur, a survivor of the Holocaust estranged from the family, has written that it is time to bury the hatchet, that he is coming to America to tell the children their family history in person. "We must learn the lessons from the fire," he writes (97). While Adam is shamed and moved by the man's letter, his cousin Sylvie sees only an old man who wants a free trip to the United States. Adam tries to break through his cousins' denial, to tell them the truths they are so unwilling to face, to bring them face-to-face with the suffering that is their legacy—pregnant wives killed, husbands forced to kill, children orphaned. "Our parents concealed everything from us," he tells them. "Too much guilt, I guess. Too much regret. We can't afford to do that again. We owe it to the children, to ourselves—there's too much at stake" (102). Across the Atlantic, Artur buys his own plane ticket and sets off for America. "Elijah had not visited the Posners that year, but Cousin Artur was on his way" (103). In "An Act of Defiance" there is no mention of Uncle Haskell having children, yet Cousin Artur comes in the next story, suggesting that perhaps there is another narrative to counterbalance Adam's: the story of Elijah, the possibility of continuity and remembrance without claustrophobic suffering.

Elijah Visible suggests that the second generation has its own stories to tell, stories that may, in fact, answer the call of memory. "I am anxious to hear you tell me your life story," Adam tells Uncle Haskell, to which Haskell replies, "And I am anxious to get to know you. There is a difference in what we seek" (66). And in "Elijah Visible," Cousin Artur tells his cousins that they carry the seeds of the memories of their dead relatives. "It is a great responsibility for you, but you must live a life that gives meaning to their death, and comfort to their souls" (96). Remembrance alone, the volume seems to warn, can lead to madness, away from life itself, which is, after everything, the most important legacy of all.

The characters of second-generation narratives sometimes seem trapped in a kind of "repetition compulsion," unable to work through the trauma of the Holocaust. Indeed, many authors continue to speak of the Holocaust as a trauma that inflicts contemporary generations. Yet, this language is not quite precise enough. To speak of contemporary generations being "traumatized" by the Holocaust threatens the specificity of the definition of trauma, generally understood as a response to an event "outside the range of usual human experience" (Caruth 1995, 3). More precisely, one might say that the second generation may be traumatized by the experience of living after the Holocaust, or, perhaps, even that the second generation may be born into trauma. Yet one needs to be cautious of pathologizing the second generation; while some children of Holocaust survivors would describe their experiences as traumatic, many would not. Similarly, although it is simplistic to suggest that after the Holocaust we are all living with trauma, we cannot know in advance the effects an encounter with the Holocaust will have on someone. Who is to say that learning about the Holocaust may not bring the nightmares and symptoms that are traditionally evidence of trauma?

Here is where the broader and narrower definitions of second generation dovetail. The protagonists of the stories I am discussing are the children of survivors, men and women who were born into confrontation with the past. Clearly, this is not true for all children of survivors, and the reader must be careful not to confuse the characters of these stories with their authors. Nonetheless, these stories suggest that, for some, the very process of identity-formation is inextricably bound up with the Holocaust. In particular, these stories suggest that the sense of one's moral self is, for many, experienced through one's relationship to the Holocaust. Many who were not born the children of Holocaust survivors may feel a connection here, if they have absorbed the lessons of Holocaust education, the lessons that insist that one's response to the Holocaust says much about the kind of person, ethically, that one is.

What I am suggesting is that rather than assume a trauma that may not exist, we look at the relationship between pedagogy and trauma. What I am arguing is that what is traumatic post-Auschwitz may not be only history itself but also *the ethical responsibility placed on one's identity*. It may be that Holocaust education itself imposes a kind of trauma on its subject, whose very identity is thrown into question. The passion to remember well enough, to be good enough, to *make something of one's life,* may be experienced as trauma. It is the responsibility, then, of Holocaust pedagogy to offer a way through an immobilizing trauma, to offer models of how to live within the knowledge of mass death. Paradoxically, second-generation stories—themselves so often laden with the difficulty of remembrance—may offer Holocaust pedagogy such a key.

For those who read them, these texts of the second generation bear an important lesson, one that rests on common memory. Those who come after the Holocaust must learn how to walk the line between duration and chronology, between inarticulable horror and shareable stories. Central to this process is the creation of a narrative about one's own relation to the Holocaust, one that differs from the relation of survivors. If we are truly to understand the Holocaust as something that is still with us, we must express that presentness in the stories we tell about ourselves. These stories should not eclipse the stories of survivors, yet they must take their place in Holocaust education.

STORIES OF SECOND-GENERATION WITNESS

For an example of how this work might progress, we can turn to what is perhaps the best-known narrative by a child of Holocaust survivors—Art Spiegelman's two-volume *Maus* (1986, 1991), written in comic book form. Having interviewed his father, Vladek, for hours about his experiences during the Holocaust, Spiegelman retells the story in the medium of his profession, with the Germans represented as cats and the Jews as mice. Throughout the two volumes, Art is self-conscious about the difficulty of representing his father's experiences, particularly when he and his father hold such different views of the world.

Like the narrator of *Nightfather*, Art speaks a different language than his father and has difficulty feeling close to him; indeed, Spiegelman suggests that were it not for the interviews, he might have been unable to speak to his father at all. Unlike the narrator of *Nightfather*, however, Spiegelman is able to reflect on his difficulties with his father, bringing them into the larger narrative about his father's experiences. What makes *Maus* so striking is its ability to tell the story of the son as well as the story of the father. Unlike Steinfeld's and Rosenbaum's characters who often have difficulty distinguishing between their lives and their parents' lives, Spiegelman uses his role as narrator to distinguish the Art character from the Vladek character. Yet there are moments where the past intervenes into the present, moments of deep memory.

In *Maus*, deep memory is not only the province of Vladek, who, in the final frame of the first volume, calls Art by the name of his dead brother, but also of Art, who has been plagued by the guilt of surviving. Deep memory cannot be sutured into the narrative, and in *Maus I*, this deep memory centers around the suicide of Art's mother, Anja. "Prisoner on the Hell Planet," a four-page comic that Art had written in 1972, tells the story of Anja's suicide, three months after Art's release from a state mental hospital. The narrative explanation for the appearance of "Prisoner on the Hell Planet" in *Maus* is that Vladek finds an old copy of the magazine, but these pages clearly stand apart from the rest of the book. Not only do they use an intense, expressionistic style, with images of humans rather than animals, but they are surrounded by a black border that marks these pages even when the book is closed.

More notably, the section begins with the only photograph in the first volume, a vacation picture presumably of a young Art and his mother labeled "Trojan Lake, N.Y. 1958." Artie crouches next to his standing mother, smiling broadly, while her hand rests on his head. His mother does not smile. The photograph is held by a drawn hand, yet its boundaries exceed the frame of the comic. In the next frame, Art stands facing the reader, wearing a concentration camp uniform, standing in what appears to be a close-up of a police line-up: "In 1968, when I was 20, my mother killed herself. . . . She left no note!" The rest of the strip tells of Art's oppressive guilt at his mother's death, his feelings that everyone blamed him for her suicide. He remembers the last time he saw her, when she came in to ask if he still loved her. "Sure, ma," he said, turning away, "resentful of the way she tightened the umbilical cord." "Well, Mom, if you're listening," the narrative ends, Art speaking from behind bars, in a large jail, "Congratulations! . . . You've committed the perfect crime. . . . You put me here. . . . Shorted all my circuits . . . cut my nerve endings . . . and crossed my wires! . . . You murdered me, Mommy, and you left me here to take the rap!" (1986, 103).

In her work on *Maus,* Marianne Hirsch (1992–1993) has pointed to the significance of the photographs, the way they stand between life and death. The photograph of Anja insists on her life, yet the next frame speaks of her death. "Poignantly," Hirsch writes, "Spiegelman juxtaposes the archival photograph with the message of death which, through the presence of the photo's 'having-been-there,' is strengthened, made even more unbearable" (18). This tension between what is and what was, between the reality of the photograph and the death that we know surrounds it, is central to Hirsch's understanding of "post-memory," the memory of the children of survivors. Through the concept of "post-memory," Hirsch attempts to describe the kind of obsessional remembrance I have been discussing in the works of Steinfeld and Rosenbaum. For Hirsch, post-memory is not beyond memory, "but is distinguished from memory by generational distance and from history by deep personal connection" (18).

Hirsch provides us a way to nuance our understanding of deep and common memory. *Maus* is predominantly a work of common memory, yet there are moments of poignancy that break through the narrative. Hirsch writes that the "fragments that break out of the frames are details that function like Barthes' *punctum;* they have the power of the 'fetish' to signal and to disavow an essential loss" (27). They are, she writes, moments of "woundedness." Through Hirsch's readings of the photographs of *Maus,* we can see the ways in which deep memory may be found even within common memory. Indeed, were it not for the narrative structure of *Maus,* the moments of wounding would not be so poignant. They are poignant precisely because in resisting the narrative fluidity of the rest of the text, they are moments that pierce.

Common memory can be understood more fully, then, as a narrative that can be shared and that, at the same time, frames our understanding of what cannot be shared or shared completely. Without common memory, deep memory keeps Art Spiegelman's character dressed in the clothes of the *Lager,* trapped behind bars of guilt and despair. Within the framework of the text, those moments become not inured, but even more poignant.

In "Hell Planet" Art has recently been released from a mental hospital and portrays himself in clothes of a concentration camp victim; in *Maus II* such pain becomes part of the narrative, as Art discusses the book with his wife, Françoise Mouly. Here, he admits to feelings similar to those of the characters of *Dancing at the Club Holocaust* and *Elijah Visible*. "I never felt guilty about Richieu," Art says of his brother, killed in the camps,

> But I did have nightmares about S.S. men coming into my class and dragging all us Jewish kids away. Don't get me wrong. I wasn't obsessed with this stuff. It's just that sometimes I'd fantasize Zyklon B coming out of our shower instead of water. I know this is insane, but I somehow wish I had been in Auschwitz with my parents so I could really know what they lived through! . . . I guess it's some kind of guilt about having had an easier life than they did. (1991, 16)

While Langer argues that common memory offers an easy way out, an escape from the direct confrontation of suffering that inheres in deep memory, the stories of the second generation add a new dimension to the draw of memory. The second generation may get stuck in the survivors' deep memory precisely because they feel that they do not have a story to tell. The stories belong to the parents, those who truly suffered, while the children can at best act as intermediaries, bringing the stories to light.

Although *Maus* allows Art to reflect on his relationship to his father and to the Holocaust, *Maus* is essentially the story of Vladek and, to a lesser extent, of Anja, to whom volume one is dedicated. The last frame of volume two pictures the Spiegelman headstone, with Vladek and Anja side by side, the dates of their lives inscribed underneath. Beneath that, Art Spiegelman's signature, with the dates 1978–1991. The book has brought an end to him as well.

Yet after the *Maus* volumes came the CD-ROM, *The Complete Maus,* and it is here, I would argue, that Art truly gets to tell his story, to narrate his own strained relationship to the Holocaust. (For clarity's sake, I will distinguish between the CD, *The Complete Maus,* and the written text, *Maus.*) The CD-ROM is an incredible piece of work, not simply because it offers the reader the opportunity to hear Vladek's actual voice and to see Art's early sketches. *The Complete Maus* is magisterial in its conception because it links the story of the first generation—the story primarily told in *Maus*—with the story of the second generation, Art's story as a successful artist and writer, contemporary Jew, child of Holocaust survivors, parent of two children. By addressing the complexities of pedagogical memory, *The Complete Maus* reflects the difficulty and necessity of creating a life within the knowledge of Auschwitz.

A CD-ROM creates the page as a multidimensional, multimedia experience. Clicking on frames of the text, readers can see Art's earlier drafts; clicking on a tape recorder, they can hear Vladek's original testimony, or Art's commentary on the particular section. *The Complete Maus* even contains video footage of Art and Françoise's trip to Auschwitz, to see the buildings that Vladek describes. Here, a new generation finds a new medium, the children telling their parents' stories in a fashion the parents would hardly recognize. More significantly, the multivocal nature of the CD-ROM allows Art to tell his own story without detracting from the centrality of Auschwitz. In this way, the CD-ROM might be seen as a supplement to the original text. The CD is the voice of the second generation, which does not occlude the original, first generation, testimony, but enhances it. Vladek's original story is present; readers can simply "page through" *Maus* on the screen as they would read the book. But we are also offered the opportunity to hear Art's perspective. And, as Art points out, the CD-ROM also allows Vladek the opportunity to speak without being translated by Art:

> I suppose the way to enter into *Maus* would be to read through it first and allow it just to enter as narrative and then to go back and pursue one's interests. . . . It seems especially useful to be able to find Vladek's version of an anecdote. That to me was one of the core appeals of what this makes possible so that rather than having me always "win" in my discussions with Vladek of how something is going to be presented, to be able to have him have the last word and to actually have it be a heard word. (audio 1)

In the book, Art is plagued not only by the enormity of his task in representing Auschwitz but also, in volume two, by the success of the first volume and the subsequent pressure of commercialization. The CD seems less tormented by these issues because it can more easily voice them. From the collage of Vladek's words, Art's representation, and Art's own commentary, *Maus* is able to evoke the complexity of Holocaust representation and testimony.

More pointedly, *The Complete Maus* gives voice to Art's concerns as a contemporary Jew, trying to live after the Holocaust, and as the child of survivors who has received much professional acclaim from telling his parents' story. In *Maus,* much of Art's sarcasm is directed toward his father, but in *The Complete Maus,* Spiegelman tackles what it means to have had his book translated into sixteen languages and to have become internationally recognized in his work. The section "Maus-related Miscellany" contains work both by and about Spiegelman, including several pieces on his ambivalent relationship to Germany. "Playing Cat and Mouse in Germany" presents Spiegelman's acceptance speech upon being granted an award at the Fourth Biannual Comics Salon in Erlängen, Germany:

> It's a strange thing for me as a Jew to be here in Germany, getting an award for describing how your parents and grandparents were accomplices in killing my grandparents and family. It's strange for you also, giving me this award—not giving it might in-

dicate a lack of sensitivity on your part, considering our history. But giving me this award could be seen as a result of a guilty conscience, a kind of war reparations to the child of a survivor. Ach! Here come the Jews again, inflicting guilt on such a pleasant evening. (*The Complete Maus*)

In *Maus,* Art struggles with his relationship to his father and his responsibility as an artist and translator of his father's story, but there is remarkably little about his relationship to the Holocaust itself. The narrative structure of *Maus* places Art very much in the role of child, even reducing him physically to a child in *Maus II,* when he is surrounded by reporters and salespeople. In the CD-ROM, Spiegelman is much more present, not only as a character of *Maus,* but as a human being. Although his father is still part of his narrative, the CD-ROM allows Spiegelman to make the story his own, to talk about what it means to live after Auschwitz, drawing from his own cultural context:

It's like the old Looney Tunes cartoons where the character runs past the edge of a cliff and keeps running through midair. It takes awhile to notice there's no ground left to walk on. Finally he notices and plummets earthward with a crash. So Western civilization ended at Auschwitz. And we still haven't noticed. I include myself, sitting here, a picture of my one-and-a-half year old baby girl in my wallet, as if there's a world after Auschwitz. *(The Complete Maus)*

It is *The Complete Maus* that allows Art to talk more fully about his mother as well. In *Maus* she is Anja, part of Vladek's story and at the center of Art's narrative as a symbol of loss. But in *The Complete Maus,* Anja becomes a supportive parent, not the "Mommy" of "Hell Planet," but "Mom," the one who encouraged Art to become an artist. Here there is another photograph of Art and Anja, the two this time joined by an issue of the comic, *Mad:*

It's Mom who complicitly feeds *Mad* love. I remember shopping with her a couple of years before this picture was taken and seeing a book on how to draw cartoons. My 25-cent allowance had long been spent, so I pleaded for another advance. She was a soft touch, but the strict household allowance Vladek kept her on didn't allow for any frills. . . . She told me the book would be a gift if I could prove it wasn't a soon-to-be discarded folly, like the marionettes she bought me the week I wanted to be a puppeteer. (*The Complete Maus*)

Were this the only story the reader had about Anja, it might be read as a common-enough story about traditional family dynamics. What makes Spiegelman's story more than that is that it, like Spiegelman himself, comes after the knowledge of the Holocaust. It is important that the reader encounter the text of *Maus* first, because that is what opens up the possibility of bringing this memory into the realm of post-memory, where the idyllic narrative is given shape by what we know surrounds it. "Later that year my mother will kill herself without leaving any note,"

Art writes, "But here in this snapshot, in my prepubescent 1960, my mother, in the shadow of a sun umbrella smiles indulgently at my beloved *Mad* while my father shows off his family and his terrace. What—us worry?" (*The Complete Maus*).

For Hirsch, the photograph is the medium that connects memory and post-memory, the memory of the parents and the memory of the children. Yet, what is implicit in Hirsch's text is that the images require knowledge in order to be read-able. Family photographs taken before the war (like Yaffa Eliach's tower of faces at the Washington, D.C., Holocaust museum) move the viewer only to the extent that the viewer knows what happened after the shutter closed. They are moments out of time, drawn from a narrative that infuses them with meaning not found ex-plicitly in the frame. To read Holocaust photographs, then, or to read prewar and postwar photographs as Holocaust pictures, requires a narrative frame. What the photographs in the *Maus* CD suggest is that the narrative frame often requires the stories of the second generation as well. The photograph of Art and his mother reading *Mad* together is not explained by Spiegelman's words, yet they provide the context that makes the photograph particularly moving. Here, in this moment, be-fore his mother's suicide, Art shares his love of comics with his mother. After this photograph will come Anja's suicide, along with the irony of Art's Pulitzer for drawing about his father's camp experiences and his mother's suicide, but for right now, a moment of tenuous happiness.

The danger of the CD-ROM, if there is one, is that it offers the illusion of mas-tery in a realm where there can be none. The viewer of *The Complete Maus* is of-fered the opportunity to switch scenes, hearing what she wants, cutting off that which she cannot handle. But perhaps this is a necessary risk, if that viewer is to find herself in the story. There is little deep memory in the *Maus* CD, not that much beyond the text itself that wounds the reader. The exceptions are the fam-ily trees of Anja and Vladek, each family member portrayed as a mouse. Half of the mice are enclosed in picture frames, and clicking on those frames reveals a pho-tograph of the actual person. These photographs do not break out of the narrative in the way that the text's photographs do, yet they remind the viewer of the ac-tual lives hidden behind the representation of mice.

The demands of pedagogical memory—that Holocaust memory can teach the present generation how to live—are not answered by *Maus*. Never does Spiegel-man suggest that there are lessons easily learned from the past. Yet by representing his own struggle as a narrator, translator, artist, child, and father, Spiegelman illu-minates the extent to which the responsibility to remember is a debt never fulfilled, only negotiated and renegotiated. In this way, he offers a model—albeit a difficult and ambivalent model—to others who struggle to live up to the ethical demands of Holocaust memory.

This is, I would like to imagine, the legacy that Art Spiegelman will pass down to his own children, Dashiel and Nadja. Although Holocaust education often speaks of passing down the story from generation to generation, the story does not remain the same. Dashiel and Nadja will have their own stories to tell; will Nadja, the first-born, remember Vladek at all? What will it be like for Dashiel to meet his grand-father through the images drawn by his father? The stories of the survivors will not be forgotten, but new stories will be added to them—are already being added, if we listen. Holocaust education must listen to these stories and hear them as Holo-caust stories because they, in most poignant and pressing ways, wrestle with what it means to live responsibly in the face of Auschwitz.

NOTES

1. "Shema," the oft-cited poem that begins Levi's *Survival in Auschwitz* begins, "You who live safe/In your warm houses/ . . . Consider if this is a man/Who works in the mud/Who does not know peace. . . ."

6

Artifactual Testimonies and the Stagings of Holocaust Memory

Andrea Liss

In one of the least sensational and arguably most revealing moments in Steven Spielberg's film *Schindler's List,* a group of women from the same town, who have been rounded up in a deportation camp, talk among themselves. They discuss how they have heard about much harsher places called concentration camps, even camps where people are murdered, although they do not call them extermination camps. The scene shows the women dismissing such received information as rumors. In the theater where I saw the film, I overheard a young woman make the following response to this scene, "Oh Mom, I didn't know they didn't know." That this commercial visual spectacle and unwitting educational forum could elicit such a suspended moment of pedagogy is crucial. In addition to making clear that the victims of the Nazi death camps did not go willingly and that not every person could believe such atrocities were taking place, this scene and its double negative response, "I didn't know they didn't know," enact the multiple layers of doubt, trepidation, and silence that surround the relay of information between the horrific realities of living through the Holocaust for survivors, the mediation of such experiences in post-Auschwitz representation, and their complex reception by the next generations.

I offer another scenario involving the pedagogy of traumatic remembrance in which the attempt to engage the contemporary subject into performing the difficult act of witnessing is troubling and convoluted. This story is closer to home. A couple of years ago, my then seven-and-a-half-year-old son came home from school with his head filled with a jumble of fragments about current events and history. Friday afternoon is usually our time together to enjoy the feeling of expansiveness that the end of the week provides, and a time when Miles often reflects on something that delights or intrigues him. On that Friday, his questions were relentless: "Why did people hate Martin Luther King? Why was President

Kennedy assassinated? And what is the 'Holycaust'?" He already had some familiarity with responses to the first two questions, but entering the realm of the Nazi-
inflicted Holocaust during World War II was uncharted territory in our relationship and in his psyche. As our discussion unfolded, Miles allowed stories to surface
slowly, haltingly. They included the clichéd images (big boots, the *Seig heil* salute)
as well as unexpected scenarios of babies stuffed into toilets. And then, finally, Miles
voiced the question I think he had really been wanting to ask from the beginning,
"Mommy, did Hitler hurt your family?"

Although I was just completing a book about the particular dilemmas and
possibilities involved in employing documentary and family photographs to represent and respectfully memorialize the victims of the *Shoah,* I was neither prepared nor willing to open this subject in depth with my son at that point (see
Liss 1998). I had thought many times about how I would begin to unravel this
history to him; now it was being forced on me because the substitute teacher
who taught in his class that day callously ignored the lesson plan his regular
teachers had prepared.

I was stunned, emotionally drained, saddened, and angry. My anxiety was not
coming from a desire for censorship; I want my son to know about events, to reflect on them, and to form his own sense of ethics, passion, and action. Most vexing for me were the psychic photographic and archival images this teacher had
unleashed, without providing a framework for helping Miles and the other children to receive them. Missing in her understanding of teaching is, in Thomas Elsaesser's apt words, that history "is not just what's past, but what is being passed
on" (1996, 145).

I consider this incident a deeply flawed pedagogic opportunity because the material was presented as an onslaught that turned the possible formation of empathy
into premature confusion and fear. Further, the substitute teacher's approach seems
particularly convoluted because I can ascertain no clear objective in her "lesson"
on the Holocaust. The degree to which each child could take in the images and the
myriad resulting interpretations would depend on his or her already formed awareness of racism and cultural identity, among many complex factors. But there was
no focus in her methodology that would even recognize such connections. Yet,
however unwittingly, the teacher's displaced concerns begin to articulate a pedagogy relevant to Holocaust representation and the problematics such representations inevitably convey. In the crucial sense of being overwhelmed and awed by
the telling of the events, fear and confusion are themselves integral to a respectful
remembrance, especially if awe can be transformed from terror into reverence and
further dialogue. I hear an echo of the denouement of Miles's questions to himself and to me, "Mommy, did Hitler hurt your family?" Although there is more to
respectful remembrance than the formation of empathy and the transposed engagement with another, an effective pedagogy of historical trauma must always
keep these desires in play against the limits of representation and the unknowability of "what happened."

It is precisely these pedagogic dilemmas and possibilities that brought home, as it were, my ongoing parallel concerns about reconsidering appropriate forms of Holocaust remembrance through representation. Indeed, the sheer horror of the events of the Shoah complicates their representation. The trauma they imprint on survivors and the post-Auschwitz generation compounds these difficulties. Yet the use of photography and artifacts as evidence of the events, the passage of events into memory, and the transference of images into post-memory are crucial bridges that help translate the history from one generation to the next. The most tense point along this fragile bridge occurs where contemporary rethinking of documentary and memorial discourse is faced with the uneasy intersection between the demand for historical accuracy and calls for respectful remembrance of those who were violated, without trespassing on the survivor's memories of trauma or metaphorically violating the contemporary listener/witness.

The public school classroom is a traditional site of pedagogy, although the complex results of the interactions that occur there are often unanticipated. Commercial films, especially those that conflate nonfiction with its dramatized reenactment, as in *Schindler's List,* implicitly insinuate their problematic documentary and pedagogic strivings. Although the scale of their memorializing tasks might differ, museum planners and contemporary artists, especially those who are children of survivors, are also faced with similar dilemmas in their representation of historical trauma. In tandem with their pedagogic and memorializing tasks, they must contend with the facts that the indirect chronicling of history is always told through an inevitable distance and that the abyss in understanding that the Shoah produces only deepens the chasm between the ones who experienced the events and distant witnesses.[1]

Those who work in the realm of translating survivors' experiences must then account for trauma's paradoxical and unaccountable results, both protective (what the survivors "forgot") and confrontational (what always remains as unforgettable and indiscriminate memories for the survivor). Classroom teachers, filmmakers, museum planners, artists, and many others might be on guard not to equate disclosure of the events with lucid understanding and to conduct their work gingerly. However, proceeding too cautiously would renounce the telling of the events to yet another doubled realm of silence. First, there is the silence that surrounded the survivors' experiences and the trauma of events after Auschwitz; and, second, the silence that the law of the voice of the legitimate witness would impose on the voice of the post-Auschwitz generation as "inauthentic." Yet the post-events' speaker's voice—in its dilemmas of inauthenticity—is inevitable, indeed necessary, for stories and memories to become public, to become part of the historical record. Cartoonist Art Spiegelman incorporates the very risk of his position as distant witness and troubled chronicler into his renowned *Maus* stories. His second book, *And Here My Troubles Began,* begins with his recognition of this inevitable dilemma. Recall Art picturing himself driving with his wife, Françoise, to visit his Auschwitz survivor father while he muses on the difficulty of working on *Maus:* "Just thinking about my book . . .

it's so presumptuous of me. I mean, I can't even make any sense out of my relationship with my father. How am I supposed to make any sense out of Auschwitz? . . . of the Holocaust?" (1991, 14).

Working with this necessary presumptuousness, some artists who are children of survivors and others who face the task of representing the Holocaust, indeed restaging the events for post-Auschwitz generations, attempt their labor through its post-memories. *Post-memories*, as I employ the term here, refers to the artists' distance from direct experience with the Shoah as well as their relation to the fallout of those events.[2] Post-memories, in the sense of acute if not blinding afterimages, constitute the imprints that photographic images of the events have created within the post-Auschwitz generation. As I intend it, the term also refers to differing and effective strategies that artists and others have formulated in their work to provoke the history and memories of the events in order to create respectful remembrance of its victims for new generations.

Some of the foundational questions that guide my inquiry into the political/theoretical issues of representing and teaching histories of trauma include: How can the dilemmas and possibilities inherent in the legacy of distant witnessing bridge the gap between firsthand experience of the trauma (itself mediated) and the desires on the part of the post-Auschwitz generation to listen to and convey what they have learned of these events? In what ways do differing strategies of interpreting and re-presenting documentary artifacts influence retellings of the histories and future generations' empathy toward or distance from the events? In this chapter, I explore the specificity of these questions through a sustained consideration of a freight car in the permanent exhibition at the United States Holocaust Memorial Museum in Washington, D.C., and an artist's book by Tatana Kellner (1992), *71125: Fifty Years of Silence, Eva Kellner's Story*. It is to these projects that I now turn.[3]

STAGINGS OF UNKNOWABILITY AT THE UNITED STATES HOLOCAUST MEMORIAL MUSEUM

Through its understated mode of approach and in its more insistent desire to "establish the physical reality of the Holocaust," the United States Holocaust Memorial Museum in Washington, D.C., reigns over the palpable inaccessibility of its historical trauma.[4] The museum's foundation literally lies over earth that has been infused with ashes collected from the Bergen-Belsen extermination camp and other sites. Indeed, the elaborated staging of the museum in its entirety is built over a set of oscillating presumptions and dilemmas to tell the untellable, "to *be* the story and to repeat its unrepeatability" (Felman and Laub 1992, 202).

The presence of artifacts within the museum's realm of re-creation falls appropriately within the traditional role of museums to exhibit "authentic objects." The work that artifacts perform, tracing the reality of events, parallels and often augments the photograph's function to document and to bear witness. Massive groupings of documentary photographs insist that viewers open their eyes to face these devastating images. Even if one chooses to turn away, the burning aftereffects of photographic images make it impossible to close one's eyes completely. With artifacts, the museum is in the business of exhibiting fragments of raw history wrenched from the authentic sites of destruction. Despite the artifacts' reference to actual human lives and previous ownership—as in the case of personal objects like toothbrushes, shoes, and eyeglasses—they are strangely devoid of the bodily presence indexed through their metonymic traces. Perhaps in part because artifacts are often denuded in this way, they gesture differently than photographs do toward the fragile and necessary possibilities of closing one's eyes to create empathic bridges through the imaginative projection of one's self into the experiences of another. Indeed, the staging of artifacts often follows photographic thinking in attempting to mirror the realities and act as supplements to the losses they stand in for. However, we must ask whether artifacts function as barriers to the events, despite the opportunities they offer to close one's eyes to be open to another's experiences. The artifact intrudes in the realm of the present through its hyperreality and, paradoxically, through the utter concreteness it signals. It brings one closer to the historical real, supposedly closer to the tangibility of the events and to the experiences of those who did and did not survive.

The freight car of the fifteen-ton Karlsruhe model stands gaping in a corner space on the third floor of the permanent exhibition at the United States Holocaust Memorial Museum in Washington, D.C. It is a frighteningly quiet space for the deafening horror of its pronouncement. The railcar, with the coy innocence of its provenance, "Donated by the Polish State Railways," once transported people to the Treblinka death camp. The provenance label and text accompanying this artifact states:

> Most deported Jews endured a tortuous train journey to death camps in bare freight cars, under conditions of hunger and thirst, extreme overcrowding, and horrible sanitation. In winter they were exposed to freezing temperatures, and in summer they were enveloped in suffocating heat and stench. Many of those deported, especially older people and young children, died during the journey. This walkway goes through a 15-ton "Karlsruhe" freight car, one of several types that were used to deport Jews. As many as 100 victims were packed into a single car. Deportation trains usually carried between 1,000 and 2,000 persons, and sometimes as many as 5,000. Their weight slowed the speed of travel to about 30 miles an hour, greatly prolonging the ordeal. Frequently, the trains halted for hours or days at a time on side tracks or in stations along the way. The freight car is standing on rails and tracks from the Treblinka camp. Donated by the Polish State Railways.[5]

The freight car is positioned to work as a dramatized object within this museologized terrain that is momentarily sealed off from the contemporary reality of

Fifteen-ton freight car of the Karlsruhe model, one of several types used to deport Jews. Donated by the Polish State Railways, and on display at the United States Holocaust Memorial Museum.

Washington, D.C. It is exhibited as part of the absolute proof of the events of the Shoah. The artifact is apprehended at this place, after a narrow pathway through displays that show the early stages of the genocide by way of photographs and films and after passageways through parts of streets and walls literally cast from ghettos that were "liquidated." This tightly packed corridor opens out onto two choices for the museum visitor in her continued journey: to bypass the freight car alto-gether, allowing the visitor to cross an almost imperceptible bridge leading to a wall of smaller intimate artifacts, or to complete the horizontal corridor leading to the car's gaping open sides.

With mixed apprehension, I approached the freight car. I cautioned myself as I prepared for what my imaginative projections might unleash, telling myself that the presence of the actual object, the vehicle that began and often atrociously ended people's journeys into the world of the unliving, will be more appropri-ate, more "effective" than any desire to artificially re-create the artifact. There were no crowds at this crucial, strangely understated point in the museum ex-cursion. I looked around, then entered the car. I stood there feeling awkward, utterly insignificant, much too visible. I waited to accommodate myself to the dimness and let it overwhelm me, making me anonymous. After a few moments, I closed my eyes. Darkness. More darkness. Then bodies. Real people crammed next to each other. Women dressed in fine suits clinging to their children, their parents, or utter strangers. People smothering each other. People trampling each other for a shard of food, a lick of water. The bestiality. The defecation. The hu-manness. I opened my eyes, embarrassed by my trespass. I was set up. In fact, the car is denuded of any such traces. It is clean. Too clean? I wonder. We can thank the museum for this discretion. I found myself leaning forward against the mu-seum railing that was blocking entry into the recesses of the train. I wanted to touch the car's wood. To caress it. Or better still, to gouge my fingers into its cruel silences.

I had been lured into the museum's logic, reaching a critical point of trespass in the obscenity of my projections. The railcar marks this perhaps necessary point of trespass. As untenable threshold, it solicited these transgressions. To trespass is to go across, to transgress, to die—that is the bottom line. Then, to exceed the bounds of what is lawful, right, or just. To offend, encroach on another's privileges, rights, *privacy*. It is, indeed, the trespass over violated rights that justifies breaking open privacy in the name of evidence that is doubly at issue here—Lyotard's insistence on the differend, or the immeasurable injustice done to the victims and the redress that representation might enact, already points to that (1988). Yet, it is the staging of the trampling on the others' privacies that tears at me; that my own little tres-pass risks conflating, even in a small way, with the original acts of violence. The complex status of the artifact itself calls forth these doubled crossings. The freight car was the Nazis' very instrument of transport to and of the destruction; now it stands in as the estranged object. The extreme circumstances of this artifact's his-tory trouble the museum visitor's perception of whether it is a precious or a reviled object. Indeed, the freight car demonstrates the tense and difficult roles that artifacts are asked to perform in bearing witness to the Shoah: to be objects of empathy and historical proof. Despite the historical authenticity of the object itself, the artifact enacts its own absolute resignation to tell. There is no a priori guarantee that it can be enacted as evidence; rather, the artifact attests to the original trauma and the post-traumatic resurfacing of the events as they recur as displaced fragments and lacerations. The indisputable presence yet utter muteness of the railcar—its uncanny objecthood—signal what we can never know, what we should not imagine we could imagine. Functioning most effectively for the museum visitor, it would mark the place of its own tragic paradox as remnant of historical and psychic trauma.

If the artifact elicits traumatic unknowability (the museum planners interestingly refer to artifacts as "object survivors"), perhaps the parallel between the artifact as remnant of the trauma and the status of human survivors needs to be made more explicit. The uncanny objecthood of the artifact stands in for deeper psychic processes that echo in part some of the experiences of trauma for the survivor. In beginning to understand trauma, through his framework of the psyche as a device based on the economy and depletion of energy, Sigmund Freud wrote about it as an experience that "presents the mind with an increase of stimulus too powerful to be dealt with or worked off in the normal way" (1968, vol. 16, 275). These stimuli create "a breach in an otherwise efficacious barrier against stimuli," in which trauma would then "set in motion every possible defense measure" (1968, vol. 18, 29). Part of this defense mechanism is the psyche's impulse to allow the organism to mime distancing and forgetting, but this is an illusive and impossible forgetting. Yet, as literary critic Cathy Caruth has noted, for some survivors, "while the images of traumatic reenactment remain absolutely accurate and precise, they are largely inaccessible to conscious recall and control."[6] As Caruth further comments on trauma's binds:

> Yet what is particularly striking in this singular experience [of trauma] is that its insistent reenactments of the past do not simply serve as testimony to an event, but may also, paradoxically enough, bear witness to a past that was never fully experienced as it occurred. Trauma, that is, does not simply serve as record of the past but precisely registers the force of an experience that is not yet fully owned. . . . For the survivor of trauma, then, the truth of the event may reside not only in its brutal facts, but also in the way their occurrence defies simple comprehension. The flashback or traumatic reenactment conveys, that is, both *the truth of an event,* and *the truth of its incomprehensibility.* (1991, 417, 419–420)

Functioning on a decidedly more conscious register, the museum's mandate warrants that it render the inaccessibility of the events into explicable narratives through the uneasy availability of the objects. The artifacts are among the key phrases that articulate the sentence "Never Forget." The imperative is designed for those who did not experience the events. Its emphasis on conscious and willful remembrance has nothing to do with survivors' painful and arduous processes of impossible forgetting, and thus reliving, of the traumatic events. Although it is not the museum's business to mime the long psychic process of trauma's protective and confrontational mechanisms, it must be asked whether the museum's necessary attempt to house memory and frame history covers over what can never be properly lodged.

The museum is faced with an enormous risk, if it chooses to acknowledge it. There is always the numbing possibility that an overly insistent focus on re-creation of the events will result in the loss of their essential and crucial incomprehensibility, what Caruth characterizes as *"the force of its affront to understanding"* (1991, 420). She further notes that "the possibility that the events will be integrated into memory and the consciousness of history thus raises the question, . . . whether it is not a sacrilege of the traumatic experience to play with the reality of the past?" (1991, 421). This crucial question is rhetorical in the sense that it depends on who responds to it. Survivors know the dilemma. The question, although psychoanalytically inflected, bears heavily on the museum's task. The duplicitous invitation to enter at the edge of the train car's abyss gives rise to the museum's vexed dilemma: How can it represent the paradoxical nature of trauma and the events themselves—inaccessible yet real—while deploying artifacts to give voice to the ineffable pain of effacement and extermination and then to employ them as the very proof of accessibility and comprehensibility?

The railcar's very intactness and muteness appropriately perform as representations of the historical trauma as well as echo the effects of psychic trauma. The artifact functions as a marker of the trauma through its status as representation—that is, as lack and loss yet also as evidence of the real—which signals its potent and ambivalent inaccessibility. The railcar's presence, in its singular and stunning objectness, avoids the problem of aesthetic display that other masses of artifacts convey in their decontextualized abjectness (shoes, teeth, eyeglasses). Such objects confront the visitor frontally, as iconic tableaux from the distant past. Yet, the railcar is apprehended through multileveled sensory and perceptual registers that project tentative bridges to the events. The visitor can guardedly engage with the artifact, touching it, walking across and around it, in charged spatial arenas in which some sense of trauma's relentless yet veiled contiguity between the past and the present is insinuated.

Although the museum is invested in the railcar's ability to testify, the pedagogic staging of the artifact defies its opaque realism through its ambiguous status as precious object and as historical proof. The mute and powerful resonance of its inability is not a marker of the collapse of evidence; it is a sign that the articulation of events calls forth an acknowledgment of the extreme difficulty of the task. Indeed, it is not a matter here of discrediting artifacts or photographs, but of reformulating assumptions about their status as accessible evidentiary devices. The representational traces of trauma demand that we face them, with our eyes both open and closed.

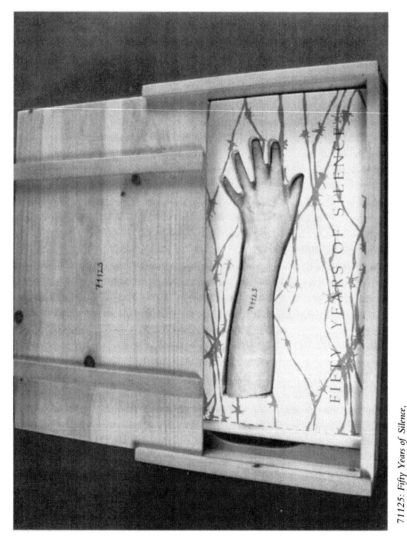

71125: Fifty Years of Silence,
limited edition artist book, silkscreen and cast handmade paper, 12" x 20" x 3", 1992.
Tatana Kellner

RESTATING TESTIMONY THROUGH
SECOND-GENERATION MEDIATIONS

Tatana Kellner's *71125: Fifty Years of Silence, Eva Kellner's Story*, 1992, is an artist's book that resulted from the artist/daughter's desire to know her mother's experiences, especially after her grandmother passed away and, as Kellner writes in the introduction to the book, "her story died with her." This book also represents Kellner's own contribution to the transmission and translation of her mother's story as daughter and artist through her design, construction, use of photographs, different textures of paper, and a key artifact to collaborate with and intervene in Eva Kellner's account.[7] My interest in discussing this unusual book in relation to the museum's display of the freight car is due to the surprising affinities they share in their approach to articulating the mute power of artifacts. Recall how the impact of the museum's freight car is supported by its powerful information label, an impact that may be further embellished by the visitor's projection of self-investment or left unarticulated by circumscribing psychic entrance into the freight car, thereby bestowing another form of respect onto the artifact and the experiences it references. *Fifty Years of Silence* is also a paradoxical representation of Holocaust history and memory. The book creates a dense overlay of Eva Kellner's memories of her experiences in Auschwitz-Birkenau and other sites of horror, yet it resonates with a profound withholding of information. When her daughter asked her to document her memories, Eva agreed on the condition that she would write them in Czech. The book includes Tatana's mother's original text, as well as Tatana's English translation. Although the text is startling in its acute detail and partial disclosure, the artifact at the visual and metaphorical center of Tatana and Eva Kellner's book represents the raw presence of knowledge that was kept silent for so many years. This artifact is a pink cast of Eva Kellner's arm.

My first impulse was to touch the cast of Eva's arm, to caress it, and as I did, I felt myself no longer refer to it as an indefinite article, as an "it," but rather as something more definitive, "her arm," and something more specific still, "Eva's arm." I slowly, cautiously placed my hand over hers, feeling an eerie affinity as my fingers slowly fit almost exactly over hers as our hands conjoined. Eva's fingers are thinner and more frail than mine, her hand slightly smaller and more childlike. Her fingers are exposed but do not seem vulnerable. The dusty rose color of the cast gives her fingers and her entire hand an ethereal quality, and yet its reality remains.

I was struck by the stunning enunciatory qualities of this replication, this cast, this mold. In the specificity of the lines, the gentle and graceful relation of one finger to the other and how they rest together, Eva's cast arm cuts through the clichés that burden so many images of tattooed numbers on survivors' arms. In the context of this heavily text-driven book, readers are reminded that this is the hand that wrote the story, that this is the humanness at the core of the book. Indeed, readers are always in relation with Eva's hand as our hands constantly cross over hers in the act of turning the pages of the book. The hand sits relentlessly at the right side, the

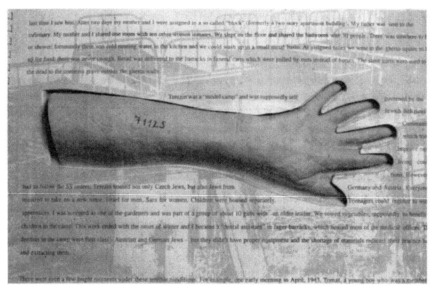

71125: Fifty Years of Silence,
limited edition artist book, silkscreen and cast handmade paper, 12" x 20" x 3", 1992.
Tatana Kellner

book's end page. The pages are all cut through at the center in the shape of the cast arm, allowing the pages to move out of the mold as we read them and turn them over to the left side. Thus, the cut out shape of the page filled with the cast at the right constantly turns into a void in the negative shape of Eva's arm as it is turned. With the turning of every page, we come closer to more knowledge of Eva's experiences and are brought into closer proximity with the full disclosure of her arm. The very enormity and detail of her stories confront readers with the utter incomprehensibility and horror that Eva lived through. In its paradoxical silence, absence and fullness, her hand stands in as the uncanny trace of impossible evidence.

As an artwork mediated through the contemporary artist/daughter's own training as a printmaker and her filtering through the material given to her by her mother, *Fifty Years of Silence* holds an unusual place in relation to traditional Holocaust memoirs and books of testimony. In addition to the remarkable cast arm and the large-scale design of the book, Kellner has inserted other visual devices of memory to emphasize her mother's implacable text and, conversely, to act as places of respite from its relentless detail. This is accomplished through the overlapping of pages that contain her mother's handwritten Czech text represented in blue ink, the daughter's English translation in black typewritten text, and the layering of silk-screened photographs onto opaque and translucent paper. These are documentary photographs of the camps her mother describes, contemporary shots of some of these sites taken by Tatana during the process of making the book, as well as family photos taken before the Holocaust up to the years her parents wrote down their

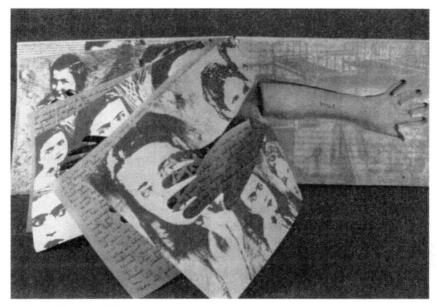

71125: *Fifty Years of Silence,*
limited edition artist book, silkscreen and cast handmade paper, 12" x 20" x 3", 1992.
Tatana Kellner

stories—picturing them as the teenagers and young adults she never knew to the middle-aged and elderly parents whose histories remained unknown to her as she grew up. The flow of the narrative is such that the opaque page with the English translation and the family photographs printed on the verso of the text are at first barely visible through the translucent page that contains photographs from the extermination sites on its recto and the blue Czech text on its verso. As the translucent page is turned, it reveals the translation, which then continuously obscures the blue handwritten text beneath it. Thus, a pause occurs every few pages, as the photographs at the left meet with the translucent page at the right, a pause that is further delineated by the arm and hand that become even more noticeable because only the obscured Czech text seen from the back surrounds them.

Kellner's strategy to emphasize and also obscure aspects of the narrative and to overlap the time zones of the unknown Holocaust past and its ever-presence recalls approaches familiar to other unusual Holocaust memoir projects by children of survivors. In Art Spiegelman's prize-winning *Maus* books, dedicated to his half-brother Richieu, who perished as a young boy, and to his mother, Anja, who lived through Auschwitz but committed suicide when Art was nineteen years old, Spiegelman recounts his father's memoirs in the nontraditional idiom of the comic book. Within the overall realm of the comics metaphor that accommodates the realm of the Holocaust by turning the world of the ordinary upside down and inside out at its seams, Spiegelman also uses irony with a vengeance. His use of animals as people, his insertions of personal commentary as the son of survivors, and his reproduction of three family photographs create a shocking contrast to the extraordinary world of the Holocaust horror. Abraham Ravett's remarkable film, *Everything's For You* (1989), is also based on his father's memories of Auschwitz. When the recounting of the worst of the events becomes too difficult, Ravett substitutes the camera's gaze on his father with powerful sketched animations of the son's own memories of his father. Similar to Spiegelman's and Kellner's layering of documentary and intimate imagery, Ravett's film also includes targeted use of both archival film footage and pre-Holocaust family photographs. And, in even closer affinity with the way Ravett uses animation and Spiegelman incorporates his precious family photos, and through the ways each project brings in the cadence and accents of the survivor's voice (Vladek Spiegelman's voice is audible on the CD-ROM, *The Complete Maus*), Kellner's reenactment of her mother's arm acts as the visible yet uncanny evidence through which every memory and document must be witnessed. As Marianne Hirsch and Susan Rubin Suleiman note, many children of survivors echo Kellner's experience of living with a silent knowledge, what the authors call an "absent memory." They write, "For Tatana, growing up, the arms may have seemed like screens which were at once masking the story and inviting a story to be projected onto them."[8]

The force of Eva Kellner's own text also accomplishes the task of documenting and memorializing the trauma that, in tandem with her daughter's highlighting and filtering, never assumes full disclosure. The distance surrounding the years of silence that encapsulates the book's story, only hinted at through its title, is still not bridged in spite of the mother's articulate handwritten testimony. As Kellner considered the process of working on the book and directly collaborating with her mother only in posing questions about the accuracy of her translation, she wrote in her introduction, "this is still not something we can talk about." One hears the daughter's trepidation in directly facing her mother, as if there was already enough trespass in having her write out her story.

Let me consider another tense point of trespass in *Fifty Years of Silence,* akin to the tension that is also evoked in the Holocaust museum's display of the freight car. Recall the pedagogic logic of how the freight car is staged at the museum. It functions as a visual artifact that both solicits the trespasser/participant's projected sense of self-investment and elicits an alternative response—one that requires keeping one's eyes open to the unrelenting emptiness of the railcar, which confronts the visitor with the very impossibility of having contained those bodies toward whom it gestures. In this way, the museum's discourse stages the impossibility of trespass, thereby circumscribing and yet realizing its own pedagogic strivings. Eva Kellner's own account of being transported in a boxcar to Auschwitz-Birkenau is strikingly circumscribed as well. Note how she offers details within a framework familiar to, if not normalized by, survivors' memoirs: "Again German and Czech police are herding us into boxcars. There are 5,000 people called for this transport. We are squeezed like sardines, sitting on the floor, one person on top of the other; a bucket sits in the corner—our toilet. No one can move. It's dark in the boxcar; light enters only through very small openings." Absent in her account is any reference to her own state of mind or body. The description seems strangely outside of herself. This is due in part to trauma's distancing and buffering mechanisms, yet also seems to be a more conscious move on Eva's part—ostensibly allowing Tatana and all other possible readers to enter, while keeping the listener/translator's eyes off of her, guarding her from trespass.

Eva Kellner's tone often emphasizes the ludicrous and understates the worst through her remarkably ironic humor. She explains how in one so-called work camp in Hamburg, the inmates received coats that were turned into odd uniforms: "Each coat must have its sleeves removed and replaced with sleeves from a different color coat. On the back of each coat a bull's eye is painted. All of this in order to find and shoot in the back prisoners in case of an escape. I wonder that no one in all this has thought of using this as a fashion statement."

The evasion and piercing irony of such accounts are nonetheless outweighed in other passages where Eva reveals experiences and transformations so intimate and so painful that one can empathize with Tatana's decision to avoid face-to-face dialogue with her mother about her narrative. Eva writes of her arrival in Auschwitz-Birkenau: "After being beaten and kicked mercilessly by the other prisoners who have been here longer . . . I lie down and am so unhappy, sad and lost that I can't even cry. I'm 16 years old and when I ask 'Why?' no one answers. This is when I lost my faith in humankind and my character was changed for the rest of my life." As if to cancel out the young woman's psychic tragedy and to make connection with the woman she knows as her mother, Tatana follows Eva's devastating admission with post-Holocaust photographs picturing her mother and father together smiling.

The rhythm of the narrative and the pacing of the photographs are punctuated throughout the book with this give-and-take between mother and daughter: Eva tentatively offering testimony and other times zeroing in on the rawest nerve of her experiences, and Tatana representing her mother's reserve and her explicit detail housed within the metaphor and material substance of the translucent and opaque pages of a book that both discloses and withholds.

Tatana and Eva Kellner's *71125: Fifty Years of Silence, Eva Kellner's Story* and the United States Holocaust Memorial Museum's display of the railcar both evidence artifactual and textual forms of bearing distant witness in which the remembrance, visualization, and pedagogy of trauma are in tension with each other, such that their commemorative functions forcefully and vulnerably allow their crucial ambivalences toward bearing witness to be palpable. These tensions and seeming contradictions are most evident and effective through their guarded and opaqued accessibility to survivors' memories. Both projects keep a respectful distance from the events yet allow the contemporary witness to face the experiences referenced in varying degrees of exposure. The museum's logic through the railcar allows for the visitor's formation of an imagined stance of engagement or effacement, while Tatana and Eva Kellner's book similarly insists on the daunting yet compelling authentic first-person voice and its second-generation mediation.

Indeed, these material projects of reluctant testimony and historical remembrance fulfill, however tentatively, some of the most crucial demands that confront the pedagogy and representation of trauma. To recall, one of the most profound tasks of this confrontation with bearing witness to the Shoah is the desire for the formation of empathy between the contemporary witness and the experiences of others and to keep this transposed engagement in tension with and against the limits of representation and the unknowability of "what happened." The effective and respectful approaches suggested by the museum's freight car and *Fifty Years of Silence* allow for reflections on the implications of how artifacts are staged for Holocaust memory. The freight car and the cast of Eva Kellner's arm demonstrate the tense and difficult roles that artifacts are asked to perform in bearing witness to the Shoah: to be objects of empathy and historical proof. As restagings, these artifacts acknowledge their desire to reveal, but not fully, leaving spaces for the contemporary visitor/reader to tentatively enter, take in some of the memories, and exit the transformed sites of trauma. In so doing, the visitor/reader can guardedly engage with the artifacts, touching them, psychically being in relation with them, in charged spatial arenas in which some sense of trauma's relentless yet veiled contiguity between the past and the present is insinuated. Thus, the contemporary spectator/witness is solicited into learning about a past he or she can never fully know, a past that cannot be fully apprehended, through artifacts that address that very unknowability. At the same time, the artifacts are designed and presented to give voice to survivors' intimate historical and personal memories.

This strategy of guardedly restaging history and more intimate stories offers what I refer to as an opaque mimesis of the events. As Kellner's book and the railcar suggest, an opaque mimesis of events might also offer the sense of touch as a crucial element in making connection with those who are no longer present, employing the metaphor and the palpable feel of the caress as a relation of both copresence and passing. In the desire to stage what can and can never be fully represented, a strategy of opaque mimesis constitutes a relation to others that refuses to claim knowledge over their experiences and seeks to retain some of the event's essential incomprehensibility. Returning to the specificity of *Fifty Years of Silence* and the museum's freight car, these overflowing and paradoxically mute artifactual testimonies trace the unbridgeable rupture that is the trauma of the events. Both projects give promise to the legacy of distant witnessing, as they work between spaces of documentation and the impossibility of knowing. In keeping with the need for representations that offer an opaque mimesis of the events, they reach tentatively and resonantly across the performative bridge of imaginative projection.

NOTES

1. Complicating this relay of traumatic experience further are the potent gaps and silences in many of the survivors' own retellings of their stories. Complex psychological and ethical

stopgaps guide their accounts, which many survivors may not theorize but which they enact, nonetheless. For important discussions on the dynamics and meanings of survivor testimonies, see especially: Ernst van Alphen 1997; Geoffrey Hartman 1996; Lawrence Langer 1991; Charlotte Delbo 1995; Cathy Caruth, ed. 1995; and Shoshana Felman and Dori Laub 1992.

2. I first used the term *post-memories* in referring to some of the most difficult of the Holocaust documentary photographs as "blinding post-memories" in my essay "Trespassing Through Shadows: History, Mourning and Photography in Representations of Holocaust Memory" (1991, 30–39). Marianne Hirsch employs this term in the singular in her essay "Family Pictures: *Maus*, Mourning, and Post-Memory" (1992–1993, 3–29). Hirsch differentiates post-memory from Nadine Fresco's notion of "absent memory," writing that "Post-memory is anything but absent or evacuated: It is as full and as empty as memory itself" (9). See Hirsch's book, *Family Frames: Photography, Narrative and Postmemory* (1997).

3. The following discussion of the freight car originally appeared in chapter four, "Artificial Witnessing as (Im)Possible Evidence," in my book, *Trespassing through Shadows: Memory, Photography, and the Holocaust* (Minneapolis: University of Minnesota Press, 1998).

4. From an interview with Martin Smith at the temporary offices of the United States Holocaust Memorial Museum, August 22, 1990.

5. For a description of the rates charged for the "journey," rates determined according to the "traveler's" age and how far he or she would travel, and for the "credits" offered the SS for one-way transport, see Michael Berenbaum, *The World Must Know: The History of the Holocaust as Told in the United States Holocaust Memorial Museum* (1993). He notes: "Reichsbahn employees used the same forms and procedures to book tourists going on vacation as they did to send Jews to Auschwitz" (115).

6. Cathy Caruth (1991, 417). In his essay, "Trauma, Transference and 'Working through'" (1992), Saul Friedlander takes issue with aspects of Caruth's thesis regarding the possibility of a delayed constitution of historical understanding, published in another essay by Caruth, "Unclaimed Experience: Trauma and the Possibility of History" (1991). However, if Friedlander questions what he calls Caruth's "redemptive theme" (following Freud's *Moses and Monotheism*), in contrast with the lack of closure offered to survivors, he nonetheless acknowledges the central theme of trauma's inaccessibility to conscious recall. In his essay, Friedlander writes, "But neither the protective numbing nor the disruptive emotion is entirely accessible to consciousness" (51).

7. Tatana Kellner created a similar book housing her father's testimony; *B-11226: Fifty Years of Silence, Eugene Kellner's Story*, 1994, which is the mate to *71125: Fifty Years of Silence, Eva Kellner's Story*, 1992. Kellner produced both books at the Rosendale Women's Studio Workshop. I would like to thank UCLA Special Collections for access to viewing and reading *Eva Kellner's Story*.

8. Marianne Hirsch and Susan Rubin Suleiman, "Material Memory: Holocaust Testimony in Post-Holocaust Art," unpublished manuscript, presented most recently at the American Comparative Literature Association Annual Meeting in Puerto Vallarta, Mexico, in April 1997. My thanks to the authors for sharing this essay with me.

7

Pedagogy and Trauma:

The Middle Passage, Slavery, and the Problem of Creolization

Rinaldo Walcott

TEACHING TRAUMA: SLAVERY AND ITS NEGATIVE ASSOCIATIONS

In "Not a Story to Pass On: Living Memory and the Slave Sublime," the last chapter of his *The Black Atlantic: Modernity and Double Consciousness* (1993), Paul Gilroy argues that Black people have not adequately dealt with the traumas of slavery. Taking Gilroy's observation as a starting point, it is the argument of this chapter that the trauma of the Middle Passage (alongside the genocide and theft of Native American lands) is a key rupture implicated in the invention of the Americas. I propose that a working through of this trauma for Black people might occasion a better understanding of the stakes of our living here, now. The impulse for this argument is the belated consideration of some generalized responses from mainly Black undergraduate students in two courses that I have recently taught. The courses were organized as responses to both the history of slavery and the ways in which Black communities make use of this history as the basis for a discourse of common community.[1] In these courses, my desire was to stage a pedagogical encounter with "neoslave narratives"[2] that might allow for a working through of the trauma of slavery and its aftermath for Black peoples. This desire rubs against the grain of historical study as salvational—that knowledge of the past will set one free and prevent future forms of racism and genocide—a perspective deeply implicated in the ways in which students tend to approach such courses. In fact, the popular

saying that "those who do not know the past are doomed to repeat it" is a main-
stay with many of my students. While most Black students are drawn to my courses
because of the redemptive promise of their content, a content they hope to be self-
affirming, many are disappointed by the points of view encountered in the texts
we study. Once students are confronted with the narrative renderings of the details of slavery, especially details that are not necessarily heroic, shame and disappointment often constitute their responses. Often this is given expression in their
suggestions that virtually any talk of slavery is an unwarranted dwelling on the
"negative" experiences of Black people. They come to claim that slavery "must be
left behind" and used only as a reminder of what was once "endured and survived."

But why is this the case? How can we account for these responses? Paul Gilroy argues that representations of slavery operate in at least two interconnected ways in
contemporary Black culture. While such representations maintain a discourse of an
invariant black tradition grounded in heroic narratives, they also signify the "site of
black victimage" (1993, 189) and the impeachability of racism. Gilroy is thus emphasizing that the "condition of being in pain" (203) circumscribes how and what
slavery means and, even more importantly for the purposes of this chapter, how slavery is made use of in contemporary Black culture. Starting from Gilroy's important
observation that there is inherent "negativity" in grappling with narratives of slavery,
I want to offer additional terms for making sense of why students respond as they do.

Afrocentric discourse has succeeded in positioning its historical narrative as redemptive. The current popularization of Afrocentrism, which pays short shrift to
slavery and its potential for other ways of seeing and knowing, results in many students having little tolerance for working through the details of slavery. Afrocentrists argue for a suppression of the traumas of slavery and their impact on the psyche of Black people in the Americas. They jettison the history of the Middle
Passage in favor of an uncomplicated and affirmative return trip to Africa. Arguing
for a centrality of African cultural memory, a memory that overshadows the experiences and legacies of slavery, Afrocentrists place the latter as merely an episode in
a larger African history. The Middle Passage tends to lie dormant in this narrative
(most of the students I have encountered are not even familiar with this phrase).
In this version of historical memory, there is a refusal to acknowledge what Stuart
Hall (1990) signals as the intervention of history, as that which constitutes identity
as "a matter of 'becoming' as well as being" (225).

Such popular Afrocentric understandings of history have clearly formed part of my
students' relation to courses on the Middle Passage. Students often interpret slavery
as a secondary historical narrative, whose meaning is inevitably imbricated with what
they perceive and articulate as "the larger concern," the founding principle of a Black
heroic story. Thus, they are often more concerned with encountering the *prehistory*
of slavery. For many students, Egyptocentric histories before "the Fall" (the transatlantic slave trade that robbed Africans of the opportunity to continue to shape world
civilization) frame their encounter with the degrading details of enslavement. On this
basis, the evidence of African cultural retentions in the Americas is understood to

speak back to the heroic qualities of Africans prior to "the Fall." Slavery becomes a sign for the remembering of courageous acts that can be traced through music, song/sound, dance, and, especially, the stories of heroic men and women.

Thus, it is not surprising that the memory of slavery exists as a difficult doubling—evidence of both heroism and Black victimage. To reinforce Gilroy's point, these two readings are not contradictory, but, rather, overlap and require each other to make sense. However, students who take courses to "learn about their past and their ancestors" often find the knowledge of the details of victimization and suffering too much to bear. The neoslave narratives that we study together do not offer easy points of identification. While this sense that painful stories of slavery are too much to bear is quite valid, it is nonetheless fraught with difficulty, because it preempts working through the trauma of slavery. It is the inability to work through this repressed trauma that leaves Black students continually repeating the condition of being in pain as the basis of identity and community formation.

Underlying all this is also the story of feeling defeated and immobilized because of this defeat. The dynamic of attraction and repulsion inherent in (neo)narratives of slavery is laden with the evidence of defeat and shame, articulating a kind of knowledge that is difficult to engage with. Deborah Britzman argues for what she calls the examination of "difficult knowledge" in pedagogical thought and practice (1998). Difficult knowledge, as Britzman sees it, "may work at the level of psychic trauma" (117). But difficult knowledge also requires educators to recognize that education is "a psychic event, charged with resistance to knowledge" (118). Difficult knowledge is thus "the demand to have hope, a compromise formation, an idealization, that in an attempt to bury actually preserves the pain of loss. What seems most crucial is a way to consider what the risk of learning has to do with the work of mourning. And perhaps the greatest risk of learning is that lonely recognition that knowledge of loss and our own insufficient response can be made only in belated time" (133). There is no doubt that students who encounter the difficult knowledge of slavery in neoslave narratives resist the attempt by authors to bring more to the story of slavery than the dichotomized expression of victimage *or* heroic transcendence. Students' reactions to such stories thus often constitute an "insufficient response." The imaginative ways in which humanity is redrawn within the contexts of slavery, the breakdown in clear delineations between hero, victim, and evildoer requires a different kind of reading. This breakdown requires an engagement that can make sense of victimization in relation to the turbulence, complicity, pleasure, and pain of the "new" invented selves—only possible in the Americas.

TOWARD A CREOLIZED PEDAGOGY

Given the pedagogical dilemmas signaled by this opening discussion, in the remainder of this chapter I mean to attempt a conceptual shift. I want to think differently about what is at stake in the difficult knowledge gestured to previously, particularly in regard to education. I will argue that "creolization" offers a possible means of coming to terms with life in the Americas by way of working through the trauma of slavery. Creolization represents a conceptual terrain that might allow for readings of slavery that enable us to think more clearly and honestly about the human condition in a time of what Wilson Harris (1990) terms "cross-cultural resonances."

What is most important about creolization (and particularly my use of it) is that it permits us to contextualize and discuss the tensions and ambivalences of what Édouard Glissant calls a "poetics of relation." Glissant writes of relation this way: "We have not yet begun to calculate their consequences: the passive adaptations, irrevocable rejections, naive beliefs, parallel lives, and the many forms of confrontation or consent, the many syntheses, surpassings, or returns, the many stubborn outbursts of invention, born of impacts and breaking . . . which compose the fluid, turbulent, stubborn, and possibly organized matter of our common destiny" (1997, 138). Glissant takes us beyond understanding creolization as merely a linguistic turn/term and embeds it in a universality from the underside, or universality seen through the eyes of the subaltern, one that demands we read pain alongside "pleasure." By this I mean that we do not only bear witness to the pain of enslavement, but we also bear witness to the ways in which the struggle to survive has forged the pleasures of cultural sharing and reinvention.

Drawing on Glissant and attempting to go beyond his early work on creolization, fellow Caribbeanists Jean Bernabé, Patrick Chamoiseau, and Raphaël Confiant, in their "In Praise of Creoleness," argue that "[c]reoleness is the *interactional or transactional aggregate* of Caribbean, European, African, Asian, and Levantine cultural elements, united on the same soil by the yoke of history" (1990, 891). Furthermore, they add: "Creoleness is an annihilation of false universalism, of monolingualism, and of purity. . . . We bend toward it [creoleness], enriched by all kinds of mistakes and confident of the necessity of accepting ourselves as complex. For complexity is the very principle of our identity" (892). In this manifesto of creolization, history, memory, and modernity are central to working out what can now be celebrated as the inventiveness of the peoples of the Americas; a peoples who must continually negotiate and "*invent the new cultural designs allowing for a relative cohabitation between them*" (Bernabé, Chamoiseau, Confiant, 893; emphasis mine). Attempting to figure out "new designs" for living with the pain and the pleasures of modernity, of which the Middle Passage and slavery are central components (both its memory and its history), is important to any project that seeks to offer complex analyses of the Americas. Making conceptual use of creolization might take us further down the road to understanding what any possible recovery from the repetitive traumas of slavery might look like. On these terms, the issue of creolization is, in effect, an issue of education. At issue is how education, in both its formal and informal manifestations, has been implicated in the making or the *re*invention of the Black/African body, effecting a transformation into an American (Black) body different from that of its African ancestor's.

Central to my argument is a reading of the Middle Passage and transatlantic slavery as the genesis of creolization in the Americas. I wonder: What might it mean to come to terms with the violent past of the Middle Passage as the grounds for inaugurating a creolized pedagogy for the Americas, one that concerns itself with an acknowledgment and working through of how intertwined our histories are? Such a pedagogy would necessarily be "a mixture of the acid and the sweet" as Derek Walcott (1974) puts it. Yet, I want to throw the net wider, to ask for a reconsideration of how we understand the Americas as an idea and a site for the working out of a sometimes dreadful experiment. Such an acknowledgment would necessitate a movement, from understanding cultural identities and practices as discreet to a working through that makes sense of the Americas as a site of multiple and conflictual renewals in the midst of violent, repetitive traumas—a traumatized, creolized space.

The importance of creolization to this issue of working through is its potential for enabling more complicated analyses of sameness and difference. The instability of identities, and the resulting possibilities of a host of identificatory moments, suggests positions and readings in excess of Afrocentric pedagogies and desires. But, more fundamentally, creolization offers a way of seeing defeat as more than lost/loss. It is a practice that may impede the transformation of defeat into (our) shame. Creolization as a concept and process highlights that life is not only lived out in mutuality, as contemporary multiculturalism suggests is possible, but also points to the aggressive ways in which life is lived and made (un)livable for some. Traumatic creolization therefore brings with it a necessity to think about both pleasure and pain: that we think of slavery as a past connection to Africa, a violent break with that continent, *and* a difficult condition of new possibilities. In this respect, creolization can offer us a way not only beyond the victim/hero binary, but also beyond the limits of shame and defeat. It requires that we think about the possibilities and turbulences of violent cultural sharing that produce new positions of identity and relation. Thus, as an educator rethinking the very project of education, I find in creolization a path of hope on which students may come to terms with the *diasporization* of Black communities as a site for the exploration of new possibilities.

THE AMBIGUITIES OF THE COUNTERNOVEL, OR, WHAT IS IT POSSIBLE TO TELL?

To further clarify the potential of creolization for working through the traumatic legacy of slavery, I turn to the literary imagination as a site for both rewriting and rereading the tensions involved in thinking about the politics of educational discourse and its still lingering thematics of elevation and racial uplift for Black people. Specifically, I am interested in neoslave narratives, narratives that might be termed "critical fictions" (Mariani 1991). Such narratives hold the intent of not only rewriting a unidimensional heroic resistance to slavery but also, and most importantly, writing slavery as a history of the everyday, forcing readers to confront the banality of evil. On these terms, critical fictions are difficult to come to terms with, particularly if one is seeking a self-affirming story. Although these works articulate pain and loss, they are not melancholic. On the contrary, these "fictions" allow for a certain kind of transformative working through of trauma, as this is instantiated by the narratives of "becoming" that their main characters often live through. Yet, students often find these works troubling and disturbing because they require that as readers students think critically about themselves in the process of engagement. Critical fictions complicate the us/them positions that students tend to bring to discussions of slavery, requiring them to confront the question of what it means to be human both in bondage and in positions of social authority. As Charles Johnson puts it, reading a critical work of fiction should challenge readers to think differently about their humanity and what it might mean (1990).

In a discussion of history and trauma, Cathy Caruth asks us to consider "what is ethical to tell?" (1991, 26). Her question is one that should be read as a kind of caution and, at the same time, as an opening that turns history into the question of ethical relations with the past, present, and future. On these terms, critical fictions representing and re-presenting slavery might be understood to provide a unique view of what it might mean to see the world "from the perspective of the species" in a postpositivist era (Wynter 1995, 8). In such moments, imaginative literature, then, is transformed in the hands of the subaltern who must make it work for more than it is generally assumed to work for. The critical fiction is multigenre: novel, history, literary criticism, social and cultural critique. The best of these literary works reinterpret and change social and psychic landscapes of Black (and all) humanity, making these novels into what Sylvia Wynter calls "counternovels" (1990, 459).

Such works address and redress the novel as a historical form and transmitter of history. As Toni Morrison states, in "The Site of Memory," the basis of the counternovel is founded on "trying to fill in the blanks that slave narratives left—to part the veil that was so frequently drawn, to implement the stories I have heard" (1990, 303). Such a practice becomes quite disturbing for Black students who encounter, in the details of these neoslave narratives, not only stories of heroics and affirmation but also stories of betrayal, pain, and contestation over community. On the surface, this is the stuff that shame can be made from. However, these critical fictions or counternovels do not rest easily here. They call into question the stability of historical knowledge and, ultimately, authoritative versions of humanity offered as conceptual ideals. The authors of these novels counter professionalized historical discourses, which depend upon and argue for the certainty, stability, and scienticity of knowing the past through the methods of history writing (De Certeau 1988). These counternovels are crucial and disturbing because they not only critique official histories but also question and refashion subaltern histories. Caruth states, "[t]he possibility of knowing history . . . is thus raised as a deeply ethical dilemma: the unremitting problem of *how not to betray the past*" (1996, 27). The counternovelists seek to bring to the writing of history the unveiling of deeply held contradictions concerning knowledge production. When they do so, students must consider the fragility of community. Such an encounter is often too difficult to bear when community authorizes in advance stories that are reductively black and white. But, sometimes, students also see these novels as having betrayed the past because of the ambivalent nature of the storytelling. History, for these novelists, then, is not an attempt to recover or recapture the past, but rather to pose the question, in the words of Michel De Certeau (1988), "what is comprehensible and what are the conditions of understanding?"

Writers such as Toni Morrison (*Beloved*), Sherley Anne Williams (*Dessa Rose*), and Paule Marshall (*Praisesong for the Widow*) do not respond to the past on the grounds of scientific rationality, but, instead, with texts of the imagination.[3] By unraveling the apparent objectivity of history, these writers demonstrate that history is not rational and scientific but an operational narrative that is constructed in the name of a given apparatus, usually the state (Deleuze and Guatarri 1987). Williams and Morrison, in particular, use hagiography and documents to construct their counternovels, in a reversal of the ways in which the archive is used to authenticate the practices of historiographic writing. Counternovelists write back to officially sanctioned histories, disturbing the popular acceptance of history as "truth." Counternovels, as neoslave narratives, might be read, then, as a response to the violence that is inflicted through various official histories, which claim to represent the past as an objective reporting of "evidence" concerning a given community. By so doing, they insist that readers (re)negotiate complex layers of identification and commonality.

Black counternovelists in their writing are thus attempting what Wynter poses as a required "closure," or bringing to end "the entire history of these past five hundred years" (1995, 6). What is crucial to note in this regard is that such closure must be accompanied by an acceptance of the Black creolized self (and therefore the condition of creolization). As Bernabé, Chamoiseau, and Confiant state, "there [can] be no interior vision without a preliminary self-acceptance. We could even go so far as to say that interior vision is a result of self-acceptance" (1990, 891). In this regard, Wynter argues for a need "to call into question the grounding premises from which the metaphysical discourses of all population groups, all human systems—including that of the West—are generated" (1990, 465). The counternovel therefore occupies a space that might be read as providing students with the tools to accomplish this, to deconstruct and simultaneously articulate the possibility of what it might mean to call a communally invested history into question.

However, it is often quite clear that many students are not ready for such a challenge. In my experience, many Black students find it quite difficult to accept that self and community are contested in these works, despite (or in spite of) their own everyday lived realities, which recognize the contestatory relations of both. Such interventions are extremely disturbing for most undergraduates who are required to reencounter history, the present, and the self. It might be said that, in the counternovel, students meet a different politicization of history. This is a politicization not structured on the basis of right or wrong, but on the tensions of what it is possible to tell. Such an encounter is "difficult knowledge" for students whose approach to history is often one of straightforward representation in which one is present in history or not. The question of *how* one is present is often not recognized until students encounter the communal representations of counternovels.

PAULE MARSHALL'S *PRAISESONG* AND
AN EDUCATION IN BEING CREOLE

In Paule Marshall's *Praisesong for the Widow,* coming to an interior self-acceptance is foregrounded as a difficult project for its main character, Avey Johnson. *Praisesong* stages the dilemma of how to live a life that recognizes blackness as integral to the Americas without jettisoning a history of oppression. On these terms, the novel highlights the ways in which interior creolized self-acceptance is a central feature of working through the aftermath of the Middle Passage and slavery, and finding one's place within the contexts of the Americas. In many ways then, the novel is a working out of the trauma of creolization. This trauma is marked by the devastating and lingering effects of the encounter, in particular between Europeans and Africans. In *Praisesong,* one of the most persistent effects of this encounter is the subordination of Black bodies and consequent attempts to live according to the standards of an imagined White populace. This desire to live on the terms of an imagined American-ness becomes one of the central problems for Avey and her husband, Jay (Jerome Johnson). In *Praisesong*'s narrative, traumatic creolization is imbricated in what has been Avey and Jay's pursuit of the impossible requirement to assimilate to a White version of what the "real" American is supposed to be. These issues come to a head as Jay Johnson becomes more formally educated and commodity minded. Marshall attempts to represent the ambivalence of formal education, which might offer an escape from difficult material conditions but might also be detrimental to one's sense of self.

> Hadn't she found it increasingly difficult as the years passed to think of herself as "Avey" or even "Avatara?" The woman to whom those names belonged had gone away, had been banished along with her feelings and passions to some far off place. . . . The names "Avey" and "Avatara" were those of someone no longer present, and she had become Avey Johnson even in her thoughts, a woman whose face, reflected in a window or mirror, she sometimes failed to recognize. (141; see also 48)

As a counternovel, *Praisesong* stages a working through of this instantiation of traumatic creolization to arrive at another practice, another form of creolization, one rooted in the art of making life livable in the Americas.

Time and memory are telescoped in the novel so that events take place over a span of two or three days, but readers encounter the life story of Avey Johnson and her ancestors. On the surface, *Praisesong for the Widow* appears to be a story about the attempt of a distressed Black, middle-class American woman (Avey) to come to terms with her widowhood and the many wasted years of accumulating wealth in marriage. Avey's life to this point, culminating in her cruise through the Caribbean, might be read as one emerging from a nightmare, only to enter a dream-world. The dreamworld aspects of the novel take place on Grenada and peak on an even smaller island, Carriacou. Marshall sends Avey on an archipelagic dream tour in which the alienated self is unraveled at its seams and reconstituted from the fragments of her repressed past.

A form of education is enacted on this voyage. Her cruise "visits" all the ports where her enslaved ancestors would have been dropped off. In this then, Avey's "cruise" is a (re)tracing and (re)visioning of the torturous journey that her ances-tors made to the Americas. While on her trip through the Caribbean, Avey be-comes possessed. Her body becomes the host for her Great-Aunt Cuney who taught her the story of the Ibos who walked back to Africa. In Avey's dreaming of her Aunt Cuney, Marshall reveals to the reader the role of mentorship, the shar-ing of knowledge and history that the older woman passes to Avey. (Avey had pre-viously repressed much of this information as the material conditions of her life changed in her transition to adulthood.) Avey's possession makes itself known through bodily symptoms, as if Aunt Cuney has invaded her. She has a pregnant bloated feeling: "The peculiar clogged and bloated feeling in her stomach and un-der her heart which could not be accounted for" (181). In her bloatedness, a sign of Avey's ancestors "speaking" to her, there are hints of an imminent rebirth.

This experience initially "forces" Avey to abandon the remainder of her trip. She disembarks from the cruise, seeking to return to her home in Manhattan. As she cannot book a flight until the following day, Avey is required to spend the night in a hotel in Grenada. That evening, her dreams and visions become so intense that she is forced to confront the return of a past that she has repressed. The next day finds Avey walking on an isolated beach where she encounters an old rum shop-keeper by the name of Lebert Joseph (a reference to the deity Legba, the god of communication and the crossroads). During their encounter, Lebert questions Avey about her people and her self:

"The Dama then . . .? The Juba . . .?"
She was about to shake her head again when she stopped herself.
"Juba? Did you say Juba?"
"Oui," he cried. "Juba! You knows it?"
"Yes . . . no . . . I mean I remember hearing or reading about it somewhere . . ."
The man's relief at this was so great it weakened him and he had to sit down.
"So you know, you remember Juba!" (177–178)

Eventually, Lebert shepherds her to Carriacou. On the journey, Avey encounters her repressed past, much like flashbacks from a traumatic experience. This encounter restages *in reverse* the trauma of the crossing of Avey's enslaved ancestors. In her "re-crossing," Marshall has Avey experience the bodily leaks of the Middle Passage:

> She vomited in long loud agonizing gushes . . . "*Bon,*" they murmured as the gouts of churned-up, liquefied food erupted repeatedly, staining for a moment the white spume on the waves below. "*Bon,*" they whispered at the loud hawking she was helpless to control and at the slime hanging in long tendrils from her mouth. "*Bon,*" at the stench . . . there followed an endless stream of fluids the color and consistency of a watery lime gelatin. "*Bon.*" The tears being forced from her eyes by the violence of each contraction mixed with the mucus streaming from her nose and the acids and bile off her raging stomach, and the church mothers, holding fast to her, murmured, "*Bon. Li bon, oui.*" (204–206)

In an effort to bring the language of the body to the unspeakable conditions of the Middle Passage, Aimé Césaire, the Martinican poet, scholar, and politician, refers to those who survived the crossing as having "slept in our shit . . . and . . . the vomit of the slave-ship" (1969, 67). Middle Passage literature, as exemplified by Marshall's novel, is populated with horrific descriptions of every bodily excretion imaginable. These bodily excretions or leaks are the leaks of history leaking into other histories. As Hayden White observes,

> the human body . . . can be defined in terms of the nature and quantity of the liquids it exudes. . . . Indeed, a whole spate of crucial taboos turns upon superstitions about the nature, quantity, and powers of bodily fluids. Perhaps it is not so much death as rather leakage of the body that is the source of ontological anxiety. What would normal tears, sweat, urine, feces, blood, snot, cerumen (earwax) consist of? The body leaks, even when it has not been perforated, punctured, or otherwise penetrated. This is the physico-ontological truth on which the fortunes, not only of the redemptive religions and the medical professions, but also and above all of the cosmetic industry, depend. The care, control, disposal, and cultivation of the body's effusions provide the basis of all "culture." (1995, 234)

Middle Passage literature's "historico-realist" and "magical" narratives are meant to shock us into the reality of the crossing and the dehumanization and suffering of the "African" body. As Césaire puts it, "For centuries [it has been] repeated that we are brute beast; that the human heart-beat stops at the gates of the black world" (67).

Avey's reenactment of the Middle Passage reverses this narrative, because she is not spewing the pain and fear of enslavement, as would have been the case with the "Africans" in the initial crossings. Instead, she is regurgitating the bile of discrimination and degradation in the Americas. Avey's vomit is the regurgitation of a life, and a history, that bears the traces of our involvement; her expelling of a repressed past implicates us in her suffering and in her becoming whole again. We (all readers) are implicated in her expelling of a repressed past, because Avey's journey is a symbolic expression of the collective repression of what slavery meant for the Americas. Her vomit is very different from Césaire's; her vomit is the beginning of her working through the trauma of creolization.

On Carriacou, Avey takes part in the "Beg Pardon," a ritual of ancestor reaffirmation, enacted once a year. The ancestors are honored as the living recall their ties to nation or tribe. The ritual is both a memory and a (re)invention of "Africa" in the Caribbean. Avey's past as it returns to her and us (all of us living in the Americas) troubles professional history writing, as the past becomes marked by our present repressions of what makes the Americas home to us all. Avey's new commitment is to spread the word of our collective interconnectedness:

> Her territory would be the street corners and front lawns in their small section of North White Plains. And the shopping mall and train station. As well the canyon streets and office buildings of Manhattan. She would haunt the entranceway of skyscrapers. And whenever she spotted one of them amid the crowd, those young, bright, fiercely articulate token few for whom her generation had worked the two and three jobs, she would stop them. As they rushed blindly in and out of the glacier buildings, unaware, unprotected, lacking memory and a necessary distance of mind (no mojo working for them!), she would stop them and before they could pull out of her grasp, tell them about the floor in Halsey Street and quote them the line from her namesake. (255)

Avey's commitment is not to share her story as cautionary tale, but as the possibility for renewal and recovery. To re-cite Nana, the matriarch from Julie Dash's film *Daughters of the Dust,* Avey's story of a revitalized creolization is made "from pieces of scrap and fragments"—that is, from recollections—fragments that give readers some sense of the (w)hole. Creolization requires that we think about how the various fragments of European domination, African, Aboriginal, and Asian retentions (at a minimum) constitute a new perspective of the subaltern in the Americas—in this case, especially, for Black Americans. This question of the whole is largely a question of interiority. To recall, as Bernabé, Chamoiseau, and Confiant suggest, creolization as a form of liberation is not possible without interior self-acceptance. Melanie Klein offers us a way to think creatively about the formation of such a "new" interior life.

In "Love, Guilt and Reparation" (1994) Klein addresses how the question of wholeness is important in another sense. She demonstrates how the relationship between the infant and the parent is, largely for the infant, one of hate, guilt, and love. As a child separates from the mother, there is a destruction and severing of emotional bonds in which the mother figures as a central site of sustenance, identification, and meaning. The work of reparation redirects the child's guilt for such destruction and poses the question of how to love. For this work to begin, one must acknowledge that something has been or would be destroyed. And, in Klein's view, the infant's work begins in the separation that enacts this destruction. Reparation becomes the means through which guilt is reduced and displaced, making the possibility to love possible at separation.

The implications of reparation are quite crucial to how the Middle Passage is imagined. I am suggesting that *Praisesong* is a novel about the making of reparation. In this, I mean to signal that New World Blacks can imagine themselves as a part of the West, and, in a manner of speaking, sever ties with Africa—while not producing guilt or denying its imaginative centrality. Reparation, in this sense, goes against the grain of centering Africa in one's historical identity and instead understands it as only one moment in the turbulent production or invention of a new self. A crucial element of this turbulence is the continued acknowledgment that separation from Africa was a violent rupture, or break. While this does not neatly fit the Kleinian model, it might be noted that separation is also often experienced by the child as a kind of violence. In the context of the forced separation of trans-Atlantic slavery, reparation is a much messier proposition. The history of slavery and the trans-Atlantic slave trade intervenes to make any return to Africa complex and contradictory, fraught with the failures, pleasures, and limitations of the (post)colonial and post-civil rights era, wherein the question of "the enemy" remains unsettled and unsettling. Reparation might be thought of as the way to resolve such ambivalent relations enacted through the re-finding of a lost object, in this case "Mother Africa," but it is also an approach to politically and conceptually engaging the failures and disappointments of a liberal modernity. This project of reparation is counter to the political desire for a reconnection with Africa as a privileged and angry rejection of Eurocentric culture, a culture that has continued the subordination of New World Black people. As a possibility of reparation, creolization takes the form of a self-actualization that suggests otherwise.

Marshall's counternovel demonstrates this for us. Because Avey does not return to Africa to work through the traumas of the Middle Passage, but instead does so in the Americas, Marshall signals that New World Black peoples must make reparation through their relation to the Americas and not merely to Africa. But I am also suggesting that Marshall stages the very dynamic that students encounter when they encounter the traumatized past of the Middle Passage and slavery: how to separate and what separation might mean? One way to answer these questions is to think about creolization. In facing a traumatized past, student responses of resistance might also be considered a trauma. It is the touch of the past within the present that makes their trauma a refusal of difficult knowledge. In this instance, creolization is difficult knowledge, as it requires all of us to think about the limits and possibilities of our current political arrangements as those arrangements echo historical violent memories.

The touch of the past within the present opens up spaces for thinking differently about the stakes of victimization and what those stakes might mean. In particular, taking seriously a relation to the Americas as home requires that Africa be placed in a different relation to New World blackness. Africa, then, might no longer signal a land or people conquered, defeated, and shamed, but might be understood as at least one source for the production of a new people. This way of thinking about New World blackness means that slavery is not merely signaled as a moment of defeat for Africans. Instead, slavery also becomes a site for signaling the various possibilities for living human life differently and for demonstrating the dynamism of human cultures in their violent and pleasurable encounters. In this regard, creolization challenges us to consider how to think beyond the framework that renders the narrative of slavery as one of defeat, rage, and shame. But creolization also allows us to consider what it might mean to resignify rage, shame, and defeat into mobilizing moments for the production of a new humanity. In this sense, history becomes a process of learning fraught with the risks of arriving at an elsewhere that cannot be known in advance.

To be a New World Black person is to be constituted through a set of ambivalences—ambivalences that are troublesome for discourses of modernity because they disrupt unproblematized ways of knowing and being. The Caribbean historian, literary scholar, and poet Kamau Brathwaite has argued that *Praisesong* and other works like it (including his own text, *The Arrivants: A New World Trilogy*) constitute "the literature of reconnection" (1993, 254)—reconnection, that is, with the severed "Mother Africa." I think that Brathwaite's insight is greatly enhanced by considering the significance of the making of reparation. The literature of reconnection is meant to convey the ways in which survival and resistance have forged a renewed and "unrepressed" reconnection with "Africa" for New World Blacks. But, I would add that the making of reparation, "which is an essential part of the ability to love" (Klein 1988, 342), brings to the fore the ways in which diasporic Blacks reconnect to "Africa" not on Afrocentric terms, but by loving their creolized selves first, by accepting the rupture and the consequent invention of the new self. Thus, for me, the capacity to make reparation is a healthy breaking away from the mother ("Mother Africa"), without fashioning a concomitant guilt (for separation) or destroying her in the process. On these terms, the mother can be loved as other. Loving the creolized self is what Afrocentrism cannot bear to tolerate, because the creolized self is a repudiation of purity, certainty, and knowability. Thus, Marshall has Avey recognize that "finally after all these decades [she had] finally made it across" (248), only when Avey is capable of making sense of what Aunt Cuney and the place Tatem (the place of Avey's childhood and her encounters with the ancestral knowledge of Cuney) mean for her sense of self.

In the case of *Praisesong,* the importance of the work of reparation is even more acute: The recovery of a historical consciousness of the main protagonist does not take place with a return to "Mother Africa," but instead with an acceptance of the creolized and syncretized life in the Americas. Thus, when Klein writes that "a good relation to ourselves is a condition for tolerance and wisdom towards others" (1988, 342) and that this ability to love has developed from those who meant much to us in the past (i.e., the mother and, in this case, "Mother Africa"), Avey's story is laid clear before us. Loving "Mother Africa" does not mean rejecting our new selves or repressing the violence that gave birth "to life upon these shores," as Robert Hayden puts it in his poem "Middle Passage" (1985, 48).

But Avey's story is also the story of many of the Black students in my courses; for, not only must they separate from "Mother Africa," but they must also separate from "Father Evil" and constitute a different relation to blackness and whiteness. In this, they are confronted with having to move beyond "the racism of skin" (Brennan 1997). The terms for this encounter are found in Avey's journey. She is only able to come to terms with herself—with being Avatara (the name she had lost long before the distance began to set in between her and Jay)—through a recognition of a past that she has repressed, but that is now revealed to be a source of love and possibility.[4] Avey's transfiguration, or transformation, is important, because it points to the ways in which the (im)possibility of representing the Middle Passage does not have to forgo the possibility of working through its trauma. The terrors of the Middle Passage "set going the drive to heal these imaginary injuries" (Marshall, 341), which, for Avey, are experienced as the psychic scars of the collective unconscious of being Black in the Americas. Students who must also heal from the psychic scars of slavery do not yet recognize that the condition of being in pain is also about how one remembers and makes use of slavery, not simply how one "forgets" it.

For Avey, this cruise is a journey "home," a return of sorts, but not a return to the ancient and towering Egyptian and Nubian images of a contemporary masculinist Afrocentrism. The trip Avey actually takes presents a critique and refutation of an Afrocentric rhetoric of the return to origins. Avey rediscovers herself and reconnects to a historical consciousness through her visit to Carriacou, rejecting a trip to Ghana. It is the experience of the visit that produces an Avey capable of thinking change not just for herself but also for others. Yet, at the same time, her trip is not suggestive of any easy notion of coming to share other cultural practices; it is not, in other words, simply a cosmopolitan sharing in Afro-Caribbean culture.[5] Instead, Avey must acknowledge repressed and returned cultural practices and work through what those practices will mean for the remainder of her life. In this fashion, Avey's idea of a kind of summer-camp remembrance for youth in Tatem is very much in keeping with the relationship between the break with the mother and the rebirth and maturity of the offspring. Avey is not suggesting a trip to Africa as the place from which a connection and respect for self might happen. Instead, she is placing the summer camp at what we might call in this case one of the originary sites of New World Black experience and history—Tatem. Her camp severs Africa from the remaking of Black identity but retains it in an interesting relation. The story of Tatem can make no sense without Africa; but trips to Africa can possibly make sense without the Tatems of the New World.

Marshall makes clear, thus, that a possible recovery from the trauma of the Middle Passage is not achieved by recrossing the Atlantic, or by some kind of gentle cultural sharing, but rather by attempting to create what we might call, following Wynter, *new forms of human life* in the Americas (Wynter 1995). Thus, Marshall does not continue to produce guilt through her narrative by suggesting that we abandon the Americas as a new "home"; rather, she offers us a way to make reparation—that is, a way to come to terms with the rupture that produced a Black diasporic population in the Americas. But, ultimately, she is concerned with all of the Americas and how to change them. That is, she challenges us to consider how to create a space for the possibility of ethical living, a living whereby our differences are not the basis upon which we are relegated to subordinate or dominating positions. In this sense, Avey is destined to become a "teacher" to children, investing promise and hope in youth. This is a pedagogical task that she could not accomplish until she had accepted her creole self.

Marshall's novel, then, is a making of reparation not only with an African past but with the bitter separation that New World Blacks experience in the Americas. In her reworking of the Middle Passage, neither as return nor recrossing, but as an inversion of the crossing and a restaging of the drop-off points, Marshall also signals the shift from "old country" to "new country." But, her reworking speaks to a much larger problematic; for, in her reworking, the Middle Passage is not just the habitus of death, suffering, and terror, it is also the painful (re)birth of something new and different. It is in this sense that the making of reparation is also important for it allows us—that is, New World Blacks—to come to terms with our love/hate relationship of the Americas. This is an interesting form of reparation—it is making reparation to ourselves, an acceptance of the ways in which the pain and the pleasures of history have intervened to invent us.

The Atlantic passage occupies the powerful imagery of the crossroads in African cosmology wherein danger is always near, but new and pleasurable possibilities also exist. Marshall, as novelist and teacher, in this instance, like her character Lebert Joseph, occupies the location of the god Shango or Legba, inciting communication and ushering in a talking cure as a working through of the trauma of the Middle Passage and slavery. Her fictive acts speak to the impossibility of discreet cultural practices and, instead, are lodged in an in-between space, one that acknowledges a lack of concern with origins in favor of a concern for making reparation with a creolized self.

CONCLUSION

The links between trauma, history, and memory are, for Black peoples who are the descendants of the enslaved, a tangle of belonging and not belonging, of losing and refinding the lost object, and of the work of making reparation. But, in occupying the space in between, what I have called elsewhere "can't return and never arriving" (Walcott 1996, 11), the descendants of the formerly enslaved recognize that, in the words of Césaire, "[t]he only thing in the world that's worth beginning:/The End of the World, no less" (1969, 60) is the only possibility for a new human species to emerge. A new form of human life becomes possible when creolization is understood as what makes the Americas possible. The shift in thinking is necessary if we are to teach with any credibility and achieve Wynter's claim that "what needs to be brought to an end is the entire history of these past five hundred years," in a manner that does not produce a new punishing humanism.

But a pedagogy of the Middle Passage and slavery must live with the possibility of risking failure. This risk might be the only possible response to such an overwhelming catastrophe. Yet, risking failure also means risking what Gayatri Spivak (1993) in another context calls "risking specialism." The irony is that slavery inaugurates a kind of "special status" for New World Blacks, but, to recover or approach anything we might dare call a cure from the repetition of this trauma, might mean risking specialism in the hopes for a new humanism. It is this risk that creolization enacts, asking us to face not our uniqueness, but our susceptibility to change both coercive and otherwise. It is painfully clear that the popular operations of history have not made available to Black students what it might mean to risk specialism. We need to figure out how to achieve a history that can doubt itself; this is what the counternovel asks us to consider. It is indeed a troubling question.

NOTES

I wish to thank the editors of the book for their guidance in helping me shape the focus of this chapter. Their help was instrumental in bringing forth what I had initially kept hidden.

1. Some of the texts taught in the courses are: Toni Morrison, *Beloved;* Charles Johnson, *Oxherding Tale;* Octavia Butler, *Kindred;* Paule Marshall, *Praisesong for the Widow;* Sherley Anne Williams, *Dessa Rose;* Ishmael Reed, *Flight To Canada;* Harriet Wilson, *Our Nig;* James Weldon Johnson, *Autobiography of An Ex-Coloured Man;* as well as the slave narratives of Frederick Douglass, Olaudah Equiano, and Harriet Jacobs.

2. For discussions of the term *neoslave narratives,* see the work of Bell, *The Afro-American Novel and Its Tradition,* and Morgenstern, "Mother's Milk and Sister's Blood: Trauma and the Neoslave Narrative."

3. In each of the novels listed, the central concern with slavery is one whereby the characters are faced with the problematics of what it means to be human in relation to a set of obstacles that are not only limited to slavery. Williams's *Dessa Rose* is an explicit engagement and response to William Styron's (1967) *The Confessions of Nat Turner* as well as an engagement with Black male historians (John Henrick Clarke, editor, 1968, *William Styron's Nat Turner: Ten Black Writers Respond*). Her project is explicitly a feminist one. Ishmael Reed's *Flight to Canada* offers us a reordering of time, history, and memory that complicates the story of slavery by making central to its telling a conversation between Black people and Native Americans. Morrison's *Beloved* writes slavery as a memory in a post-Civil War United States. While it is a memory that cannot be put behind, Morrison challenges us to think about the relationship between memory, the writing of history, and the creation of fiction from the fragment of a fact. In Morrison's case the reported incident concerning Margaret Garner, who was put on trial for murdering a child she would not allow to be returned to slavery, is the impetus for her text. Williams also makes use of a newspaper account to imagine a meeting between a Black woman who helped to lead a rebellion on a slave coffle and a White woman she read about, who used her farm as a sanctuary for escaping slaves. She wonders about and then explores in her text what might have occurred had those two women met.

Charles Johnson's *Oxherding Tale* reverses the role that White women played in the sexual economy of slavery. In this regard, the practice and evidence of miscegenation is everywhere bringing to the fore the possibilities of cultural sharing of various kinds. Johnson sees the possibility of a role for White women that is also one of sexual domination, but he also offers us a window into the more intimate confines of the pleasure and pain of domination and subordination. His text provokes us to think about cross-cultural resonances in numerous ways.

4. As Patrick Taylor points out, Avatara with the "A" at the end dropped, is "Avatar the Hindu term for incarnations of the deity Vishnu" (198), adding yet another layer of New World Black Creole culture—the Indian subcontinent.

5. For example, Avey's college-educated daughter Marion, a schoolteacher, was quite taken by the Afrocentric return and had tried to persuade her mother to take a trip to Ghana, or as a compromise, to Brazil. Similarly, Thomasina Moore, one of Avey's traveling companions on the cruise, is a good example of a multicultural cosmopolitan.

8

Loss in Present Terms:

Reading the Limits of Post-Dictatorship Argentina's National Conciliation

Mario Di Paolantonio

The nation binds affectively. It does so not (merely) through a facile dispensation of its force, but rather by attempting to answer the subject's desire for identification. Yet, for nations that stand on the crypt of past ontological violence(s), the answer (which always shelters an identity) dissipates before the apparition of the question: How are "we" responsible for the remains of the other?[1] Hence, a crucial moment in a post-trauma society occurs when a (revenant) question surfaces in the "we." Margarete Mitscherlich-Nielsen uncovers the heavy consequence of the question when she asks, "what does a [nation], a whole society, do when confronted with crimes of such a magnitude and the incalculable scope of its own part in them, crimes that are irreversible, for which there can never be 'appropriate' reparation?" (1989, 412). Any answer is impossible. For the question does not make an answer ever-finally-possible, rather it signals that behind the nation's stage a specter awaits to enter.[2] The impossible question—that, rather than seeking an answer, ends up unhinging the very binding of the nation—will inevitably haunt and challenge the binding collective's imaginary basis for sustaining its fantasies of identification across time and space. It is this collective's narcissistic desire for self-vindication and integrity that is rendered vulnerable by the apparition of this question.

The question, really, is about the possibility of mourning—about the possibility of a "society" ever being able to mourn not only the victims of its past violence but also the loss of an imaginary (ontological) identification: its appeal to the imagined "we." Freud spells out that mourning is not only "the reaction to the loss of a loved person" but also a response to the loss "of some abstraction which has taken the place of one, such as one's country, liberty, an ideal and so on" (1917, 252). In the case of national desires that have wielded violence against the other, the work of mourning necessarily involves confronting the horrible, while simultaneously parting with ontological ideals and a narcissistic self-enclosure. But this is a painfully heavy process that may trigger "an extraordinary dimunition" of (the group's) self-esteem (Freud 1917, 254). How can the "we" face and eventually learn to "come to terms" with its murderous history if it still finds the basis of its identification within the nation? How can a society mourn, Mitscherlich-Nielsen clarifies, "if it wishes to preserve a nationally viable continuity?" (1989, 411).

My discussion of these issues initially begins with quite an abstract discussion of how the return of the abject—of what has been discarded in the name of some ontological claim—disrupts the imaginary plenitude of a self-enclosed identity. First, I trace how this encounter with "loss" might allow for a move away from a narcissistic identification. Yet, I also focus on how this opening toward a beyond to the self-same is a threatening moment that calls up a series of artifices for assuaging the worrying erosion of identity. Through these concerns, I hope to prepare the way for a "reading" of the specific problematics involved in the politics of representation in post-dictatorship Argentina. In contrast to those claims that invoke the legal-representational means for "coming to terms with the past," I point to the *ethical limits* of using truth commissions and trials as a pedagogical means of telling and cultivating "a national narrative that can effectively foster discursive solidarity and liberal memory [after an episode of state-sanctioned violence]" (Osiel 1997, 283). My concern here is that representing the violent event through a national conciliatory lesson ultimately relies on a way of understanding without facing loss, without confronting how this event challenges, or exceeds, the symbolic economy of the "we." Paying attention to what remains on the way to reconciliation, to what is now abjected by the present desire to "come to terms with the past," points to an ethical practice that is able to read the limits of representation—where something that should be put into phrases cannot yet be phrased in the accepted terms. Finally, I attempt to expose the ethical necessity for bearing witness to an alien imperative, to a disavowed affect, which is resistant to the equivalence of symbolic exchange, or to anything that we might share in common. A perturbing yet potentially availing opening of the present boundaries of identity is afforded by bearing witness to an affect that exposes the loss of our terms. I end with some remarks on how we may draw an ethical lesson from the limits of translation; that is, on how our encounter with the problematics of translation, through our reading and writing, provokes the present to become vulnerable to another (forgotten) imperative.

I

Matters of Horror: The Return of the Abject

In "post-dirty war" Argentina, bodies "were found floating in the Rio de la Plata, or buried in mass graves, often with hands and heads cut off to prevent identification" (Speck 1987, 498). *"Look, here are his legs, severed, cut and torn but they are his legs or perhaps the legs of another. Don't be afraid"* (Agosin 1992). The image taunts us—we are afraid! The return of the "bits and pieces," the return of the inerasable trace, the cinders of the disappeared ignite a real fear of the uncontainable. The absence of a formal death ritual, the symbolic's utter failure in protecting and responding appropriately and singularly to death, incites a fear beyond words. Death can never be interchanged with the word *disappeared;* nor can "the disappeared" ever be equivalent to the word *death*. Because the remains (literally) move, because they cannot embody/contain themselves (in a name or body), they are a menace to the symbolic order. An uncanny encounter between life and death keeps washing away the shoreline where we stand. Their return from the sea calls into question the symbolic's grip on the fundamental boundaries that separate/protect/identify. How impossible is it to cease the haunting for a nation that does not have a tombstone and a name for each of its ontological victims? Here we fear the dread that ghosts translucently emblemize—that the dead (wronged) may never be able to die. Neither alive nor sufficiently (ever) dead it signals us to a nonspace, a gaping zone where we fall upon the pieces of the naked Real (cadaver). "[I]n that thing that no longer matches and therefore no longer signifies anything, I behold the breaking down of a world that has erased its borders: fainting away" (Kristeva 1982, 4). To see the corpse, according to Kristeva, "without God and outside of science [without the shelter of the symbolic], is the utmost of abjection" (1982, 4).

But allow me to trace the "power of this horror": the force of the return of what has been cast out. There is something about the abject, something about its ceaseless disturbance of "identity, system, order" that obliges the "we" to think its limit. "The abject does not cease challenging its master" (Kristeva 1982, 2). True, the abject is sickening, repulsive, and ultimately horrific, but a space—through its encounter—does open: A perturbing yet potentially availing decomposition of the common boundaries of identity is afforded/confronted by our *falling* through this opening. The "power of this horror" may force us to confront the unsealed (burial) grounds of the "we." Can it be that a significant encounter with the horror of the abject may (also) facilitate an internal struggle/confusion that requires a reexamination of any self-enclosed composition of identification? For after all, "abjection is . . . a kind of narcissistic crisis" (Kristeva 1982, 14). Given the violence(s) that have been committed through a narcissistic desire for (national) identification, the issue here is critical. Can it be that in the very encounter with its abject, the "we"[3] (necessarily) confronts the question—how are "we" responsible for the remains of the other? How are "we" responsible for what "we" have cast out? In what follows, I mobilize a particular reading of Kristeva's notion of the abject, one that traces the inevitable consequences it implies for what claims to possess a coherent and complete identity.

The expulsion of "impure" internal-matter affords the ego its hold on a stable identity: "I expel *myself,* I spit *myself* out, I abject *myself* within the same motion through which 'I' claim to establish *myself* " (Kristeva 1982, 3). But although the self (individual or national) attempts to define and seal its image against the "waste material" that has been abjected or expelled, the residue of "waste" is never wholly expunged. Ultimately, the abject returns as one's own corpse, as one's own (constant) waste that blurs the borders between being and nonbeing: "It is something rejected from which one does not part" (Kristeva 1982, 4). What has been cast out as the "not me" returns to haunt the ego with "one of those violent, dark revolts of being . . . [where] a vortex of summons and repulsion places the one haunted by it literally beside himself" (Kristeva 1982, 1). As symbolic exclusions fail to maintain any hard borders between "identity" and "waste," "outside" and "inside," the force of the abject pounds back through the ego's hold on a unified identity. Kristeva writes, "[t]he abject shatters the wall of repression and its judgments. It takes the ego back to its source on the abominable limits from which, in order to be, the ego has broken away—it assigns it a source in the non-ego, drive, and death. Abjection is a resurrection that has gone through death (of the ego). It is an alchemy that transforms death drive into a start of life, of new significance" (1982, 15).

The encounter with the abject induces not merely bewilderment and regression but an instance of disorganization and reorganization (transformation) that demands a type of death for the ego. We have come full circle. While the ego's claim to identity is established by "casting out" its "impurities," the remains that return demonstrate that the exclusionary imperative that upholds the ego's past in significance does not possess the sufficient fortitude to confine the abject. The double aspect of this uncanny encounter thoroughly decenters subjectivity. The abject—that which initially is cast out in order to define the border between "identity" and "waste matter"—proves ultimately *not* to be under the control of the ego. The ego fails to turn the abject into an object (relation): "The abject is not an object facing me, which I name or imagine . . . [t]he abject has only one quality of the object—that of being opposed to I" (Kristeva 1982, 1). Conversely, the double movement of the abject ends up *subjecting* the ego to "death" while (simultaneously) transforming the death drive into life—into significance.

Kristeva tells us that "the abject is the violence of mourning for an 'object' that has always already been lost" (1982, 15). Encounters with the abject bring the ego face-to-face with its own loss of control and cohesion: with *the limits of its narcissistic (self-enclosed) identification.* Because this loss signals an ongoing process that obliterates the ego's claim to master its own integration, it becomes the locus of its transformation. The ego is thus subjected to death—the uncontrollable (drive)—and dies (generates) into the subject of scission. Hence, exposure to the abject—to what is non-ego, drive, death (loss)—unleashes the perpetual destructuring or restructuring of subjectivity: It unleashes a subject of scission, a subject-in-process, whose post in the symbolic (the place of significance) is always subjected to pressures from the drives, to what is repressed and horrifying (the abject).

This reading of Kristeva's notion of the abject—albeit a truncated one—seems to afford a way of breaking out of a self-enclosed, narcissistic identification. What are the implications of this? Allow me to quickly reconsider the movement of the abject with some brief notes on how it informs a reading of Argentine national identity.

Nation and Abjection

As I have suggested previously, the desire for a self-enclosed identity attempts to limit or cast out what is construed as the "not-me," as the nonidentical other. Along these lines, we may read the sociosymbolic order of the Argentine nation as explicitly constructed on the repression and dejection (abjection) of what is considered other to its illusion of a self-same identity. According to Javier Torre and Adriana Zaffaroni, "even if we bracket its apogee under regimes of military dictatorships, . . . [i]ntolerance, elitism, denial of ideological plurality, visceral rejection of change and of anything 'different' . . . has a long tradition of prevalence in Argentina" (1989, 14). Throughout its history, Argentina has engaged in maniacal political rituals and tropes to ward off the perceived pollution and decay of its national body by "waste material." The Kristevan abject has an uncanny resonance here; for a concern with defilement by "waste matter," and hence "purgation," became historically literalized in Argentina. In the early part of this century, during a tense period of labor unrest, police records were issued describing immigrants as the "debris rejected by other countries, who take refuge in our bosom but constitute an exotic factor, not assimilable to our sociability" (Graziano 1992, 19). The defilement within the very "bosom" of the national body, by foreign bodies, would continue to be invoked throughout the twentieth century, with its most manic force (and, of course, consequences) unraveling during the military's "dirty war." Diana Taylor cites a pro-military political advertisement that was circulated days before the March 1976 coup that ushered in the period of systemic "disappearances." In an "emphatic tone" that addresses the imagined community through its guardians, a line from the ad reads: "Yes, your fight isn't easy, but knowing that you've got *truth on your side* makes it easier. Your war is *clean*" (Taylor 1997, 64, my emphasis). Indeed, a ceremonial purgation of the most horrific kind was staged in order to "cleanse" Argentina of what one of the architects of the terror described as "a minority [who] we do not consider Argentine . . . those whose ideas are contrary to [and, hence, defile] our Western, Christian civilization" (cited in Feitlowitz 1992, 41).[4] The Kristevan abject does not totalize that which has been expelled; for the abject is that which can never be totally restrained or ever fully cast out: It always returns. The literal return of the "disappeared," as undistinguished cadavers, made it impossible for the nation to imagine itself as sharing in a common ideal narrative or destiny. National identity was revealed to be historically tarnished by rituals of violence that literally "dismembered" its social body. As well, the Argentine illusion of being "superior," or "more Western" than the rest of Latin America could no longer hold currency amid the barbaric ruins of "torture centers," "concentration camps," "mass graves," and the "horror of testimonies" that were uncovered in the "post-dirty war" period. With the return of the repressed on its shoreline, Argentina did not just see the cadavers of its "disappeared" but also gawked at its national cadaver. Like all waste matter that reveals the inherent porousness of the body, the sight of corporeal (national) disintegration worryingly subjected the borders of an enclosed (illusory) identity to the force of the other, to a relentless relation to loss.

Being subjected to death means being subjected to a loss that is beyond the mastery of the ego: It is a reminder that the ego can neither master nor fulfill its narcissistic ideal. There is a suggestion here that this space of loss is a disturbing yet potentially transformative moment for significance, where the self-same boundaries of identity become subjected to what is beyond the control/will of the ego—to difference. As the Argentine cultural critic Fernando Reati acknowledges: "Violence fractures personal and collective identity and forces an ontological transformation where old assumptions [about a self-same identity] are shattered" (Reati 1989, 33). The ideal of a common national "we" gives way to the realization that the imagined nation is inevitably imperfect, violently fragmented, and riddled with difference. Facing the "uncanny strangeness" of the abject is a confrontation with the inherent loss at the core of national identity. Hence, the imaginary plenitude of a narcissistic national ego has to face that its ideals for fusion and mastery are always already lost. In this sense, violence forces the "we" to confront the content of its appeal to an imaginary community. Is it in this *apparently* self-reflexive moment that the "we" can ask: How are "we" responsible for the remains of the other? How are "we" responsible for what "we" have cast out?

In a later work, Kristeva notes that the shock of this "uncanny strangeness, . . . is a *destruction of the self* that may either remain as a psychotic *symptom* or fit in as an *opening* toward the new, as an attempt to tally with the incongruous" (1991, 188). The ceaseless movement of the abject does not guarantee self-reflexivity in the "we." For the encounter with the abject is a moment of horror, loss, and pain that takes us to the threshold between renewal and regression. It might be that such an encounter facilitates a reexamination of the complex process of identification. (And what this self-reflexive moment might be, or how it might take shape, is something that I will visit later in the chapter.) Yet, the return of the abject that provokes an "opening towards the new," toward an unnamable that cannot presently be, threatens a structure intent on denying its loss. Thus, it might equally signal, and this is the concern to which I now turn, a project that attempts to ward off the horror, loss, and pain in order to secure and protect its identity (symptom).

Assuaging Identity

Facing loss is a profoundly painful process that may unleash "an extraordinary diminution [of] self-regard, an impoverishment of [identity] on a grand scale" (Freud 1917, 254). Vamik Volkan notes that "it is more difficult to mourn loss and humiliation wrought by a human agency than to mourn a natural disaster since the former brings about a loss of self-esteem and group identity" (1996, 272). To the extent that group identity depends upon an ideal (sacred) narrative that avoids examining its claims to grandeur and unity, the encounter with events that signal the loss of self-integrity are bound to be painfully felt by those that identify with the group image. The reassertion of the abject, of what was rejected in the name of an imaginary unity (identity), reveals an unmendable tear in the group's narrative of itself: an exposure of the vulnerable seam of self-constitution. To the extent that the group's imaginary homogeneity/integrity (ego) becomes vulnerable to disintegration (loss), a state of anxiety takes hold. Anxiety, of course, is more frightening than fear; for whereas "fear requires a definite object of which to be afraid" (Freud 1920/1984, 282), the state of anxiety (as fright) lacks a definite object (Freud 1923/1984, 399). The very indeterminacy of this "object-less" state—which accentuates the gap, and threatens a dizzying assent into the Real—proves to be an intolerably baffling and painful moment for the group.

Speaking about post-Holocaust Germany, Alexander and Margarete Mitscherlich make an apparently similar claim: "[G]iving up the quasi-primary process of a commonly shared ego-ideal [an imaginary unity of identity] involved considerable anxiety for a great part of the population. Bewilderment and disorientation reigned" (Mitscherlich and Mitscherlich 1975, 23). Their thesis proposes, albeit in a hypostatized manner, that because a propensity toward anxiety accompanies the process of giving up the national "ego-ideal," a self-protective mechanism is put in place. In a later paper, which summarizes and reflects on the above work, Margarete Mitscherlich-Nielsen tells us that the ability to mourn implies that one "is able to part with *open eyes* not only from lost human objects but also from lost attitudes and thought patterns that governed [one's] life" (1989, 408, my emphasis). This is supplemented by her claim that only through this *conscious effort* will one be able to "think new thoughts, perceive new things, and alter one's behavior patterns" (1989, 408, my emphasis). Conversely, as post-Holocaust Germany severs the affective links to its immediate past, it ends up enclosed within an "autistic state" that can neither unravel its unconscious motivations nor imagine another possibility. To counter the dangers of this state, the Mitscherlichs' work proposes a restorative ego function that can slowly and painfully come to terms with the past. "Instead of irrationally rejecting existing conditions," the Mitscherlichs hold to the hopes of "an ego interested in self-correction [that] will learn to reflect step by step on the circumstances under which it developed" (1975, 253). Accordingly, then, "change for the better" can only come about when the "we" ends up "living more by the critical lights of the ego" (1975, 253). Through the work of the "critical-ego," which reveals a referent that grounds the process for coming to terms with the past, the elusive state of anxiety and its defense mechanisms can be mastered: For "one can 'radically overcome' only on the basis of knowledge firmly anchored in consciousness" (1975, 66).

The logic of this therapeutic model is stitched by a faith in the ego's ability to distinguish itself from the imaginary identifications that constitute it. This faith in the ego's autonomous strength must overlook how (as discussed previously through

Kristeva's abject) the ego is radically decentered and always already *subject to loss*. As well, the retrenchment of the ego as a "rational" structure that can uncover a "knowledge" apart from its imaginary identification does not consider how its very claims, how its production of knowledge, may function as *an adaptive protective-maintenance for its imaginary investments.* Whereas the Mitscherlichs' scheme proposes knowledge (the critical-ego function) as a neutral means for the "we" to overcome its narcissistic self-enclosure, recent work on historical trauma often points out how the practice of knowledge/remembering "may be a highly charged tool to legitimate new forms of reification" (Antze and Lambek 1996, xxv). Volkan speaks of historically traumatic events that become "chosen trauma," insofar as they are reworked/remembered by the group to relegitimate and reestablish its identity. He writes, "the event in question becomes psychologized, and the way the people share mental representations of it marks their [national] identity. . . . The affect it evokes is congruent with issues of shared identity rather than with the historical truth" (Volkan 1996, 270, 272). Hence, knowledge/representation as a means for coming to terms with the past, as a means to symbolically settle anxiety, can be hyper-cathected in such a way that it conforms to the group's imaginary captivation.

This suggests that, for the national "we," introspective knowledge is inevitably governed by retrospective "artifices" or "screen memories" that work to overcome those anxieties that threaten the fantasies of group identification. In this sense, knowledge is bound in terms of what simultaneously stabilizes the anxiety and the ontological basis of the "we." "Knowledge firmly anchored in consciousness" is thus subject to the imaginary frame of group identity: The power of knowledge hence lies in the confirmation/reflection of the group's identification. Far from "overcoming the self-protective forces of forgetting," the production of knowledge can work to cover over those contradictions that painfully expose the seams of the "we": the loss of an imaginary (ontological) identification. Thus, the use of knowledge as a means for coming to terms with the past—which implicitly or explicitly extols the restorative function of the ego—cannot be a means for the "we" to encounter the question: How are "we" responsible for the remains of the other? The ego's captivation within the imaginary does not afford such self-reflexivity; rather its encounter with the abject, with what was rejected in the name of its identity, sends it scurrying before the mirror to represent what it needs to see: that which will confirm its integrity and assuage the anxiety of fragmentation (loss).

II

The above explanatory and prepositional concerns prepare the way for what the remainder of this chapter will unravel within the specific problematics that have emerged in post-dictatorship Argentina. Namely, as the nation's narcissistic desire for self-vindication and integrity becomes vulnerable to the apparition of the horror of the abject, it turns to knowledge and away from the other: It turns away from what questions its ontological self-enclosure. Marcelo Suarez-Orozco points out that in post-dictatorship Argentina "what had been previously denied and forbidden returned in the form of an almost exaggerated need to read and talk about the atrocities committed. In post-dirty war Argentine folk speech this became known as 'the horror show' period" (Suarez-Orozco 1990, 370). This cathartic yet ambivalent moment produced a series of highly charged and conflictual discourses that exceeded the tightly drawn boundaries of "understanding," or of cognitively coming to terms with the past. Rather than constative representations of the event, the "horror show" mobilized a series of affective responses that exposed the contradictions and differences underlying national identity. Indeed, a "crisis of identity" gripped and questioned post-dictatorship Argentina with the limits of its being. As the Argentine literary critic Beatriz Sarlo wrote, "at the present time . . . the Argentine question is focused not only on how we were constituted but on why we broke apart" (Sarlo 1992, 240).

My argument, which unfolds through the example(s) of legal representation, is that the desire to preserve an ontological continuity—or in other words, "a nationally viable continuity"—assuaged the anxiety of this moment with an "objective" and technically "neutral" means for understanding the past. The issue is not simply with remembering or forgetting, but rather with *how* the nation remembers to forget, with how, that is, the representations of a remembered past serve an imaginary coherence that remains closed to the other. My focus will be with the legal means for coming to terms with the past, since the law, in Argentina, came to play a central role in screening the encounter with the abject.

Mourners-in-Waiting

"Coming to terms" with state-induced trauma has in our time increasingly involved the constitution of quasi-legal investigatory commissions, often known as "truth commissions," which may lead (in rare cases) to the prosecution of those deemed responsible.[5] These commissions are instituted in order to "know exactly what happened, to tell the truth, to face the facts" (Cohen 1995, 12). Why is the representation of "truth," "facts," and "knowledge" of critical importance to a post-trauma society? Moises Kijak and Maria Lucila Pelento, two Argentine psychoanalysts who have worked on the issue of social trauma and state sanctioned violence, have presented a paper entitled "Situaciones de Catastrofe Social" ("Social Catastrophic Situations").[6] The paper implies that the significance of our social bonds and personal lives are established and confirmed through the mourning of life lost (cited in Andersen 1993, 17). Their work acknowledges that because social significance depends on the ability to stretch backward into a society's ancestors and forward into future generations, all societies maintain their symbolic order through "common points of griefwork": namely, through the feasibility of locating and/or visiting the remains, and through the possibility of the mourner to express their grief in a social environment that can confirm and sustain it (cited in

Andersen 1993, 17). They point out that—because the violation of the mourning process would create a symbolic gap in the social continuity, throwing us into psychic chaos—the social order is expected to master and structure any situations that would threaten this organizing ritual. Thus the amorphous anxiety that takes hold on a social and personal scale when the mourning process is blocked—such as in wartime, or aviation/maritime/natural catastrophes—is usually rerouted through institutional mechanisms that offer official information/confirmation about the instant and circumstances of death. And, in those circumstances where it is impossible to retrieve the remains in order to conduct funeral services, there are commemorative events and monuments that publicly sanction the course of grief.

But in a society where "disappearances" were once part of the contraption of the state, the very material for the work of mourning is hauntingly displaced; indeed, the very networks of the social order become an elusive labyrinth that ensnares us in uncertainty. Because, in this instance, there is literally no *body* to confirm death—for there is no physical body or any body of the state to verify the death—an intolerable vagueness encircles those who search for the whereabouts of those who are supposed to be, according to the Argentine dictatorship's description of a "disappeared": "absent forever," "neither here nor there, neither past nor present."[7] Kijak and Pelento acknowledged that in post-trauma Argentina, mourners-in-waiting are still waiting. Without the remains, and with the only information consigning the disappeared to a limbo outside of life and death ("absent forever"), these mourners-in-waiting (relatives and friends of the disappeared) found themselves "submerged in a situation of panic, impotence, and abandonment. The need for survivors to try to accept the possible death of a loved one while holding out hope that he/she will reappear alive operated violently . . . [and] successively, exposing the psychic apparatus to a high degree of disintegration" (cited in Andersen 1993, 17). Another psychoanalyst who has commented on mourners-in-waiting in Argentina, Nancy Caro Hollander, similarly defines the possibility of mourning as depending on the possibility of knowing the certainty of death, in order to disengage from a person who no longer exists: "This kind of psychological separation, which allows gradual decathexsis from the lost object and the resumption of life in the present, is impossible when a family member has disappeared. That individual has simply vanished and no confirmation of his or her whereabouts is possible" (1992, 282). According to Hollander, the possibility of mourning as a ceremonial and significant passage, where one may come to accept the separateness and otherness of the dead, is arrested in a state of fear and guilt. To mourn under these nebulous conditions might be read (symbolically) as a kind of murder. But to go on with life with the image of a disappeared who is still alive but in prison brings about "acute anxiety and can result in the wish to free the victim from such suffering through the fantasy of his or her death, a wish that produces intolerable guilt feelings" (Hollander 1992, 283). In order to harness this objectless fear, the unknown and cryptic state of the disappeared must be reassembled in a topography that can confirm and sustain the "reality" of the fate of the loved and lost person; otherwise, paradoxically, there results (for both the present and the absent) a live entombment in some uncertain realm without any mark of separation/death (without a burial place).

A Liturgy of Facts

I want to suggest that a "truth commission" gains its appeal (although not officially recognized in this way) largely on its claims to "master" in a linear, quantitative, and rationally organized way this imponderable conception of death. In other words, by producing claims on "reality," it attempts to provide a type of "factual liturgy" for mourning the other—who can have no "proper" funerary rites, who does not have the political power to erect monuments or preserve spaces for its memories, who remains outside of the symbolic. But because the "factual liturgy" can only reinstate "reality"—that which allows us to separate/disengage from the past—via "knowledge," it inevitably comes to interpret and order the "facts," according to a regime of truth and rationality that functions to legitimate and reproduce the moral terms that justify our present. For a "truth commission" does not only have to enunciate the "facts" via the internal discursive conditions for presenting and verifying evidence. It must also *justify* the "facts" by references to moral claims that condone and make viable certain (often dominant) patterns of signifying the world.

The "truth commission's" moral oration proposes that "by knowing what happened, a nation is able to debate honestly why and how dreadful crimes came to be committed" (Neier, cited in Jelin 1994, 51). Further, it is proposed that this knowledge may "help reduce the likelihood of future abuses simply by publishing an accurate record of the violence, with the hope that a more knowledgeable citizenry will recognize and resist any sign of return to repressive rule" (Hayner 1994, 609). These claims imply that the appropriate outcome of this mourning process must unambiguously serve a pedagogical purpose for reestablishing the present's sense of itself: a moment for self-recovery, a national commemorative lesson for developing a "moral sensibility" that can immunize the present against forgetting and repeating the wrongs of the past. Thus, by exhuming and absorbing "knowledge" from a period that defies simple "comprehension," it not only attempts to sustain a rite of passage (integration into the symbolic) for those who have been "directly affected" by a period of disappearances, but it also attempts to mend the tears in the social order's desire to fill and master what is beyond its capacity to define/understand/reconcile. Hence, implicated in the "factual liturgy" are the configurations of the present's concern to exhume (to know the horror), in order to reconcile and expunge that which cannot be incorporated into the *body* of its *identity*.

In this therapeutic model, a *wrong* to the other is committed. The *wrong* is committed by the inappropriate application of a "factual strategy" (a descriptive) to a situation that demands a prescriptive response from the present.[8] The call of the other, which insistently demands the present keep its promise (to care for the remains, to honor the singularity of the dead) above all else, is subsumed within descriptive regimes of truth that seek to establish the "facts" and "reality" of the past. Whereas the memorial grounds of the "truth commission" aim to heal the wound that the trauma opened in the symbolic order by recording the "facts" or sublating that which is beyond its concerns, the immemorial call of the other demands a response prior to any "facts" or purposes. Thus, an endeavor that tries to make this prescription subject to a process of verification before a "truth tribunal" strips the exigencies of the obligation before us into a derivative discourse that must now deal with the authentication of its "truth" (descriptive) claims (Lyotard 1989, 283). The prescription, which comes and obligates before any "verification" that the addressee can have, is now drained of its commanding force: The "what ought to be" becomes condensed to the "what is," to the "what I know" and "what we are." This abolishes the critical asymmetrical relationship that must be maintained between the addressor (the other) and addressee in a plea (in a prescription), consequently allowing the addressee to hold the privileged position as it asks the other (the one making the plea) to descriptively prove itself (Lyotard 1989, 287). In other words, the strategies of representation with which the present comes to order (to know and legitimize) itself have swallowed the obligating force of the before and beyond itself.

What I am suggesting here is that, within this form of commemoration (the "factual liturgy"), the other has become an object of/for knowledge. This violates the ethical grounds upon which our relation to the other is possible. For an (ethical) encounter with the other requires an "epistemic lack" (a suspension of the descriptive regime) on the part of the addressee. For the addressor (of a prescription) must be before and beyond the present empire of knowledge, in order to be otherwise than the present/same. To consider the other as an object of/for knowledge is to smother the asymmetrical relationship within a finite (representable) set of "traits" or "features" that the present can instrumentally "utilize" for itself. Because the other is commemorated with facts, it readily becomes a means for satisfying the desire of the present: as a way of "coming to terms with the past" in order to assuage any anxiety; as a scheme for developing a "moral sensibility"; as an exercise (we will notice below) for confirming the present's "identity."

As the military's legitimacy disintegrated and democracy began to establish itself, the discourses circulating about how to "come to terms with the past" were replete with the need to "uncover knowledge" that could once and for all exorcise the "national spirit" of its ghosts (Donghi 1988, 14). The public rituals of producing "evidence"/"facts"/"truth" about the past trauma became a key means in the will to disinter "the true identity of the nation." As author Santiago Kovadloff claimed: "[T]he trial [of the junta] is founding the Republic. We, through this trial . . . are founding the Republic" (cited in Brysk 1995, 225 n. 81). The longing for the absent "imagined community" ("who we *really* are") was linked with the will to "know"; the "facts" and the "truth" that would be *gotten* from the traumatic event were ultimately to serve in separating and thus abjecting the "false" and "aberrant" values of Argentine identity from the "true" and "original" ones. Hence, the will to "come to terms with the past," to make the other into an object of knowledge, reveals the desire in the formation of a redeemed national identity: an opportunity for self-confirmation, a history lesson on "who *we* really are."

What, then, attracts and satiates the present's will to "know" is what appeases its identity. The foundational search for "*who* we really are" supplants the immemorial obligation that asks us to consider "*where* are the remains." The claim that moral reflection commence from the present's concern to recover/justify its identity (as being a Republic: "democratic"/"civilized"/"just") not only neutralizes the distinctive call of the prescriptive but produces a narrative that yearns for a unified and totalized "we." This, of course, smothers difference, reconciling or excluding the other, those who do not share in the harvest of the "we." In this sense, there is a very real danger that the present will "comprehend and englobe all possible reality; that nothing [will be] hidden, [that] no otherness [will] refuse to give itself up [to it]" (Critchley 1992, 6).

Yet every "understanding" that settles the trauma into the present's desire for presence owes its existence to its other, the remains that remain in every claim to re-presentation. In what follows I will give an account of how the representative strategy of the Argentine "truth commission" (CONADEP) and "the trial of the junta" were mainly informed and motivated by the protocols for national reconciliation. My concern for discussing the limits of these representative strategies does not gesture toward rectifying the "truth" through mending the commission's and the law's capacity for distribution or retribution. Rather, my regards are with the remains that remain other to this means for "coming to terms with the past." Thus, in contrast to any "abiding lesson" for reconciliation, *it is possible and necessary to develop an ethical reading practice* that interrupts the immanence in any claims to representing "truth" and "justice."

The Limits of the CONADEP

In a paper entitled "The Politics of Measurement: The Contested Count of the Disappeared in Argentina," Alison Brysk provides an analysis of how the "politics of measurement" structured the CONADEP's mandate and final report. Her work makes evident that the "facts"—specifically the aggregate body counts meant to evidence the extent of the state-sanctioned violence—that were collected by the "truth commission" and subsequently became the monumental account of the disappeared were "politically framed, limited, and deployed" (1994, 692). As she states at the start of her paper, "(b)eyond its historical/interpretive function, investigation often catalyzes a politics of information, in which various political forces in the subject state use the figures to argue their own . . . policies" (Brysk 1994, 677–678). The CONADEP, which gathered the testimonies and accounts of witnesses, relatives of the missing, and survivors, was the most comprehensive endeavor to produce "knowledge" of the military's "dirty war." Although the commission's time limit allowed it to file and write up only about 30 percent of the material received during its nine-month appointment, it published a multivolume report with a list of the documented disappeared that put the preliminary figure at 8,960. Another significant limitation of the CONADEP's report on the extent of the state-sanctioned violence is its inability to add to its record the evidence of "disappearances" that gradually surfaced from poor and isolated areas. As late as 1988, "scattered and new reports of disappearances," which had taken place during the last dictatorship, were uncovered in different rural locations. This new evidence, however, did not alter the official figure. Adding to this is the exclusion of reports emanating from grassroots activists who, through their work in poor urban neighborhoods, provided "local figures which far exceeded those officially registered for their area" (Brysk 1994, 683).[9] Because of the limitations and the obvious fact that "the predominant tactic of disappearance is inherently difficult to document and even to define," Brysk cautions that "there is no clear way to determine definitely how many people disappeared permanently in Argentina or who they were" (1994, 681, 682).

Yet despite these limitations on knowing the "final" and "true" figures, "the 1984 CONADEP report has been widely adopted by researchers, foreign observers, and domestic political forces in Argentina" as the final and verifiable account (Brysk 1994, 683).[10] The deeply rooted positivist belief that numbers are a form less subject to "biased" influences than other sources of representation provided a powerful technology for informing and confirming a narrative of the events, which could "heal" and "reconcile" the exposed gaps in the "imagined community." In an interesting play of logic, the figure became a semantically powerful mechanism that was often cited by those discourses that insisted on "redeeming" the nation. The CONADEP figure was large enough to justify the broad reforms needed to legitimize a post-dictatorship "redeemed" national identity, but "it was not on the same scale as other mass [state-sanctioned] murders," which could demand an exposure and dislodging of those national rhetorical tropes, norms, and conventions that sanctioned the violence (Brysk 1994, 686).[11] The period of disappearances was thus to be viewed as an aberration from the "national character" that needed only to "deal" with these "criminals" and reclaim itself. The exorcism that aimed at "healing" the "fragmented nation" attempted to police the narrative borders around a numerical figure (and therefore did not include the disproportionate disappearances amongst rural and urban poor), so as to reconcile or expunge that which threatened to remind the nation of its remains. We should think of this mechanism of exclusion as a technology for the *reproduction and relegitimation* of a coherent (national) identity.

The Law, National Reconciliation, and Its Limits

In perhaps a more spectacular manner, the trial of the military dictatorship attempted to maintain and extend this mechanism for defending the nation against the loss of its imaginary coherence. Allow me to contextualize the desire for reconciliation that became expressed and motivated by the apparently "neutral" mechanism of the law.

In "post-dirty war" Argentina, grassroots human rights groups and many cultural workers endeavored to launch a general effort to probe the social milieu that made the extensive state violence possible. One of the most riveting issues that emerged from this process was the recognition that the "dirty war" was fueled by and based on the nation's obsessive drive to erect a unified and transparent "we" that would not tolerate any sense of otherness (Masiello 1987). For those seeking to work for a society where such horror would *"Nunca Mas"* (Never Again) take place, it became urgent to recognize the other—as that which has been excluded from the "we"—and the ways in which one is implicated in relation to this ineliminable otherness.[12] Obviously this would involve an ongoing process that would seek to expose and dislodge those national rhetorical tropes, norms, and conventions that sanctioned the violent episode. Javier Torre and Adriana Zaffaroni gesture toward such an expansive and ongoing process when they write:

> the authoritarian politics of the recent military governments in Argentina was not a meteorite in the midst of a sky of freedom or a sudden and unilateral decision by a small group of Fascist conspirators. Rather, it was simply the most recent and acute cultural transformation of the intolerance that enjoys a long tradition in Argentina. If this is true, the passage to democracy, as much in the cultural sphere as in others, will require an attempt at comprehension and political imagination that go far beyond institutional recuperation. (1989, 16)

But precisely because the recognition of the other is bound to open up a space for dislodging the fixed and bounded assumptions of national identity, intense effort to confine this process took place. Proposing that the fragile new democracy would not endure such an ordeal, an "official" human rights strategy moved to bracket any discussion of the authoritarian ethos that lurks within Argentine identity in favor of reestablishing the "rule of law" (Brysk 1995, 67).[13] To this end, the official rights strategy answered the "crisis of identity" that hovered over "post-dirty war" Argentina by framing the discussion within the questions and protocols for how the legal norms of the nation can come to terms with the past. The liturgical-performative power of this mechanism for bracketing the contradictions and differences of the imagined community is implicitly noted by Luis Roniger and Mario Sznajder, who write: "the process [the trial] itself would be signaled by its high visibility and the ritual, symbolic representation of the supremacy of the rule of law. Accordingly, it was common to find in reports of the trials detailed descriptions of their liturgic, ritual and ceremonial aspects; they were depicted as a 'moral *mise-en-scene*' or as a 'dramatization of the ethical conflict involving the whole community'" (Roniger and Sznajder 1998, 143). Thus, through the protocols of the law, the fragmented community could ceremonially redeem itself.

Of course the initiation of the trial was and should be broadly welcomed: However, an excessive legalism encroached upon public debate in Argentina, draining the redemocratization process of its broader political imagination while entrenching a facile, institutionally contained ritual for "coming to terms with the past." The legal frames for "remembering the past" tended to feed into the national longing for a reverential precept that would synthesize the exposed differences, subduing them within an all-encompassing resolution. The "treacherous assault on the law" was invoked repeatedly as the explanation for what promoted the "dirty war": The law was the victim of "terrorisms" from both the left and from the right.[14] Although caught in the middle of the senseless violence, the law inevitably endured and was able to once again establish normalcy to the nation. For most Argentines who remained docile during the horrors committed by the state, the presentation of the law as being "caught in the middle," as being unable to convince "the *two* violent groups" of its decency, provided powerful tropes for identification. For it bespoke their desires to appear righteous while being absolved of any implications with this period: "Our" morals, it could be claimed, were held hostage by rival extremists who were completely irrational. Viewing the "dirty war" as a period of "barbarism and chaos" that was the result of a "minority" of people brought about the need to now redeem the "true" identity of the nation.

Invoking the trial within the continuum of the nation's "founding norms" thus provides the national imaginary with a means of bracketing its authoritarian ethos as a "regretful and aberrant period" that can now be overcome by (affectively) remembering its "true"/"original" values in the law. This reverence for the law, as the "founding" terrain of the nation, shelters the national imaginary from the recognition that an authoritarian legacy has often accompanied the populist desires and claims of Argentine identity:[15] The violent past is now not only presented as an abhorrent event, but it is also displayed as an ephemeral episode—one that is aberrant to the Argentine community. Hence, this reverence assuages the necessary introspection and possible disruption of identity that, according to Gottfried Appy, would come from admitting that "these [authoritarian] ideals had been loved by us, although they were also hated, and that they are still parts of ourselves" (cited in Wangh 1996, 296). He continues, "[t]o declare them [these authoritarian ideals] only as being 'out there' [or as an aberrant past episode] denies our identification with them. . . . Only after this sort of recognition of an inner conflict can a renewed separation from them take place" (cited in Wangh 1996, 296). Appy's concern, although referring to post-war Germany, is also relevant to Argentina since it points to what Mitscherlich-Nielsen describes as "a particular kind of memory work [that] is needed [in order] to develop the ability to mourn . . . not only for the loss of persons, but also for [national] ideals and narcissistic self-love"; this would be "less a matter of recalling facts and events," than of remembering and reconsidering the national community through its "ways of behaving, value judgments, feelings, and fantasies" (1989, 407).[16]

However, the desire for national self-vindication and integrity can avoid its disturbing implications with the now abject authoritarian ideals by drawing on the symbolic blanket of the law. By promising a "neutral" means for producing knowledge of the past, the trial—symbolically—*attempts* to contain the anxieties that are riddling the nation. Following Foucault's claims on the production of discourse, we can see the trial as attempting to produce knowledge that "is at once controlled, selected, organized and redistributed according to a number of procedures whose role is to avert its powers and its dangers, to master the unpredictable event" (cited in Gaete 1993, 52). By bracketing the discussion within legal (supposedly "technically neutral") questions and protocols, the possibilities of recognizing the other—both the victims and the now abject authoritarian ideals—can be more or less framed so as to avoid those "dangerous" and "unpredictable" instances that would contradict the national imaginary and consequently problematize the process for reconciliation.[17] Indeed, the legal strategy hinged on the conciliatory assumption that "trials for human rights violations committed in the past are great occasions for social deliberation and for collective examination of the moral values underlying public institutions" (Nino 1996, 131). To frame the legal strategy in this way is clearly to grant a privileged, determining role to what brings about "social deliberation," to what continues the nation's "institutions," rather than to what problematizes, contradicts, or ruptures their vocabulary and cohesion. Since this is a mechanism for assuaging the "crisis of identity" through social and institutional reconciliation, we need to ask: What are the limits to this "great occasion"? What remains other to the "deliberation"? Who fails to speak in the moral voice of the "we"? What is now abject?

The Remains of Reconciliation

The belief that the "dirty war" was an aberrant episode that was mostly propagated by "a few extremists" tacitly sanctioned the need to reclaim the "true" identity of the nation. To this end, the law becomes the unquestionable principle or unimpeachable terrain upon which Argentina can establish its (moral) sense of itself. As public prosecutor Julio Cesar Strassera claimed, "this trial could enable the Argentine people to recover their self-esteem and their trust in the values on the basis of which they had constituted themselves as a nation" (Amnesty 1987, 43). Thus, at the core of the nation, is the "original position" of law, a unifying and essential ground where "we" dwell in a situation of complete equality and sameness. To bring the incomprehensible before the law thus provides a retrospective lesson on the founding values of the nation. This retrospective artifice had an incredible force in the "official narrativization" of the "dirty war." For, it was from behind this "veil of ignorance" that the law would provide a record that could "distinguish dispassionately the legitimate aims of the antiterrorist campaign from the illegitimate means adopted for its realization" (Osiel 1986, 155). Working from these presumptions, there seemed to be no exegetical (legal) way for the trial to read the whole "antiterrorist campaign" as being itself wholly "illegitimate" and a means to institutionalize class war by the state; this would have breached the discursive framework ushered in by the process of national reconciliation. Hence, the trial "steered clear of judging the legitimacy of the junta as a government or its deci-

sion to combat subversion, [the court] confined itself to judging the defendants for
the commission of well established crimes and struggled to make the proceeding
resemble an average criminal trial" (Speck 1987, 494).[18]

Because the boundaries within which the criminal case must organize its "facts"
assume that behind the "veil of ignorance" all are equal, that the social differences
of race, class, gender, and religion are unimportant, the trial produced a decidedly
disconnected and individualized narrative of the event. As Carina Perelli observes,
"the collective dimension of repression tended to be lost in this bleak recitation of
individual pain and despair" (1992, 435). Because the extensive documentation of
kidnappings, murders, and torture were presented without any deliberate attempt at
formulating the connections between them, a despairingly discrete picture was
drawn of a process that was ultimately methodical/dogmatic in its selection of victims. In not considering the broader social milieu, "the trial failed to provide an out-
let for the feeling of personal inadequacy, anger, and frustration repressed during the
years of extreme individualization, under the culture of fear" (Perelli 1992, 435).
The trial was particularly vexing, for although there was evidence that the military
was involved in a specific "cleansing" policy against different groups (against inde-
pendent labor unions, social movements, certain religious groups, and other political "undesirables"), the issue of "genocide" was excluded from the criminal case. In
proposing to be drawing on the assurance of a technically "neutral" mechanism for
coming to terms with the past, to be hence administering the unifying and original
position of law "blindly" and with an even measure against all the *individuals* who
had violated it, the trial could/would not seriously probe the extensive "social or
ideological" dimensions that were imbricated with the "criminal case."

Thus the very confines within which the criminal law produces its knowledge
and judgments, the very means of uncovering "evidence" through discontinuous
accounts (with disregard for historical-ideological motivations), secured for the
"nation" an artifice for assuaging those "dangerous" and "unpredictable" moments
that threatened the conciliatory process. Hence, we see the "prosecution failing to
pursue the periodic suggestions of anti-Semitism among the torturers, offered spon-
taneously at the trial by several prosecution witnesses" (Osiel 1986, 163, n. 64).
Mark Osiel notes that "the fear that the trial might come to be labeled and dis-
credited as 'the work of the Jews' may have restrained the prosecutor from such
questions" (1986, 163, n. 64). Because anti-Semitism was (and continues to be) another facet of the "ideology" prevailing within the officer corps, any implication
about its motivating the "crimes" of the "antiterrorist campaign" had to be disregarded in favor of the prudential consideration for consolidation. Moreover, since
the exemplary trial was implicitly producing a narrative that was attempting to stabilize "the crisis of identity," the issue of anti-Semitism, which called up a long
history of national fragmentation, threatened to remind the "nation" of its excluded others.[19] It is important to note, then, that the way that the trial's narrative
framed the 1976–1983 period as an aberrant and isolated episode of state violence
dehistoricizes the authoritarian ethos that has been entrenched in Argentine soci-

ety since its inception. Jaime Malamud-Goti reaffirms this: "Both official and popular versions of recent Argentine history suggest that state sponsored human rights violations were the results of the military regime's strategy following the 1976 takeover. However, situating the massive abuses between March '76 and December '83, when the military was formally in power, is a misguid[ed] version of history" (1995, 166).

Differends before the Law: Reading the Other

When we consider that many of the disappeared are still and probably will forever be undocumented, that their remains REMAIN unburied, we realize that no legal endeavor (whether it be exemplary, prudential, or retributive) can ever really do justice to this event. Even if the trial could be staged so that it would not be marred by the presumptions and constraints for national reconciliation, even under the most "objective" procedures, justice would still be lacking. For the unrepresentability of this violent "nondeath" is such that it necessitates a permanent deferral of any coherent and integrated conclusions, because it also raises its incommensurable relation with the current conventions of any given society. Legal representation is limited here not only because it operates inevitably from the present norms and desires for order and closure, but because its terms "run out" when it wants to condemn or punish something as imponderable as mass murder and torture. Hence, to call the violence of disappearances "criminal" and, thus, a "problem" that can be settled or repaired through litigation risks diminishing its incommensurability. The extreme suffering involved and the wholly odious acts of mass murder and torture completely disrupt our self-understanding and the understanding of our immediate social world. Truly, then, we are confronted with something that calls us beyond our present terms, beyond our moral and legal ways of speaking. But since this nonunderstanding provides no evidence in a court of law, the sense in which the event is incommensurable with our present categories remains unrepresentable.

This unrepresentable (abject) instance threatens any structure intent on denying its loss to another possibility. If the trial was a means of privileging national reconciliation so as to avoid the self-reflective concern for the other and the possible disruption of national identity, this gap that breaks the continuity of national institutions, norms, and ways of speaking is a threatening moment that must be filled over with what "we" understand. The discrepancies and limits of the trial must be covered over with claims that console the desire for "a national narrative that can effectively foster discursive solidarity" (Osiel 1997, 283). Rather than think through the ways in which the gaps and ruptures in the trial shatter, confront, and invoke the nation/state beyond its self-understanding, recent scholarship, which explicitly reflects upon the trial of the military in Argentina (Nino 1996, Osiel 1997), has tended to emphasize the pedagogical benefits of retelling the past within the vocabulary of the rule of law. Clearly aware of the limits of an exemplary trial, Osiel nevertheless proposes that "the orchestration of criminal trials for pedagogic purposes—such as the transformation of a society's collective memory—is not inherently misguided or morally indefensible. The defensibility of the practice depends on the defensibility of the lessons being taught—that is, on the liberal nature of the stories being told" (1997, 65). As long as the trial stages an opportunity to repair and continue the telling of the "liberal tradition," the limits of this form of representation can be justified. Osiel continues, "whether show trials are defensible depends on what the state intends to show and how it will show it. Liberal show trials are ones self-consciously designed to show the merits of liberal morality and to do so in ways consistent with its very requirements" (1997, 65). With this criterion in mind, he informs us that "in recounting the tale of the crimes the Juntas had ordered, the obedience of their underlings, and the suffering of their victims, the military trials in Argentina told such liberal stories" (1997, 73).

This justification for the trial seems rather incapable of acknowledging those instances of excess, those other dejected ways of speaking that, in their very "incapacity" to provide "evidence," signal to what cannot be defined or discoursed within the vocabulary of liberal morality, or within legal protocol. To justify the commemorative lesson of the trial within the principles of institutional coherence, and within the grounds of liberal morality, necessarily totalizes one memory of the past over those excluded from the trial's performativity. Hence, those instances that contradict or complicate the desire to bracket the Argentine authoritarian ethos as an aberrant period are smothered by the conciliatory memory of "our" true and founding values in the law—"our" (imagined) liberal institutions, traditions, and norms. The other remains unrepresented and unrepresentable by a "truth commission" or trial (by a form of collective memory) that is celebrated for its pedagogical ability to tell "a larger story about the community, its history, and its evolving normative [liberal] commitments" (Osiel 1997, 73). And yet the other remains (returns). For, quite obviously, the fragments and traces that unwork the certainties of a narrative that fosters discursive solidarity and liberal norms can always be "read" through what remains. But this "reading" is never a straightforward one. Rather, it is stirred (affected) by a recognition of the limits and the ruptures that reemerge from what was cast out. This "reading" involves one in a process of "bearing witness" to those enunciations that cannot be represented by what "we" understand. Thus, when we "read" a narrative that claims to have disclosed a "truth" that "feeds public discussion and generates a collective consciousness" (Nino 1996, 147), or when we "read" the trial as a mnemonic device for staging the principles of liberal morality (Osiel 1997), we realize that a *wrong* has been committed against those (non)utterances that unwork the certainties of our vocabulary. In realizing that a *wrong* has been committed, that a narrative that aspires to condense the multiple discrepancies and (non)utterances into any "discursive solidarity," into any unifying project, does *violence* to the other, we are summoned or stirred by the specter of "justice."

Lyotard's work is quite useful in helping us develop a sense of what it means to "read" the ruptures and gaps, of what it means to "bear witness" to that which has not been given its "say in court." In the claims that "[i]ndividuals who seek to inject their personal stories into the public realm—stories at odds with currently prevailing official narratives—are free to invoke the law to that end" (Osiel 1997, 263), Lyotard would detect what he calls a *differend:* "As distinguished from a litigation, a *differend* would be a case of conflict between (at least) two parties, that cannot be equitably resolved for lack of a rule of judgment applicable to both arguments" (Lyotard 1988, xi). His project points to the ethical work of exposing the implicit instability in what has been repressed or supposedly resolved by representation, by what has become knowledge. For a *differend* occurs when the representational conflict/complexity in two different ways of speaking is settled by the assumption that their terms are interchangeable. Under such a consolatory resolution, under the belief of an economy that expunges any consideration of difference or power relations in favor of the equivalence of symbolic exchange, the loss inevitably suffered by the other in such an exchange or substitution cannot be signified or argued within the regimen of the language that is reputedly to "settle" the conflict. As we have seen, the discursive regulations of the trial/legal strategy were such that only one kind of voice, the "we" of the national reconciliation project, could be signified as "legitimate." The other—that which interrupts the conciliatory narrative—"is divested of the means to argue and becomes for that reason a victim" (Lyotard 1988, 9). Subsumed under the rule of judgment or exchange imposed by the "we," the other is discarded and rendered unrepresentable. The ability to "read" the *differend* would activate and bear witness to this *wrong,* to what has been smothered or purportedly resolved within the claims of the trial. By drawing attention to the excess/dejection of what is to be said, over what can presently be settled by any "official narrative," we bear witness to the *incommensurability* that exists between the "remains" of the other and the discursive confines of the trial. Thus, the "reading" of the *differend* opens onto the limits and gaps inherent in any representational system, and so demands the respect for idioms that do not yet exist (Lyotard 1988, 13). In other words, the *differend* summons us to respect that which cannot be symbolically exchanged or substituted, that which is unrepresentable and therefore not related to our *present* faculty of understanding, to our *present* ways of speaking. This is not a call to establish an unpresentable reality, but to *"read" the unpresentability of the unpresentable* as a means to recall the limits of our "self-subsistent present." This widens the ruptures and gaps in what is presentable in order to expose the norms and conventions of the present as NOT a closed totality. In the context of "post-dirty war" Argentina, where the "official narratives" and the ensuing pardons effectively seal off the past event from the present, the need to disrupt the self-enclosure of the present is a pressing matter.

III

The Obligation to the Unsaid: Bearing the Weight of an Affliction

I have proposed that the legal narrative strategy of the post-dictatorship (transition) period in Argentina expressed the desire to reconcile and mend the fragmented imaginary "we" in the face of imponderable violence. In its attempts to respond to this liminal state and so limit its own loss of legitimacy, the nation (primarily through the institution of law) transcribes the "incomprehensible" into a legal narrative that offers an official representation of the "facts," and eventually a verdict that can provide some sense of closure. By exhuming and absorbing "knowledge" from a period that defies any simple "comprehension," it is hoped that a rite of passage (a mourning ritual/"factual liturgy") can be performed on behalf of the imaginary "we," and simultaneously for those who have been "directly affected" by the evasions of a period of disappearances. The performative power of this rite of passage lies in its ability to reinstate a way of understanding (through the language of rights) that ultimately makes sense of the event through the continuity of "our" terms. Osiel writes,

> The liberal state can thus provide an institutional mechanism for mourning not only the deprivation of a victim's abstract moral rights, but the fully-developed life she might have lived in exercising those rights. In so doing, criminal law contributes significantly to the social solidarity that is based on shared commitment to liberal principles of mutual respect and concern among individuals. This communal mourning is one important role that collective memory may legitimately play in a liberal society, or within a society aspiring to liberalize itself. (1997, 68)

By writing the event through the evidential rules of relevance and admissibility that pertain to the institution of law, a "collective" healing process (also read, a "liberalizing process") is proposed.

However, this process for reconciliation has been constantly interrupted (during and after the trials) by the unending rage and lament of the Mothers of the Plaza de Mayo. Still, every week on Thursdays at 3:30 in the afternoon, the Mothers assemble and publicly display their grief in the political and economic center of the country—the Plaza de Mayo. Their refusal to weave themselves within the process of reconciliation, their persistent public displays of rage and suffering tear at the symbolic fabric of the "we." The assurance of "our" coming to terms with past ontological violence dissipates before the apparition of a rage and suffering that refuses to settle in any present reparation. Their demands are impossible; they call out: *"Con vida los llevaron, con vida los queremos!"* (They took them away alive, we want them back alive!). The call can never be answered. And so the call is made over and over. It persists in reminding all those at home in the present that behind their comfort, behind any settlement, a specter is lurking. This call inevitably haunts any "new" or "old" imaginary basis for sustaining "a nationally viable continuity." In the very binding of the nation, in the public square of its history, the neither alive nor sufficiently ever dead call out.

The desire for collective vindication, which the legal means for coming to terms with the past enacted, is rendered vulnerable by the weekly apparition of the Mothers. Although political rationality insists on the need to *heal the wounds of the nation,* the Mothers' agony bursts through any solution. "Let there be no healing of wounds," they argue. "Let them remain open. Because if the wounds still bleed, there will be no forgetting and our strength will continue to grow" (cited in Bouvard 1994, 152). The attempt to come to terms with the abject by submerging/assuaging its affect into an explanatory economy is interrupted by a call that seems to gesture in the opposite direction. This call, which in its very (impossible) claim dejects itself from the symbolic economy (where this loss, this affect, can be metaphorically exchanged or substituted like any other loss), works to halt the equivalence of symbolic exchange. Its very abject manifestation (as a type of bleeding) signals that this loss is not an ordinary loss that can be substituted and once again absorbed by or stitched into the symbolic order—for there is no death when someone "disappears," only an open wound that grieves. The abject and uncontainable material of this call not only points beyond the political light of the present but attempts to shelter an affect that thwarts the symbolic economy. In this sense, the call breaks the economy of the "we"; it ruptures the assumptions that allow the caller and the addressee to correspond/signify by means of a familiar and exchangeable set of norms or terms. In other words, unlike a political project that builds a consolatory frame around what "we" share in common, that inoculates the kinship of the "we" from its festering abject, the call (as a dejection from the symbolic) remains unabsorbable, and so beyond this present: It thus remains as a call that necessarily returns to ask us to think beyond the present understanding.

But the price of this call that is resistent to direct symbolization is quite high; for it weighs too much on the scale of the present and so becomes resented, pathologized, and ultimately excluded from the "new" Argentina. Marguerite Guzman Bouvard tells us that "when the mothers first voiced this cry [*Con vida los llevaron, con vida los queremos!*] many supporters of the [new democratic] government criticized them as crazy, obstinate women who refuse to accept the reality of their children's deaths" (Bouvard 1994, 147).[20] Yet, what makes their cries different from any simple "denial" or "melancholic pathos" is that they are "acting to preserve something in the midst of unbearable destruction, *to honor obligations* [to the remains] that cannot be annihilated by brute force"(Elshtain 1989, 231, emphasis mine). Their rhetorical dismemberment of any political settlement unearths the revenant question that lies in the imaginary "we"—*How are "we" responsible for the remains?*

> The Mothers explained that their demand was in truth "asking a question of those who do not wish to answer it and questioning a whole system which generated a savage repression. . . ." The slogan was a response to the junta's mythologizing of reality, most especially to its campaign of denials during the terror. It was also a reaction to the legislation under Alfonsin transforming the "disappeared" into victims of *murder* and to the official pronouncement of the theory of the two devils. [See n. 16 this chapter.] In demanding the return of their children alive, the Mothers insisted upon recreating and reasserting the complexity of reality, the shades of differentiation that the junta's reduction and simplification had sought to eliminate. "Our children are not dead," one of the Mothers insisted. "They are 'disappeared.'" (Bouvard 1994, 147, emphasis mine)

These "mourners-in-waiting" who perform their ascribed private gender roles ("the grief of a mother") in the most public space of the country come to embody the "repulsion" of boundary transgression, of not remaining in the folds of the present rationality. Thus, "just as Creon aimed to portray Antigone as mentally deranged, the Mothers were labeled 'las locas,' the madwomen—beyond the pale, outside the boundaries of legitimate politics" (Elshtain 1989, 231–232).[21] As new boundaries establish and redeem the institutions and "character" of the nation from the supposed anomaly and aberration of the past violence, these "mourners-in-waiting" who refuse to "let go of the past" cross the normative boundaries of time and space and are thus dejected into the fringe of society or rendered "crazy." After the return of democracy, Jean Bethke Elshtain notes the ambivalence and embarrassment that often accompanied those Argentines who spoke to her of the Mothers (see Elshtain 1994, 77–78). The attitude attests to the intensity of the anxieties and tensions that lurk under the desire for reconciliation. Whatever remains outside of the process of reconciliation, whatever interrupts the concerns of the here and now, of the law, is a deviation so profound, an encounter so strange, that it must be abjected, considered as "too crazy" and "embarrassing" to be able to participate under the light of "legitimate politics."[22]

Clearly the wrong suffered by these "mourners-in-waiting" cannot be justly translated into a litigation. Despite Osiel's assurance, their affliction resists being retold and "woven into a larger story about the community, its history, and its evolving normative commitments" (1997, 73). If their suffering served such purposes, it would be a gross injustice, a condensation of the imponderable into a tidy moral telos: a way of understanding without loss, without leaving one's ground. The intertextual fabric of the "we" literally rips apart when it encounters the Mothers' insistence: *"Con vida los llevaron, con vida los queremos!"* For the Mothers' *call* (as abject matter) does not provide anything that confirms or settles into my vocabulary; rather it signals an affliction, a sentiment, a "feeling," that is unable to phrase what must be phrased: a mnemonic rupture that displays the *differend*. A *differend* which I *read* and therefore become *obligated* to (somehow) *transmit* or put into phrases.

> The differend is the unstable state and instant of language wherein something which must be able to be put into phrases cannot yet be. This state includes silence, which is a negative phrase, but it also calls upon phrases which are in principle possible. This state is signaled by what one ordinarily calls a feeling [a sentiment]: "One cannot find the words," etc. A lot of searching must be done to find the new rules for forming and linking phrases that are able to express the differend disclosed by the feeling, unless one wants this differend to be smothered right away in a litigation and for the alarm sounded by the feeling to have been useless. What is at stake in literature, in a philosophy, in a politics perhaps, is to bear witness to differends by finding idioms for them. (Lyotard 1988, 13)

Without trying to "understand" the Mothers' impossible call, that is, without reducing their claims to the "irrational" or to the psychological category of a "defense mechanism," the stakes for bearing witness (reading) is to write (transmit) the sentiment and obligation in this call that has no present possibility, that remains abject to the symbolic. Writing must bear witness to how "this present 'society' has no need for this affection [sentiment] nor for its preservation, [how] it forecloses it more than any other" (Lyotard 1990, 40). This writing writes, then, to transmit something that "alarms" but that risks being forgotten, risks being "smothered" by "our" terms. Indeed, since it is beyond "our" terms "a lot of searching must be done": for, how to bear witness, how to write/transmit, how to find idioms, for an unappeasable (abject) sentiment without reducing, smothering, forgetting its provocation within "our" terms of representation.

The pedagogical task here is most pressing and, yet, because we are dealing with a crisis at the very border of articulation, most difficult to spell out. Lest we smother the provocation, the difficult obligation to think the unthought, we cannot venture directly into an answer, or any formulaic resolution on how to properly write/transmit the remains. Yet, it is rightly asked, indeed it must be asked in order to push thought to account for itself, what does this writing, what does this searching and caring (this acknowledging of what is at stake), in what remains unphrased, teach us, now, here, in the particular present problematic? Ending this chapter, I do not aspire to any overall conclusion, but rather seek to underline the *ethical lesson* that ensues from a *reading* that comes upon a distress in language that is beyond the equivalence of symbolic exchange. The suggestion here will not at all be about how to represent (write/transmit) the remains but, more allusively, it will gesture to how a *reading* that comes to feel obligated to transmit what is presently vulnerable/inconvenient ultimately comes upon the vulnerability of "our" terms. It is from this vexing encounter with the limits of translation (which displays the lack in our present terms/settlements) that we may call our present historical projects/writing into question. Thus, the pressing problematic to be addressed concerns a self-recapitulative re-presentation that forecloses those unreconcilable tensions and memories that inconvenience the present.

Given the context of post-dictatorship Argentina the need to disrupt the self-enclosure of the present (through a reading of the limits of what is claimed as history) is a pressing matter. For today in Argentina (more often than not) the present remembers to forget the past.[23] There is a general danger in Argentina of not only forgetting the ongoing work that is needed to challenge the authoritarian legacy that still dwells in its institutions, but there is also the peril of forgetting the obligation that is still due to the unburied remains. This danger is present not because the state has failed to produce representations and validations (a history) of the past, but, ironically, because the state (or anyone else for that matter) can cash in on these former representations by suggesting that the nation has already sufficiently come to terms with its past. Through the *National Commission on the Disappeared* (CONADEP) and through the trial of the former dictatorship, it officially *appears* as if the nation has already faced its problems, established reconciliation, and can, now, assured that the violent past is an aberrant episode, learn how to "turn the page." Writing about how truth commissions face the violent past (although taking his argument into a very different direction than mine), Michael Ignatieff writes, "the societies in question used the truth commissions [and I would add here the trial in Argentina] to indulge in the illusion that they had put the past behind them. The truth commissions allowed exactly the kind of false reconciliation with the past they had been expressly created to forestall" (1996, 112). Anyone who would claim that past injustices have been adequately discoursed or catalogued as a historical lesson on "who *we* really are" would end up sheltering the present from confronting the limits of its (burial) grounds: the remains that can never be buried or sown into "our" historical ground. In other words, to believe that the past has been legitimately represented by "our" terms, or consequently to propose a redeemed national identity, implies "finishing off" the past's force (claims) on the present. This would close off any ethical consideration of that which exceeds or might be excluded from the present empire of knowledge. In this sense, history is ossified within the norms and conventions of the present; it could very well be, then, that accounts that inconvenience, the flow of present exchange would have no recognition in this scheme.

Overcoming the problematics of this self-enclosure depends on the ability to acknowledge the limits of the present's norms, to encounter how the "we" is subject to loss. This concern points to an ethical reading practice that—instead of identifying with that (knowledge) which fills up "our" loss—teaches us how to take "our time," how to give attention to the scandal of what cannot at this time be fully discoursed or settled with the currency of "our" terms: This is a reading, read again, of the *differend*—an attentive reading, as I previously discussed, which alerts us to what remains in the margins of any writing of the past that funds the metonymies of a normative tradition. But, at this point, I need to be a bit more precise about what this reading implies for writing; hence, what does this reading of the limits transmit? If this reading seeks to point out that which exceeds "our" vocabulary, that which puts us at a loss, what (lesson) is *being* transmitted here?

Allow me to approach this matter through that instance of vulnerability that initiated this discussion, with the weight of that affliction that breaks the economy of the "we" as it calls out: *"Con vida los llevaron, con vida los queremos!"* This sentiment, this distress in language, which does not make itself understood, which cannot simply transfer itself into the currency of any present exchange or contract, comes before me in its utter vulnerability. In its radical singularity to suffering—and not because of its identity—this distress in language demands that I become vulnerable to its vulnerability. In facing these words I become caught and obligated, powerfully affected, not by the comfortable "we-intentions" that weave "our" identification/kinship/politics/history, but by what puts me at a loss, by "another imperative, [that] contests the [same] imperative my thought has always obeyed" (Lingis 1994, 29). This other imperative exposes the heavy load, the inherited debt, in any claims to the "we"; for the provocation that I become vulnerable to the other's vulnerability inevitably implies something beyond the self-assurance of pity, that I ask *how my terms to the "we" are grounded on the overturned burial grounds of the other.* In more searing terms, it compels me to consider how "[m]y being-in-the-world . . . [has] been the usurpation of spaces belonging to the other man whom I have already oppressed or starved, or driven out into a third world; are they not acts of repulsing, excluding, exiling, stripping, killing?" (Levinas 1989, 82).

With the above metaethical encounter in mind, I want to suggest that reading is explicitly implicated within the problematics of historical transmission as soon as it comes upon a distress, an "unstable state and instant of language" (Lyotard 1988, 13), which signals the sentiment of an affliction (a vulnerability) that *prescriptively* obligates me to respond. An attentive reading that (now) feels obligated to respond must necessarily ask (problematic) questions about how to translate this sentiment, of how to find phrases for what inevitably resists "our" terms. Yet, because this sentiment cannot justly be condensed or settled into our terms of exchange, an "unstable state and instant in ['our'] language" (Lyotard 1988, 13) moves us toward the realization that we cannot phrase what is presently unphrasable before we sense that "our" very present terms are incapable of carrying across (translating) the weight of the sentiment. Thus, self-reflexively, our attempt to respond (to write) comes upon the re-cognition that "our" terms are at a loss, that they are therefore vulnerable (lacking), yet open (hopeful) to something other than what they already know/claim. The problematics of translation necessarily lead to our vulnerability to the other's vulnerability, to a spectral noncontemporaneity, that bursts into "our" time with another imperative that affords the hope of thinking and asking something altogether differently: not what "we" are, but rather how "we" are responsible for the remains of the other. I am suggesting—if not overstating—that this coming upon a vulnerability, which in turn makes us vulnerable (that is, this reading that acknowledges that it must respond yet realizes—by its being *vexed*— that there is no shared epistemological ground that will guarantee our being able to translate this affliction into "our" terms), necessarily implies an ethical instance for calling "our" time into question, for the possibility of "allowing ['our'] language to be powerfully affected [frustrated and obligated] by the foreign tongue" (Benjamin 1968, 81).

To stage the problematics of translation through our reading and writing is to begin manifesting the very material, the very distress and compelling questions that unwork the terms of "our time." Asking how the claims of the other affect and vex "our time" is crucial for any pedagogical endeavor that seeks to keep "the past" alive without reconstructing or cannibalizing it into some ontological project or lesson on "who *we* really are." In present-day Argentina, being able to ask *how the terms of the "we" are grounded on the overturned burial grounds of the other* is a vitally charged instance. For the very *matter* of this haunting question becomes eerily explicit when we consider how the present terms of national reconciliation constantly threaten to demolish the past's force (claims) on the present. Assuming that the translation of the past horror is interchangeable with the present terms of conciliation, the government of Argentina recently proposed (in light of "present accomplishments") to tear down a building in Buenos Aires that had been previously used by the former dictatorship as a torture center.[24] Literally, in the overturned burial grounds of the disappeared the redeemed "we" sought to monumentalize itself: "Menem said the site would be turned into a park, which, he said, would be a monument to national unity" (*BBC News Online: World Americas,* January 8, 1998).

This is a blatantly grotesque example of how the terms for national redemption attempt to edify/represent themselves through the obliteration of the unreconcilable tensions and memories that cut across the "we." Given the danger of using the same grounds of a past atrocity in order to justify the terms of the present, there is an urgent pedagogical task in mobilizing a form of study that is able to witness those unstable and unappeasable instances that render our present terms vulnerable and at a loss. In other words, because the strategies and tropes of reconciliation continue to be invoked, it becomes crucial to interrupt this assumption in historical translation (which renders the past horror interchangeable with our present terms and desires) with a reading of the *differend:* a reading that feels obligated to respond (write/transmit) to a distress in language, yet recognizes the inadequacy of "our" present terms in any translation of social suffering.

NOTES

1. This self-reflexive question unearths the grounds for "propping up"/"erecting" Being. Following Levinas, this is ultimately a concern for how ontological claims or props displace and usurp "the spaces belonging to the other man" (Levinas 1989, 82, 86).

2. The specific specter of ontological violence that haunts contemporary Argentina is termed the "dirty war." This term refers to a violent period that was systematically wielded by the state after a military junta deposed the government of Isabel Perón and brought an era that they extolled as the *Proceso de reorganizacion nacional* (Process of National Reorganization). Because the term *dirty war* invokes the idea of a "war" it mistakenly gives the impression that there was an actual war between two self-defined hostile forces. I want to avoid giving this impression and instead read the term as that period (between 1976 and 1983), when the Argentine military proclaimed a total war on what they termed "subversives." In explicitly ontological terms, a "subversive," was described by Videla as "a minority [who] we do not consider Argentine, . . . those whose ideas are contrary to our Western, Christian civilization" (cited in Feitlowitz 1992, 41). Claims of the military's ontological crusade to establish "Christian morals, national tradition, and dignity of the Argentine Being" can also be found in Andres Avellaneda, *Censura, autoritarismo y cultura: Argentina 1960–1983,* (2 V). Buenos Aires: Biblioteca Politica Argentina/CEDAL, 1986. The "war against subversion" established a national network of underground detention centers, where victims were held after being "disappeared," to be tortured and usually murdered. Frank Graziano tells us that the "purported intelligence function of torture is untenable. . . . It was not the information itself but like the medieval inquisitors, [the torturers] altered the very fabric of reality by scripting roles [identities] and making those summoned before them play these pre-assigned and largely pre-written parts" (Graziano 1992, 38). All those who were "discovered" as hav-

ing "subversive characteristics" (and this would prove to be an ever-expanding ontological definition), were contaminated and thus had to be ritually "cured" through torture, or, if that failed, abjected from the national body "without a trace." "The junta vowed to operate and clean the public sphere, exterminating the germs that threatened the well-being of the fragile organism. The offending body was literally under the knife or picana electrica [an electric cattle prod which the military used for torture]. Those who were not deemed recoverable died. The well-being of the nation/patient often called for drastic measures" (Taylor 1997, 97).

3. My concern for and use of this hypostatized notion of the "we" is a rhetorical attempt to not only address this conventional liberal trope with the limits of its "own" words but also to entangle and confound *any* "identity-logical" thinking—any mind-set that proposes an ontological binding to the constitutive self-understandings of a common vocabulary or tradition—with what is buried under its ground. By addressing the "we" through a metaethical opening, by exposing this necessarily imaginary identity to that which haunts and tears its ground, I do not *directly* address any (one) specificity but an "identificational fantasy." That is to say, I address an imaginary ideality (the fantasy/thought of a continuous, self-present identification—a "we") that can never be established empirically. For obviously the boundedness of any particular "we" is never an accomplished and given fact, as contradictions and permeations cut through its illusory homogenous image. Thus, the interface (the rhetorical encounter) between this illusory identification and the metaethical language of the other does not take place *directly* in the empirical; rather it stages an *obligation in thought*—an encounter of the limits—that cannot be considered *purely* in constative or descriptive terms. Rhetorically (through sentences that do not have a direct referent to the empirical, but that still take place as sentences, as thought) it stages the necessary movement from ontology to ethics, where thought thinks the limits of its (identity-logical) thinking. Throughout the chapter I will place the imaginary "we" in quotation marks so as to recall/perform the above-mentioned concerns. However, there is an interesting tension/conflation that instantly develops between the imaginary national trope ("we") and the personal pronoun (we) that evokes my (imaginary) readers. It seems to me that this initially unintentional slip, between the *"we"* and *our* allocation as readers, incorporates the potential of returning the ethical critique of the "we" to the very moment of our "reading." Thus, as the chapter proceeds to trouble the "we" it also, implicitly, provokes the reader who is allocated by the pronominal deployments within the text: Given that our reading is rhetorically involved within the problematics it explores, the very metaethical encounter, the very necessity for self-reflexivity, will implicate our reading—our allocation.

4. Frank Graziano has observed that the portrayal of "subversives" as nonbeings (as abjects)—"as antinational beings, as the enemies of 'Western and Christian civilization', as germs alien to the *corpus mysticum*"—was an attempt at purifying "the social body as the externalized and isolated defilement 'disappeared'" (Graziano 1992, 217–218).

5. Priscilla B. Hayner documented and analyzed a total of fifteen truth commissions between the period of 1974–1994 (Hayner 1994, 597–655). I, of course, will limit myself to commenting on the case of Argentina, where after the restoration of "democracy" President Alfonsin and the human-rights community initiated the grounds for bringing to terms the "crimes" of the past through an "impartial" investigation that sought to learn who in fact disappeared and what circumstances they suffered. This work was delegated to a special government-appointed commission—the National Commission on the Disappeared (hereafter referred to as the CONADEP).

6. The paper was presented to the World Congress on Psychoanalysis in August 1985 (cited in Andersen 1993). For an essay that quotes and expands on "Situaciones decatastrofe social," see: Julia Braun's and Maria Lucila Pelento's "Les vicissitudes de la pulsion de savoir dans certains deuils speciaux," in Janine Puget, *Violence d'etat et Psychanalyse*. Paris: Bordas 1989, 86–104. Also see Oscar Abudara (et al.), *Argentina psicoanalisis repression politica*. Buenos Aires: Ediciones Kargieman, 1986.

7. Then-commander of the Argentine Army Roberto Viola provided this profoundly cruel and absurd definition of a "disappeared."

8. Matilde Mellibovsky, one of the mothers of the Plaza de Mayo, reflects on the painful process of attempting to make her call (her insatiable demand for justice and her "rage") fit into the present "descriptive" structure. She writes, "[w]ords used to make me choke up; I had so much to tell, so many emotions, so much pain. So I said the hell with sentence structure. . . . With thirty thousand 'disappeared' there was no time for syntax. . . . What use did we have for syntax when every testimony, every 'habeas corpus,' every letter got only silence for an answer? You don't need syntax for shouting and cursing" (1997, ix). Although Mellibovsky herself goes on to speculate about the political necessity of trying "to pause and think syntactically" (ix), I want to propose that it would be a *wrong* to respond to this "rage" by *demanding* that it present itself "descriptively"—within the present structures of sense. Thus, rather than asking this "rage" to order itself within a "descriptive" economy (of "facts," "reality," and "politics") so that "we" may properly grasp it, there is the ethical necessity of hearing how this "rage" prescriptively calls on "us" to respond beyond "our" terms. This would imply respecting the accent of "rage" as that which bursts through the present and *calls us* to remember what was left behind on the way to the "facts" or "truth." Following Lyotard (1989) I sketch the ethical consequences (the *wrong*) of subsuming a "prescriptive" within a "descriptive" regime. I then extend the implications here to read how the CONADEP and the trial of the military junta proliferated this *wrong*.

9. Yet another example of how the report was flawed in its account of the "disappeared" is provided in Brysk 1995. In that work, she cites Graciela Fernandez Meijide, the CONADEP secretary, who reports that "since the Commission did not directly investigate the repressive forces and relied on reporting by victims, cases with no witnesses or cases in which whole families disappeared would also not be reported" (1995, 216, n. 48).

10. The way in which the CONADEP report has been officially catalogued betrays the state's desire to hold on to this number (8,960) as the final version, despite the obvious discrepancies. Brysk tells us that the government of Alfonsin

> sought to close the book on human rights investigations with the CONADEP report. The raw CONADEP records were closed, filed with an Executive branch Under-Secretary for Human Rights, and sealed to all but government officials and a handful of designated representatives of human rights organizations. The original CONADEP files are not available to scholars, journalists, or international organizations, and it is unclear whether records have been preserved outside of Argentina. (Brysk 1994, 687–688)

11. In this regard, we witness the circulation of discourses that justified the limited and exemplary trials strategy (only a handful of officers where tried), by "favorably comparing the ratios of victims . . . in Argentina with that of the Nuremberg trials" (Brysk 1994, 686).

12. Being able to recognize the responsibility to the other (to those who fall outside of any "we") is especially significant for Argentina where the quiet and unreflective desire for

normalcy, more or less made possible the state-sanctioned violence against those who threatened to expose the lack/gaps in the realization of a "pure Argentine identity." Although of course many Argentines attempted to establish normalcy in the face of terror out of fear, it must also be acknowledged that "in many cases their acquiescence in the means bespoke the intensity of their commitments to the ends" (Osiel 1986, 153). For lest we forget, the *"Proceso de Reorganizacion Nacional"* was not only a strategy for "ridding" the nation of its foreign "diseases," but it was accompanied by an economic policy that delighted those of the middle class who reveled in what was known as *"la plata dulce"* (the sweet money).

13. Mark Osiel notes that, official human rights groups believed that to "prosecute society" beyond the exemplary and limited legal frame would amount to the nation "tearing itself apart with a decade of mutual recrimination" (Osiel 1986, 154).

14. The "antiterrorist campaign" was often invoked, by the Alfonsin government that had initiated the trials, and by the prosecution, as a "regretful and aberrant episode" that was the *fault* of "two terrorisms," one emanating from certain segments of the military and the other from the "guerrillas." Interior Minister Antonio Troccoli and Luis Moreno Ocampo, assistant prosecutor in the trial of the juntas, both expressed that the military and "the left" were "twin sides of the same coin" (cited in Osiel 1986, 158). This would become known as the "doctrine of the two demons/devils." According to this doctrine, the recent violent episode emanates "from the combined evils of two demons: the revolutionary guerillas and the armed forces set to combat them. Both were a manifestation of a dangerous authoritarian mentality that had taken the rest of society hostage" (Perelli 1992, 433). Despite the fact that the "guerrilla struggle" was all but eradicated at the time of the 1976 coup and that the violence that the state wielded was incomparably more damaging than that of the sparse "guerrilla struggle," both the (phantom) "guerrillas" and a handful of overly zealous military officers were—according to this formulation—equally to blame for the "dirty war," and hence equally responsible before the law (see Osiel 1986).

15. Even if we were to overlook (and this surely would be quite irresponsible) the atrocities that were committed during Argentina's early formation, recent history cannot justify a time when "democracy" and respect for "human rights" were "the norm": Consider that between 1955 and 1983 Argentina had only six years of freely elected governments. Of course, the repressive strategy of "disappearance," between 1976 and 1983, was both abhorrent and unprecedented in the way it affected and implicated large sectors of the population; yet, the authoritarian conceptual framework (that tolerates no sense of otherness) that fueled the military's "dirty war" does not stand as an anomaly within Argentine history, but is continuous with its uncompromising quest for "national purity" (Graziano 1992).

16. This comprehensive process, with all its ensuing ambivalences, was, as I have already mentioned, officially designated as being quite risky for the "precarious new democracy." Although we can understand—within the logic of "real politics"—why the decision to frame the introspective process took place within the law, I am proposing that we also take note how the law serves the *desire* to bracket the Argentine authoritarian legacy, in order to continue the integrity of the national imaginary. Because state legitimation often depends on "what is perceived as the nation's grand heritage," the re-legitimation project not only takes place within the strategic maneuverings of political alliances/conciliations but *affectively* seeks to preserve a nationally viable imaginary in spite of its being inextricably tied to a violent past.

17. Although "mass support of the citizenry of the dictatorship's campaign of terror demonstrate that responsibility was shared by many sectors of society" (Malamud-Goti 1995,

167), the intention was to bring to trial only a handful of high-ranking officers. The desire for a contained and exemplary lesson that would reestablish the rule of law made it inconceivable to bring to trial any of the institutions, groups, ideologies, or other wide-ranging social concerns that were directly or indirectly implicated in the campaign of disappearances. For if the trials were to do so they would certainly run the risk of exposing the conflicting aspirations and interests within, what Ronald Dworkin exultantly described as, "the fresh sense of community [that] Alfonsin's victory had produced" (CONADEP 1986, xviii). The desire to consolidate the military (which was still largely made up of officers who were schooled or had served during the repression) within the "fresh sense of community" depended on carefully bounding the issue of criminal responsibility. Hence, the legislative package that initiated the criminal proceedings against the military focused on the nine commanders of the first three military juntas from 1976 to 1983. In accordance with Alfonsin's prudential call for "justice," the legal strategy severely confined further trials against the military as it sanctioned, for those who did not occupy its commanding offices, an automatic presumption of due obedience—the so-called taking orders defense (see Nino 1996, 69). This overly prudential and limited strategy would prove to be quite contentious. However, despite initial modifications it ultimately asserted itself, drowning any legal claims that exceeded the desire for reconciliation. On December 22, 1986, the "punto final" law (full stop) was passed. This law specified a sixty-day limit for submitting charges against the military; after that date all charges would once and for all be extinguished. After Alfonsin negotiated with the leaders of a serious military rebellion, the "due obedience" legislation was introduced and subsequently passed (June 4, 1987) by Congress; the law revised the due obedience defense to favor a perfunctory closure for the trials.

18. In its concluding remarks about the trials Amnesty International made a statement about the possible problematics of attempting to seek justice through the procedural peculiarities of a "criminal" case: "The Court was guided by the basic principle in criminal law that liability and the corresponding sentence must be assessed individually and not collectively. Collective entities cannot stand trial, only individual persons, and this poses major difficulties in cases of offenses planned or perpetrated by groups. Although the question of collective responsibility was resolved in the case of this particular trial, it will undoubtedly continue to provoke disagreement in legal and moral discussions" (Amnesty International 1987, 86).

19. For a bibliography that details different works around this general issue, see Allan Sheldon Metz, "La semana tragica: An Annotated Bibliography," *Revista Interamericana de Bibliografía* (1990, 51–91). For a specific account of anti-Semitism during the military's "dirty war," see "Jewish Victims of Repression in Argentina under Military Rule," *Holocaust and Genocide Studies* (1989, 479–499).

20. The claim that held the Mothers to be "crazy" was of course initiated by the very military dictatorship that "disappeared" their sons and daughters. A military spokesperson was quoted as saying, "this matter is of no concern to us. These women are mad" (cited in Elshtain 1994, 82). Thus, the claim that the Mothers are "crazy" by the democratic government or its supporters carries a particularly malicious tone. In fact, both President Alfonsin and President Menem drew on the extremely explosive discourse of "national interest" and "national threat" (against subversives who threaten the nation) in order to delegitimate the Mothers from the political arena (see Fisher 1989, 142; Bouvard 1994, 200, 214).

21. With the return to democracy the state emphasized a "new public rationality" that excluded the Mothers' rage from the institutionalization of liberal (individual) rights. The

narrow legalistic frames for retelling the traumatic past privileged the Oedipal script, "which focuses on generational father-son conflict and the male rulers' attempts to put an end to social crisis and *disease* through self-knowledge and the discovery of the Truth" (Taylor 1997, 208), over Antigone's imperative to care for the remains beyond Creon's "rationalist politics"—beyond the logos of any state. Elshtain tells us that Antigone's imperative, like the Mother's protest, "embodies a civic revolt, action undertaken in the public sphere in defense of exigencies that emerge from the private sphere" (1989, 229). Hence, this imperative does not situate loss around an idealized private ego (melancholia), but rather publicly mourns or expresses a grief/rage that interrupts the symbolic with ever being able to simply claim "death" or "murder" over the imponderable violence of "disappearance."

22. The way in which the Mothers have been closed off from the "legitimate" political discourse of Argentina is made painfully obvious by an important demonstration that literally took place in the dark. Bouvard recounts, "I was with them on one of these marches and observed that city officials had turned off the lights in the Plaza and the people closed their windows or turned away as the Mothers passed by. The only television coverage was from abroad, and the following day none of the newspapers carried stories about the march" (Bouvard 1994, 210).

23. Unfortunately Argentina is not only inclined to forget the past, but, as Jaime Malamud-Goti discusses, there are "present indicators that the populace is ready to elect authoritarian rulers and acquiesce again to police brutality. A new campaign of police abuse has met with little public reaction, and in 1991 elections, candidates representing extremely authoritarian views had an astonishing appeal" (Malamud-Goti 1995, 160). His assessment is even more striking in a later work where he writes,

> after the formal restoration of constitutional rule, general respect for individual liberties was neither visible nor evident in Argentina's life. For advocates of individual rights, the Argentine situation in the mid-1990s is bleak. By and large, the citizenry is apathetic in the face of renewed police brutality. Since the late 1980's, abuse has once more become widespread. . . . I contend that the new violence is merely a continuation of the practices and beliefs acquired during the stages of terror; the small minority that opposed brutality in the 1970–80 period seems not to have grown any larger. (Malamud-Goti 1996, 147, 148)

24. Early in 1998 President Carlos Menem announced his government's plan to demolish the Navy School of Mechanics (ESMA) building, which had served as a torture center and mass gravesite during the military's "dirty war." Menem proposed to replace this notorious symbol of the past state-sanctioned violence with a monument to "national reconciliation." "His proposal was defeated by rights groups who want the ESMA left standing as a reminder of the horror. . . . A court ruled that forensic anthropologists can dig up the grounds and search for victims' remains at the most infamous torture center of the [military's] 'dirty war'" (*CNN On Line: World: Americas,* September 3, 1998).

9

Beyond Reconciliation:

Memory and Alterity in Post-Genocide Rwanda

Jody Ranck

> How can I be responsible for a face that is perhaps only a likeness of the face I attribute to him? The true face is an absence—face of the man who has been flayed—absence of face becomes face of my responsibility. Faces deported to Auschwitz and all the other camps of humiliation and extermination scattered over the world. Face of the non-face. Non-face of the Face.
> —Edmond Jabes, *A Foreigner Carrying in the Crook of His Arm a Tiny Book*

In 1998, the world community celebrated the fiftieth anniversary of the United Nations Declaration of Human Rights and the creation of the statute for the establishment of the International Criminal Court. These celebrations were marked by ritualistic exhortations of "progress" over the past half century and the triumph of international legal norms. Taken as a further step in the evolution of international law and human rights, the two events appear as landmarks in the humanist endeavor to "come to terms" with the violence of World War II and the *Shoah*, foundational events leading to the creation of the United Nations. However, if one reads these events through a different prism, one that problematizes the present through a suspension of the humanist assumption of progress, a very different picture may emerge.

My estrangement from the assertion of a humanist metanarrative of moral progress emanates from the fault lines etched into it by the contemporary presence of genocide. The contrast of the progress of international law amid ongoing efforts at mass annihilation provides a crucial site for reexamining not only our present but also the pedagogical lessons that might be drawn from the memory of genocidal practices. My interest specifically in this regard is with the recent genocide in Rwanda. The stakes here are not about the search for redemptive meaning in the murder of nearly one million Rwandese—while the international community watched, refusing to intervene. Instead, at issue is the challenge this genocide submits to traditional humanist ethics, the foundational moral codes on which the institutions of international law are built. Inherent in this challenge is the articulation of a radical ethics of responsibility to the Other. What this chapter begins to explore is how such an ethic might be brought to bear on the question of memory. In doing so, it draws inspiration from Emmanuel Levinas (1978/1991, 27), who rejected humanism for not being human enough, who mourned philosophy for fleeing the Shoah, and whose work provides important insights into the relation of memory and alterity that genocide brings to the fore.

In Kigali, Rwanda, in July 1997—as I was beginning my research on the effects of the genocide and how individuals and communities confront this ongoing tragedy—I was confronted by the shock of a juxtaposition of two images that testified, on very different terms, to the events in Rwanda in the spring of 1994. The first of these images were the small plaques, placed outside the offices of the U.S. Agency for International Development and the United Nations Development Program, listing the names of the Tutsi employees killed during the 1994 genocide. By themselves, these commemorative plaques are unremarkable, particularly in contrast to the memorial complex of mass graves and churches filled with decaying bodies that remain scattered throughout the Rwandan countryside. Nearly a week later, however, I came across other images that brought home the significance of these commemorative plaques. On a visit to the International Criminal Tribunal for Rwanda (ICTR), I viewed two documentary videos that unsettled the apparently benign and generous nature of the plaques. The first of these videos contains scenes of Rwandese pleading to be rescued by UN peacekeepers and diplomatic corps evacuating Western individuals in April 1994, days after the genocide had begun. In the second video, a French military officer discusses the "humanitarian intervention" of the French government in setting up the *Zone Turquoise,* a so-called safe haven, which served as a buffer to protect the Hutu army that had just participated in the murder of nearly one million civilians.

These video clips aligned over and against the commemorative plaques pose the question of what it means for humanism and the practice of humanitarianism, when nearly fifty years after the Shoah, a genocide is *allowed* to take place under the watchful eyes of the "humanitarians"? What is the significance of war crimes tribunals and humanitarian relief programs in this context? What rationalities are involved here when responsibility to the other has become disregarded to the extent that this disregard is not viewed as a crime?

The gaze of the international community has been too long diverted to rendering justice and seeking causes for mass violence without looking further. Perhaps, this "community" might take to heart its own complicity with the "power effects" or sovereign exception critiqued by Giorgio Agamben. It does not take a leap of the imagination to grasp the relevance for the Rwandan genocide of Agamben's observation that

> the correct question to pose concerning the horrors committed in the camps is, therefore, not the hypocritical one of how crimes of such atrocity could be committed against human beings. It would be more honest and, above all, more useful to carefully investigate the juridical procedures and deployments of power by which human beings could be so completely deprived of their rights and prerogatives that no act committed against them could appear any longer as a crime. (1998, 171)

In the age of CNN, the abrogation of responsibility can rarely, if ever, be attributed to a lack of knowledge. We must remember the notorious press conference at the U.S. State Department when a spokesperson for the government delivered the most blatant display of rhetorical cynicism in the midst of the genocide, announcing that "[a]lthough there have been acts of genocide in Rwanda, all the murders cannot be put into that category."[1]

Contemporary practices of humanitarianism, Agamben observes, "maintain a secret solidarity with powers they ought to fight" since they have yet to confront the implications of late modern forms of power constitutive of the separation of humanitarianism from politics (Agamben 1998, 132). Agamben cites this as the extreme phase of the separation of the rights of man from the rights of the citizen whereby humanitarian organizations can only "grasp life in the figure of bare or sacred life," that is, life that can be killed without being considered a crime.

In the discussion that follows, we must keep in mind that the Rwandan genocide was one that could have been stopped. Indeed, the genocide was a "policy success" in that Western powers, having the ability to put an end to the killings, intentionally chose not to. With a multitude of legal instruments available, such as the Geneva Conventions and the United Nations Genocide Convention, what forms of reason and emergent hierarchies allowed nearly one million Rwandans to be killed—with Western complicity—after fifty years of "Never Again"? These are the questions a critical praxis of remembrance of the Rwandan genocide might very well take up in an insistence on a problematization of the present.

HISTORY OF THE CONFLICT

History in Rwanda is a central site of struggle where power and memory converge in the constitution of subjectivities. From the early colonial period, the search for "origins" has occupied a central place in representations of the past. The assertion of putative origins has been implicated in the struggle for a governing legitimacy in both colonial and postcolonial contexts. As Ana Maria Alsonso notes, "[r]e-presentations of the past, whether professional or popular, printed or spoken, are defined as specific sorts of performances or texts through a series of framing devices.

The way such reconstructions are framed configures their truth value by bringing into play the ideologically constituted status of different forms of knowledge" (1988, 34). As elsewhere, knowledge of the past in Rwanda has been used by governments and political leaders to foster the illusion of legitimate authority as "naturally occurring," an illusion that evokes forms of memory that render social formations as organically whole. Primordialist notions of ethnicity have been deployed by ethnic nationalists in the struggles over history and memory to buttress claims of autochthony in the creation of national selves and others (Boyarin 1994). As such, one must approach the question of "majorities" and "minorities" that we see in Rwanda as products of particular historically inflected forms of governmentality (Foucault 1991), deployed by the modern state and supported through disciplines such as ethnology, history, linguistics, and other human sciences.

Over time, the performative dimensions of memory and identity have worked to produce fixed and hardened boundaries in political and cultural struggles in Rwanda. These performances have been intertwined with practices of colonial administration and international diplomacy, practices that have also worked to reinscribe primordialist assumptions in their efforts to promote, first, a harmonious colonial regime and, subsequently, a postcolonial "peace." The Arusha Accords[2] in 1993, for example, attempted to broker a power sharing arrangement that ultimately led to the political crisis preceding the genocide. These accords can be clearly criticized for the manner in which they upheld notions of ethnicity that, in the search for peace, reinscribed the very terms that have provided the deep structure of the conflict. As Bhabha (1994, 66–70) explains, colonial discourse depends on the concept of "fixity" in the ideological construction of otherness and the ambivalence of anxiety-producing stereotypes that persist into the present. This is a crucial point, frequently overlooked by many journalists, political scientists, and others concerned with the practices of attempted "peace and reconciliation" in Rwanda, which endeavor to reconcile political subjectivities produced through violence and governmentality.

The first Europeans arrived in Rwanda and Burundi in 1892 at a time when, through war with surrounding chiefs, the Mwami (King) Rwabugiri had successfully extended and centralized his authority. That said, Rwandan society was still quite decentralized with numerous chiefdoms and client systems centered around kinship relations (Newbury 1988). The kingdom of Rwabugiri was far more complex than the caricatures found in much of the ethnohistory that informs contemporary ethnic extremist propaganda in Burundi and Rwanda. To consider the kingdom as singularly securing Tutsi sovereignty over Hutu subjects smooths over important aspects, such as the following (Newbury 1988; Vidal 1985):

1) rule was largely based on clan and lineage rather than racialized notions of ethnicity;
2) to the extent that "ethnicity" can be understood as a social category in this context, it was quite fluid and depended on the number of cattle owned and could fluctuate with one's (mis)fortune;

3) rule of the territory was shared by several chiefs who had power over various aspects of production such as cattle, people, and land;

4) political violence was more often between clans and lineages than between "Tutsis" and "Hutus";

5) patron-client relationships were not uniform and did not always include the worst off.

As the object of study of colonial administrators, historians, and anthropologists, the fluid and variegated social institutions and relations described above were increasingly codified, fixed, and inserted into forms of representation useful to a colonial governmentality directing and dominating social life. As Bhabha notes, "colonial discourse produces the colonized as a social reality which is at once 'other' and yet entirely knowable and visible" (1994, 70).

Throughout both the precolonial and colonial eras, numerous rebellions against the central authorities erupted, particularly in the north, and were frequently associated with various spirit mediums (Berger 1981). By 1894 Rwabugiri had died and, following a violent overthrow of the apparent heir (Linden 1977), an illegitimate successor claimed the sacred drum (the symbol of the monarch's legitimacy and domination). German authorities intervened to uphold the coup. Despite the illegitimate successor, a bureaucratic political structure, a legacy of Rwabugiri, endured. Included in this structure were defined provinces, a designated responsibility for collecting taxes, inscription for military service, and the *ubuhake* patron-client relationship (which particularly marked the beginning of notions of ethnicity as having political saliency).

It was during the early decades of colonialism that fluid notions of ethnicity began to be displaced by a more racialized connotation. The hardening of identity boundaries had begun under Rwabugiri; however, this was extended most dramatically with the imposition of indirect rule under the Germans and Belgians. Central to this process was the so-called Hamitic hypothesis developed by European academics and theologians. In its most common form, the Hamitic hypothesis postulates that cattle breeding nomads arrived in Africa from the Caucasus with the ability to elevate African societies from their "primitiveness" (Sanders 1969; Spottel 1998).[3] Although considered inferior to white Europeans, the Hamites' civilizing capacity was buttressed by a presumed patrimonial lineage to the biblical Noah's son Ham (who, the myth postulates, transgressed by uncovering his father's nakedness, and thus was cursed with darker skin). However, it is important to stress that this Hamitic hypothesis was, at root, part of a discourse of origins and purity (Spottel 1998). Bhabha (1994, 74–77) suggests that we read these stereotypes as a practice of fetishism whereby the myth of historical origins produced in relation to the colonial stereotype functions to normalize multiple beliefs and split subjects. The fetish or stereotype is both a recognition and disavowal of difference that assumes fixity in facilitating colonial realities and forms of racial and cultural opposition, precisely the terms through which colonial power is exercised.

In Rwanda and Burundi, the Hamitic hypothesis served as the legitimating basis for indirect rule of the Tutsi lords over the Hutu masses. When Rwanda and Burundi became Belgian protectorates after World War I, power became increasingly centralized in the hands of a small Tutsi elite (two out of a total of more than thirty clans that existed at the time), under a form of colonial governmentality that abolished the previous regime of rule in which different chiefs had controlled different productive aspects of social life. The new system concentrated power in the hands of a single local chief. As Mamdani (1996a) notes, room for greater exploitation by despotic local administrators thus increased dramatically. Mandatory identity cards with ethnic categorizations became an effective means to crystallize identities. This effectiveness was secured as access to education, jobs, and power was based on these ethnic identifications. As Appadurai notes, colonial classifications of social groups worked with the aid of enumerative strategies used for tax collection, demographic surveys, and so on, to reconfigure communal identities (1996). Rwandans, to varying degrees, were complicit in this process. For example, the Rwandan philosopher and historian Alexis Kagame, claiming unique access to the secret knowledge of the royal court, contributed to notions of Tutsi superiority by identifying the Rwandan nation-state with Tutsi nationalism (de Lame 1996).

As alienation grew among those identified as Hutus, a historical consciousness of oppression and a call for the end of Tutsi hegemony grew ever louder, strengthened by a new class of Belgian missionaries who supported the Hutu masses after World War II. "Majority rule" (*rubanda nyamwinshi*) became the rallying cry for the newly emerging Hutu intellectuals headed by Gregoire Kayibanda. He would come to power through the 1959 Hutu Social Revolution, which ushered in independence, but an independence based on ethnic politics and exclusion. The form of democracy that emerged from this revolution was largely founded on a politics of *ressentiment*, which institutionalized a form of reverse discrimination. The invocation of "Revolution" in 1959 thus became a performative speech act that constituted its own aura of authority through self-proclamation. As a foundational myth contaminating all spheres of authority in the postcolonial state, it permeated not only political discourse, but also state practices of control and surveillance.

The ethnic violence that accompanied decolonization resulted in tens of thousands of deaths and the creation of a large diasporic community of Tutsis in neighboring countries. The violence continued throughout the 1960s as threats to the legitimacy of Kayibanda's rule, stemming from regional and class fissures, were parlayed into the scapegoating of Tutsis. Kayibanda, coming from the south, was overthrown in 1972 by Juvenal Habyarimana, a Hutu army chief representing northern landowners (Prunier 1995).

From the outset, Habyarimana called on the discourse of development as a legitimating tool. At birth, all Rwandans were compelled to join the Mouvement Revolutionnaire Nationale pour le Developpement (MRND). As elsewhere, mobilization of the discourse of development in Rwanda led to the translation of social problems into technical issues solvable through the rational management of resources—a discourse that rarely contributes to the alleviation of poverty and suffering, but successfully enhances the power of the state (Ferguson 1994). Development, with its notions of progress and communal harmony, effectively constituted a form of antipolitics (Ferguson 1994) in that the body politic became increasingly depoliticized while the state's reach extended into the everyday lives of most Rwandans. This occurred through "development" programs such as compulsory labor (*umuganda*), the co-optation of cooperatives, and a patronage system supported by foreign aid (Uvin 1998). In Rwanda, the discourse of development was deployed in such a way as to cast those questioning the state's legitimacy as "foreigners," traitors to communal harmony and solidarity (de Lame 1996).

In addition, Habyarimana played the role of symbolic god-king appropriating symbols of the Tutsi monarchy: the *intore* (court dancers of the Tutsi monarchy) at public ceremonies, *seances d'animation* during compulsory communal labor, and, the exchange of gifts (*amaturo*) in communal ceremonies marking the king's ownership and absolute control over his territory. The appropriation of religious motifs to enhance the aura of the president was manifest in the declaration of one propagandist for the newspaper *Umurava:* "It is God who has given Habyarimana the power to direct the country, it is He who will show him the path to follow" (Chretien 1995, 46; des Forges 1999, 72). Each of these rituals had a performative dimension that played a role in the spectacle of the state, a spectacle that would make the propaganda and terror of 1994 all the more feasible. During the 1980s, the tensions and contradictions of development emerged as world coffee prices plummeted, a famine struck the south and central regions, and Tutsis in the diaspora (under the Rwandan Patriotic Front—the RPF) incessantly pressured the regime for the right of return. These tensions erupted into a civil war in 1990 when the RPF decided to force the issue through armed struggle. These tensions and the ensuing struggle were signs that the illusion of a unified nation-state was dissipating—except, of course, to the international donor community who continued to hold Rwanda as the "model" development state in Africa. Resistance to the state resulted in a growing political crisis that threatened the legitimacy of the regime as well as the veil of solidarity among Hutus that had been forged through state violence and memory of the 1959 Revolution.[4] Pressures for democratization led to the establishment of new political parties and an increasingly critical press that further exacerbated the political crisis. In this context, a hate media emerged that would play an instrumental role in the genocide of 1994.

PROPAGANDA

The period between the RPF invasion on October 1, 1990, and the genocide in 1994 was a time of increasing violence, in which terror was used to silence a body politic that had become increasingly restless. As criticism of the regime and of the narrow clique of the president, his wife, and their allies (or the *Akazu,* literally, "the lit-

tle house") grew, the regime took a heavy hand against its opponents and supported
the establishment of a Hutu extremist media, primarily the newspaper *Kangura*
("Wake Him Up") and *Radio-Television Libre Milles Collines* (RTLM). Both of
these sources relied on a melange of rumor, political humor, and traditional cultural forms to criticize and demonize the RPF and other potential adversaries. In a
manner similar to the Nazi use of pseudo-historical myths, those Hutu in power
used the media to make reality itself a form of theater (Buck-Morss 1993). The
performative power of language worked to fashion a vision of the body politic as
a unified whole, in which those who resisted could be sacrificed to guard the purity of that whole.

In December 1990, *Kangura* published an influential article by Hassan Ngeze,
one of the chief propagandists, which detailed the basic ideology of Hutu Power
(Chretien 1995). The article, "The Bahutu 10 Commandments," is notable for the
prominent position of Tutsi women in four of these commandments. Here, Tutsi
women became a central target, positioned as "spies and seductresses"—a threat to
the masculinized Hutu social body vulnerable to the sexuality of Tutsis. Tutsis were
portrayed as power hungry and clever and capable of using "their" women in the
service of acquiring power. In contrast, there were frequent references to the
virtues of Hutu women as good mothers and honest guardians of their Hutu husbands, who are depicted as always vulnerable to the beauty of Tutsi women. In this
propaganda, the female body became the privileged site for the creation of ethnic
identities and purity. The obsessive concern with the power of Tutsi women
worked not only to construct Tutsi women as dangerous but also to construct specific notions of Hutu masculinity that would figure in the centrality of rape during the genocide. The final commandment stressed the need to teach and dissem-
inate the ideology of the 1959 Social Revolution. The connection of the state's
founding mythology with a religious motif demonstrated the marriage of the secular and religious elements in the ideology of Hutu Power.[5]

Using the technology of identification initiated by the identity cards instituted
during the era of Belgian colonialism, Hutu Power deployed these cards to block
many Tutsis from access to education and government positions.[6] Commentary in
the extremist press stressed that the RPF term *Banyarwanda* (the Kinyarwanda term
for Rwandan) was a Tutsi fabrication and that history of Rwanda had always been
a history of three separate peoples.[7] This form of primordialist argument was also
captured by the international media in which the Rwandan genocide was, and continues to be, referred to as a result of "ancient tribal hatreds." Ironically in June
1994, nearly two months after the genocide began and the bulk of the killings were
over, the UN Commission of Experts delivered their report on the genocide, and
RTLM used this report as proof of the primordialist argument, arguing that in order for there to be a genocide one must establish the existence of distinct ethnicities with a biological basis.[8]

Cartoons in *Kangura* depicted the *kalinga*, or ceremonial drum, of the Tutsi
monarchy as containing the dried testicles of slain (Hutu) chieftains. This was of-

fered as a symbol of the humiliation of Hutus and the desire of Tutsis to dominate. Cartoons of Tutsi women engaged in sex acts with UN peacekeepers, or Hutu moderates, such as Prime Minister Agathe Uwilingiyimana, in bed with various political leaders, were part of the semiotics of terror that labeled Tutsi women (or those who posed a threat to the boundaries of Hutu/Tutsi) as spies/seductresses, both desired and feared (Chretien 1995). Other cartoons represented the RPF as cannibals and rapists of Hutu women—the bearers of Hutu tradition. These cartoons often portrayed acts of violence on specific body parts such as genitalia and mouths. It is noteworthy that during the genocide, fingers, legs, noses, and other specific body parts of Tutsis were often mutilated in specific patterns that formed what Malkki (1995) has termed "necrographic maps," inscribing particular memoro-logics on the bodies of the victims. The semiotics of torture thus reflected the physiognomic stereotypes produced under colonial rule.

The aesthetics of the radio broadcasts are equally important in demonstrating how myth and memory worked during the genocide. As Chretien notes, singer Simon Bikindi's music was particularly effective in blending popular Zairean rhythms and choral verses with long passages from divination rituals such that "one could dance to the passionate call to ethnic mobilization" (Chretien 1995, 342). The songs mobilized images of mythical Hutu heroes and included lyrics that emphasized previous Hutu servitude and the need "to wake up" the "majority people" to put past humiliation at the hands of Tutsis as far behind as possible (Chretian 1995, 353).

In summary, the propaganda deployed by the extremist media relied on hybrid cultural forms that fused traditional myths, created primarily under colonial rule and memory, with modern forms of state power and messianic religious themes. Hutu Power propaganda created an assemblage of historical fictions that came to assume the appearance of the real. Difference was constituted through "scientific" proof of the foreignness of Tutsis coupled with fears of miscegenation. The distinction between Tutsi and Hutu was positioned as a given, as men are to women. Myths of origins, colonial historiography, and propaganda worked as forms of knowledge of the other. In so doing, the Hutu ethnic self was constructed, a self that had come under increasing threat and yet was integral to the tenuous founding mythology of the 1959 Social Revolution.

On April 6, 1994, the plane carrying the presidents of Rwanda and Burundi was shot down over Kigali. Within hours, the killings and rapes of Tutsis and Hutu moderates began. While this violence continued into June, most of the killings and rapes took place during the first three weeks. Within hours of the shooting down of the presidential plane, roadblocks appeared functioning as checkpoints for ferreting out Tutsis and Hutu moderates on the basis of identity cards and death lists. Extensive death lists detailing who was to be killed in each commune were signs of a well-organized genocidal plan that enabled the murder of several hundred thousand Rwandans in a few weeks. One of the primary strategies of the genocide was to destroy the homes of murdered occupants. Attempts were even made to destroy the ruins of these homes in order to obliterate all memory of the victims. Clearly the genocide was meant not only to cleanse the social body of the Rwandan state of Tutsis but to remove all traces and consign to oblivion the entire Tutsi community.[9]

THE POLITICS OF MEMORY AND TRAUMA
IN POST-GENOCIDE RWANDA

The belated experience of trauma . . . suggests that history is not only the passing on of a crisis but also the passing on of a survival that can only be possessed within a history larger than any single individual or any single generation.
                                              —Cathy Caruth, *Unclaimed Experience*

I will now turn to the politics of memory in post-genocide Rwanda. In the discussion that follows, I will examine the "trauma" programs that were instigated as forms of humanitarian aid. I will argue that these programs may be understood as technologies of memory, which, although applied with the intent of alleviating suffering, have the potential to displace other ways of thinking and doing memory work. Of key concern here is how biomedical practices in the context of liberal-humanist projects of reconciliation may submerge the ethico-political dimensions of remembrance.

Trauma interventions provide a window into the dynamics of the negotiation of political subjectivities of survivors, perpetrators, and bystanders, in the context of their ethnic and gender identities and in relation to the question of justice. In such interventions, trauma is understood as an experience to be contained rather than an ethical calling to be heard, one that would challenge assumptions of responsibility, politics, and subjectivity. Thus, one must begin to ask the question of how a rethinking of trauma itself may reconfigure the (im)possibilities for justice, history, mourning, and memory work. In such questioning, the traumatic insists on an interrogation of the status of culture in the theories and practices of mental health and healing. In this there is an undoing of the binaries of the universal/particular and the autonomous individual/social body that have plagued many debates on psychiatry, human rights, and memory.

Shortly after the RPF assumed power, and after the humanitarian organizations were no longer preoccupied with the fiasco of the refugee camps in Zaire (which had increasingly become advantageous to the organizers of the genocide),[10] the international community finally began to address the emotional needs of the survivors who remained in Rwanda. The recognition that the needs of genocide survivors are not simply material but also encompass psychosocial recovery is a new step in humanitarianism, but one fraught with many ethical and political questions. As technologies of memory, the discourses of psychology and psychiatry rely on particular configurations of power/knowledge deployed in particular contexts, often as a means to contain memory and trauma rather than respond to them as a form of witnessing. Numerous assumptions shaping prevalent understandings of trauma are linked to hegemonic biomedical discourses. Post-traumatic stress disorder (PTSD) forms the primary body of knowledge used by humanitarians to treat the emotional impact of war. While PTSD by no means constitutes a unified or universal construct that exists outside of those practices and technologies used to study and treat it (Young 1995), there is an underlying theory of causality that assumes "time moves from the etiological event to post-traumatic symptoms" (Young 1995, 135). On these terms, a normative description of PTSD commonly refers to post-traumatic stress as a normal reaction to abnormal events. The *Diagnostic and Statistical Manual* (DSM), which serves as the handbook for psychotherapeutic diagnosis in the United States and elsewhere, defines PTSD as caused by a traumatic event that manifests itself through the following symptoms: a reexperiencing of the event, the avoidance of situations that may trigger the event, the numbing of responses, and forms of arousal upon exposure to triggering phenomena.

The DSM is principally informed by the notion of an autonomous, universal individual located at the center of Western morality and cosmology (Bracken et al. 1995). The assumed universalism of the DSM obscures the ways in which PTSD is an effect of specific forms of power/knowledge. As Young (1995) has shown, the DSM emerged from a specific historical and cultural context that valued such positivist epistemologies as those espoused by Kraepelin (1973). Kraepelinian psychiatry constitutes symptoms as signs of underlying pathological structures in which symptoms are arranged in stable formations or syndromes (Young 1995, 96). This discourse constitutes pathology as exterior to the historically and culturally informed subjectivity of the individual patient. As Bracken and Petty (1998, 49) note, in regard to the underlying cognitivist philosophy of Western psychiatry, trauma is assumed to act on individuals; thus therapy is oriented toward restoring schemata in discrete individuals through the talking cure. While terms on which PTSD is conceptualized are worth critical consideration in general, PTSD as a framework for addressing suffering in Rwanda is further limited by its assumption of a "post" to the violence that may continue to threaten many individuals and communities (Becker 1995). The emphasis on the finite character of traumatic events silences the realities of ongoing structural violence. Furthermore, as Bracken and Petty (1998) note, therapeutic practices in response to a diagnosis of PTSD do not address the mechanisms through which people might work through the political failures that resulted in violence in the first place. These limitations result in a depoliticization and medicalization of suffering.

The diagnosis of PTSD excludes the possibility of recognizing the historical-political dimension of suffering when the overwhelming emphasis on ameliorative treatment relies on a set of universal symptoms that miss an encounter with the moral and social imperatives that emerge from the wound. Traumatization becomes a pathological condition to be treated rather than experiential knowledge demanding legitimation in terms that exceed biomedical discourse. Kleinman (1988, 28) has rightly pointed out that biomedicine and the behavioral sciences limit contemplations of trauma and suffering to one of understanding. However, he stops short of addressing deeper challenges to claims of knowledge and reason in the wake of mass violence. In the analysis that follows, I will attempt to point out the limitations of psychotherapeutic interventions with an eye to the ethico-political imperatives of witnessing and, in turn, consider how these issues relate to questions of justice and reconciliation.

In the months following the genocide, UNICEF created a comprehensive program to address the problems of trauma in Rwanda. At unaccompanied children's centers and orphanages, UNICEF officials conducted surveys informed by the psychological constructs embodied in the DSM. The stated purpose of the UNICEF surveys was to ascertain the "magnitude of exposure to traumatic events and frequencies of traumatic reactions" (Jensen et al. 1997, 86). From this baseline survey of trauma exposure, a National Trauma Center (CNT) was created to train social workers, teachers, and clergy on the symptomatology of PTSD and techniques for encouraging children to tell their stories through art and verbal exchanges. Radio vignettes, role playing exercises, and a tertiary care center for severely traumatized children were all components of the comprehensive mental health program, which was lauded by UNICEF as a culturally appropriate intervention. However, on these terms, the issue of cultural competence has largely been framed in terms of the successful translation of survey instruments and vignettes into Kinyarwanda and the employment of Rwandan professionals with training in psychology and psychiatry. Working as a legitimating discourse, the use of the notion of "culturally appropriate practice" may produce culture as fetish, serving as a mask for a wound or void created through loss. There is little mention of the power relations and sociopolitical context that were implicated in the genocide and continue, in transformed ways, in its aftermath.

These "culturally appropriate" programs have rarely addressed how trauma is locally constructed, an inquiry that would have to consider how local cultural forms and power relationships conceptualize the psychic and social wounds of mass violence. Proceeding as if this is a nonissue, the globalizing practices of humanitarian organizations may actually be working to marginalize local knowledges and practices for dealing with grief and loss. For example, when I interviewed two Rwandan mental health professionals, raising the question of the role spirit possession and indigenous healers may have in mediating suffering and memory, I was met with an incredulous look and the response, *"Á'est sauvage et incivilisé."* The CNT and related programs have importantly contributed to dispelling notions that flashbacks, nightmares, social withdrawal, or intrusive thoughts are signs of madness, a madness that could further evoke social disharmony, marginalization and revictimization of individuals.[11] However, it is incumbent on those attempting to provide aid to victims of mass violence to listen and respond to suffering in a manner that enables the possibility for the reconstitution of speech and subjectivity. This practice remains absent from the aid discourse on trauma in Rwanda. While this issue is considered by many practitioners as merely academic, it actually strikes at the heart of the crisis of suffering and its ethico-political demands. The hegemony of Western biomedical thought, which emphasizes talking cures, can marginalize other practices that place the origins of distress and healing therapies in the social body.

Counter to the dominance of the PTSD framework, many anthropologists have emphasized the role of "traditional" healers in mediating trauma through ritual, which may restore communal bonds through the exorcism of violent or malingering spirits from the body (Nordstrom 1997), or provide other nondiscursive forms of healing (Bracken et al. 1995). These works raise the persistent question of culture and its place in healing, suffering, and memory, a question that has plagued discourses such as ethnopsychiatry since the colonial era. At issue, though, is just how such healing practices are to be understood and what their relation to the social body might be. As Hayes (1998) notes, both psychological reparation and political reconciliation are *historical* projects, each in need of unpacking. On these terms, an overly rigid evocation of this dichotomy between healing therapies that address "the social body" and therapeutic discourses founded on an individualized, universal self risks an orientalist reduction. Moreover, embracing this dichotomy threatens to delegitimize the suffering of individuals by subsuming individual testimonies to the collective, social "Other." Rather than positing an opposition between the individual and society, one must begin to think of the imbrication of the two in theorizing a cultural politics of trauma.

To begin to get some sense of the implications of this rethinking, it is important to consider how the customary place of traditional healers in contemporary Rwanda has been destabilized. The Habyarimana regime attempted to co-opt such healers through the creation of a traditional medical center that attempted to limit the impact of these therapies while simultaneously asserting their authenticity (Taylor 1992). Since the colonial era, the Catholic Church had sought to suppress indigenous forms of religion that competed with the church and had actually formed the basis of numerous rural revolts against central authorities. After a century of increased pressures from both capitalism and Christianity the traditional therapeutic modalities have become fragmented, reworked, and, at times, resemble confessionary practices associated with Western psychiatric discourses (Taylor 1992). In addition, the genocide itself has affected these therapies as many traditional healers did not survive the violence.

That said, traditional healing practices are not unheard of in post–genocide Rwanda. One Rwandan social worker working with a genocide survivor organization related the following:

> There is a woman, Alphonsine, who comes here every week who lost her 3 year old son when the *interahamwe* attacked her hill. After torturing his father in front of him he was also killed with machete blows. Alphonsine rarely sleeps at night because the spirit of her child runs around her *urugo* (home with enclosure) all night long and his cries keep her awake. When she went to one of the trauma programs with counselors trained in western psychology they provided little assistance for her. Therefore she came to us to see if we could find a way for her to communicate with her son. Normally she could find an *umupfumu* (witch doctor) in her sector but they were all killed or fled as refugees. Therefore we must help her find another.

The survivor mentioned here ultimately resorted to the use of both traditional healers and trauma counselors. The counselor I spoke with also suspected that this woman was a practitioner of *kubandwa,* or spirit possession, which she shyly admitted one day after many therapy sessions. As a form of remembrance, spirit possession establishes a link between the dead and the living, present and past, as a form of embodied memory. What is enacted in spirit possession is a memorial practice of relation between people across time, rather than the notion of memory as a databank that predominates in most Western societies (Lambek 1996, 239). Taylor's (1992) study of indigenous healing in Rwanda reveals the historical importance of spirits who embody particular historical agents ranging over decades. As Lambek suggests, the dead can speak for themselves. Throughout much of Sub-Saharan Africa, spirit possession, or *ngoma* (particularly as these practices occur in social settings), can serve as therapeutic circles where individual suffering can be articulated in public spaces, even though such spaces in the Rwandan context are in the cover of darkness, away from the gaze of the church. As such, spirit possession can be a confirmation of continuity (memory) and discontinuity (mourning), where remembrance serves as a moral claim rather than a neutral representation (Taylor 1992).

However, a total reliance on spirit possession, or traditional medicine, for practices of memory work (in opposition to psychotherapeutic counseling) is not uncontested. While several Rwandan trauma counselors have complained to me in interviews that Belgian ethnopsychiatrists have preached that traditional healers "are the way to go in trauma counseling," these counselors have far more nuanced positions. They recognize, on the one hand, the propensity for quackery to fill the void left by the genocide and hence possibly furthering the exploitation of sufferers. On the other hand, these counselors recognize the need for encouraging patients to discuss their experiences with healers and pursue practices that they find effective.

Up to this point, I have been attempting to complicate the dichotomies that have driven polemics and policy in the delivery of trauma support programs in postgenocide Rwanda. This discussion becomes further complicated when one critically considers the evocation of "the social" in therapeutic modalities. First of all, therapeutic programs tend to rely on community-based mental health care in which community leaders are trained to recognize the symptoms of trauma in order to refer the most severely traumatized individuals for individual therapy at survivor organizations or the CNT. However, the idea of community in these programs generally is viewed as innocuous: defined through spatiality, devoid of power relations and undifferentiated by gender, class, clan, or ethnicity. The fact that virtually every community in Rwanda was the site of massacres and displacement dramatically complicates what the idea of community means and who it is that can stand as a "community leader." What happens to the social idea of "community" when neighbors, priests, nuns, doctors, and children have taken part in killing hundreds of thousands of individuals?

Indeed, talk of "reintegrating" traumatized individuals into communities begs the question of what precisely it means to speak of community in the wake of the genocide. The structural violence that is implicated in the genocide has become further entrenched with the destruction, physical insecurity, and emotional distress that exist in many parts of the country. What these concerns gesture to is the recognition that the question of community is also a question of how mourning, memory, and knowledge are related (Benjamin 1997). This questioning demands a rethinking of trauma that moves beyond the discourse of PTSD into the realm of ethics.

According to Caruth's reading of Freud's *Moses and Monotheism,* the belatedness of the traumatic experience creates a situation where the traumatized become a symptom of a history they cannot possess (1996, 71). Present concerns with justice and the liberal ideal of reconciliation are based on the notion that evidentiary knowledge will provide truths capable of assigning guilt and mastering the past through the accumulation of knowledge. But what might the possibility for history and justice be if trauma is unknowable, an event that happened too soon to be grasped (Caruth 1996, 71)? In this dilemma, one faces the question of the relation between speech and truth, of what words are to be found that could utter experiences that cannot be known and yet remain imbricated with issues of culture and power (Bertoldi 1998). What kind of psychoanalytic discourse can counter the reification of "culture" legitimated in the totalizing forms of universalism or the exclusivist particularisms that reassert boundaries and forms of (mis)identification? What has been lacking in these mental health programs is a discussion of how the work (or play) of mourning may be untethered from a priori foundations or universal stages of mourning.

During the genocide, bodies were thrown into mass graves and rivers, mutilated, burned, or lost in the ensuing massive displacement of communities, leaving many survivors without access to the necessary rituals of mourning. The absence of bodies emerges as a presence and continual source of suffering, but as well poses very specific problems in regard to what mourning can mean and how it might take place. Gasibirege (1995) points to the debate on PTSD in the Rwanda context and how applied psychology has marginalized the question of the work of mourning. The homogenizing effects of trauma programs have silenced the multitude of individual practices of mourning and the incommensurability of experiences of traumatic loss. In a discussion with a Rwandan trauma counselor, I learned of a well-known British psychologist working on community-based trauma programs in Rwanda. He made the assertion that all trauma programs were largely equivalent so it would be a worthwhile endeavor to attempt to further standardize programs and training; after all, he argued, grieving processes are generally the same. This is a clear example of how the rationality of humanitarian discourses attempts to overcome difference and depoliticize the politics of mourning. The more one tries to impose sameness on cultural practices the greater the potential for silencing the Other. However, the solution to the problem does not lie purely in the realm of a particularistic, yet homogenized and fetishized notion of mourning rituals in "Rwandan culture." The question of the universal and the particular in these political contexts must move beyond the notion of pure sameness or difference. As Ernesto Laclau has astutely recognized:

> An appeal to pure particularism is no solution to the problems we are facing in contemporary societies. The assertion of pure particularism, independent of any content and of any appeal to a universality, is a self-defeating enterprise. . . . If particularity asserts itself as mere particularity, in a purely differential relation with other particularities, it is sanctioning the status quo in power relations between groups. This is exactly the notion of "separate developments" as formulated in apartheid. (1996, 87–88; see Bertoldi 1998, 129)

In beginning to rethink what is necessary to support the work of mourning in post-genocide Rwanda, I remain haunted by my conversations with Elizabeth, a survivor of the 1994 mass atrocities: "When my children grow up how will I explain why their father was killed? Because he was Tutsi? All of this is meaningless. I never cared about ethnicity and neither did he. In the end I need to forget but I know that we can never forget what happened here." "I need to forget but we can never forget"—who is the "we" of this address? Elizabeth still lives in the home where she was raped by numerous *interahamwe* for one hundred days and where a mass grave containing the bodies of her husband and neighbors was dug several feet from the front of her home. On our occasional walks through the neighborhood, she narrated the events of the genocide as they took place on this hill, literally producing a cartographic map of terror that she continues to inhabit.[12] The dead, you see, continue to defy death and haunt the present as an absence, thus blurring the boundary between life and death. The forgetting that Elizabeth references is a necessary part of understanding, of speaking beyond the very impossibility of knowing, of bringing to light new modes of hearing and witnessing (Caruth 1996, 32–56). Andrew Benjamin brings to light the central concern here through a meditation on Blanchot's *The Writing of Disaster* that asks how we can accept not knowing in the wake of Auschwitz while simultaneously addressing the imperative of not forgetting. Genocide as a limit experience defies knowledge. However, this impossible possibility opens up for Benjamin a space where loss can be rethought as a type of intellectual and political activity demanding vigilance and recognition of the impossibility of mastering what took place (Caruth 1996, 22). This rethinking demands an ethical form of hearing, one that brings to light Caruth's (1996, 24) insight of how "trauma is never simply one's own . . . history is precisely the way we are implicated in each other's traumas."

Elizabeth's struggle to make sense of her trauma is one of the issues that Caruth (1996) brings to light in her rereading of Freud's writings on trauma. Trauma in her reading is "a wound with a voice that cries out," but this is a paradoxical wounding in that it is produced by an event that "has been experienced too soon to be fully known and it is this unknowability that returns to haunt the survivor." Here the traumatic experience is located in the beyond or is ungraspable. Such experiences demand our listening. Trauma is more than "an escape from death"; it is "the ongoing experience of having survived it" and the "oscillation between a crisis of death and the correlative crisis of life" (Caruth 1996, 65). However, banishment from language and knowledge opens up the possibility of a return, of something new. Life does go on. Elizabeth immediately began organizing circles of children—both those who had witnessed the violence and those belonging to Hutu and Tutsi families that had not experienced violence. Resisting recommendations to take her children to one of the trauma centers, she has, through both writing and bringing her neighbors together, begun to explore ways to forge life beyond the violence. This entails the weighty task of how to live with the memories of the past and reconcile community and identities inscribed through a mass violence that has rendered the everyday unfamiliar.

It is precisely the voices of women like Elizabeth that disrupt the triumphalism of the State, its foundational myths and the sacrificeablity of women. Her dilemma of how to remember and forget brings to mind Benjamin's notion of the play of mourning (Benjamin 1963/1998). Benjamin's notion of mourning is one that defies a collective working through of grief. The loss of the object must be preserved, not reconciled with an experience that is inherently unreconcilable (Jay 1996). Forgetting here means active forgetting of the Nietzschean sort, which opens up the possibility for other forms of knowledge and belonging rather than a nostalgic attempt to recover "history as it was." Benjamin is cautious to avoid a form of mourning that falls into a paralyzing form of despair or what he called "tortured stupidity" or melancholic subjectivity that remains subjugated to the dead and detaches itself from political action (Pensky 1993, 11). Voices such as Elizabeth's cry out for a form of remembrance that pays its debts to the dead while not claiming to speak on their behalf. Flashes such as these, Benjamin hoped, would provide the inspiration for social and political movements rather than become appropriated in the monumental history of the state (Buck-Morss 1993). For Benjamin, forms of insightful remembrance that make fragments of the past visible in the present as traces work against uncritical monumentalist forms of memory and disrupt the chronological forms of history. The juxtaposition of the past and present holds within it the potential for liberating oppressed moments of history in the present, moments that may become sites of resistance.

JUSTICE, MOURNING, AND COUNTERMOURNING

"Justice," she said. "I've heard that word. It's a cold word. I tried it out," she said, still speaking in a low voice. "I wrote it down. I wrote it down several times and always it looked like a damn cold lie to me. There is no justice."

—Jean Rhys, *Wide Sargasso Sea*

Can there ever be justice for the nearly one million killed in Rwanda and for those who witnessed the unthinkable? In the 1990s, there has been a remarkable attention to the prosecution of those accused of having committed crimes against humanity in conflicts around the world. Following in the wake of the truth and reconciliation commissions in Argentina and Chile, and the prosecution of the Vichy leaders in France, the creation of the International Criminal Tribunal for the Former-Yugoslavia (ICTY) has been considered a sign of moral progress. This tribunal is widely embraced as a major development in the legitimation of international human rights and the formation of institutions concerned with the establishment and adjudication of laws of war. However, one might argue that, despite the persistent belief in the progress of international law, there is little reason to celebrate. Clearly in Rwanda, what we have seen is the persistence of war crimes and a profound indifference by those institutions created to protect "international civil society" from the evils of totalitarianism and mass death. Despite these realities, there remains a profound faith in the power of international law and its juridical mechanisms to not only prosecute war criminals but also master or transcend the past. It is to this "article of faith" (Ignatieff 1996) that I now turn, a faith that the narrative memories articulated within legal proceedings can put the past to rest and lead to a more secure present and future. In the discussion that follows, I am not positing an either/or scenario in which the prosecution of war criminals would be neglected in the name of an ethics of alterity. Such an argument would merely perform the humanist lie that Foucault cautions us against. Indeed, Foucault himself did not preclude rights discourse (Foucault 1988 and 1984; Keenan 1997). Instead, the discussion that follows is meant to alert us to the conditions of possibility for rethinking notions of memory, community, and justice that may emerge from the site of trauma, leading to other forms of subjectivity that problematize and transcend the present.

A key theoretical analysis of the importance of war crimes tribunals and truth and reconciliation commissions remains Mark Osiel's (1997) *Mass Atrocity, Collective Memory, and the Law*. Written from a liberal legal position, Osiel's text supports the assertion of the return of the rule of law in the wake of mass atrocities. Central to his argument is an understanding of trials as public spectacles, in which "moral entrepreneurs" (i.e., liberal legal representatives) stage a public reckoning that will, it is hoped, generate a pedagogical narrative memory guided by liberal values of tolerance and respect. The desire here is that this narrative will contribute to a national, collective memory that may transcend the authoritarian practices of the past. Osiel's thinking assumes a detached Archimedean point from which society can be viewed in its totality and in which a "liberal show trial" (judged by the liberal metanarrative produced and orchestrated through the guidance of the "enlightened" legal profession) can flourish. The tribunal as a liberal text guides the nation-state's mourning process, a process it is assumed that will initiate a rupture with the past in guiding the way to a future.

This conceptualization certainly requires problematization.[13] The internal contradictions within Osiel's text, and liberal formulations of human rights law in general, clearly reveal the inability to take into account alterity and thus undermine attempts to pursue justice as a form of critical practice. Through an analysis of the assumptions of Osiel's text and how these assumptions frequently unfold in practice in the Rwandan context, I will attempt to demonstrate the inconsistencies in the hegemonic discourse of justice and reconciliation. On these terms, I offer an understanding of how practices of countermourning and countermemory contest the metanarrative of liberalism, the state, and difference in an effort to direct attention to other forms of justice and memory that may better address alterity.

My critique of the liberal metanarrative of justice in international and human rights law will heed the call of Sophocles' Antigone, who "demands our recognition irrespective of any legal code" (Douzinas and Warrington 1994, 20). The call of the other, prior to the law, the state, or the metanarrative of liberalism, is one that demands to be heard rather than appropriated as "Sameness." Levinas's call for an ethics of alterity here resonates with Benjamin's warning that "even the dead will not be safe from the enemy if he wins" (Benjamin 1968, 255)—a calling that resists subsuming the memory of the dead (and the living) under the weight of monumental history. The imperative then is to demand a form of justice that lies in the beyond, never satisfied, always vigilant; one that resists the closure that liberalism desires. As Douzinas and Warrington (1994, 150) argue, modern law has abandoned ethics through the impersonal exercise of power in the quest for the *administration* of justice rather than seeking a form of justice infused with the ethico-political demands of a critical practice.

Osiel's desire for the forging of a collective memory based on metaphysical foundations not only denies space for competing "truths" and counternarratives but runs the risk of espousing forms of community based on origins. Communities of memory (Wyschogrod 1992, 170) that value the act of knowing—a form of representation based on the self-deception that one can know the unknowable—have been central to the mobilization of memory in nationalist and ethnic violence in Rwanda and elsewhere. Furthermore, Osiel's liberalism lacks the reflexivity needed to interrogate the effects of power that result from particular forms of universalism that naturalize the nation-state as the primary form of identification, and in which dis-identifications may be enforced. This can be seen in the case of Rwanda, in which the nation-state succeeded—with the complicity of the West—in the extermination of nearly one million individuals no longer identified as legitimate citizens. A form of justice that opens the possibility for alternative forms of identification is therefore demanded. Memory, rather than being mobilized to fill the homogeneous, empty time of the state, can offer a way to explore the "multiple pulls and trajectories of hegemony . . . which carries within it a system of differentiated subjectivities as reconstituted in the present" (Frazier 1998, 115). This notion of a reconstitution of differentiated subjectivities undoes any straightforward notion of a "collective memory." It prompts the question: Who is included in the collectivity or who is the "we" involved here, and how was this entity produced? Justice viewed in merely its institutional context as such works to obscure the multitude of cultural practices and sites where memory and justice are thought and practiced.

The Rwandan state's attempt at trying the perpetrators of the genocide and initiating reconciliation brings home the imperative of collective memory as critical practice. Since 1996, the RPF has sought to reform the judicial apparatus and bring to trial those accused of having participated in the genocide, while forging a "government of unity and national reconciliation." The genocide resulted in 80 percent of the lawyers and judges either being killed or having fled the country, a country where tens of thousands are accused of having participated in the genocide. Clearly the task of ending impunity is overwhelming. Mamdani (1996b) points out that the Rwandan state has historically been characterized as one where the identity of one group is that of power and the other has the fate of the subject. The RPF has attempted to transcend this historical precedent through the ideology of pan-Africanism. One manifestation of this ideology is the effort to remove ethnic identity from identification cards, through stressing that Rwandans are all *Banyarwanda*. On the surface, this appears to be a rather harmless gesture; however, it evokes a discourse that veils the power relations that still work to constitute a humiliated subjectivity for Hutus (always potentially tainted as bystanders or supporters of the genocide). A fitting note on the potential for continuing conflict within Rwanda is offered by Appiah (1992, 176), who highlights the underlying problematic with reductive aspects of pan-Africanism(s) based on race. He argues, "'[r]ace' disables us because it proposes as a basis for common action the illusion that black (and white and yellow) people are fundamentally allied by nature and, thus, without effort; it leaves us unprepared, therefore, to handle the 'intraracial' conflicts that arise from the very different situations of black (and white and yellow) people in different parts of the economy and of the world."

In the past year, a Commission on Unity and National Reconciliation has been created to formulate a political agenda to promote reconciliation. Coupled with the ideology of unity is a form of ethnohistory that stresses the harmonious relationship of the three ethnicities prior to colonialism. It is argued that the root of division within Rwanda lies with European colonialism. The colonial history of Rwanda is certainly of central importance, but to ignore the agency of Rwandans in their own history risks an externalization of responsibility obscuring the necessity of thinking politically about the present. Accompanying the task of rethinking identity/difference must be a critical project of reexamining long-held notions of responsibility, justice, and democracy. When the wounds of the genocide are still raw, the political expediency of this approach may be a pragmatic move, but one that risks fetishizing ethnic origins and elevating the desire for a nostalgic past that is not that different from the forces that should be opposed. In this regard, an internal contradiction has emerged in that the RPF has used the term *umuryango* to identify itself—a term literally meaning a lineage or kin group denoting common origins (des Forges 1999, 693). As such the RPF's discourse of reconciliation fails to rethink the political identities necessary to transcend the violence of the past (Mamdani 1996b).

The experience of the tribunals and memorial practices over the past several years actually works to undermine the reconciliatory ideology of the RPF, which increasingly appears to espouse a strictly punitive notion of justice. Mamdani (1996b) raises the issue of how claims to truth may actually breed self-righteousness and humiliation of the other. The execution of four convicted war criminals in April 1998 demonstrates the dangers of the national tribunals. The executions in the Nyamirambo stadium in Kigali of those convicted of genocide drew large crowds, which reportedly showed great enthusiasm for the executions, the first act of state punishment four years after the genocide. Responding to international criticism of the executions, the government claimed that these executions would be a first step in healing the nation as Rwandans could finally witness the punishment of those responsible for their suffering. The umbrella organization for all of the genocide survivor organizations, IBUKA ("Remember"[14]) supported the executions, arguing that they would be a cathartic experience for the country. The public spectacle of executions, however, can be read as much more than an attempt at reconciliation or an evocation of a cathartic experience. Rather, they are a spectacle aimed at displaying the power of the state. The executions as a performative act are examples not of the power of violence, but rather the violence of power. Arriving in Rwanda barely two months after the executions, I came across many who felt that the death sentences had dissipated much of the frustration emerging from the slow pace of the tribunals and fears of impunity. However, beneath the surface, other narratives appeared. One afternoon on a hill, barely two kilometers from the stadium, I asked a group of women what they thought of the executions. Immediately, frowns appeared on their faces and one began wagging her finger with an air of authority. "I am a Christian[15] and we do not kill like this. The *interahamwe* killed my husband and sons but I never want to become like them!" she exclaimed. "Killing doesn't bring back my family. We need to learn to live together and stop killing each other, what have we become?" another added. In its attempt to orchestrate a spectacle capable of recreating an "imagined community," the violence of the state—while intending to create a unifying spectacle through the exercise of power—produced, in these cases at least, further fractures.

One needs, thus, to be suspicious of reconciliatory claims within a discursive complex where notions of justice and memory are deployed as practices of power that justify the present. But it is at the margins of these discourses where other competing conceptualizations frequently emerge. Unproblematic appropriations of the language of reconciliation thus become implicated in neoliberal and authoritarian practices that may be less distinct from what they critique than is generally assumed. As Benita Parry (1995), writing on the question of reconciliation and remembrance in South Africa, states:

In this new world order, the power of capital looms over the rhetoric of reconstructed and "people-driven" programmes devised by governments of national unity in recently-liberated states. Thus the critical question to be asked of an official ideology of reconciliation, with its language of consensus and settlement, is that it is deployed within social formations that remain fissured by class divisions and conflicts. In which case, is it not premature to command concord when the circumstances making for discord remain in place? And is it not inequitable for governments and intellectuals to entreat gestural atonement from the strong, whose privileges are intact, while the aspirations of the dispossessed who are enjoined to pardon their expropriators and exploiters, continue to be unappeased? The problem for theoretical work then presents itself not as one of aligning reconciliation with remembrance, but rather of joining remembrance of the past with a critique of the contemporary condition. This suggests that we need to recall the long histories of injustice, and to remember the obstacles in the way of building a just society. For our best hope for universal emancipation lies in remaining unreconciled to the past and discontented with the present. (95)

CONCLUSION

Throughout this chapter, I have attempted to highlight some of the shortcomings of hegemonic discourses of justice, reconciliation, and healing within liberal and humanitarian practices. The analysis is not meant merely to deconstruct these concepts, but rather to open up spaces for their rethinking. The underlying assumptions in much of the talk on justice and reconciliation reflect a desire to produce closure, to know the past as it was, without coming to terms with the political inscription of violence and one's complicity within structures that carry great potential to reinscribe violent discourses under the guise of peace or justice. The assumption that the "veil of ignorance" of law can posit a position outside of the conflict is no longer tenable (Campbell 1998a). There is no exteriority from which to speak. Therefore, responsibility emerges from within as a question of proximity (Keenan 1997, Levinas 1978/1991). By problematizing justice, thinking of it as an ideal, we can "hope" to displace justice from its institutional context to the realm of the everyday, as an effort to open up the present, in a restaging of a multitude of sites for the praxis of memory, memory as justice. The necessity of thinking beyond merely the reinstallation of the rule of law responds to Foucault's observation that "the rule of law does not replace warfare: humanity installs each of its violations in a system of rules and this proceeds from domination to domination" (Foucault 1977, 150–151).

There are many spaces in Rwanda where mourning and voice have become central organizing elements of social practices. Less than a year after the genocide, Beatrice Mukansinga returned to Rwanda from Kenya to find much of her family had been brutally murdered during the genocide. After learning of her father's death and many who had lost entire families, as well as discovering that many women had been raped and had borne the children of these rapes, her despair was overwhelming. In response, she organized groups of women survivors to come together to tell their stories, to pray, to sing, and to dance. These groups eventually evolved into an organization called *Mbwira Ndumva* (Speak, I'm Listening). This organization works to provide housing, micro-credit, and trauma counseling, but, most importantly, to create a space where women can tell their stories. Moreover, *Mbwira Ndumva* welcomes anyone, regardless of ethnicity, to join their circles; thus hybrid spaces not belonging to any preconstituted community are emerging. Revenge, or the ranking of other people's suffering, does not belong to the vocabulary of the organization. In spaces such as this, we see the Levinasian embrace of alterity through the recognition of the human in the other. We see as well in this space the slow building of the foundation of an alternative politics of democracy, far more profound than the textbook notions of civil society and institutional democracy espoused by the dominant version of liberal human rights discourse. Beatrice and her colleagues remain fierce critics of the ICTR, for they remain unreconciled with the past and present. The language of institutional justice remains far removed from their everyday struggles of survival and the refashioning of selves and communities.

Frequently throughout my research in Rwanda, I have been told of spontaneous groups, such as *Mbwira Ndumva,* which remain informal entities that began as associations of Tutsi women raped or widowed during the genocide. However, in 1996, when repatriated Hutus began returning from Zaire, some of these associations of Tutsi women embraced Hutu women, traumatized by the experience of forced exodus and the conditions in the refugee camps where they faced death, sexual violence, and deprivation. These associations rarely appear in human rights reports and other writings on Rwanda, but constitute powerful acts of remembrance and resistance to the violence that has caused their suffering. As these groups of individuals meet to tell their stories, to listen to the wounded words of their neighbors, these "wounded spaces" become sites where the dominant narrative of Rwandan history can be disrupted and the collective traumas of precolonial, colonial, and postcolonial violence can be transformed. In these sites, the history of women's oppression and suffering promises to become a source of imaginative power and forge new languages of social suffering, democracy, and justice (McLaren and da Silva 1993). Here, the nation-state's project of "Out of the Many One" becomes unraveled, revealing "the ethnography of its own historicity [opening] up the possibility of other narratives of the people and their difference" (Bhabha 1990, 294–300).

A critical politics of remembrance necessarily implies a decolonization of imagination that scrutinizes the discourse of (neo)colonialism for its contamination of the politics of the present. Memory as critical praxis resists a search for origins or authenticity, or homogenizing calls for unity that negate difference. As Davies (1998) notes, this must entail foregoing notions of "origins and exclusivity" produced by colonial historians such as Speke (1863) and moving toward the decolonization of the fetish. The European appropriation of the fetish resulted in its use by the dominant to legitimize their rule; however, an alternative notion of the fetish would recognize its double meaning as a metaphor for another reality where the taboo, the unspoken, can be named and unveiled. In the space of silence between domination and subordination lies the conditions of possibility for new languages and ways of belonging, or nonbelonging, "a being radically devoid of any representable identity" (Agamben 1993, 85). From these spaces, Benjamin's notion of "redemptive remembrance" can be articulated, where a form of countermemory emerges that moves beyond history and myth, where the seamless narrative of the state and its violence can be disrupted, where a dialogue that embraces alterity (registering the ways in which "we" are all caught up in and disproportionately constituted by dominant discourses) can provide a critique of the present (McLaren and da Silva 1993).

Perhaps this is where the final lesson of trauma lies. For Levinas, the subject is trauma (Critchley 1999, 186), "a gaping wound that will not heal." Critchley concludes that "[t]he passage to justice in Levinas—to the third party, the community and politics—passes through or across the theoretical and historical experience of trauma" (1999, 195). Arising from this obligation may also lie the possibility for hope and an ethos of democracy that sustains a notion of identity indebted to the other rather than at the expense of the other. The spaces created by *Mbwira Ndumva* and others may then constitute what Blanchot termed "the unavowable community" (Blanchot 1988, Wyschogrod 1992, 174–175), where the victim deprived of language can articulate her claims—a right to rights or new forms of experience yet unrealized in "human rights" (Keenan 1997), a dream for justice on the horizon embodied in a community without foundations.

NOTES

1. Speech by State Department spokesperson Christine Shelly. *International Herald Tribune,* June 13, 1994.

2. The Arusha Accords was the UN-sponsored attempt to put an end to the civil war by brokering a power-sharing arrangement between the Habyarimana regime and the RPF that initiated the war in 1990 (see Prunier 1995).

3. In the eighteenth century, biblical interpretations of the Hamitic hypothesis were increasingly replaced by scientific notions used by social scientists to explain the seemingly paradoxical situation of Egyptian civilization. Throughout the early twentieth century, ethnologists continued to study the Hamites and their inherent "will to dominate" such that the discourse of Hamitism became part of discussions of Euro-American geopolitics and anti-Semitism. Social scientists such as Maquet (1954) also produced essentialist interpretations of ethnicity based on stereotypes and character traits.

4. The 1980s to early 1990s saw growing resistance by various sectors of society. One group in particular, coffee farmers, began uprooting coffee trees in symbolic protest. The existence of such widespread discontent should provoke some wariness when approaching the oft-cited notion that the genocide in Rwanda occurred because of the proclivity of Rwandans to obey authorities, one of the causes that Prunier (1995) emphasizes most often.

5. The origins of Hutu Power, according to its ideological founders, is the Black Consciousness Movement, but, as is apparent from its content, this is a fallacy (Chretian 1995).

6. Rwanda also had one of the most authoritarian policies regarding spatial mobility of the population, more so than South Africa under Apartheid (see Prunier 1995).

7. The three ethnicities being Hutu, Tutsi, and Twa.

8. The Kinyarwanda term for genocide is *itsembabwoko,* which is derived from the verbs *gutsemba* (to exterminate) and *ubwoko* (ethnicity). This is slightly different from the English or Latin derivative used by international law, which is not limited to ethnicity alone.

9. For those wanting a more detailed analysis of the genocide, the works of African Rights (1995) and Prunier (1995) are the most authoritative accounts at present.

10. The refugee camps in the bordering countries were largely created by the forced exodus of the Hutu population under the leadership of the FAR. Once the refugee camps were created, it is estimated that 60–70 percent of the $1 million/day food aid was diverted for the purchase of weapons and support of the leadership of the genocidal regime. The effects of the "humanitarian" policies have contributed to the long-term instability and present war in the Democratic Republic of Congo, which began in August 1998.

11. Rwanda's only psychiatic hospital, L'hopital psychiatriqu de Nedra, was established under Belgian rule to treat prisoners.

12. The first time I met Elizabeth she recounted the story of how, several months after the genocide, a Tutsi man from Uganda (upon hearing her story) accused her of being an *ibyitso,* or accomplice, for having survived the genocide. She must have collaborated with the *interahamwe,* he argued, or how else had she survived? Falling into despair for weeks after this accusation, Elizabeth feared for her life and her children. In the immediate aftermath of the genocide, such false accusations were rife. Often to take someone's home, all a person had to do was accuse another of being a *genocidaire* and the accused could find himself in prison. But more than the immediate threat this accusation raised, this experience was felt, she explained, as the "second rape" or "death." Her experience of rape, widowhood, and mass killings came to resemble a form of social death.

13. Throughout Osiel's text, there are constant references to "postmodernists" as facile relativists. Although a common move in many liberal and human rights discussions, this form of polemic does little justice to a broad literature falling under the headings of poststructuralism, postcolonialism, certain forms of feminist theory, etc. A close reading of the very theorists he criticizes, such as Foucault and Lyotard, would reveal a deep commitment to justice, however, a justice reconfigured in a very different manner to the understanding he articulates.

14. IBUKA maintains a political position viewed by many as one seeking revenge and unable to think critically about its memory politics. One informant noted that IBUKA strongly resists the notion that Hutu survivors of the genocide should be eligible for reparations or benefits that Tutsi survivors are eligible to claim. When the government has sought to release prisoners lacking dossiers or evidence of their participation in the genocide, IBUKA protests the release. The rights of the defendants do not appear to be an issue in their understanding of justice. As an umbrella for all of the survivor organizations, it should not be viewed as the singular voice of the much contested and negotiated subjectivity of genocide survivors.

15. The Christian communities are also in disarray because of the complicity of both Catholic and Protestant denominations in the genocide. The RPF has long been at odds with the church; human rights groups such as African Rights have documented the extent of the participation of the Catholic hierarchy and the Vatican's refusal to acknowledge the role of its leadership, both European and Rwandan, in the conflict. Nevertheless, most Rwandans still remain members of various churches, yet religious practices are undergoing scrutiny and change in post-genocide Rwanda.

10

Relearning Questions:

Responding to the Ethical Address of Past and Present Others

Claudia Eppert

> To read a text . . . means bearing some burden of responsibility, believing oneself ad-
> dressed, and thus answerable—to the text itself, or to one's reading of it.
> —Adam Zachary Newton, *Narrative Ethics*

At a critical point in Joy Kogawa's narrative *Obasan* (1981), a novel dealing with the difficult remembrance of the internment and forced dispersal of Japanese-Canadians during and following World War II, the central character, Naomi Nakane, dreams of her dead mother. She has just come to learn that her mother had experienced the nuclear bombing of Nagasaki when Naomi was a child, and that it was for this reason that she had never returned to Canada and to Naomi. In this dream, her mother is performing a dance of love in a courtyard, alias graveyard, in the presence of soldiers and family. As Naomi attempts to draw near to her, the dream turns to nightmare. A dark ominous cloud in the shape of a great cape ascends from a valley and descends over them. Naomi identifies the overshadowing presence as that of the Grand Inquisitor. With his large hands, the Grand Inquisitor struggles to pry open Naomi's mother's mouth and Naomi's eyes. At this point, Naomi literally and symbolically "awakens" from her nightmare, falling and crying out, called by her mother to attend to what the dream communicates (228). She observes that "[t]he Grand Inquisitor was carnivorous and full of murder. His demand to know was both a judgment and a refusal to hear. The more he questioned [Naomi's mother], the more he was her accuser and murderer. The more he killed her, the deeper her silence became" (228).

In reading this passage, I suddenly and unexpectedly felt myself accused and interrogated. To what extent, I wondered, had my own reading of Naomi's and Kogawa's narrative been inquisitorial, constructed out of a demand to know that was both a judgment and a refusal to hear? In this moment, I was struck with the singular awareness that my questions of a text, of others, could never be fully realized in an answer. Insofar as my questions constituted the pursuit of a particular conclusive truth, they would always be insufficient and require more questions. I learned that the subject to which my questions were directed would never be reducible to them, that *I would never know*. In this context, I began to wonder more centrally what it means to question, what and how one learns from questioning, and how the orientation of questioning enables or obstructs responsible engagements with others.

Such responses to *Obasan* did not emerge from a vacuum but, rather, were framed by prior concerns with what might encompass a responsive and responsible reading of what I call contemporary North American "narratives of historical witness." The scope of these narratives includes, but is not limited to, the following: 1) the narration of factual and counter-factual complexities of sociohistorical moments of violation and violence instituted by events of colonialism, genocide, and nationalism; 2) the provision of testimony set against the exclusionary dominant grammar and methods of history as framed by the project of modernity; 3) the factual detailing of such legacies wrought by these historical events as the disintegration of communities, family, friendships, and the destruction of personal and social identities; 4) the detailing of the depth and extent of the physical and psychological infliction and effects of personal and social suffering undergone not only by those who lived this oppressive past but also by subsequent generations; 5) the undertaking of the arduous task of working through remnants of the past and of setting/settling the grounds for an affirmative redefinition of individual, familial, communal, and collective identities; and 6) the ongoing challenging not only of antiquated but also contemporary hegemonic framings of what might designate a North American national or multicultural historical consciousness. Individual texts might thus attempt any one or more of these tasks of witness.[1]

I call this literature one of historical witness, as opposed to what has variously been called "ethnic literature," "testimonial literature," or "trauma literature." In doing so, I wish, in part, to reference those texts that specifically engage the subject of traumatic history and to include works by those, such as Toni Morrison, who write about events in the past without necessarily having experienced them firsthand. But, principally, I use this conceptual phrasing to emphasize that this literature constitutes itself within the social form and framework of an ethico-pedagogical address to readers. The "claim" of address both staked and exerted by this literature calls upon readers not to read indifferently or purely for pleasure but to themselves become answerable—both to this literature and to its historical referents (Newton 1995, 11). As Robert Brinkley and Steven Youra maintain, "To receive the words of a witness is to find that one has also become a witness, that one's responses are there for others to witness as well. Once the transmission begins, one cannot stand outside its address" (1996, 23). I contend that this "becoming" of address frames witnessing as an interminable learning practice, a learning of what it means to be answerable to the address of past and present others.

In this chapter, I further this examination by considering the relationship between the practice of questioning and the task of learning. Such consideration bears significantly not only upon the individual reading of witness literature but also upon this literature's introduction in North American high school, college, and university classrooms. How, as educators and students, might we ask questions of this literature that is responsive/responsible to its learning address? While a significant body of work is developing that wrestles with pedagogies of ethical remembrance and response to past social suffering and injustice, what needs concurrent consideration is how the questioning of (textual) others is implicated in such pedagogies. As Robert Gibbs contends, "We have much to learn about . . . how one questions oneself by asking a question of another; and how another's questions of me are my questions for myself" (1992, 104). Gibbs's observation seems particularly insightful insofar as learning is centrally perceived as proceeding through a dialogic questioning engagement.

Posing this question of the (learning) question is, on the one hand, to constitute questioning as a promising transformative endeavor. Commonly questions are endowed with such possibility in their dynamic communicative and interruptive orientation, in their characteristic ability to initiate engagements with others and to interrogate assumptions, statements, expectations. Robert Eaglestone asserts that "unlike a statement . . . a question starts a dialogue. An idea phrased as a question resists closure and begs not only an answer but another question, an interruption" (1997, 139). On these terms, learners might productively be defined as communities of rigorous questioners. One might also contend that, in this spirit of coming to know, there can be no illegitimate question. Along these lines, Vladimir Jankélévitch maintains that, in study, one must be responsive to "everything that is thinkable in a question, thoroughly, at all costs. You must entangle the inextricable and only ever stop when it becomes impossible to go any further" (cited in Ouaknin 1995, 62). On the other hand, it must be cautioned here that what Eaglestone and Jankélévitch are pointing toward is the ethical potential/potency of the question. Naomi's dream of the Grand Inquisitor stands as a crucial reminder that questioning is by no means always and entirely responsive/responsible. Any community of questioners thus must first interrogate the question itself, must offer the question as an open question.

REMEMBRANCE AND *BILDUNG*

For the purposes of this chapter, I pursue these concerns specifically through a discussion of Kogawa's *Obasan*, from a particular interest in and response to this narrative's compelling pedagogical structure. First, as with other witness narratives, such as Leslie Silko's *Ceremony* (1977) and Paule Marshall's *Praisesong for the Widow* (1984), *Obasan* might readily be read as a *Bildungsroman*. However, in marked contrast to a tradition of *Bildungsromane*, in which the protagonist's learning is fashioned as a heroic narrative of progress constituted through the *Erfahrung* (experience) of an unanticipated series of adventures, the formative road traveled by the protagonists in witness narratives is contrastingly headed back in time toward a series of experiential confrontations with a traumatic history that they did or did not live and have largely denied or repressed. The principle vehicle for this *Bildung* is remembrance or, more specifically, what Toni Morrison describes as an inconsolable memory that is always "there for you, waiting for you" (1987, 36). The return to memory in these narratives testifies to its struggle to come out from beneath the service and shadows of history to act against the grain of an objectifying and oppressive historical grammar. In a realization that the project of modernity has gone horribly wrong through the events of fascism and the violences of imperialism, remembrance has been hailed as a reparative act of vigilance against the methods of history and in honor of those who suffered its consequences. David Palumbo-Liu points out that "ethnic writing as revision of history points to this term [memory], for it is through memory alone, as the repository of things left out of history, that the ethnic subject can challenge history" (1996, 212). Remembrance in these *Bildungsromane* thus becomes the predominant means for the protagonists' learning. Each is variably summoned and guided by one or more unorthodox mentors to a radical "remembrance-learning" that constitutes a resolute working through of traumatic experience, initiating a marked transformation in their complex lives. The learning is "radical" in part in that it critiques notions of education extrapolated within the conservative epistemological paradigms of *Bildung,* and proceeds less through cognitive language or informational learning than through processes equivalent to the dreaming and transferential relations of psychoanalytic encounters.

The pedagogical structure of these *Bildungsromane* encompasses this literature's witnessing address to readers. As the protagonist is called to a remembrance-learning, so too are we as readers asked to learn, asked in several respects to accompany the protagonist on his or her formative journey, to *learn from* his or her engagements with a traumatic history in ways that not only inform us about events in the past and their psychological legacy but fundamentally alter our relationship with past events and modes of social interaction. Yet, this transactionality is not unproblematic. It introduces pedagogical concerns with respect to what such an alignment encompasses and what its implications might be for how we respond to the text. For instance, in what measure does an answerability to this literature's address involve readers in practices of empathetic identification with the remembrance-learning of the protagonist? Insofar as we are called upon to participate in the protagonist's learning, how and on what terms might we question it? How does the protagonist's remembrance-learning engage us in a practice of questioning ourselves—our identities, our relationships to past and present others, and the individual, social, and institutional practices of reading/learning/questioning we bring to a text?

There is a second reason for my attention to *Obasan*. What so compellingly distinguishes it from other *Bildungsromane* that attempt a remembrance-learning on radical terms is the significant role questions play in Naomi's formative education and in this narrative's address. *Obasan* might significantly be regarded as a book of (learning) questions asked by Naomi and directed variably to herself, to other characters in the narrative, and principally to readers. In what follows, then, I elaborate upon the memorial pedagogical and "questioning" structure of Kogawa's narrative, and introduce what it might mean for readers to respond to its learning address through their own questions. To this latter end, I draw upon Emmanuel Levinas's philosophical writings in the consideration of a responsive/responsible questioning practice. Principally, my purpose in this chapter is to mark an *anagnoretic* shift in Naomi's remembrance-learning and questioning, and subsequently to suggest that this "ethical learning moment" has key implications for how we as readers and learners might approach witness narratives. To this end, I begin with a background detailing of Naomi's remembrance-learning throughout the first two-thirds of the novel.

THE DIFFICULT LEARNING OF NAOMI NAKANE

Obasan's prologue introduces the pedagogical structure in and against which Naomi's remembrance-learning and the readers' learning is to take place. Kogawa writes:

> There is a silence that cannot speak.
> There is a silence that will not speak.
> Beneath the grass the speaking dreams and beneath the dreams is a sensate sea. The speech that frees comes forth from the amniotic deep. To attend its voice, I can hear it say, is to embrace its absence. But I fail the task. The word is stone.
> I admit it.
> I hate the stillness. I hate the stone. I hate the sealed vault with its cold icon. I hate the staring into the night. The questions thinning into space. The sky swallowing the echoes.
> Unless the stone bursts with telling, unless the seed flowers with speech, there is in my life no living word. The sound I hear is only sound. White sound. Words, when they fall, are pock marks on the earth. They are hailstones seeking an underground stream.
> If I could follow the stream down and down to the hidden voice, would I come at last to the freeing word? I ask the night sky but the silence is steadfast. There is no reply.

The narrative's learning address is introduced in the hidden voice of an Other that calls from an amniotic deep for attendance, but "cannot" and "will not" speak because of the failure of the contemporary educational terrain of listening and

questioning to enable its telling. Indeed, the present terms of learning produce for
Naomi and, I suggest, for readers, only resistance and resentment of the impene-
trability and enormity of what needs to be confronted. The ambiguous "I" con-
joins narrator and readers consequently to the task of a radical learning, articulated
in the narrative's first and organizing pedagogical question: "If I could follow the
stream down and down to the hidden voice, would I come at last to the freeing
word?" The question reads simultaneously as preparation and warning. We must
be prepared to "follow" this stream to its unknown source without familiarity and
without assurance. While the risks of this learning are considerable, Kogawa suggests they are not refusable. Without this learning there is no communication, no
living: "Unless the stone bursts with telling, unless the seed flowers with speech,
there is in my life no living word." Kogawa thus introduces, in ways that I will
elaborate upon in the discussion of Levinas that follows, the necessary terms for a
learning that is answerable to the address of another. The question becomes the
measure in which Naomi's learning is characterized by this risk, a question I return
to following a brief introductory framing of Naomi's remembrance-learning.

The novel opens in August 1972, on the same night twenty-seven years after
the bombing of Nagasaki, and introduces Naomi as a Japanese-Canadian elemen-
tary school teacher in Cecil, Alberta. We observe that her life has been largely one
of an indeterminate repression of her past, a repression that has left her at the age
of thirty-six "unable to either go or stay in the world with even a semblance of
grace or ease" (50). A question that haunts Naomi and structurally propels the narrative is that of the whereabouts of her mother, a question that Naomi incessantly
has asked but to which she has never been given a definitive answer. Her uncle's
death from unknown causes, a month after the novel's opening events, becomes
the occasion not for her return to teaching, but rather for her own contentious remembrance-learning, a remembrance-learning that finally provides her with the
answer to the question of her mother's absence. Naomi is prepared to receive this
answer through the disparate teachings of Obasan and her Aunt Emily. She comments on their contrariness: "How different my two aunts are. One lives in sound,
the other in stone. Obasan's language remains deeply underground but Aunt Emily,
BA, MA, is a word warrior. She's a crusader, a little old grey-haired Mighty Mouse,
A Bachelor of Advanced Activists and General Practioner of Just Causes" (32).
Obasan is the embodiment of traumatic memory, locked into a remembrance she
can neither consciously recollect nor unconsciously forget (Caruth 1995, 4–5). Unable to cry because of clogged tear ducts and rarely speaking, she wanders in a "different dimension of time" (44) in which "[e]verything is forgetfulness" (30).
Obasan shows Naomi that while the discourse of trauma is elliptical, burrowing in
danger and threat, it nevertheless possesses its own syntactical and semantic grammar: "[T]he language of her grief is silence," Naomi says of Obasan. "She has
learned it well, its idioms, its nuances" (14). While Obasan importantly teaches
Naomi the language of suffering, she does not, however, call her to a practice of remembrance, as she herself is unable to confront and work through her memories.

Rather it is her Aunt Emily who initiates Naomi into a learning about and from her past, passionately invoking her to "remember everything" (50). Naomi describes her as a single-minded and determined academic, activist, and pedagogue enraged by any injustice (34), who has devoted her life to telling "of the lives of the Nisei [second generation] in Canada in an effort to make familiar, to make knowable, the treacherous yellow peril that lived in the minds of the racially prejudiced" (40). For Aunt Emily, making "known" encompasses a blaze of sociopolitical activity: attending conferences, writing letters of protest, lecturing, producing pamphlets, and generally "rushing from trouble spot to trouble spot with her medication pouring into wounds seen and not seen" (34). At the same time, her ways of making "known" become the crucial means for an uncompromising remembrance of the past. Her motivation to make past injustices a "live issue" is therefore rooted not only in the belief in the need for public—communal and national—acknowledgment and reparation. It also echoes Nicholas Abraham and Maria Torok's (1994) notion of the "transgenerational phantom," that traumas not voiced and worked through are incorporatively passed down to subsequent generations. Aunt Emily insists: "We have to deal with all of this while we remember it. If we don't we'll pass our anger down in our genes. It's the children who'll suffer" (36).

In efforts to compel Naomi to confront her past, she sends her a parcel "for [her] education" (188) so that she might come to "know everything" (43). The parcel, which Naomi reads before her uncle's funeral and while taking care of Obasan, functions as Naomi's (and the readers') primary text. It contains a series of material traces of the past as well as more current documents, displacing conventional "textbook" teaching: an old scrapbook full of newspaper clippings, Aunt Emily's diary dated 1941 composed in the form of letters to Naomi's mother, conference papers, government and family letters from her grandmother Kato, copies of telegrams and memorandi. Among other historical moments, the contents of the documents recount the progressive events of discrimination and persecution following the bombing of Pearl Harbor: the confiscation of property—radios, businesses, fishing boats, furniture, homes—by the Canadian government, increased censorship and segregation, the internment of Japanese-Canadians to work camps and concentration camps, the forced relocation of others to ghost towns, the bombing of Nagasaki.

The documents in the parcel, as well as family photographs in Obasan's home, not only become for Naomi the vehicle for an informational coming to know about the events of the war but also spawn the recollection, contextualization, and telling of her childhood memories: the dispersal of her family, her abandonment by her mother, her experience of sexual abuse, her relocation to the ghost town of Slocan, B.C., and the hardships she endured in the years following the war when her family was required to work on a beet farm in southern Alberta. To an extent, Naomi shares a traumatic memory with Obasan: "But we're trapped, Obasan and I, by our memories of the dead—all our dead—those who refuse to bury themselves. Like threads of old spider webs, still sticking and hovering, the past waits for us to submit or depart" (26). Reading the contents of the parcel not only prompts the return to and narrativization of Naomi's traumatic memories but also alerts her to the terrible innocence of aspects of her young memory. Immersing herself in Aunt Emily's journal entries, dated December 25, 1941, to May 21, 1942, she remarks that "Aunt Emily's Christmas 1941 is not the Christmas I remember. . . . Sick Bay, I learned eventually, was not a beach at all. And the place they called the Pool was not a pool of water, but a prison at the exhibition grounds called Hastings Park in Vancouver" (79, 77). The documents also finally provide Naomi with insight as to the reasons behind certain familial decisions, such as the injunction by her mother that Naomi not be told what happened to her at the close of the war: "The orders, given to Uncle and Father in 1945, reach me via Aunt Emily's package in 1972, twenty-seven years later. The delivery service is slow these days. Understanding is even slower" (173). Naomi's difficulty in understanding introduces and underscores a central challenge faced in pedagogical attempts to make events of historical trauma "knowable" not only to those who underwent them but even more so to those who witness them later in time. How and under what conditions can pedagogy "deliver"—that is, deliver on its conventional imperative as well as its goals of social justice—when its subject matter at every turn points to "the obscenity of the very project of understanding"? (Lanzmann 1995, 205).

How might we characterize Naomi as a learner? Naomi undoubtedly finds herself compellingly addressed by her aunt's parcel. In addition to an injunction by her aunt in a note addressed ambiguously to either Naomi or Aunt Emily herself, to "[w]rite the vision and make it plain. Habakkuk 2:2," Naomi concedes that the contents of the package themselves ignite her attention: "on my lap, her papers are wind and fuel, nudging my early thoughts to flame" (32). For the most part, however, her remembrance-learning is met with considerable instances of ambivalence, denial, and evasiveness, responses that issue understandably from the traumas of Naomi's life. Naomi herself acknowledges that she is by no means a model student, insofar as this is defined through an unquestioning enthusiasm and receptivity. She observes the difference between herself and her Aunt Emily: "Write the vision and make it plain? For her, the vision is the truth as she lives it. . . . The truth for me is more murky, shadowy and grey" (32). Early on she confesses that "[t]he very last thing in the world I was interested in talking about was our own experiences during and after World War II" (32). As Aunt Emily refuses to indulge Naomi in her escapist desires, insisting that she "remember everything" and that "denial is gangrene," Naomi participates reluctantly. Called upon to recollect her life in Alberta she remarks, "The fact is I never got used to it and cannot, I cannot bear the memory. There are some nightmares from which there is no waking, only deeper and deeper sleep. . . . Aunt Emily, are you a surgeon cutting at my scalp with your folders and your filing cards and your insistence on knowing all?" (197, 194).

At the source of Naomi's resistance is not only her pain but, importantly, an inability to articulate a reason for her and others' remembrance-learning. Indeed, this inability haunts Naomi as illustrated through her persistent questioning, a questioning that is invested in seeking justifications for the evasion of questions:

Crimes of history, I thought to myself, can stay in history. What we need is to concern ourselves with the injustices of today. Expedience still demands decisions which one day will be unjust. Out loud I said, Why not leave the dead to bury the dead? . . . Life is so short . . . the past so long. Shouldn't we turn the page and move on? . . . All this belongs to yesterday and there are so many other things to attend to today. All the details of death that are left in the laps of the living. . . . Some memories, too, might better be forgotten. Didn't Obasan once say, "It is better to forget"? What purpose is served by hauling forth the jar of inedible food? If it is not seen, it does not horrify. What is past recall is past pain. Questions from all these papers, questions referring to turbulence in the past, are an unnecessary upheaval in the delicate ecology of this numb day. (41–45)

For Naomi, initially it is the present that preoccupies her, remembrance of the past serving only to detract from attention to contemporary injustices, burdening the present with unnecessary emotion. At a further point in the novel, when character and reader alike have been more definitively subjected to the details of the senseless atrocities against Japanese-Canadians, Naomi again asks herself, "do I really want to read all these? . . . I am tired, I suppose, because I want to get away from all this. From the past and all these papers, from the present, from the memories, from the deaths, from Aunt Emily and her heap of words" (182–183). Her resistance is perhaps most acutely expressed in an imaginary conversation with Aunt Emily in which she contemplates: "What is done, Aunt Emily, is done is it not? And no doubt it will all happen again, over and over with different faces and names, variations on the same theme. . . . Or are you thinking that through lobbying and legislation, speech-making and story-telling, we can extricate ourselves from our foolish ways? Is there evidence for such optimism?" (199). Naomi's resistance betrays despair, not only the fear and doubt that her own and others' remembrance-learning is a futile endeavor but also the anxiety of the sufficiency of storytelling and sociopolitical action to overturn grammars of violence and violation.

THE QUESTION OF ANSWERABILITY

I return at this point to the notion outlined in the beginning of this chapter that, as the protagonists of the *Bildungsroman* are called to a transformative remembrance-learning, so too are we as readers addressed to learn from the protagonists' learning. Insofar as we maintain this parallel, we might subsequently consider Naomi's questions as questions both from and for ourselves as readers. Not only might her questions plausibly echo our own resistance to reading about a traumatic past, but they also challenge us to attempt a response to Naomi's evasions and hopelessness.[2] They ask us to become answerable to Naomi's suffering and distress, to the text, and to its historical referents. How might we consider these questions? And what might the implications of such a response in turn be for a learning and questioning practice with regard to the reading of historical witness narratives such as *Obasan?*

In this context, I reference the thought of Emmanuel Levinas—his critique of ontology and the radical ethics he introduces. Levinas contends that Western traditions of epistemology and ethics—how we know and engage others—have manifested an ontological imperialism. Knowing has encompassed the mastery and comprehension of the Other through thematizing processes that neutralize "it." The Other on these terms is affirmed only through the deprivation of its alterity and independence. Ethics has been predominantly defined through dual notions of human freedom: as moral action determinable through self-evident and intrinsically intelligible universal laws of reason and, in its utilitarian sense, as the pursuit of personal fulfillment. Levinas defines this "autonomous freedom" as determined in the consolidation and maintenance of the self in the midst of and against the Other (1969, 46). Against this, Levinas offers a contestative radical ethics. Against the primacy and sovereignty of the same, he posits an a priori structure of relationality and obligation for others. He maintains that before the pretensions of ontology, the "face" (not as visual image but as an infinite relation with an alterity that comes from without and exceeds my conceptual capacities) of an other person calls me to attention, summons me to an infinite and absolute responsibility for that person, a responsibility that is always more dire than the other's responsibility for me. In this respect, we are always already obligated to another before our being in the world. Against the construct of an "autonomous freedom," Levinas poses the paradox of a "difficult freedom," in which we find ourselves free only to the extent that we are infinitely and absolutely responsible for others before ourselves.

Effected in Levinas's ethics is an important pedagogical reversal (Handelman 1996, 222–228). He shows the real structure of learning to proceed not from the self but from one's encounters with the alterity of a unique other. The other thus becomes the teacher who teaches me a responsive/responsible relation with him or her. On these terms, terms that prioritize ethics over epistemology, the alterity of another remains irreducible to the learning subject, incapable of being masterfully "known" or incorporated by the subject. Because we are continually subjected to this alterity that exceeds the resources of consciousness, learning thus is always incumbent upon an encounter of "surprise." Learning is not the recollection of something already known, but more fundamentally the learning of something new (Gibbs 1997, 53). Levinas deploys the phrase "traumatism of astonishment" to describe, more specifically, the learning of responsibility in the encounter with another. The learning is astonishing because it is the experience of something radically foreign (Levinas 1969, 73). It is traumatizing because the subject learns that "[t]he Me before the other is infinitely responsible. . . [and that] [t]o be myself signifies, then, not to be able to get out from under responsibility" (Levinas 1966, 41). The learner finds herself always already commanded by the Other before and despite herself, learns that the "I" is nothing but that which is established in relation to this obligation.

In this respect, Levinas also crucially redefines the terms for questioning. On the one hand, he presents responsibility for another as unquestionable, as prior to subjectivity and prior to questioning (Attridge 1995, 225). Responsibility is not a question justifiable in principles or consciousness (Gibbs forthcoming, 3). Yet, at the same time, the very priority of responsibility points to the centrality of a questioning practice, though one importantly redefined within the learning of this relationality and obligation for it. Learning that the subject is always unquestionably responsible for another exposes the subject to its own spontaneous egoism and violence. In the facing relation, the subject finds itself accused, the violence of its own will irrevocably and traumatically experienced. Richard Cohen writes that the Levinasian subject "recognizes its powers as violent, [and] its authority as imperial . . . it recognizes itself as murderous and the Other as vulnerable or destitute, the object of the subject's actual or potential violence, the object of irresponsibility and injustice" (1987, 17). The subject thus is decentered and displaced; interrogated on every level: cognitively, affectively, bodily. Levinas asserts: "The subject is in the accusative . . . [n]ot at rest under a form, but tight in its skin, encumbered and as it were stuffed with itself, suffocating under itself, insufficiently open, forced to detach itself from itself, to breathe more deeply, all the way, forced to dispossess itself to the point of losing itself" (1978/1991, 110). The result is a profound reorientation that commands a subjectivity for the Other, an absolute attendance and answerability to the Other that contains within it the obligation that "thou shall not commit murder." Rather than questioning being inquisitorially directed at and upon the Other, on these Levinasian terms, it therefore now encompasses the Other calling me (and the world in which I find myself) into question, wounding me. Questioning becomes reconfigured as a "calling into question" of the self-same. Susan Handelman emphasizes that, for Levinas, "the consciousness of questioning is the question of conscience. This means an overturning of the egoism and the narcissisms of consciousness, of its autonomy and self-coincidence, its identity and repose" (1991, 192).

NAOMI'S CRISIS OF LEARNING

The ontological imperialism Levinas critiques is precisely that which has produced the Grand Inquisitor referenced in Naomi's dream and his silencing and murderous questioning practices. The Grand Inquisitor's grand interrogatives seek to conquer, judge, and convict, encompassing processes of inquiry that deny and condemn difference. The content and manner of his questions are set within investments of power, mastery, and ownership; they are questions that may function as forms of defense, even of repression, questions that deflect and disavow any self-interrogative responsibility for the question itself. Naomi feels herself as a thirty-six-year-old unmarried Japanese-Canadian continually subject to his categorical questioning. She witnesses the pejorative inquisitiveness of her young students when they define her as a "spinster" and inquisitively ask if she plans to be married. This prompts her remembrance of a date with the widowed father of one of her students, who assumed she was a foreigner and "was so full of questions that

I half expected him to ask for an identity card" (7). The widower asks those same "incessant" and "well-intentioned" interrogatives of strangers: "'How long have you been in this country? Do you like our country? You speak such good English.' . . . Does it so much matter that these questions are always asked? Particularly by strangers? These are icebreaker questions that create an awareness of ice" (225).

But what of Naomi's own (refusals of) questions? While she observes and experiences inquisitorial questions directed at her, in what measure is her own questioning practice—whether those questions be of the whereabouts of her mother or of the why of a remembrance-learning—framed equally within the ego boundaries of the inquisitorial? In what follows, I reexamine Naomi's dream of the Grand Inquisitor and consider the learning that takes place in the final third of the novel. The Grand Inquisition scene occurs formally at the "crisis point" of Kogawa's narrative. On an immediate and structural level, Naomi's crisis is that of discovering that her mother had experienced the bombing of Nagasaki and had died not long after. This revelation ends the riddle that has plagued Naomi since her childhood. But, on a much deeper level, I argue that Naomi's crisis comes not from this information so much as from the radical dream-learning that follows it. In this sense, while Naomi's remembrance-learning throughout the narrative represents a working through of the traumatization she experienced as a child (the expression of which is Naomi's dispossession of self-identity, and her experience of the limits of knowing and being), her dreaming, opened up by her mother, initiates a subsequent traumatization of a radically instructive nature.

The dream (the dream of the dance) is a ceremony of both initiation and teaching: The dance that Naomi's mother dances in the center of the graveyard is a radical "dance of learning." In this scene, her mother is the teaching Other, a phantom voice that addresses Naomi from the other shore, from the distance of Japan and the infinity of death. Naomi receives her mother's dance as a ceremony of love. In recalling the dream, she remembers two Japanese ideographs for the word *love* that she once came across: "The first contained the root words 'heart' and 'hand' and 'action'—love as hands and heart in action together. The other ideograph for 'passionate love', was formed of 'heart', 'to tell', and 'a long thread'" (228). Naomi recognizes that the dance ceremony combined the meaning of these two ideographs to represent a teaching of three women: Obasan, Aunt Emily, and Naomi's mother. She observes: The ceremony is a "slow and courtly telling, the heart declaring a long knotted thread knotted to Obasan's twine, knotted to Aunt Emily's package" (228).

The dream profoundly alerts Naomi, crucially interrupting the intent and grammar of her own questioning. Upon awakening, she recognizes her former self—as child, learner, and schoolteacher—as also inquisitorial: "How the Grand Inquisitor gnaws at my bones. At the age of questioning my mother disappeared. Why, I have asked ever since, did she not write? Why, I ask now, must I know? Did I doubt her love? Am I her accuser?" (228). Naomi experiences the hypocrisy of her own questioning and the shattering of her own narcissistic unity, her complacency in the world. In this self-accusatory moment, what Naomi accomplishes, therefore, is a taking on of responsibility for her own questioning practice, something she hasn't done earlier on in her life narrative.

This learning moment seizes Naomi with a nonindifference that challenges her to read and question the traces of her mother *other-wise*, in ways that come out of a relationality with her mother and that are interruptive of the ostracizing and leveling discourses of the Grand Inquisitor. She realizes that this reorientation insists on a responsiveness to an alterity irreducible to the language of the Grand Inquisitor: "What the Grand Inquisitor has never learned is that the avenues of speech are the avenues of silence. To hear my mother, to attend her speech, to attend the sound of stone, he must first become silent. Only when he enters her abandonment will he be released from his own" (228). This attentiveness, a vulnerable attentiveness, is foreshadowed in the prologue to *Obasan,* in the address to hear and learn from what the stone "cannot or will not tell." It is also signaled when Naomi is told by her Anglican minister to attend to the trace of her mother in the reading of Grandma Kato's letters of 1949 that detail the horrors of Nagasaki and resolve the mystery of Naomi's mother's disappearance. Before reading them aloud, Nakayama-sensei says softly, "Naomi . . . your mother is speaking. Listen carefully to her voice" (233).

The need for such an attentiveness is alternately signaled in Naomi's dream. In her dance ceremony of the dead, Naomi's mother carries in her mouth the tangled string stem of a rose. Moving her fingers skillfully from knot to knot, she assigns her daughter's attention to this knotting, teaching her that to approach her mother, Naomi must attend to these knots. While the string stem may be read as signifying the weave of continuity and commonality in Naomi's remembrance-learning, the knots represent a binding tangle of inexplicability and interruption. While made of thread, the knots constitute an instructive disruption of it, precisely a calling into question of the very terms of continuity and commonality.

Naomi learns that to become answerable to her mother, she must aspire to withdraw herself from and put into question her own projections, investments, and suspicions. To learn from her mother requires from her the im/possible attempt to let her mother speak independently from any aim Naomi might have with regard to her (Gans 1988, 86). She must listen and learn from her mother in ways that are not dominant and assertive but are receptive to the Other's teaching authority, in ways that signal an availability to hear what is exterior to the self (Gibbs 1997, 53). Open to this listening and learning, she signals her availability to her mother as well as her experience of her mother's teaching authority, in the form of another question:

I close my eyes. Mother. I am listening. Assist me to hear you. . . . Silent Mother, you do not speak or write. You do not reach through the night to enter morning, but remain in the voicelessness. From the extremity of much dying, the only sound that reaches me now is the sigh of your remembered breath, a wordless word. How shall I attend that speech, Mother, how shall I trace that wave? (240–241)

Naomi's question of "how shall I attend that speech?" (the trace of her mother's "remembered breath") is one that proceeds from a learning orientation radically different from that which prompted her inquisitorial questions. Rather than being situated within oppressive terms of mastery, this question comes from her mother's nuclear suffering, from the "extremity of much dying" (241) and attempts to be responsible/responsive to this devastation. The question not only betrays the realization that Naomi's mother's address is traceable within this very question, but that what is consequently required from Naomi is responsible and responsive action. The question marks the absence of Naomi's authority and, in so doing, opens her to a relationship with her disfigured mother, in the aftermath of Nagasaki: "In the dark Slocan night, the bright light flares in my dreaming. I hear the screams and feel the mountain breaking. Your long black hair falls and falls into the chasm. My legs are sawn in half. The skin on your face bubbles like lava and melts in your bones. Mother I see your face. Do not turn aside" (242).

QUESTIONING *OTHER-WISE*

What I have attempted is a reading of Kogawa's *Obasan* that points to Naomi's crisis of learning as a crisis of responsibility. Through this reading, and by referencing Levinas's critique of ontology and his radical ethics, I have sought to open up the question of the question in pedagogical remembrance practices. Levinas's ethics and my reading of Naomi's dream significantly frustrate assertions concerning the legitimacy of all questions for a learning about and from past and present others. They open us up to the realization that the "legitimate" question is not any question insofar as "any question" issues from and is directed toward the establishment and maintenance of the sovereign self. Legitimacy defined on ethical terms shows questioning, on the contrary, to be an interminably responsive/responsible "calling into question" of the "I" and its sovereignty.

By way of conclusion, I introduce what might be some practical implications of these insights with respect to an answerability to the ethical address of narratives of historical witness in the context of the classroom. The challenge of learning posed here, in some respects, is twofold. On an initial level, it entails a critical reading in which we call into question the concretization of themes and identities as these are introduced through particular narratives. With regard to Kogawa's *Obasan,* this more specifically might involve a calling into question of history, memory, identity, suffering, racism, love, silence, empathy, and trauma (concepts and emotions that the narrative itself questions), examining how these "themes" are transposed into "saids" (Levinas 1991) in life and literature. For example, such a reading practice opens up for questioning the very questions Naomi repeatedly asks herself and us as readers; namely, why remember, and whether, in doing so, can we extricate ourselves from our foolish ways? What becomes attempted here is not simply a response to these questions, but rather the very calling into question of these questions' foundational terms.

A practice of "calling into question," however, concurrently returns us to a reflexive interrogation of ourselves as readers. It involves us in a critical vigilance on levels of both readership and personhood as to how we interpret or "solicit" texts (Handelman 1991, 315). It focuses us on an examination of how we impose meanings on texts and the ways in which we fail in our impositions—a process that unquestionably returns me to my own partial reading of *Obasan*. Such self-interrogation might involve asking questions of the personal, social, and historical origins of such "impositions of meaning" and our investments in them. Why, for instance, is it that students in my English classes, in their reading of *Obasan,* so often accuse the text through such repeated and forcefully-held questions as: Why does Naomi complain so, and why does she not know the details of Japanese-Canadian history, particularly considering that she is a schoolteacher? Even though Aunt Emily was the only one given official permission and even though she had hopes that she could eventually free her family, why did she abandon them in order to move to Toronto rather than join them in their forced relocation to the ghost town of Slocan? Why did she not visit them again for twelve years? These charges by students tend to be linearly directed against the characters, and Kogawa, rather than returning dialogically back to them/us in the questioning frame of their/our reasons for and aggressive investments in asking such questions.

An interrogative reflexivity is equally called for in our emotional responses to texts, responses such as fascination, sympathy, empathy, and abjection, in the realization that these feelings themselves are "saids" implicated in sociohistorical conventions of appropriation and exclusion. As Deborah Britzman contends, "feelings . . . cannot exist without narrative conventions and their own structures of intelligibility and unintelligibility . . . structures of intelligibility that depend upon historically specific spheres" (1998, 84). She consequently points to the need for contemporary pedagogical theory and practice not to constitute feelings as "the royal road to attitudinal change . . . [but] as a curious reading practice, as a problem of ethical conduct" (1998, 84). In putting our feelings into question through their discursive contextualization and critique, what then is able to become of issue is the measure in which our feelings enable or obstruct attentive engagements with others.

A critical reflexive attention is by no means to render reading solipsistically performative, as this attention remains in response to the address of the other, bound to its exigencies. As Annette Aronowicz reinforces in her discussion of Levinas, a personal reading "requires as its corollary that intense attention to the object, not only in what it manifests but also in what, through its manifestations, it hides . . . this . . . helps to make the relation of the interpreter to the text something other than mere whim, for it forces him out of his private universe into a life he shares with others" (1990, xx). In this respect, the learning subject never loses sight of its answerability to the other. The experiential remains inextricably bound with the social, the cultural, and the historical in terms of both the specific details of the text and (non)thematic issues that concern the world at large. Nor does such a reading practice construct the narrative as outside of a critical questioning. Indeed, this recognition is constituted in the realization that a learning of answerability is responsive to (and at times, in tension with) the address of the text and its historical referents.

These "calling into question" practices move in an opposite direction from common practice in English classrooms. Rather than seeking to ascertain and master the themes of a literary work through hermeneutic practice, what is aspired to here is their interminable undoing. Moreover, rather than a practice of reading that seeks an experiential commonality with the narrative that calls upon readers (imaginatively) to know and comprehend the experiences of others on one's own contemporary terms of understanding, or that deploys the text as a means for the recovery of readers' own identities, a reading for alterity conversely beckons an approach paradoxically situated in a withdrawal from the text, from the presumption that a reader can possess or "relive" the experiences of another. Complicated here, then, is the notion put forth earlier that the remembrance-learning of the protagonist is our learning as readers. With respect to a narrative such as *Obasan,* an ethical responsivity to its address acknowledges the necessity of a humility before Naomi's historical experiences. While we as readers may experience horror, shock, and distress upon learning of the reasons for Naomi's mother's disappearance, Naomi's testimonial dream and our responses to it require an answerability that cannot come at the expense of the difference of her experience as both told and not told. In this respect, our witnessing obligations require a withdrawal from potentially imagining ourselves into the particularities of Naomi's Japanese-Canadian experiences, her traumatic childhood abandonment and subsequent loss of her mother, or her mother's suffering during and after the nuclear bombing of Nagasaki. Nor, for that matter, can we project a presumptive equivalency between Naomi's learning and our own. While Naomi and readers both learn what it might mean to witness, to hear/bear the testimony of another's suffering, the specific context, expression, and relevance of this learning remain markedly separate.

But is there not something more fundamental at issue here that needs reinforcement? An ethical questioning is crucially implicated in a crisis of learning, an *anagnorisis.* Naomi's dream-learning is one of an a priori responsibility not *to* but *for* another. Hers is not the learning of an answerlessness in response to mass violence, but, conversely, an answerability in the face of answerlessness. This answerability comes out of Naomi's recognition that her fulfillment is not what is at issue in her remembrance but rather the unquestionable burden of responsibility she bears for her mother. In certain respects, her learning of responsibility is an answer to the very interruptive question of *why learn?* This question might be read as one that comes from her mother—a question that is asked *of* Naomi not *by* her—and one that is concurrently located deep in the shadow of Naomi's despair as to whether we can "extricate ourselves from our foolish ways." I suggest that Naomi's dream awakens her to two possible responses to this question; namely, "I learn for myself" or "I learn for another." Naomi's radical learning is that she experiences the legitimacy of only one response. Levinas maintains that "[t]rue learning consists in receiving the lesson so deeply that it becomes a necessity to give oneself to the other. The lesson of truth is not held in one . . . consciousness. It explodes toward the other" (1994, 80). Prior to her dream, Naomi's questioning of the purpose of her own remembrance-learning came out of an egoism in denial of her relationality with past and present others. She asks, "Why not leave the dead to bury the dead? . . . Life is so short . . . the past so long. Shouldn't we turn the page and move on?" (42). Even when she reluctantly comes to acknowledge later in the narrative that "I suppose I do need to be educated. I've never understood how these things happen" (188), her concession, it seems, issues more from the recognition of the need for an informational learning about the past, a content learning for explanatory purposes, than the impossible refusal of address. Her learning to this point is one in which her learning "I" remains intact, unquestioned. The dream, however, reveals Naomi to *be* only in relation to another, and always already responsible for that other.

Her realization of the answerability required from her directs Naomi to a different questioning, one that acknowledges the alterity of the other always already in everything she says and does, and embraces her interminable subjection before this alterity. As it is the other that is the cause of her (and our) questioning, the face of the Other is always traceable in the question, inhering in its dynamic qualities. This fact Naomi acknowledges in her question to her mother, "How can I hear you?" The question signals her willingness and capacity to learn out of and from the demands of an infinite and absolute responsibility, to learn not for herself but for her mother. It is a question Naomi risks, unable to guarantee that she will be able to be meaningful for her mother. But the question is hopeful; not in the sense of a wish but rather as the reality and action of hope. It marks not a negativity but a positive turning point. The novel ends early in the morning with Naomi donning Aunt Emily's coat and returning to coulee, the novel's opening scene. She observes the dynamic scene before her: "Above the trees, the moon is pure white stone. The reflection is rippling in the river—water and stone dancing. It's a quiet ballet, soundless as breath" (247).

NOTES

1. This genre testifies to such historical moments of discrimination and persecution as the Middle Passage and its subsequent history of slavery, the mass deaths of Chinese-Americans and Chinese-Canadians in the building of the transnational railroads, the internment and forced dispersal of Japanese-Canadians during and following World War II, the persecution of the indigenous peoples of North America, North American anti-Semitism, and symbolic and physical violence against women and refugees. Literature that bears witness to these historical events includes, among a wealth of others, novels such as Toni Morrison's *Beloved* (1987), Maxine Hong Kingston's *The Woman Warrior* (1975) and *China Men* (1977), Leslie Marmon Silko's *Ceremony* (1977) and *Almanac of the Dead* (1991), Paule Marshall's *Praisesong for the Widow* (1983), Sherley Anne Williams's *Dessa Rose* (1986), and children's/young adult fiction such as Margaret Craven's *I Heard the Owl Call My Name* (1973),

Marlene Nourbese Philip's *Harriet's Daughter* (1988), Kogawa's *Naomi's Road* (1995), and Beatrice Culleton's *April Raintree* (1995).

2. It is important to note here that Kogawa was among the first to voice the experiences of Japanese-Canadians. She was writing *Obasan* at a time when Japanese-Canadians were petitioning for an official apology and compensation from the Canadian government. This public apology came only in 1988, from then Prime Minister Brian Mulroney, when the Canadian government agreed to pay $21,000 to each of those surviving Japanese-Canadians (approximately 12,000 people) who had had their possessions confiscated and had been interned during the war.

Bibliography

Abraham, Nicolas, and Maria Torok. 1994. *The Shell and the Kernel: Renewals of Psycho-analysis*. Vol. 1. Edited and translated by Nicholas Rand. Chicago: University of Chicago Press.

Abrams, M. H. 1993. *A Glossary of Literary Terms*. 6th edition. Fort Worth: Harcourt Brace Jovanovich College Publishers.

Abrams, Philip. 1988. "Notes on the Difficulty of Studying the State." *Journal of Historical Sociology* 1, 1: 58–89.

Adorno, Theodor. 1998. "The Meaning of Working through the Past." In *Critical Modes, Interventions and Catchwords*. Translated by Henry W. Pickford, 89–103. New York: Columbia University Press.

African Rights. 1995. *Rwanda Death, Despair and Defiance*. Revised ed. London: African Rights Publications.

Agamben, Giorgio. 1998. *Homo Sacer: Sovereign Power and Bare Life*. Stanford: Stanford University Press.

———. *The Coming Community*. Minneapolis: University of Minnesota Press.

Agosin, Marjorie. 1992. *Circles of Madness: Mothers of the Plaza de Mayo*. Translated by Celeste Kostopulos-Cooperman. New York: White Pine Press.

Alber, Beth. n.d. *Design Proposal to the Women's Monument Project*. Unpublished document.

Alonso, Ana Maria. 1988. "The Effects of Truth: Re-Presentations of the Past and the Imagining of Community." *Journal of Historical Sociology* 1, 1: 33–57.

Amnesty International. 1987. *Argentina: The Military Juntas and Human Rights Report of the Trial of the Former Junta Members, 1985*. London: Amnesty International Publications.

Andersen, Martin Edwin. 1993. *Dossier Secreto: Argentina's Desaparecidos and the Myth of the "Dirty War."* Boulder: Westview Press.

Anderson, Benedict. 1991. *Imagined Communities*. 2nd ed. London: Verso.

Antze, Paul, and Michael Lambek. 1996. "Introduction: Forecasting Memory." In *Tense Past: Cultural Essays in Trauma and Memory*, edited by Michael Lambek and Paul Antze, xi–xxxxviii. New York: Routledge.

Appadurai, Arjun. 1996. *Modernity at Large: Cultural Dimensions of Globalization*. Minneapolis: University of Minnesota Press.

Appiah, Kwame Anthony. 1992. *In My Father's House: Africa in the Philosophy of Culture*. Oxford: Oxford University Press.

Arendt, Hannah. 1963/1979. *Eichmann in Jerusalem: A Report on the Banality of Evil*. New York: Penguin.

————.1954/1993. *Between Past and Future*. New York: Penguin Books.

Aronowicz, Annette. 1990. "Translator's Introduction." *Nine Talmudic Readings by Emmanuel Levinas*. Bloomington: Indiana University Press.

Attridge, Derek. 1995. "Ghost Writing." In *Deconstruction Is/In America*. Edited by Anselm Haverkamp, 223–227. New York: New York University Press.

Avellaneda, Andres. 1989. "The Process of Censorship and Censorship of the Proceso: Argentina 1976–1983." In *The Redemocratization of Argentine Culture: 1938 and Beyond*. Edited by David William Foster, 23–47. Tempe: Arizona Board of Regents.

Avni, Ora. 1995. "Beyond Psychoanalysis: Elie Wiesel's *Night* in Historical Perspective." In *Auschwitz and After: Race, Culture and "The Jewish Question" in France*. Edited by L. D. Kritzman, 203–218. New York: Routledge.

Bar-On, Daniel. 1995. *Fear and Hope: Three Generations of the Holocaust*. Cambridge: Harvard University Press.

Becker, David. 1995. "The Deficiency of the PTSD Concept When Dealing with Victims of Human Rights Violations and Other Forms of Organized Violence." In *Beyond Trauma*. Edited by R. Kleber, 99–110. New York: Plenum Press.

Becker, Jurek. 1996. *Jacob the Liar*. Translated by Leila Vennewitz. New York: Arcade.

Behar, Ruth. 1996. *The Vulnerable Observer: Anthropology That Breaks Your Heart*. Boston: Beacon Press.

Bell, Bernard. 1987. *The Afro-American Novel and Its Tradition*. Amherst: University of Massachusetts Press.

Benjamin, Andrew. 1997. *Present Hope: Philosophy, Architecture, Judaism*. New York: Routledge.

Benjamin, Walter. 1968. *Illuminations*. Translated by Harry Zohn. New York: Schocken Books.

————. 1963/1998. *The Origin of German Tragic Drama*. London: Verso.

————. 1920/1996. "Critique of Violence." In *Walter Benjamin: Selected Writings*. Vol. 1, 1913–1926. Edited by Marcus Bullock and Michael W. Jennings, 236–252. Harvard: Belknap.

Berenbaum, Michael. 1993. *The World Must Know: The History of the Holocaust as Told in the United States Holocaust Memorial Museum*. Boston: Little, Brown.

Berger, Iris. 1981. *Religion and Resistance: East African Kingdoms in the Precolonial Period*. Tervuren: Musee royal de l'Afrique centrale.

Bernabé, Jean, Patrick Chamoiseau, Raphaël Confiant. 1990. "In Praise of Creoleness." Translated by M. B. T. Khyar. *Callaloo* 13, 4 (Fall): 886–909.

Bertoldi, Andreas. 1998. "Oedipus in (South) Africa?: Psychoanalysis and the Politics of Difference." *American Imago* 55, 1 (Spring): 101–134.

Bettelheim, Bruno. 1979. "The Ignored Lesson of Anne Frank." In *Surviving and Other Essays*, 246–257. New York: Vintage Books.

Bhabha, Homi K. 1996. "Unpacking My Library . . . Again." In *The Post-Colonial Question: Common Skies, Divided Horizons*. Edited by Iain Chambers and Lidia Curti. New York: Routledge.

————. 1994. *The Location of Culture*. New York: Routledge.

_____. 1993. "Beyond the Pale: Art in the Age of Multicultural Translation." In *1993 Biennial Exhibition: Whitney Museum of American Art.* Edited by Elisabeth Sussman, Thelma Golden, John G. Hanhardt, and Lisa Philips. New York: Whitney Museum of American Art.

_____. 1990. "DissemiNation: Time, Narrative, and the Margins of the Modern Nation." In *Nation and Narration.* Edited by Homi K. Bhabha. London: Routledge.

Blanchot, Maurice. 1988. *The Unavowable Community.* Barrytown, New York: Station Hill Press.

_____. 1986. *Writing the Disaster.* Lincoln: University of Nebraska.

Blumenthal, Ralph. 1998. "Five Precious Pages Renew Wrangling over Anne Frank." *New York Times* (September 10): A6.

Bociurkiw, Marusia. 1990. "Je me Souviens: A Response to the Montreal Killings." *Fuse* XIII, 4 (Spring): 6–10.

Bollas, Christopher. 1987. *The Shadow of the Object: Psychoanalysis of the Unthought Known.* New York: Columbia University Press.

Bouvard, Marguerite Guzman. 1994. *Revolutionizing Motherhood: The Mothers of the Plaza de Mayo.* Wilmington: Scholarly Resources, Inc.

Boyarin, Jonathan. 1994. "Space, Time, and the Politics of Memory." In *Remapping Memory: The Politics of TimeSpace.* Edited by Jonathan Boyarin, 1–37. Minneapolis: University of Minnesota Press.

Bracken, Patrick, Joan Giller, Derek Summerfield. 1995. "Psychological Responses to War and Atrocity: The Limitations of Current Concepts." *Social Science and Medicine* 40, 8: 1073–1082.

Bracken, Patrick, and Celia Petty, eds. 1998. *Rethinking the Trauma of War: Save the Children.* London: Free Association Books.

Brantley, Ben. 1997. "Review." *New York Times* (December 5): B1, 5.

Brathwaite, Kamau. 1993. *Roots.* Ann Arbor: University of Michigan Press.

Brennan, Timothy. 1997. *At Home in the World: Cosmopolitanism Now.* Cambridge: Harvard University Press.

Brickman, Julie. 1992. "Female Lives, Feminist Deaths: The Relationship of the Montreal Massacre to Dissociation, Incest, and Violence against Women." *Canadian Psychology* 33, 2: 128–139.

Brinkley, Robert, and Steven Youra. 1996. "Tracing Shoah." *Publications of the Modern Language Association of America* (PMLA) 111, 1: 108–127.

Britzman, Deborah P. 1998. *Lost Subjects, Contested Objects: Toward a Psychoanalytic Inquiry of Learning.* Albany: State University of New York Press.

Brook, Peter. 1993. *The Open Door: Thoughts on Acting and Theatre.* New York: Pantheon Books, Random House.

Brooks, J. A. 1992. "Freud and Splitting." *International Review of Psychoanalysis* 19: 335–350.

Brown, Wendy. 1995. *States of Injury: Power and Freedom in Late Modernity.* Princeton: Princeton University Press.

Brysk, Alison. 1995. *The Politics of Human Rights in Argentina: Protest, Change, and Democratization.* Stanford: Stanford University Press.

_____. 1994. "The Politics of Measurement: The Contested Count of the Disappeared in Argentina." *Human Rights Quarterly* 16, 4: 676–692.

Buck-Morss, Susan. 1993. *The Dialectics of Seeing: Walter Benjamin and the Arcades Project.* Cambridge: MIT Press.

Buruma, Ian. 1998. "Anne Frank's Afterlife." *New York Review of Books* (February 19): 4–8.

Butler, Judith. 1997. *The Psychic Life of Power*. Stanford: Stanford University Press.

Butler, Octavia E. 1988. *Kindred*. Boston: Beacon Press.

Campbell, David. 1998a. *National Deconstruction: Violence, Identity, and Justice in Bosnia*. Minneapolis: University of Minnesota Press.

———. 1998b. "Why Fight: Humanitarianism, Principles and Post-Structuralism." *Millenium* 27, 3: 497–521.

Canby, Vincent. 1997. "A New 'Anne Frank' Still Stuck in the 50s." *New York Times* (December 21): AR 5, 6.

Carroll, David. 1990. "The Memory of Devastation and the Responsibilities of Thought: 'And let's not talk about that.'" Forward to Jean-Francois Lyotard's *Heidegger and 'the jews.'* Translated by Andreas Michel and Mark S. Roberts. Minneapolis: University of Minnesota Press.

Caruana, John. 1996. "Mourning and Mimesis: The Freudian Ethics of Adorno." *Canadian Journal of Psychoanalysis* 4, 1: 89–108.

Caruth, Cathy. 1996. *Unclaimed Experience: Trauma, Narrative and History*. Baltimore: Johns Hopkins University Press.

———. 1991. "Introduction." *American Imago* (Special Issue on "Psychoanalysis, Culture and Trauma: II) 48, 4 (Winter).

———. 1991. "Unclaimed Experience: Trauma and the Possibility of History." *Yale French Studies* 79: 181–192.

Caruth, Cathy, ed. 1995. *Trauma: Explorations in Memory*. Baltimore: Johns Hopkins University Press.

Certeau, Michel de. 1986. *Heterologies: Discourse on the Other*. Translated by Brian Massumi. Minneapolis: University of Minnesota Press.

Césaire, Aimé. 1969. *Return to My Native Land*. Translated by John Berger and Anna Bostock. Baltimore: Penguin Books.

Chretien, Jean-Pierre. 1995. *Rwanda: Les médias du génocide*. Paris: Karthala.

Clark, Candice. 1997. *Misery and Company: Sympathy in Everyday Life*. Chicago: University of Chicago Press.

Clarke, John Henrik, ed. 1968. *William Styron's Nat Turner: Ten Black Writers Respond*. Boston: Beacon Press.

Codere, H. 1973. *The Biography of an African Society: Rwanda 1900–1960*. Tervuren: Musee Royal de l'Afrique centrale.

Cohen, Richard A. 1994. *Elevations: The Height of the Good in Rosenzweig and Levinas*. Chicago: University of Chicago Press.

———. 1987. "Introduction." In *Emmanuel Levinas: Time and the Other*. Translated by Richard Cohen. Pittsburgh, Pa.: Duquesne University Press.

———. 1986. "Introduction." In *Face to Face with Levinas*. Edited by Richard Cohen. Albany: State University of New York Press.

Cohen, Stanley. 1995. "State Crimes of Previous Regimes: Knowledge, Accountability, and the Policing of the Past." *Law and Social Inquiry* 20, 1 (Winter): 7–50.

Comaroff, John. 1998. "Reflections on the Colonial State, in South Africa and Elsewhere: Factions, Fragments, Facts and Fictions." *Social Identities* 4, 3: 321–361.

CONADEP 1986. (National Commission on Disappeared Persons). *Nunca Mas: The Report of the Argentine National Commission on the Disappeared, with an introduction by Ronald Dworkin*. New York: Farrar, Straus, Giroux.

Connerton, Paul. 1989. *How Societies Remember*. Cambridge: Cambridge University Press.

Cooper, Frederick, and Ann Laura Stoler. 1997. "Between Colony and Metropole: Rethinking a Research Agenda." In *Tensions of Empire: Colonial Cultures in a Bourgeois World*. Berkeley: University of California Press.

Cotler, Irwin. 1999. *Canadian Jewish News*. May 13, 1 and 34.

Craven, Margaret. 1973. *I Heard the Owl Call My Name*. New York: A Laurel Book.

Critchley, Simon. 1999. *Ethics-Politics-Subjectivity*. London: Verso.

———. 1992. *The Ethics of Deconstruction: Derrida and Levinas*. Oxford: Blackwell.

Culleton, Beatrice. 1995. *April Raintree*. Winnipeg, Manitoba: Peguis.

Dafoe, Chris. 1994. "Life and Death in Pink Granite." *The Globe and Mail* (October 22): C16.

Das, Veena. 1995. *Critical Events*. Oxford: Oxford University Press.

———. 1995. "Voice as Birth of Culture." *Ethnos* 60, 3–4: 159–179.

Davies, Ioan. 1998. "Negotiating African Culture: Toward a Decolonization of the Fetish." In *The Cultures of Globalization*. Edited by Frederic Jameson and Masao Miyoshi, 125–145. Durham: Duke University Press.

De Certeau, Michel. 1988. *The Writing of History*. Translated by Tom Conley. New York: Columbia University Press.

de Lacger, Louis. 1961. *Ruanda*. 2nd ed. Kabgayi: Vicariat.

de Lame, Danielle. 1996. *Une colline entre mille ou le calme avant la tempete: Transformations et blocages du Rwanda rural*. Tervuren: Musée Royal de l'Afrique Centrale.

d'Hertefelt, Marcel. 1971. *Les clans du Rwanda ancien: Elements d'ethnosociologie et d'ethnohistoire*. Tervuren: Musée Royal de l'Afrique Centrale.

Delbo, Charlotte. 1995. *Auschwitz and After*. Translated by Rosette C. Lamont. New Haven: Yale University Press.

Deleuze, Gilles, and Felix Guattari. 1987. *A Thousand Plateaus: Capitalism and Schizophrenia*. Translated by Brian Massumi. Minneapolis: University of Minnesota Press.

Derrida, Jacques.1994. *Spectres of Marx: The State of the Debt, the Work of Mourning and the New International*. Translated by Peggy Kamuf. New York: Routledge.

———. 1987. *The Post Card: From Socrates to Freud and Beyond*. Translated by Alan Bass. Chicago: University of Chicago Press.

des Forges, Alison. 1999. *Leave None to Tell the Story. Genocide in Rwanda*. Paris: International Federation of Human Rights.

Destexhe, Alain. 1994. *Rwanda: Essai sur le genocide*. Brussels: Complexe.

Diamond, Elin. 1997. *Unmaking Mimesis: Essays on Feminism and Theater*. London and New York: Routledge.

———. 1992. "The Violence of 'We'." *Critical Theory and Performance*. Edited by Janelle G. Reinelt and Joseph R. Roach, 390–398. Ann Arbor: University of Michigan Press.

Doneson, Judith. 1987. "The American History of Anne Frank's Diary." *Holocaust and Genocide Studies* 2, 1: 149–160.

Donghi, Tulio Halperin. 1988. "Argentina's Unmastered Past." *Latin American Research Review* 23, 2: 3–24.

Douzinas, Costas, and Ronnie Warrington. 1994. *Justice Miscarried: Ethics, Aesthetics and the Law*. New York: Harvester Wheatsheaf.

Eaglestone, Robert. 1997. *Ethical Criticism: Reading After Levinas*. Edinburgh: Edinburgh University Press.

Edelstein, Susan. 1994. "Untitled." *Border/Lines* (Supplement) 34/35: 02.

Eliach, Yaffa. 1998. *There Once Was a World*. Boston: Little, Brown.

Elsaesser, Thomas. 1996. "Subject Positions, Speaking Positions: From *Schindler's List*." In *The Persistence of History: Cinema, Television and the Modern Event*. Edited by Vivian Sobchack, 145–183. New York: Routledge.

Elshtain, Jean Bethke. 1994. "The Mothers of the Disappeared: Passion and Protest in Maternal Action." In *Representations of Motherhood*. Edited by Donna Bassin et al., 75–91. New Haven, London: Yale University Press.

――――. 1989. "Antigone's Daughters Reconsidered: Continuing Reflections on Women, Politics, and Power." In *Life-World and Politics: Between Modernity and Postmodernity*. Edited by Stephen K. White, 222–235. Notre Dame: University of Notre Dame Press.

Feitlowitz, Marguerite. 1992. "Night and Fog in Argentina." *Salmagundi* 94–95 (Spring-Summer): 40–74.

Felman, Shoshana. 1992. "Education and Crisis." In *Testimony: Crises of Witnessing in Literature, Psychoanalysis and History*, by Shoshana Felman and Dori Laub, 1–56. New York: Routledge.

――――. 1987. *Jacques Lacan and the Adventure of Insight: Psychoanalysis in Contemporary Culture*. Cambridge: Harvard University Press.

Felman, Shoshana, and Dori Laub. 1992. *Testimony: Crises of Witnessing in Literature, Psychoanalysis and History*. New York: Routledge.

Ferguson, James. 1994. *The Anti-Politics Machine: "Development," Depoliticization, and Bureaucratic Power in Lesotho*. Minneapolis: University of Minnesota Press.

Fink, Ida. 1997. *Traces*. Translated by Philip Boehm and Francine Prose. New York: Metropolitan Books.

Fisher, Jo. 1989. *Mothers of the Disappeared*. Boston: South End Press.

Forché, Carolyn. 1993. "Introduction." In *Against Forgetting: Twentieth Century Poetry of Witness*. Edited by Carolyn Forché. New York: W.W. Norton.

Foucault, Michel. 1997. "Nietzsche, Genealogy, History." In *Language, Counter-Memory, Practice: Selected Essays and Interviews by Michel Foucault*. Edited by Daniel Bouchard. Ithaca: Cornell University Press.

――――. 1997. *The Politics of Truth*. Edited by Sylvere Lotringer and Lysa Hochroth. New York: Semiotext(e).

――――. 1991. "Governmentality." In *The Foucault Effect: Studies in Governmentality*. Edited by Graham Burchell, Colin Gordon, and Peter Miller. Chicago: University of Chicago Press.

――――. 1988. "Technologies of the Self." In *Technologies of the Self: A Seminar with Michel Foucault*. Edited by Luther H. Martin, Huck Gutman, and Patrick Hutton. Amherst: University of Massachusetts Press.

――――. 1984. "Face aux governments: les droits de l'homme." *Liberation* (June-July): 22.

――――. 1980. *Power/Knowledge: Selected Interviews and Other Writings*. Edited and translated by Colin Gordon. New York: Pantheon Books.

Frank, Anne. 1995. *The Diary of a Young Girl: The Definitive Edition*, by Otto Frank and Mirjam Pressler. Translated by Susan Massotty. New York: Doubleday.

Frazier, Lessie Jo. 1998. "'Subverted Memories': Countermourning as Political Action in Chile." In *Acts of Memory: Cultural Recall in the Present*. Edited by Mieke Bal, Jonathan Crewe, and Leo Spitzer, 105–119. Hanover, N.H.: Dartmouth College.

Frazier, Lessie Jo, and Joseph Scarpaci. 1998. "Landscapes of State Violence and the Struggle to Reclaim Community: Mental Health and Human Rights in Iquique, Chile." In

Putting Health into Place. Landscape, Identity & Well-Being. Edited by Robin Kearns and Wilbert Gesler, 53–74. Syracuse: Syracuse University Press.

Fresco, Nadine. 1984. "Remembering the Unknown." *International Review of Psychoanalysis* 11: 421.

Freud, Sigmund. 1984. *On Metapsychology: The Theory of Psychoanalysis. Vol. 2.* Harmondsworth: Penguin Books.

———. 1968. *Standard Edition of the Complete Works of Sigmund Freud.* Translated by James Strachey. In collaboration with Anna Freud. Assisted by Alix Strachey and Alan Tyson. 24 vols. London: The Hogarth Press and the Institute of Psychoanalysis.

———. 1933. "Introductory Lectures on Psychoanalysis." *Standard Edition.* Vol. 22, 3–182.

———. 1930. "Civilisation and Its Discontents." *Standard Edition.* Vol. 21, 59–145.

———. 1920/1984. "Beyond the Pleasure Principle." In *Volume 11, On Metapsychology: The Theory of Psychoanalysis: The Pelican Freud Library.* Edited by Angela Richards; translated by James Strachey, 275–338. New York: Penguin Books.

———. 1923/1984. "The Ego and the Id." In *Volume 11, On Metapsychology: The Theory of Psychoanalysis: The Pelican Freud Library.* Edited by Angela Richards; translated by James Strachey, 350–407. New York: Penguin Books.

———. 1919. "The Uncanny." *Standard Edition.* Vol. 17, 219–252.

———. 1917/1915. "Mourning and Melancholia." *Standard Edition.* Vol. 14, 239–258.

Friedlander, Saul. 1994. "Trauma, Memory, and Transference." In *Holocaust Remembrance: The Shapes of Memory.* Edited by Geoffrey H. Hartman, 252–263. Oxford, UK: Blackwell.

———. 1992. "Trauma, Transference and 'Working Through' in the Writing of the History of the Shoah." *History and Memory* 4, 1 (Spring/Summer): 39–59.

Friedman, Carl. 1994. *Nightfather.* Translated by Arnold and Erica Pomerans. New York: Persea.

Gaete, Rolando. 1993. *Human Rights and the Limits of Critical Reason.* Brookfield: Dartmouth.

Gale, Henry. 1994. "Not Collective Guilt, but Collective Responsibility." *The Globe and Mail* (November 23): A24.

Gans, Steven. 1988. "Levinas and Pontalis: Meeting the Other as in a Dream." In *The Provocation of Levinas: Rethinking the Other.* Edited by Robert Bernasconi and David Wood. New York: Routledge.

Gasibirege, Simon. 1995. État des lieux de "La santé mentale communautaire" au Rwanda en avril et mai 1995. Texte provisoire (unpublished manuscript).

Gibbs, Robert. Forthcoming. *Why Ethics: Signs of Responsibilities.* Princeton: Princeton University Press.

———. 1997. "Asymmetry and Mutuality: Habermas and Levinas." *Philosophy and Social Criticism* 3, 6: 51–63.

———. 1995. "Philosophical and Historical Witness." Paper delivered to the Faculty of Divinity, Cambridge, England, January.

———. 1992. *Correlations in Rosenzweig and Levinas.* Princeton: Princeton University Press.

Gilroy, Paul. 1993. *The Black Atlantic: Modernity and Double Consciousness.* Cambridge: Harvard University Press.

Glissant, Édouard. 1997. *Poetics of Relation.* Translated by Betsy Wing. Ann Arbor: University of Michigan Press.

Graver, Lawrence. 1995. *An Obsession with Anne Frank: Meyer Levin and the Diary.* Berkeley: University of California Press.

Graziano, Frank. 1992. *Divine Violence: Spectacle, Psychosexuality and Radical Christianity in the Argentine "Dirty War."* Boulder: Westview Press.

Green, André. 1986. *On Private Madness.* Madison: International Universities Press.

Guillaumin, Colette. 1991. "Madness and the Social Norm." Translated by M. Lakehead. *Feminist Issues* 11, 2: 1–15.

Haas, Aaron. 1990. *In the Shadow of the Holocaust*. Ithaca: Cornell University Press.

Hall, Stuart. 1990. "Cultural Identity and Diaspora." In *Identity, Community, Culture, Difference*. Edited by Jonathan Rutherford, 222–237. London: Lawrence & Wishart.

Hammelburg, Bernard. 1997. "A Fresh Look at 'Anne Frank': In Search of the Historical One." *New York Times* (November 30): AR 4, 12.

Handelman, Susan. 1996. "The Torah of Criticism and the Criticism of Torah: Recuperating the Pedagogical Moment." In *Interpreting Judaism in a Postmodern Age*. Edited by Steven Kepnes, 221–239. New York: New York University Press.

Handelman, Susan A. 1991. *Fragments of Redemption: Jewish Thought and Literary Theory in Benjamin, Scholem and Levinas*. Bloomington: Indiana University Press.

Harris, Wilson. 1990. "In the Name of Liberty." *Third Text* 11 (Summer): 7–15.

Hartman, Geoffrey H. 1996. *The Longest Shadow: In the Aftermath of the Holocaust*. Bloomington: Indiana University Press.

Haver, William. 1996. *The Body of this Death: Historicity and Sociality in the Time of AIDS*. Stanford: Stanford University Press.

Hayden, Robert. 1985. "Middle Passage." *Collected Poems: Robert Hayden*. Edited by Frederick Glaysher, 48. New York: Liveright.

Hayes, Grahame. 1998. "We Suffer Our Memories: Thinking about the Past, Healing, and Reconciliation." *American Imago* 55, 1 (Spring): 29–50.

Hayner, Priscilla B. 1994. "Fifteen Truth Commissions—1974–1994: A Comparative Study." *Human Rights Quarterly* 16: 597–655.

Hecht, David, and Abdoumaliqalim Simone. 1994. *Invisible Governance: The Art of African Micropolitics*. Brooklyn, N.Y.: Autonomedia.

Hirsch, Marianne. 1997. *Family Frames: Photography, Narrative and Postmemory*. Cambridge: Harvard University Press.

———. 1992–1993. "Family Pictures: *Maus*, Mourning, and Post-Memory." *Discourse: Theoretical Studies in Media and Culture* 15:2 (Winter): 3–29.

Hirsch, Marianne, and Susan Rubin Suleiman. 1997. "Material Memory: Holocaust Testimony in Post-Holocaust Art." Unpublished manuscript presented at the American Comparative Literature Conference, April 1997.

Hoagland, Molly Magid. 1998. "Anne Frank on and off Broadway." *Commentary* 105: 58–63.

Hollander, Nancy. 1997. *Love in a Time of Hate: Liberation Psychology in Latin America*. New Brunswick: Rutgers University Press.

———. 1992. "Psychoanalysis and State Terror in Argentina." *The American Journal of Psychoanalysis* 52, 3: 273–289.

Huyssen, Andreas. 1993. "Monument and Memory: In a Postmodern Age." *Yale Journal of Criticism* 6, 2: 249–261.

Ignatieff, Michael. 1996. "Articles of Faith." *Index: On Censorship* 25, 5: 110–122.

Jaar, Alfredo. 1988. *Let There Be Light: The Rwanda Project 1994–1998*. Barcelona, Spain: ACTAR.

Jay, Martin. 1996. *Walter Benjamin, Remembrance, and the First World War*. Madrid, Spain: Instituto Juan March de Estudio e Investigaciones.

Jefremovas, Villia. 1991. "Loose Women, Virtuous Wives, and Timid Virgins: Gender and the Control of Resources in Rwanda." *Canadian Journal of African Studies* 25: 378–395.

Jelin, Elizabeth. 1994. "The Politics of Memory: The Human Rights Movement and the Construction of Democracy in Argentina." *Latin American Perspectives* 21, 2 (Spring): 34–58.

Jensen, Soren Buus, Richard Neugebauer, Torben Marner, Susan George, Logan Ndahiro, and Eugene Rurangwa. 1997. *The Rwandan Children and Their Families: Understanding, Prevention and Healing of Traumatization*. Copenhagan, Denmark: European University Center for Mental Health and Human Rights.

Johnson, Charles. 1991. *Oxherding Tale*. New York: Grove Weidenfeld.

———. 1990. *Being and Race: Black Writing since 1970*. Bloomington: Indiana University Press.

Johnson, James Weldon. 1989. *Autobiography of an Ex-Colored Man*. New York: Vintage Books.

Kaplan, Robert. 1994. "The Coming Anarchy: How Scarcity, Crime, Overpopulation and Disease Are Rapidly Destroying the Social Fabric of Our Planet." *Atlantic Monthly* (February): 44–76.

Keenan, Thomas. 1997. *Fables of Responsibility*. Stanford: Stanford University Press.

Kelley, Caffyn. 1995. "Creating Memory, Contesting History." *Matriart* 5, 3: 6–11.

Kellner, Tatana. 1994. *B-11226: Fifty Years of Silence, Eugene Kellner's Story*. New York: Rosendale Women's Studio Workshop.

———. *71125: Fifty Years of Silence, Eva Kellner's Story*. New York: Rosendale Women's Studio Workshop.

Kingston, Maxine Hong. 1989. *China Men*. New York: Vintage International.

_____. 1989. *The Woman Warrior: Memoirs of a Girlhood among Ghosts*. New York: Vintage International.

Kleber, Rolf, Charles Figley, and Berthold Gersons. 1995. *Beyond Trauma: Cultural and Societal Dynamics*. New York: Plenum Books.

Klein, Melanie. 1994. *Love, Guilt and Reparation and Other Works 1921–1945*. London: Virago.

Kleinman, Arthur. 1988. *The Illness Narratives: Suffering, Healing and the Human Condition*. New York: Basic Books.

Kogawa, Joy. 1981. *Obasan*. Ontario: Penguin.

Kohli, Rita. 1991. "Violence against Women: Race, Class and Gender Issues." *Canadian Woman Studies* 11, 4: 13–14.

Kraepelin, Emil. 1973. "Comparative Psychiatry." In *Themes and Variations in European Psychiatry*. Edited by S. R. Hirsch and M. Shepherd, 7–30. Charlottesville: University of Virginia.

Kristeva, Julia. 1991. *Strangers to Ourselves*. Translated by Leon S. Roudiez. New York: Columbia University Press.

_____. 1982. *Powers of Horror: An Essay on Abjection*. Translated by Leon S. Roudiez. New York: Columbia University Press.

LaCapra, Dominick. 1996. *Representing the Holocaust: History, Theory, Trauma*. Ithaca: Cornell University Press.

Laclau, Ernesto. 1996. *Emancipation(s)*. London: Verso.

Lakeman, Lee. 1992. "Women, Violence and the Montreal Massacre." In *Twist and Shout: A Decade of Feminist Writing in This Magazine*. Edited by Susan Crean, 92–102. Toronto: Second Story Press.

Lambek, Michael. 1996. "The Past Imperfect: Remembering as Moral Practice." In *Tense*

Past: Cultural Essays in Trauma and Memory. Edited by Paul Antze and Michael Lambek. New York: Routledge.

Langer, Lawrence L. 1998. "Pre-empting the Holocaust. "*Atlantic Monthly* (November): 105–115.

———. 1995. *Admitting the Holocaust: Collected Essays*. New York: Oxford University Press.

———. 1991. "Deep Memory: The Buried Self." In *Holocaust Testimonies: The Ruins of Memory*, 1–39. New Haven: Yale University Press.

———. 1991. *Holocaust Testimonies: The Ruins of Memory*. New Haven: Yale University Press.

Lanzmann, Claude. 1995. "The Obscenity of Understanding: An Evening with Claude Lanzmann." In *Trauma: Explorations in Memory*. Edited by Cathy Caruth, 200–220. Baltimore: Johns Hopkins University Press.

Larson, Jacqueline. 1994. "Taking It to the Streets." *Border/Lines* (Supplement) 34/35 : 03–12.

Laub, Dori. 1992. "An Event without Witness: Truth, Testimony and Survival." In *Testimony: Crises of Witnessing in Literature, Psychoanalysis and History*, by Shoshana Felman and Dori Laub, 75–92. New York: Routledge.

Levin, Meyer. 1992. *The Obsession*. New York: Simon & Schuster.

Levinas, Emmanuel. 1998. "Useless Suffering." In *Entre nous: On Thinking of the Other*. Translated by Michael B. Smith and Barbara Harshaw, 91–101. New York: Columbia University Press.

———. 1996. "Peace and Proximity." *Basic Philosophical Writings*. Edited by Adrian T. Peperzak, Simon Critchley, and Robert Bernasconi, 161–169. Bloomington: Indiana University Press.

———. 1994. *Beyond the Verse: Talmudic Readings and Lectures*. Translated by Gary D. Mole. Bloomington: Indiana University Press.

———. 1990. *Nine Talmudic Readings by Emmanuel Levinas*. Bloomington: Indiana University Press.

———. 1989. "Ethics as First Philosophy." In *The Levinas Reader*. Edited by Sean Hand, 76–87. Oxford: Blackwell.

———. 1987. "Diachrony and Representation." In *Time and the Other*. Translated by Richard A. Cohen, 97–120. Pittsburgh: Duquesne University Press.

———. 1985. *Ethics and Infinity: Conversations with Phillip Nemo*. Translated by Richard A. Cohen. Pittsburgh: Duquesne University Press.

———. 1978/1991. *Otherwise Than Being or Beyond Essence*. Translated by Alphonso Lingis. Dordrecht: Kluwer Academic Publishers.

———. 1969. *Totality and Infinity: An Essay on Exteriority*. Translated by Alphonso Lingis. Pittsburgh: Duquesne University Press.

———. 1966. "On the Trail of the Other." Translated by Daniel Hoy. *Philosophy Today* 10: 34–36.

———. 1961. *Totality and Infinity: An Essay on Exteriority*. Translated by Alphonso Lingis. The Hague: Martinus Nijhoff.

Linden, Ian. 1977. *Church and Revolution in Rwanda*. Manchester: Manchester University Press.

Lingis, Alphonso. 1994. *The Community of Those Who Have Nothing in Common*. Bloomington: Indiana University Press.

Liss, Andrea. 1998. *Trespassing through Shadows: Memory, Photography and the Holocaust*. Minneapolis: University of Minnesota Press.

_____. 1991. "Trespassing through Shadows: History, Mourning and Photography in Representations of Holocaust Memory." *Framework* 4, 1: 30–39.

Lowenthal, David. 1985. *The Past Is a Foreign Country*. Cambridge: Cambridge University Press.

Lyotard, Jean-Francois. 1991. *The Inhuman*. Translated by Geoffrey Bennington and Rachel Bowlby. Stanford: Stanford University Press.

_____. 1990. *Heidegger and "the jews."* Translated by Andreas Michel and Mark S. Roberts. Minneapolis: University of Minnesota Press.

_____. 1989. "Levinas' Logic." In *The Lyotard Reader*. Edited by Andrew Benjamin, 275–313. Cambridge: Basil Blackwell.

_____.1988. *The Differend: Phrases in Dispute*. Translated by G. Van Den Abbeele. Minneapolis: University of Minnesota Press.

Malamud-Goti, Jaime. 1996. *Game without End: State Terror and the Politics of Justice*. Norman: University of Oklahoma Press.

_____. 1995. "Punishing Human Rights Abuses in Fledging Democracies: The Case of Argentina." In *Impunity and Human Rights in International Law and Practice*. Edited by Naomi Roht Arriaza, 160–170. New York: Oxford University Press.

Malette, Louise, and Marie Chalouh, eds. 1991. *The Montreal Massacre*. Translated by Marlene Wildeman. Charlottetown: gynergy books.

Malkki, Liisa. 1996. "Speechless Emissaries: Refugees, Humanitarianism, and Dehistoricization." *Cultural Anthropology* 11, 3: 377–404.

_____. 1995. *Purity and Exile: Violence, Memory, and National Cosmology among Hutu Refugees in Tanzania*. Chicago: University of Chicago Press.

Mamdani, Mahmoud. 1996a. "From Conquest to Consent as the Basis of State Formation: Reflections on Rwanda." *New Left Review* 216: 3–36.

_____. 1996b. "Reconciliation without Justice." *Southern African Review of Books* (November-December).

Mann, Laurin. 1998. *Actor Training in Toronto: Theory in Practice*. Unpublished doctoral thesis. University of Toronto.

Maquet, Jacques Jérôme Pierre. 1954. *Le systeme des relations sociales dans le Rwanda ancien*. Tervuren: MRCB.

Mariani, Philomena. 1991. "God Is a Man." In *Critical Fictions: The Politics of Imaginative Writing*. Edited by Philomena Mariani, 3–12. Seattle: Bay Press.

Marshall, Paule. 1984. *Praisesong for the Widow*. New York: E. P. Dutton.

Masiello, Francine. 1987. "La argentina durante el proceso: las multiples resistencias de la cultural." In *Ficcion y politica: La narrativa argentina durante el proceso militar*. Edited by Daniel Balderston et al., 11–29. Buenos Aires: Alianza Editorial.

Mbembe, Achille. 1992. "Provisional Notes on the Postcolony." *Africa* 62, 1: 3–37.

McDowell, Deborah. 1995. *"The Changing Same": Black Women's Literature, Criticism, and Theory*. Bloomington: Indiana University Press.

McCulloch, Jock. 1995. *Colonial Psychiatry and "The African Mind."* Cambridge: Cambridge University Press.

McLaren, Peter, and Tomaz Tadeu da Silva. 1993. "Decentering Pedagogy: Critical Literacy, Resistance and the Politics of Memory." In *Paulo Freire: A Critical Encounter*. Edited by Peter McLaren and Peter Leonard, 47–89. New York: Routledge.

Mellibovsky, Matilde. 1997. *Circle of Love over Death: Testimonies of the Mothers of the Plaza de Mayo*. Translated by Maria and Matthew Prosser. Willimantic: Curbstone Press.

Melnick, Ralph. 1997. *The Stolen Legacy of Anne Frank: Meyer Levin, Lillian Hellman, and the Staging of the Diary*. New Haven: Yale University Press.

Mendes-Flor, Paul. 1987. "History." In *Contemporary Jewish Religious Thought*. Edited by Arthur A. Cohen and Paul Mendes-Flor, 371–387. New York: Free Press.

Metz, Allan Sheldon. 1990. "La semana tragica: An Anotated Bibliography." *Revista Interamericana de Bibliografia* 40, 1: 51–91.

———. 1989. "Jewish Victims of Repression in Argentina under Military Rule." *Holocaust and Genocide Studies* 4, 4: 479–499.

Millar, Morgan, et al. 1998. *"Marker of Change": The Story of the Women's Monument* [video recording]. Canada: The May Street Group.

Minow, Martha. 1998. *Between Vengeance and Forgiveness: Facing History after Genocide and Mass Violence*. Boston: Beacon Press.

Mitscherlich-Nielsen, Margarete. 1989. "The Inability to Mourn—Today." In *The Problem of Loss and Mourning: Psychoanalytic Perspectives*. Edited by David R. Dietrich and Peter C. Shabad, 405–426. Madison: International Universities Press.

Mitscherlich, Alexander, and Margarete Mitscherlich. 1975. *The Inability to Mourn: Principles of Collective Behavior*. Preface by Robert Jay Lifton. Translated by Beverley R. Placzek. New York: Grove Press.

Morgenstern, Naomi. 1997. "Mother's Milk and Sister's Blood: Trauma and the Neoslave Narrative." *differences* 8, 2: 101–126.

Morrison, Toni. 1990. "The Site of Memory." In *Out There: Marginalization and Contemporary Cultures*. Edited by Russel Ferguson, Martha Gever, Trinh T. Minh-ha, and Cornel West, 299–305. New York: The New Museum of Contemporary Art and the MIT Press.

———. 1987. *Beloved*. New York: A Plume Book.

Moses, Raphel. 1986. "Projection, Identification and Projective Identification: Their Relation to Political Process." In *Projection, Identification, Projective Identification*. Edited by Joseph Sandler, 133–150. London: Karnac Books.

Nelson-McDermott, Catherine. 1991. "Murderous Fallout: Post-Lépine Rhetoric." *Atlantis* 17, 1 (Fall/Winter): 124–128.

Newbury, Catherine. 1988. *The Cohesion of Oppression: Clientship and Ethnicity in Rwanda, 1860–1960*. New York: Columbia University Press.

Newton, Adam Zachary. 1995. *Narrative Ethics*. Cambridge: Harvard University Press.

Nino, Carlos Santiago. 1996. *Radical Evil on Trial*. New Haven: Yale University Press.

Nordstrom, Carolyn. 1997. *Another Kind of War Story*. Philadelphia: University of Pennsylvania Press.

Osiel, Mark. 1997. *Mass Atrocity, Collective Memory, and the Law*. New Brunswick, N.J.: Transaction Publishers.

———. 1986. "The Making of Human Rights Policy in Argentina: the Impact of Ideas and Interests on a Legal Conflict." *Journal of Latin American Studies* 18: 135–180.

Ouaknin, Marc-Alain. 1995. *The Burnt Book: Reading the Talmud*. Translated by Llewellyn Brown. Princeton: Princeton University Press.

Ozick, Cynthia. 1997. "Who Owns Anne Frank?" *New Yorker* (October 6): 76–87.

Pagès, A. 1933. *Au Ruanda sur les bords du lac Kivu (Congo belge): Un royaume hamite au centre de l'Afrique*. Brussels: Institut royal colonial belge.

Pagis, Dan. 1981. *Points of Departure*. Translated by Stephen Mitchell. Philadelphia: The Jewish Publication Society of America.

Palumbo-Liu, David. 1996. "The Politics of Memory: Remembering History in Alice Walker and Joy Kogawa." In *Memory and Cultural Politics: New Approaches to American Ethnic Literatures*. Edited by Amritjit Singh, Joseph T. Skerrett Jr., and Robert E. Hogan, 211–226. Boston: Northeastern University Press.

Parry, Benita. 1995. "Reconciliation and Remembrance." *Pretexts* 5, 1–2: 84.

Pensky, Max. 1993. *Melancholy Dialectics*. Amherst: University of Massachusetts Press.

Perelli, Carina. 1992. "Settling Accounts with Blood Memory: The Case of Argentina." *Social Research* 59, 2 (Summer): 414–451.

Plank, Karl A. 1994. *Mother of the Wire Fence: Inside and Outside the Holocaust*. Louisville: John Knox Press.

Prunier, Gerard. 1995. *The Rwanda Crisis: History of a Genocide*. New York: Columbia University Press.

Rancière, Jacques. 1994. *The Names of History: On The Poetics of Knowledge*. Translated by Hassan Melehy. Minneapolis: University of Minnesota Press.

Reati, Fernando. 1989. "Argentine Political Violence and Artistic Representation in Films of the 1980's." *Latin American Literary Review* 17: 24–39.

Reed, Ishmael. 1977. *Flight to Canada*. New York: Avon Books.

Renan, Ernest. 1990. "What Is a Nation?" In *Nation and Narration*. Edited by Homi Bhabha, 8–22. New York: Routledge.

Reynjens, Filip. 1997. "L'Afrique des Grands Lacs." *Annuaire 1996–1997*. Paris: L'Harmattan.

Rich, Frank. 1997. "Anne Frank Now." *New York Times* (December 21): A 21.

Ring, Jennifer. 1997. *The Political Consequences of Thinking: Gender and Judaism in the Work of Hannah Arendt*. Albany: State University of New York Press.

Roniger, Luis, and Mario Sznajder. 1998. "The Politics of Memory and Oblivion in Redemocratized Argentina and Uruguay." *History and Memory* 10, 1 (Spring): 133–169.

Rosenbaum, Thane. 1996. *Elijah Visible*. New York: St. Martin's.

Rosenberg, Sharon. 1997. *Rupturing the "Skin of Memory": Bearing Witness to the 1989 Massacre of Women in Montreal*. University of Toronto, Unpublished dissertation.

Rosenberg, Sharon, and Roger I. Simon. 1999. "Beyond the Logic of Emblemization: Rethinking Remembrances of the Montreal Massacre." Unpublished manuscript.

Rosenfeld, Alvin. 1993. "Anne Frank—And Us: Finding the Right Words." *Reconstruction* 2, 2: 86–92.

_____. 1991. "Popularization and Memory: The Case of Anne Frank." In *Lessons and Legacies: The Meaning of the Holocaust in a Changing World*. Edited by Peter Hayes, 243–278. Evanston: Northwestern University Press.

Rosenzweig, Franz. 1972. *The Star of Redemption*. Boston: Beacon Press.

Sanders, Edith. 1969. "The Hamitic Hypothesis: Its Origins and Functions in Time Perspective." *Journal of African History* 10, 4: 521–532.

Sarlo, Beatriz. 1992. "Strategies of the Literary Imagination." In *Fear at the Edge: State Terror and Resistance in Latin America*. Edited by Juan E. Corradi et al., 236–249. Berkeley: University of California Press.

Scanlon, Jennifer. 1994. "Educating the Living, Remembering the Dead: The Montreal Massacre as Metaphor." *Feminist Teacher* 8, 2 (Fall/Winter): 75–79.

Scarry, Elaine. 1985. *The Body in Pain*. Oxford: Oxford University Press.

Scott, David. 1995. "Colonial Governmentality." *Social Text* 43 (Fall): 191–220.

Segal, Hannah. 1997. *Psychoanalysis, Literature and War: Papers of Hannah Segal, 1972–1995*. Edited by John Steiner. London: Routledge.

Silko, Leslie Marmon. 1991. *Almanac of the Dead: A Novel.* New York and London: Penguin.

———. *Ceremony.* 1977. New York and London: Penguin.

Silverman, Kaja. 1996. *The Threshold of the Visible World.* New York: Routledge.

Simon, Roger I., and Claudia Eppert. 1997. "Remembering Obligation: Pedagogy and the Witnessing of Testimony of Historical Trauma." *Canadian Journal of Education/Revue canadienne de l'éducation* 22, 2 (Spring): 175–191.

Simon, Roger I., Claudia Eppert, Mark Clamen, and Laura Beres. 1999. "Witness-as-Study: The Difficult Inheritance of Testimony." Unpublished manuscript.

Singer, Isaac Bashevis. 1998. *Shadow of the Hudson.* Translated by Joseph Sherman. New York: Farrar, Straus, Giroux.

Smith, Jonothan. 1993. "The Lie that Blinds: Destabilizing the Text of Landscape." In *Place/Culture/Representation.* Edited by J. Duncan and D. Ley, 78–92. New York: Routledge.

Soelle, Dorothy. 1990. *The Window of Vulnerability: A Political Spirituality.* Translated by L. M. Maloney. Minneapolis: Fortress Press.

Speck, Paula K. 1987. "The Trial of the Argentine Junta: Responsibilities and Realities." *The University of Miami Inter-American Law Review* 18, 3: 491–534.

Speke, John Hanning. 1863/1969. *Journal of the Discovery of the Source of the Nile.* London: Dent.

Spelman, Elizabeth. 1997. *Fruits of Sorrow: Framing Our Attention to Suffering.* Boston: Beacon Press.

Spiegelman, Art. 1991. *Maus: And Here My Troubles Began, Vol. 2.* New York: Pantheon Books.

———. 1986. *Maus: A Survivor's Tale, Vol. 1.* New York: Pantheon Books.

Spivak, Gayatri. 1993. *Outside the Teaching Machine.* London: Routledge.

Spottel, Michael. 1998. "German Ethnology and Antisemitism: The Hamitic Hypothesis." *Dialectical Anthropology* 23:131–150.

Steinfeld, J. J. 1993. *Dancing at the Club Holocaust: Stories New and Selected.* Charlottetown, P.E.I.: Ragweed.

Styron, William. 1967. *The Confessions of Nat Turner.* New York: Random House.

Suarez-Orozco, Marcelo. 1990. "Speaking of the Unspeakable: Toward a Psychosocial Understanding of Responses to Terror." *Ethos* 18, 3: 353–383.

Talkback: Women's Monument. On *As It Happens* [radio programming]. Canada: CBC Radio, August 11 1994.

Taussig, Michael. 1995. *The Nervous System.* New York: Routledge.

———. 1993. "Maleficium: State Fetishism." In *Fetishism as Cultural Discourse.* Edited by Emily Apter and William Pietz, 217–247. Ithaca: Cornell University Press.

Taylor, Christopher. 1992. *Milk, Honey and Money: Changing Concepts in Rwandan Healing.* Washington, D.C.: Smithsonian Institution Press.

Taylor, Diana. 1997. *Disappearing Acts: Spectacles of Gender and Nationalism in Argentina's "Dirty War."* Durham: Duke University Press.

Taylor, Patrick. 1996. "Post-Colonial Encounters: Paule Marshall's 'Widow's Praisesong' and George Lamming's 'Daughter's Adventure.' In *"And the Birds Began to Sing": Religion and Literature in Post-Colonial Cultures.* Edited by Jamie Scott, 195–207. Amsterdam and Atlanta: Editions Rodopi.

Torre, Javier, and Adriana Zaffaroni. 1989. "Argentina: Its Culture During the Repression and During the Transition." In *The Redemocratization of Argentine Culture: 1938 and Beyond*. Edited by David William Foster, 11–21. Tempe: Arizona Board of Regents.

Uvin, Peter, 1998. *Aiding Violence: The Development Enterprise in Rwanda*. West Hartford, Conn.: Kumarian Press.

van Alphen, Ernst. 1998. "Symptoms of Discursivity: Experience, Memory and Trauma." In *Acts of Memory: Cultural Recall in the Present*. Edited by Mieke Bal, Jonathan Crewe, and Leo Spitzer. Hanover: Dartmouth College.

———. 1997. *Caught by History: Holocaust Effects in Contemporary Art, Literature, and Theory*. Stanford: Stanford University Press.

Vaughan, Megan. 1991. *Curing Their Ills: Colonial Power and African Illness*. Cambridge: Polity Press.

Vidal, Claudine. 1985. "Situations ethniques au Rwanda." In *Au coeur de l'ethnie*. Edited by Jean Loup Amselle and Elikia M'Bokolo. Paris: La Decouverte.

Volkan, Vamik D. 1996. "Intergenerational Transmission and 'Chosen' Traumas: A Link between the Psychology of the Individual and that of the Ethnic Group." In *Psychoanalysis at the Political Border*. Edited by Leo Rangell and Rena Moses-Hrushovski, 257–282. Madison: International Universities Press.

Walcott, Derek. 1974. "The Muse of History." In *Is Massa Day Dead?: Black Moods in the Caribbean*. Edited by Orde Coombs, 1–27. Garden City, N.Y.: Anchor/Doubleday.

Walcott, Rinaldo. 1996. "Tom Say: A Preface." In *The Austin Clarke Reader*. Edited by Barry Callaghan, 11–13. Toronto: Exile Editions.

Wangh, Martin. 1996. "The Working through of the Nazi Experience in the German Psychoanalytic Community." In *Psychoanalysis at the Political Border*. Edited by Leo Rangell and Rena Moses-Hrushovski, 283–302. Madison: International Universities Press.

Werbner, Richard, ed. 1998. *Memory and the Postcolony: African Anthropology and the Critique of Power*. London: Zed Books.

White, Hayden. 1995. "Bodies and Their Plots." In *Choreographing History*. Edited by Susan Leigh Foster, 229–234. Bloomington: Indiana University Press.

White, Ted. 1994. "Letter to the Editor." *The Globe and Mail*, December 6: A24.

Wiesel, Elie. 1992. *The Forgotten*. Translated by Stephen Becker. New York: Summit.

Williams, Raymond. 1977. *Marxism and Literature*. Oxford: Oxford University Press.

Williams, Sherley Anne. 1986. *Dessa Rose*. New York: William Morrow.

Wilson, Harriet E. 1983. *Our Nig*. New York: Random House.

Wilson, Richard, ed. 1996. *Human Rights, Culture and Context*. London: Pluto Press.

Women's Monument Project. n.d. Design Competition Guidelines. Unpublished document.

Wynter, Sylvia. 1995. "1492: A New World View." In *Race, Discourse, and the Origin of the Americas*. Edited by Vera Lawrence Hyatt and Rex Nettleford, 5–57. Washington, D.C.: Smithsonian Institution Press.

———. 1992. "Rethinking 'Aesthetics': Notes Towards a Deciphering Practice." In *Ex-Iles: Essays on Caribbean Cinema*. Edited by Mbye B. Cham, 237–279. Trenton, N.J.: African World Press.

———. 1990. "On Disenchanting Discourse: 'Minority' Literary Criticism and Beyond." In *The Nature and Context of Minority Discourse*. Edited by Abdul R. JanMohamed and David Lloyd, 432–469. New York: Oxford University Press.

Wyrd Sisters, The. 1992. "Leave a Little Light" [sound recording]. Winnipeg, Manitoba: Oh Yah! Records.

Wyschogrod, Edith. 1998. *An Ethics of Remembering: History, Heterology, and the Nameless Others*. Chicago: University of Chicago Press.

_____. 1992. "Man-Made Mass Death. Shifting Concepts of Community." *Journal of the American Academy of Religion* 63, 2: 165.

Yerushalmi, Yosef. 1989. *Zakhor: Jewish History and Jewish Memory*. New York: Schocken Books.

Young, Allen. 1995. *The Harmony of Illusions: The Invention of PTSD*. Berkeley: University of California Press.

Young, James. 1998. "The Holocaust as Vicarious Past: Art Spiegelman's *Maus* and the Afterimages of History." *Critical Inquiry* 24 (Spring): 666–699.

_____. 1993. *The Texture of Memory: Holocaust Memorials and Meaning*. New Haven: Yale University Press.

_____. 1988. *Writing and Re-writing the Holocaust: Narrative and the Consequences of Interpretation*. Bloomington: Indiana University Press.

Young, Robert. 1990. *White Mythologies: Writing History and the West*. London: Routledge.

Index

About the Editors and Contributors

Rachel N. Baum teaches at the University of Wisconsin-Milwaukee, where she is director of the Edison Initiative, a program that works on improving undergraduate education. She has presented papers on the Holocaust nationally and is a participant in the Pastora Goldner Holocaust Symposium, which meets biennially in Wroxton, England. Her research on the Holocaust focuses on the connections between pedagogy, remembrance, and the emotions.

Deborah P. Britzman is author of *Practice Makes Practice: A Critical Study of Learning to Teach* (1991) and *Lost Subjects, Contested Objects: Toward a Psychoanalytic Inquiry of Learning* (1998) and is associate professor at York University in Toronto.

Claudia Eppert recently completed her doctoral dissertation at the Ontario Institute for Studies in Education of the University of Toronto. Her work considers the ethico-pedagogical possibilities for a responsive/responsible practice of reading contemporary literature of historical witness. She is currently teaching English education at Louisiana State University.

Mario Di Paolantonio is a Ph.D. candidate at the Ontario Institute for Studies in Education of the University of Toronto. He is also a part-time literature teacher at the School of Experiential Education and a member of the Testimony & Historical Memory Project of OISE/UT. His current research explores how posttraumatic societies use truth commissions and trials as a pedagogical mode for repairing and assuaging national identity. At issue in his work are a series of questions that concern themselves with the ethical transmission/representation of that which remains other to national commemorative projects.

Andrea Liss is the contemporary art historian and cultural theorist in the Visual and Performing Arts Program at California State University-San Marcos. Her teaching focuses on contemporary representations of history and memory, the history and criticism of photographically based artwork, and feminist theory and practice. She has recently published *Trespassing through Shadows: Memory, Photography and the Holocaust* (1998) and is currently working on *Reconceiving the Maternal Image: Feminist Art and the Politics of Care,* a book on contemporary representations of feminist motherhood.

Jody Ranck is a research and teaching fellow at the Human Rights Center at the University of California. He teaches interdisciplinary courses on human rights that draw on critical theory and anthropology. Ranck is writing a book on memory and genocide in Rwanda as well as directing a project with Rwandan academics and genocide survivors on gender violence, memory, poverty, and human rights. He has a doctorate in public health.

Sharon Rosenberg is assistant professor at York University in Toronto, where she teaches in the School of Women's Studies. Her scholarly work attends to questions of feminist remembrance practice in the wake of ongoing traumatic violences against women. Rosenberg's writing has appeared previously in *Hypatia, Resources for Feminist Research, Borderlines,* and the *Canadian Journal for Community Mental Health.*

Julie Salverson is a playwright and a doctoral candidate at the Ontario Institute for Studies in Education of the University of Toronto. She has published articles on testimony, ethics, and performance in *Theatre Topics, Canadian Theatre Review,* and *Theatre Research in Canada* together with a number of plays published by Playwrights Canada. She is artistic director of Flying Blind Theatre Events in Toronto. Salverson currently is assistant professor in the Department of Drama at Queen's University.

Roger I. Simon teaches at the Ontario Institute for Studies in Education at the University of Toronto. He has written extensively in the area of critical pedagogy and cultural studies and is the author of *Teaching against the Grain: Texts for a Pedagogy of Possibility.* Simon's recent work has addressed the formation of public memory and the pedagogical character of various forms of remembrance.

Rinaldo Walcott is assistant professor in the Division of Humanities, York University, Canada. He is the author of *Black Like Who? Writing Black Canada* (1997). He is currently working on a book tentatively entitled *ReCrossings: Languages of the Middle Passage.*

Breinigsville, PA USA
08 September 2010
245006BV00002B/7/P